PERSPECTIVES ON DRAMA

PERSPECTIVES ON DRAMA

EDITED BY

JAMES L. CALDERWOOD

AND

HAROLD E. TOLIVER

UNIVERSITY OF CALIFORNIA, IRVINE

NEW YORK

OXFORD UNIVERSITY PRESS

LONDON   TORONTO

1968

Copyright © 1968 by Oxford University Press

Library of Congress Catalogue Card Number 68–19763

Printed in the United States of America

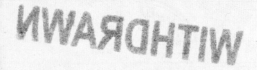

PREFACE

Using the term "perspectives" for a collection of essays on dramatic theory is less an exercise in the art of editorial evasiveness than an acknowledgment of the polymorphic monstrousness of drama itself. Spawned apparently by Dionysus the shape-changer, its emblem the mask, its identities ranging elusively between mime and dramatic monologue, the dramatic monster has lent itself much more readily to the quick critical snapshot than to synoptic overviews and definitive portraits. The editorial task, therefore, is to assemble some sort of quasi-coherent image out of a great many ways of looking at the creature. Part of the problem has been to do justice to both the literary and the theatrical aspects of drama, to avoid treating it on the one hand as closet drama and on the other as show business. The introductory essays by Wilder, Ghéon, and Duerrenmatt, the essay on "Origins" by Southern, those on "Illusion" by Koestler, Williams, and Langer, and those on "Imagery" by Downer and on "Enactment" by Frisch and Bentley give ample scope to the concept of drama as one of the performed arts. We have assumed, however, that one of the major uses of this book would be as a supplementary text to an anthology of plays. Thus, if we have neglected essays that focus primarily on such matters as directing, acting, costuming, stage designing, and so on, it is not because we consider them irrelevant to dramatic theory but because they are less available than the literary aspects of drama to analysis and illustration outside the theater.

The first half of the book looks at drama primarily within the context of cultural and historical change. The opening essays attempt some general observations about the nature of drama, the section on "Origins" speculates about its evolution from ritual to art, and the remaining three sections all deal with varying conceptions of dramatic "form." The second half of the book attempts to dissemble and inspect the constitutive elements of drama. If you are going to dissect something, Plato advises, "chop at the joints"—which is all very well, provided you know where they are. Like all art, however, drama makes a practice of concealing its joints in the process of bringing all its formative parts into athletic co-ordination. Any line-up of elements is bound to be arbitrary, and we are quick to deny any deep emotional involvement in the one used here. However, critics have singled out certain dramatic features that merit attention, and we have tried to reflect the critical practice without implying hard and fast categories. Hence the headnotes to each section frequently include cross-references to other essays that lead into or out of the area under discussion.

Acknowledgments to authors, translators, and publishers who gave us permission to reprint essays here are recorded on the first page of each selection or on the copyright page. We should also like to thank Mrs. Betty Becker, Mrs. Diana Ewing, Mrs. Virginia McQuaid, and Mrs. Sue Smith for their generous assistance in preparing the materials for this collection.

J. L. C.
H. E. T.

University of California, Irvine
December, 1967

CONTENTS

ELEMENTS OF DRAMA

PERSPECTIVES ON DRAMA

GENERAL

Drama is the most combinative of the arts, bringing together at times such disparate enterprises as literature, dance, music, painting, tableau, ritual, mime, and so on. Determining the essential nature of so variable a form is no easy task. Thornton Wilder, the American scholar, novelist, and Pulitzer prize-winning playwright of *Our Town* (1938) and *The Skin of Our Teeth* (1942), seeks to isolate four distinguishing characteristics of drama. Although he uses the terms "drama" and "theater" interchangeably, it may be argued that theater is not drama itself but its major mode of existence, as it is for all of the performing arts. Opera, for instance, shares with drama Wilder's four characteristics, but that does not mean that opera *is* drama. Henri Ghéon (a pseudonym for Dr. Henri Vangeon, a physician, music critic, painter, director, and dramatist who delivered the following lecture in 1923 at the theater of the Vieux-Colombier) prefers to emphasize the heterogeneity of the form, recognizing that a certain impurity is built into drama and needs to be accepted as a working condition by both playwright and director. For as an "art" drama longs for the purity of timelessness, the permanence of print or stone or even canvas and oil, but as a *performing* art drama suffers the continuous fate of dissolving in its very moments of fulfillment, as though Sisyphus, instead of Dionysus, were its mythic sponsor.

3

Friedrich Duerrenmatt, the contemporary Swiss dramatist, also shies away from the task of finding pure essences in a form that is reconstituted in each changing age. The modern theater is especially ambiguous in that it must be capable of embracing all previous dramatic forms and at the same time of creating through constant experimentation its own forms. Duerrenmatt's remarks about the modern playwright's manipulations of time, place, and action are most profitably read in light of the later section called "Form: The Unities."

THORNTON WILDER

Some Thoughts on Playwriting

Four fundamental conditions of the drama separate it from the other arts. Each of these conditions has its advantages and disadvantages, each requires a particular aptitude from the dramatist, and from each there are a number of instructive consequences to be derived. These conditions are:

1. The theatre is an art which reposes upon the work of many collaborators;

2. It is addressed to the group-mind;

3. It is based upon a pretense and its very nature calls out a multiplication of pretenses;

4. Its action takes place in a perpetual present time.

I. THE THEATRE IS AN ART WHICH REPOSES UPON THE WORK OF MANY COLLABORATORS

We have been accustomed to think that a work of art is by definition the product of one governing selecting will.

A landscape by Cézanne consists of thousands of brushstrokes each commanded by one mind. *Paradise Lost* and *Pride and Prejudice*, even in cheap frayed copies, bear the immediate and exclusive message of one intelligence.

It is true that in musical performance we meet with intervening executants, but the element of intervention is slight compared to that which takes place in drama. Illustrations:

1. One of the finest productions of *The Merchant of Venice* in our time showed Sir Henry Irving as Shylock, a noble, wronged and in-

From *The Intent of the Artist*, edited by Augusto Centeno; Princeton University Press. Copyright, 1941, by Thornton Wilder. Reprinted by permission of Brandt & Brandt.

dignant being, of such stature that the Merchants of Venice dwindled before him into irresponsible schoolboys. He was confronted in court by a gracious, even queenly, Portia, Miss Ellen Terry. At the Odéon in Paris, however, Gémier played Shylock as a vengeful and hysterical buffoon, confronted in court by a Portia who was a *gamine* from the Paris streets with a lawyer's quill three feet long over her ear; at the close of the trial scene Shylock was driven screaming about the auditorium, behind the spectators' back and onto the stage again, in a wild Elizabethan revel. Yet for all their divergences both were admirable productions of the play.

2. If there were ever a play in which fidelity to the author's requirements were essential in the representation of the principal role, it would seem to be Ibsen's *Hedda Gabler,* for the play is primarily an exposition of her character. Ibsen's directions read: "Enter from the left Hedda Gabler. She is a woman of twenty-nine. Her face and figure show great refinement and distinction. Her complexion is pale and opaque. Her steel-gray eyes express an unruffled calm. Her hair is an attractive medium brown, but is not particularly abundant; and she is dressed in a flowing loose-fitting morning gown." I once saw Eleonora Duse in this role. She was a woman of sixty and made no effort to conceal it. Her complexion was pale and transparent. Her hair was white, and she was dressed in a gown that suggested some medieval empress in mourning. And the performance was very fine.

One may well ask: why write for the theatre at all? Why not work in the novel where such deviations from one's intentions cannot take place?

There are two answers:

1. The theatre presents certain vitalities of its own so inviting and stimulating that the writer is willing to receive them in compensation for this inevitable variation from an exact image.

2. The dramatist through working in the theatre gradually learns not merely to take account of the presence of the collaborators, but to derive advantage from them; and he learns, above all, to organize the play in such a way that its strength lies not in appearances beyond his control, but in the succession of events and in the unfolding of an idea, in narration.

The gathered audience sits in a darkened room, one end of which is lighted. The nature of the transaction at which it is gazing is a succession of events illustrating a general idea—the stirring of the idea; the gradual feeding out of information; the shock and countershock of circumstances; the flow of action; the interruption of action; the moments of allusion to earlier events; the preparation of surprise, dread, or delight—all that is the author's and his alone.

For reasons to be discussed later—the expectancy of the group-mind, the problem of time on the stage, the absence of the narrator, the element of pretense—the theatre carries the art of narration to a higher power than the novel or the epic poem. The theatre is unfolding action and in the disposition of events the authors may exercise a governance so complete that the distortions effected by the physical appearance of actors, by the fancies of scene painters and the misunderstandings of directors, fall into relative insignificance. It is just because the theatre is an art of many collaborators, with the constant danger of grave misinterpretation, that the dramatist learns to turn his attention to the laws of narration, its logic and its deep necessity of presenting a unifying idea stronger than its mere collection of happenings. The dramatist must be by instinct a storyteller.

There is something mysterious about the endowment of the storyteller. Some very great writers possessed very little of it, and some others, lightly esteemed, possessed it in so large a measure that their books survive down the ages, to the confusion of severer critics. Alexandre Dumas had it to an extraordinary degree, while Melville, for all his splendid quality, had it barely sufficiently to raise his work from the realm of nonfiction. It springs, not, as some have said, from an aversion to general ideas, but from an instinctive coupling of idea and illustration; the idea, for a born storyteller, can only be expressed imbedded in its circumstantial illustration. The myth, the parable, the fable are the fountainhead of all fiction and in them is seen most clearly the didactic, moralizing employment of a story. Modern taste shrinks from emphasizing the central idea that hides behind the fiction, but it exists there nevertheless, supplying the unity to fantasizing, and offering a justification to what otherwise we would repudiate as mere arbitrary contrivance, pretentious lying, or individualistic emotional association spinning. For all their magnificent intellectual endowment, George Meredith and George Eliot were not born storytellers; they chose fiction as the vehicle for their reflections, and the passing of time is revealing their error in that choice. Jane Austen was pure storyteller and her works are outlasting those of apparently more formidable rivals. The theatre is more exacting than the novel in regard to this faculty, and its presence constitutes a force which compensates the dramatist for the deviations which are introduced into his work by the presence of his collaborators.

The chief of these collaborators are the actors.

The actor's gift is a combination of three separate faculties or endowments. Their presence to a high degree in any one person is extremely rare, although the ambition to possess them is common. Those who rise to the height of the profession represent a selection and a struggle for survival in one of the most difficult and cruel of the artistic activities. The three endowments that compose the gift are observation, imagination, and physical co-ordination.

1. An observant and analyzing eye for all modes of behavior about it, for dress and manner, and for the signs of thought and emotion in one's self and in others.

2. The strength of imagination and memory whereby the actor may, at the indication in the author's text, explore his store of observations and represent the details of appearance and the intensity of the emotions—joy, fear, surprise, grief, love, and hatred, and through imagination extend them to intenser degrees and to differing characterizations.

3. A physical co-ordination whereby the force of these inner realizations may be communicated to voice, face and body.

An actor must *know* the appearances and the mental states; he must *apply* his knowledge to the role; and he must physically *express* his knowledge. Moreover, his concentration must be so great that he can effect this representation under conditions of peculiar difficu'ty—in abrupt transition from the non-imaginative conditions behind the stage; and in the presence of fellow-actors who may be momentarily destroying the reality of the action.

A dramatist prepares the characterization of his personages in such a way that it will take advantage of the actor's gift.

Characterization in a novel is presented by the author's dogmatic assertion that the personage was such, and by an analysis of the personage with generally an account of his or her past. Since, in the drama, this is replaced by the actual presence of the personage before us and since there is no occasion for the intervening all-knowing author to instruct us as to his or her inner nature, a far greater share is given in a play to (1) highly characteristic utterances and (2) concrete occasions in which the character defines itself under action and (3) conscious preparation of the text whereby the actor may build upon the suggestions in the role according to his own abilities.

Characterization in a play is like a blank check which the dramatist accords to the actor for him to fill in—not entirely blank, for a number of indications of individuality are already there, but to a far less definite and absolute degree than in the novel.

The dramatist's principal interest being the movement of the story, he is willing to resign the more detailed aspects of characterization to the actor and is often rewarded beyond his expectation.

The sleepwalking scene from *Macbeth* is a highly compressed selection of words whereby despair and remorse rise to the surface of indirect confession. It is to be assumed that had Shakespeare lived to see what the genius of Sarah Siddons could pour into the scene from that combination of observation, self-knowledge, imagination, and representational skill, even he might have exclaimed, "I never knew I wrote so well!"

II. THE THEATRE IS AN ART ADDRESSED TO A GROUP-MIND

Painting, sculpture, and the literature of the book are certainly solitary experiences; and it is likely that most people would agree that the audience seated shoulder to shoulder in a concert hall is not an essential element in musical enjoyment.

But a play presupposes a crowd. The reasons for this go deeper than (1) the economic necessity for the support of the play and (2) the fact that the temperament of actors is proverbially dependent on group attention.

It rests on the fact that (1) the pretense, the fiction on the stage would fall to pieces and absurdity without the support accorded to it by a crowd, and (2) the excitement induced by pretending a fragment of life is such that it partakes of ritual and festival, and requires a throng.

Similarly the fiction that royal personages are of a mysteriously different nature from other people requires audiences, levees, and processions for its maintenance. Since the beginnings of society, satirists have occupied themselves with the descriptions of kings and queens in their intimacy and delighted in showing how the prerogatives of royalty become absurd when the crowd is not present to extend to them the enhancement of an imaginative awe.

The theatre partakes of the nature of festival. Life imitated is life raised to a higher power. In the case of comedy, the vitality of these pretended surprises, deceptions, and the *contretemps* becomes so lively that before a spectator, solitary or regarding himself as solitary, the structure of so much event would inevitably expose the artificiality of the attempt and ring hollow and unjustified; and in the case of tragedy, the accumulation of woe and apprehension would soon fall short of conviction. All actors know the disturbing sensation of playing before a handful of spectators at a dress rehearsal or performance where only their interest in pure craftsmanship can barely sustain them. During the last rehearsals the phrase is often heard: "This play is hungry for an audience."

Since the theatre is directed to a group-mind, a number of consequences follow:

1. A group-mind presupposes, if not a lowering of standards, a broadening of the fields of interest. The other arts may presuppose an audience of connoisseurs trained in leisure and capable of being interested in certain rarefied aspects of life. The dramatist may be prevented from exhibiting, for example, detailed representations of certain moments in history that require specialized knowledge in the audience, or psychological states in the personages which are of insufficient general interest to evoke self-identification in the majority. In the Second Part of Goethe's *Faust* there are long passages dealing with the theory of paper money. The exposition of the nature of misanthropy (so much more drastic than Molière's) in Shakespeare's *Timon of Athens* has never been a success. The dramatist accepts this limitation in subject matter and realizes that the group-mind imposes upon him the necessity of treating material understandable by the larger number.

2. It is the presence of the group-mind that brings another requirement to the theatre—forward movement.

Maeterlinck said that there was more drama in the spectacle of an old man seated by a table than in the majority of plays offered to the public. He was juggling with the various meanings in the word "drama." In the sense whereby drama means the intensified concentration of life's diversity and significance he may well have been right; if he meant drama as a theatrical representation before an audience he was wrong. Drama on the stage is inseparable from forward movement, from action.

Many attempts have been made to present Plato's dialogues, Gobineau's fine series of dialogues, *La Renaissance,* and the *Imaginary Conversations* of Landor; but without success. Through some ingredient in the group-mind, and through the sheer weight of anticipation involved in the dressing up and the assumption of fictional roles, an action is required, and an action that is more than a mere progress in argumentation and debate.

III. THE THEATRE IS A WORLD OF PRETENSE

It lives by conventions: a convention is an agreed-upon falsehood, a permitted lie.

Illustrations: Consider at the first performance of the *Medea*, the passage where Medea meditates the murder of her children. An anecdote from antiquity tells us that the audience was so moved by this passage that considerable disturbance took place.

The following conventions were involved:

1. Medea was played by a man.

2. He wore a large mask on his face. In the lip of the mask was an acoustical device for projecting the voice. On his feet he wore shoes with soles and heels half a foot high.

3. His costume was so designed that it conveyed to the audience, by convention: woman of royal birth and Oriental origin.

4. The passage was in metric speech. All poetry is an "agreed-upon-falsehood" in regard to speech.

5. The lines were sung in a kind of recitative. All opera involves this "permitted lie" in regard to speech.

Modern taste would say that the passage would convey very much greater pathos if a woman "like Medea" had delivered it—with an uncovered face that exhibited all the emotions she was undergoing. For the Greeks, however, there was no pretense that Medea was on the stage. The mask, the costume, the mode of declamation, were a series of signs which the spectator interpreted and reassembled in his own mind. Medea was being re-created within the imagination of each of the spectators.

The history of the theatre shows us that in its greatest ages the stage employed the greatest number of conventions. The stage is fundamental pretense and it thrives on the acceptance of that fact and in the multiplication of additional pretenses. When it tries to assert that the personages in the action "really are," really inhabit such and such rooms, really suffer such and such emotions, it loses rather than gains credibility. The modern world is inclined to laugh condescendingly at the fact that in the plays of Racine and Corneille the gods and heroes of antiquity were dressed like the courtiers under Louis XIV; that in the Elizabethan age scenery was replaced by placards notifying the audience of the location; and that a whip in the hand and a jogging motion of the body indicated that a man was on horseback in the Chinese theatre; these devices did not spring from naïveté, however, but from the vitality of the public imagination in those days and from an instinctive feeling as to where the essential and where the inessential lay in drama.

The convention has two functions:

1. It provokes the collaborative activity of the spectator's imagination; and

2. It raises the action from the specific to the general.

This second aspect is of even greater importance than the first.

If Juliet is represented as a girl "very like Juliet"—it was not merely a deference to contemporary prejudices that assigned this role to a boy in the Elizabethan age—moving about in a "real" house with marble staircases, rugs, lamps, and furniture, the impression is irresistibly conveyed that these events happened to this one girl, in one place, at one moment in time. When the play is staged as Shakespeare intended it, the bareness of the stage releases the events from the particular and the experience of Juliet partakes of that of all girls in love, in every time, place and language.

The stage continually strains to tell this generalized truth and it is the element of pretense that reinforces it. Out of the lie, the pretense, of the theatre proceeds a truth more compelling than the novel can attain, for the novel by its own laws is constrained to tell of an action that "once happened"—"once upon a time."

IV. THE ACTION ON THE STAGE TAKES PLACE IN A PERPETUAL PRESENT TIME

Novels are written in the past tense. The characters in them, it is true, are represented as living moment by moment their present time, but the constant running commentary of the novelist ("Tess slowly descended into the valley"; "Anna Karenina laughed") inevitably conveys to the reader the fact that these events are long since past and over.

The novel is a past reported in the present. On the stage it is always now. This confers upon the action an increased vitality which the novelist longs in vain to incorporate into his work.

This condition in the theatre brings with it another important element:

In the theatre we are not aware of the intervening storyteller. The speeches arise from the characters in an apparently pure spontaneity.

A play is what takes place.

A novel is what one person tells us took place.

A play visibly represents pure existing. A novel is what one mind, claiming omniscience, asserts to have existed.

Many dramatists have regretted this absence of the narrator from the stage, with his point of view, his powers of analyzing the behavior of the characters, his ability to interfere and supply further facts about the past, about simultaneous actions not visible on the stage, and above *all* his function of pointing the moral and emphasizing the significance of the action. In some periods of the theatre he has been present as chorus, or prologue and epilogue or as *raisonneur*. But surely this absence constitutes an additional force to the form, as well as an additional tax upon the writer's skill. It is the task of the dramatist so to co-ordinate his play, through the selection of episodes and speeches, that though he is himself not visible, his point of view and his governing intention will impose themselves on the spectator's attention, not as dogmatic assertion or motto, but as self-evident truth and inevitable deduction.

Imaginative narration—the invention of souls and destinies—is to the philosopher an all but indefensible activity.

Its justification lies in the fact that the communication of ideas from one mind to another inevitably reaches the point where exposition passes into illustration, into parable, metaphor, allegory, and myth.

It is no accident that when Plato arrived at the height of his argument and attempted to convey a theory of knowledge and a theory of the structure of man's nature he passed over into story telling, into the myths of the Cave and the Charioteer; and that the great religious teachers have constantly had recourse to the parable as a means of imparting their deepest intuitions.

The theatre offers to imaginative narration its highest possibilities. It has many pitfalls and its very vitality betrays it into service as mere diversion and the enhancement of insignificant matter; but it is well to remember that it was the theatre that rose to the highest place during those epochs that aftertime has chosen to call "great ages" and that the Athens of Pericles and the reigns of Elizabeth, Philip II, and Louis XIV were also the ages that gave to the world the greatest dramas it has known.

HENRI GHÉON

The Conditions of Dramatic Art

I am going to talk to you about my favorite theories, my own thoughts about the theatre. They won't be anything new; they have grown out of the thoughts of many men. The only value thought has is to belong to the common tradition, to prolong it, to carry on that great spiritual continuity that links us still to our very sources. In all ages the masters were once disciples; receptivity is no hindrance to bold innovation. Good students do not necessarily become great masters, but at least they have the chance.

One reservation: I shall speak of the theatre only as a playwright and a director. My whole life has been dedicated to the writing and production of plays. Aside from my religion, this has been the center of my deepest thought and concern. I shall try now to focus these thoughts for you. The professional critic from his seat on the aisle may well disagree with me. True, he can see what escapes me; but I speak of what I know, and know from experience, as no critic can. If our viewpoints conflict, they may also complement each other.

What is dramatic art in its traditional form? *What* has it become? What *should* it become, what do we hope it may become? I shall speak on these three points. My words may not convince all, but they may perhaps open the way to men of greater genius.

I

Let us first lay down some principles. Today, for lack of guiding principles, much good will, talent, even genius goes to waste; self-flattery, self-conceit, and self-preservation dominate all man's activities and especially literature and the arts. Even if it means being labeled dogmatic or pedantic, we must state boldly any truth we find of value. To drift aimlessly to and fro in the equivocal is the surest way to get nowhere.

Theatre is an *art*. Let us recall briefly the fact that art has two aspects: absolute and relative. It must be absolute: that is demanded by its very nature. An art that does not tend to the absolute, denies itself. Art is born in the mind and nowhere else; it is the ideal, the idea. Yet for all its philosophical and transcendental affinities, art is also relative because it is a technique, a craft that exists only in so far as it is practiced. If the work of art does not emerge from the mind to take perceptible form, it remains unfulfilled. The idea can be judged only by its execution, the genius only by his work. We have all dreamed marvelous poems that will never exist—because they remain a dream. That is the paradox: absolute in theory, art is relative in actuality; execution imposes on it conditions that are inevitably relative—relative to man, to his limitations, to his needs, to his means. That is what the Scholastics teach us, i.e., Aristotle as interpreted by Saint Thomas. It does not seem to me that, in aesthetics at least, we can reject their general conclusions. These conclusions, formulated in a subtle and profound little book, *Art and Scholasticism*, by Jacques Maritain, are exactly what experience teaches; they are not only the wisdom of the ages but also plain common sense.

"All art is free . . . and as art, it is disinterested. . . . The virtue of art looks only at one thing: the goodness to be created, the beauty to shine out from matter, to come into existence according to its own laws, independent of all else." Yet this theoretically pure art must meet something foreign, something opposed to itself, i.e., its instrument, its material. The art is in the artist, the artist in the man. "If there is no man, there is no artist"—and consequently no art. The man who wishes to create will meet a double resistance: the resistance of his own limited nature unable to subject itself wholly to what the mind demands; and the resistance of matter—the indocility of color, marble, sound, or word. He must compromise, he must also use violence; but if he goes too far, forcing the instrument to a note beyond its range, forcing matter into a form alien to its nature, then the instrument, matter itself, will take its own revenge. By all means let art tend to the maximum of freedom, to the absolute; such is its duty. But this maximum has a limit; beyond that limit lie meaninglessness, deformity, cacophony.

In a truly human and therefore relative aesthetic, it would be possible to classify the arts by that degree of the absolute to which they attain, and consequently by the sum of external factors which restrict them. On what level of this hierarchy is dramatic art?

Since Richard Wagner's ambition to restore the Greek tragic poets' concept of drama in "total theatre," such "total theatre" has been exalted as the shrine sacred to the meeting, the marriage, the fusion of all the arts. I do not deny that this point of view has its legitimacy and its grandeur. It is a fact that theatre alone can at one and the same time delight the eye and ear and heart in a balanced harmony of plastic movement, music and poetry.

Does, then, a union of all the arts necessarily produce a super-art? If they are truly united, yes.

Does it produce a purer art? Certainly not.

Each art sharing in this ideal synthesis under an expert hand must look to the other arts for support, inspiration, *élan*, emphasis: gesture must accentuate word, music prolong voice. Nowhere else are so many means available . . . not to mention the chief instrument—the living man, the actor, in whose spirit and flesh the work is given form and movement. But the more complex the material, the greater its resistance to one who seeks to mold it. As the means multiply, so do the servitudes. The result is that "total dramatic art" just because of its great resources becomes in fact the most confused, the most contingent of all arts, impeded by the heaviest passive resistance, balked at every step by massive obstruction.

Does that mean that Aeschylus and Sophocles were not able to master their material, that their greatest achievements were perhaps only brilliant compromises? We cannot know: the major part of their performances—the music, the dance—is forever lost. However, there is no doubt that Wagner in seeking to follow them destroyed all equilibrium in the arts: one art alone, music, submerges the whole drama. In my opinion there is more balance in Gluck and Mozart, in Debussy, and Monteverdi. But that is not our subject here; at the moment I had better not go into the question of "total drama."

I do not mean that music ought never to be used to illuminate or to emphasize, but that it must always be as accompaniment, as relief or as interlude and no more. However, my subject here is literary drama in the form in which it has come down to us and is in actual use today: *the spoken drama.* Does that change the terms of our problem? No, for there is no theatrical art, however stylistic, abstract, intellectual, that does not participate in the other arts, that does not speak through eyes and ears to mind and heart, and that therefore does not demand of the playwright not only concern for good writing—a demand made equally on essayist, poet, novelist—but also an ear for musical order (rhythm, intonation), and an eye for plastic order (movement, image). We find here, then, the same contingencies as in "total drama," the same servitudes, the same "impurity." We must admit this honestly and try to work out a healthy dramaturgy; but first let us look at the causes for the sterility of modern theatre; i.e., our book-centered approach to drama.

II

There is some excuse for this long misunderstanding of the first principles of drama. Where could we learn save from books? The works of great playwrights survive only in the writings that record them. And as they come to us in the most abstract form, we are tempted to look on them as we do on masterpieces of poetry and fiction. Are they not only one more literary form among all the others—comedies of Aristophanes and tragedies of Sophocles, blood brothers to the *Eclogues* of Virgil and the *Dialogues* of Plato? Creon speaks to Antigone as Tityrus to Meliboeus, as Socrates to Alcibiades, though with perhaps a little more pathos. As we read, the drama takes shape in our head. But the laws that shape this drama hold good only for production inside our head and not outside it. Such imaginations are as far from the dramatic truth as the inner world is from the outer world. Don't imagine you have been present in spirit at the authentic drama of Aeschylus or of Shakespeare as Aeschylus or Shakespeare conceived it.

For neither Aeschylus nor Shakespeare, nor Sophocles, nor Calderon wrote plays for us *to read;* they wrote plays *to be acted on the stage* and on a *special* stage, plays for an audience and a special audience, plays for immediate production, immediate and evanescent. A few centuries later, even with the most reliable tradition and incontestable documents, we cannot even begin to imagine the way in which Champmeslé or Duparc interpreted Racine. The most skilful revivals are and can be nothing more than adaptations. What relation is there between the original *Antigone* of the theatre of Dionysus and the academic *Antigone* of the Comédie-Française, even when revived by the genius of Mounet-Sully and Julia Bartet? What the true *Antigone* was, we will never know, nor the *Passion* of Gréban, nor *Othello,* nor *Phaedra,* nor *The Misanthrope.* All we have left is a dead book, a text, a skeleton, a blueprint; admirable as this may be, it is not the total living pattern created by those who conceived it and gave it life. The theatre has joined the "classics" in textbooks and lectures, for the esoteric pleasure of a few highbrows: it has become "literature." It is true that the highest form of theatre does deserve a place among literary forms, yet, I repeat, it is a unique literary form that curiously escapes from the printed page. If it does not overflow the page, it does not really exist at all, it has lost its own reason for existence, or if you prefer, has only a semiexistence. Like oratory, it leads a double life, in books and out of books. It would sacrifice the former rather than the latter, give up the library rather than the stage. We may study it in texts, but the text is only a fragment.

I do not deny its importance. It is the kernel, the mother cell, and nothing can replace it. "In the beginning was the Word . . ."—and this has universal validity. When thought renounces the word, it renounces its own definition; and to drive thought from the theatre would be to empty the theatre of substance, to degrade it. But granted that, we must also hold that drama has its own thought which is not that of poetry or of the novel, thought that must escape the written word if it is to have any life or power.

Book-life is enough for a poem, at least as poetry is conceived today —unfortunately perhaps—less and less for recitation and reading aloud, more and more for the silent, intimate joy of a solitary reader, a secret delight and song, murmured deep in the heart. Some even hold that no audience is needed at all, but this is extreme, monstrous—for the *sine qua non* of all art is to be communicable. Without going that far, let us say that, once recorded in a book, a poem can wait for its reader. We all know that Stendhal wrote his novels for readers to come a half-century after his death. Any purely literary work is almost completely achieved in its book, subject only to contingencies of grammar, logic, and, for poetry, of prosody. More or less beautiful typography changes nothing in the intrinsic value of the words as signs of things or of thoughts.

The playwright who thinks only in the written word as does a poet or novelist, who shapes beautiful forms vibrant with book-contained life, runs the risk of creating museum pieces, lifeless and incapable of life, with no momentum beyond the printed page. Of course, there is such a thing as an "armchair theatre" for those with enough imagination, and plays for such readers do exist, though they are really dialogue-novels. This is an essentially falsifying makeshift, one that hampered the career of the most genuine and perhaps the only truly dramatic writer of the nineteenth century, Alfred de Musset.

Another indefensible attitude is that of the playwright who polishes his sentences and hands them over to the director saying: "Here it is—I've done the words, the rest is your job." The words may be there, but they do not yet exist. Could an author who thus abandons his play once written, fancying that the text is enough, ever have put into the text what his art demands? Could he ever have charged the words with the power potential that alone makes them words of drama, dynamic, expressive, explosive? If so, would he not have wanted to make them come to life himself?

The word indeed rules all things, in the theatre as in books; it is the spirit's ambassador. But in the theatre it must be uttered by a human mouth, it must be incarnate in beings of flesh, it must live and move in them; it dictates the act and is the act (the *act* not in a Thomistic sense, but in the mechanical sense of movement). Before it touches and possesses the hearer, it must touch and possess a composite, indocile, and rebellious instrument: the stage, this particular concrete stage, with all its resources and all its resistances. When the playwright has trapped in written words the always relative absolute of his vision, that dream-group of personalities who meet, love, hate, live, and die at his good pleasure—he has as yet done nothing. He owes it to his art and to himself to design a dream that is realizable, viable, playable, and, if I may coin a pretty poor word, "exteriorizable." I repeat, he must not say, "Here are words, give them life, form, gesture, movement, action!" If that were enough, a scenario would do and drama would amount to no more than that embryo called *commedia dell'arte*. His very words must of themselves evoke image, gesture, movement, action, life; to add all this afterward is a poor artifice. Not that he must calculate them all ahead of time with implacable precision, leaving no room for the actor's imagination: this would paralyze the play. The life he must infuse is an appeal to the living actor; it calls out to another life, to life itself for its own accent and intonation. The playwright implicitly suggests to the interpreter a series of possibilities among which he need only choose. The playwright gives hints, fragments; the interpreter must put them together, give them sense.

But such foresight supposes that the author has complete grasp of technique. Even if he has an inborn feeling for the stage—he'll never write a play unless he has that—even so he must acquire its techniques humbly and perseveringly. Experience is indispensable. The stage offers itself to him as clay to the potter, stone or wood to the carver. Perhaps he will be tempted to take a part himself. . . . If he can, he should; then he truly becomes master craftsman, master of the work. Who should be that master, if not the one who has conceived it? A Shakespeare, a Molière—author, director, and actor—that is the complete playwright.

Here you will quote my own words against me: "That is to canonize the ephemeral, the impermanent." This is exactly our difficulty. For posterity, the writer alone survives, as the material conditions of dramatic art are ever changing with the times. But my point is this: the dramatic writer does not write only for posterity, and to my way of thinking, he'll never reach it at all unless he first writes for his own time. I do not say that he should not seek to be a good writer; I mean that he must accept and embrace what is most transitory in his art, the only substances he can grasp, essentially evanescent as they are. I say that it is in them alone that he will make his drama a reality. I say that only in using them, with all their plus and minus qualities, their possibilities and their limitations, will he create a living thing, dramatically speaking. I say it is only at this price that after one century or ten, when nothing remains of his work but the words, those words will still keep a little of the dynamic power proper to drama and to drama alone. For if today we cannot revive the original *Antigone,* or the original *Macbeth,* or even the original *Polyeucte,* nevertheless, they still have power to move us, fragmentary and changed though they may be; and they can move us in a way that no *Aeneid* or *Divine Comedy,* no *Don Quixote* or Platonic *Dialogue* can. Had the plays been conceived and executed in the abstract, they would perhaps have beauty, but another kind of beauty. The profound life hidden within them, still welling up within them, springs from their vital origin, for in their own day they were conceived in terms of living elements, they were lived out on a stage by men of flesh and bone. Written words, they were written for men's voices, for their masks and their bodies, and the words are still impregnated with this memory. Given such conditions, the play will be what it should be: a drama. Suppress this need of the playwright for immediate concrete realization and he loses his true being; he had better get another job.

There is nothing equal to the stage as a school for humility. The author is essentially dependent on the possibilities of the actor. In accord with the style, with the laws of the dramatic action (plastic form, movement, development), he must further appeal to the costumer, the set designer, the electrician, the mechanic, the director—if he does not himself direct—above all, to the actors. I should insist here on the harm done to dramatic art when the perilous harmony of these instruments is shattered, when the inadequacy of the play, of the playwright's skill, tempts one or another—director, designer, actor—to work on his own. That is the reason for the too-frequent failures in our contemporary theatre. . . . Do we then conclude that when the spirit of the play has fused author and actors into a living whole and the curtain goes up, then at last the work has come to life? . . . No, not at all—as yet, nothing has been done: there has to be an audience.

For dramatic art is not achieved by an author writing his play in a corner, nor by a group of trained actors giving it life on the stage; it requires also an audience to receive it. It is author, actors, audience. We cannot eliminate any one of these three elements: they are integrally bound together.

You can imagine a picture that an artist paints for himself alone. You can imagine a poem that the poet recites to himself from morning to night but never repeats to other men. You can imagine a novel that has never been read, asleep in a desk drawer. But you cannot imagine a play, written, rehearsed, staged, finally produced, and then acted before empty chairs. At least when this does happen, it is far from pleasing to actors and author; for a play is not an end in itself. I mentioned above the strange liberty of novelist and poet in regard to their public. In our time this has turned into contempt for the public. It is true that to run after the public, to flatter its prejudices and weaknesses, is not the best way for an author to deepen and perfect his art. But it is quite another thing to despise the public, to discourage it, to slam the door in its face and refuse to speak to it. The writer who seeks publication wants to be read, otherwise he would write only to give form to his own ideas, his dreams; no need to go into print. All art is essentially social. But as I have also said, he who writes books is absolutely free to wait for his public. They may come or not, many of them or few, today, tomorrow, in ten years or in a century. It does not matter. The poem, novel, essay, remains printed on the pages of its book; it exists now and will not exist with any more reality on the day when it has ten thousand, twenty thousand, a hundred thousand readers. It is not influenced by the eventual reader; he cannot change it either before or after (I am not speaking of commercial literature); it is the reader alone who is influenced, more or less deeply, sooner or later. Great writers, like our classic writers, will show a certain elementary and courteous consideration for their public, being careful in grammar, syntax, logic, using language not too remote from common speech. But they know too that a book can be reread, picked up when one wishes, put aside again, returned to, opened and closed again; hence they will not dilute their thought because it is difficult, nor their style because it is elliptical. If the reader complains, so much the worse for him—he is not worthy to understand! No poem or novel or essay need be popular.

The case is quite different with dramatic work. It is like a book that is being read aloud, its pages turned remorselessly from the first to the last chapter. When a word has been spoken, it has been spoken; you cannot ask the actor to repeat it. That certainly would be a rich comedy, if you could imagine a difficult play punctuated by spectators rising in turn, demanding a replay of some fragment of the first act, a monologue in the third—they had missed the point at the time. The more intelligent—and those longing to seem intelligent—would protest with indignant "shushes!" Altercations, disorder, fist-fights! The drama would move off the stage into the house: action on the stage would stop. I am not fooling. Whether he pays for his seat or not, the spectator wants to understand, right on the spot, what the actor is saying. Hence the need of clarity, of intelligibility. The theatre is the very shrine of the manifest. This is the first servitude that the playwright must accept, willingly or not: no matter how exquisite, stylized, erudite, significant, image-flowered it may be, the language he uses must be understandable by all.

A second servitude is no less rigorous. We must go beyond the letter and the word to the object which they signify. It is no use for the words to be exact, the sentences well constructed, the ideas logically and clearly developed, if the thought or feeling touches no chord in the minds and hearts of the audience and calls forth not even a faint echo of that feeling and that thought! Still worse if they call out a contrary reaction. That can happen; in fact it happens frequently. Some weep, and others laugh at the same thing; two plays are being performed at the same time, one comic, one pathetic. Which is the true play, tell me? The one the author intended? In that case, let him keep it to himself. He is expressing feeling and thoughts to his contemporaries that they do not share. "Excuse me," you may object, "do any two men ever have even one emotion or one idea exactly alike?" Certainly not, in details. But in general, yes. For there are certain intellectual and moral values on which the majority agree in any real society: good and evil, true and false (I do not say beauty and ugliness; these are aesthetic values, and as such are subject to variation in the best of societies; let us not get involved in pure aesthetics, please). Agreement on what is good, agreement on what is true: the man who writes for the theatre must create at least that minimum of communion between his work and his audience. Only then will he touch feelings and win the assent he desires. A play really exists, lives and really lives, only when its life-spark leaps from the stage and from the playwright's soul across to the audience in a moment of vital contact. That is why Jaques Copeau said in a phrase I love to quote:

> There will never be a new theatre (meaning a reaction against today's falsified theatre in a return to tradition) until the day comes when the man in the audience murmurs in his heart and with his heart the same words spoken by the man on the stage.

Yes, the day when author and spectator—and I may add, actor also, for he is the hyphen between them—are one, and stand together on the same intellectual and moral ground. For communion we need such ground. But it can exist only in a truly organic society, by which I mean a society that has a center, a coherence and unanimity: it recognizes one good as *good* and one truth as *true*.

But if society is not organic, or if there is no society at all—what happens? Well, there will not be any theatre, or at the most a fragmentary, stammering, time-serving theatre. There will be no understanding, no communication, no communion. The play will have to crawl into the book, and wait for better days.

It cannot wait too long; for in the theatre, too long a delay in realization alters the concept itself. While the author is working on his play, unless he has at hand and under his control all the elements of language and technique as well as actors and audience, the validity of his "creative activity," as Maritain says, will be hopelessly falsified. He is not one, but two, or rather three; what matters is not only that many speak his name, but that all should answer him.

There is a school that conceives the stage as a room with one wall removed where something happens. I imagine it more as a platform set up in the midst of a crowd, a place of perpetual barter. A dramatic author must make a practical study of the conditions of that barter, discover its laws, make sure that it is possible, that he is not speaking a tongue alien to his public.

Thus dramatic art presupposes both in theory and in fact the existence of a homogeneous society, a "people" in the noblest meaning of the word. It is not a closed art, nor a long-range art, but an open, immediate art. Pity the author who feels within himself power to give substance to a dream that haunts him, yet who can find nothing outside to help him. It would be a miracle if he could create life in the present only by his hope for the future. True, there are certain great works that for special reasons did not succeed in their author's lifetime, even though they were essentially in accord with their age; their dramatic success was only a little deferred. But no plays of real vitality were misunderstood and rejected in their own day only to grip the emotions of an audience centuries later. Plays that survive or revive, as I have said, are plays that have once been alive.

Such are the essential conditions for drama. It depends on its own lifetime to exist or not. No talent, not even genius is enough: good luck is needed too.

You understand that all these principles call for qualification. There are special cases that escape the general rule and to which I shall return. The important thing is that the problem be established on solid ground. I take back nothing essential. The born dramatist may also be a great poet or a great creator of characters; his art may embrace beauties that poetry and novels can possess only fragmentarily, for being neither poet nor novelist, he can call a whole world into life and movement. Yet by this very fact he must work in a relative medium with substance that is in part perishable. No withdrawal to his tower will safeguard purity. Unless he comes down again, the work will not be a play. The dramatist is imprisoned in the contingencies of theatre and of society; the character of his art is essentially social.

FRIEDRICH DUERRENMATT

Problems of the Theatre

Behold the drive for purity in art as art is practised these days. Behold
this writer striving for the purely poetic, another for the purely lyrical,
the purely epic, the purely dramatic. The painter ardently seeks to
create the pure painting, the musician pure music, and someone even
told me, pure radio represents the synthesis between Dionysos and
Logos. Even more remarkable for our time, not otherwise renowned
for its purity, is that each and everyone believes he has found his
unique and the only true purity. Each vestal of the arts has, if you think
of it, her own kind of chastity. Likewise, too numerous to count, are
all the theories of the theatre, of what is pure theatre, pure tragedy,
pure comedy. There are so many modern theories of the drama, what
with each playwright keeping three or four at hand, that for this reason,
if no other, I am a bit embarrassed to come along now with my theories
of the problems of the theatre.

Furthemore, I would ask you not to look upon me as the spokesman
of some specific movement in the theatre or of a certain dramatic technique, nor to believe that I knock at your door as the traveling salesman of one of the philosophies current on our stages today, whether as
existentialist, nihilist, expressionist or satirist, or any other label put on
the compote dished up by literary criticism. For me, the stage is not a
battlefield for theories, philosophies and manifestos, but rather an instrument whose possibilities I seek to know by playing with it. Of
course, in my plays there are people and they hold to some belief or
philosophy—a lot of blockheads would make for a dull piece—but my
plays are not for what people have to say: what is said is there because
my plays deal with people, and thinking and believing and philosophiz-
ing are all, to some extent at least, a part of human nature. The prob-

From *Tulane Drama Review*, Vol. 3, No. 1 (1958). Translated by Gerhard
Nellhaus. Copyright © 1958 by *Drama Review*. Reprinted by permission of
Verlag Der Arche, Zurich, Jonathan Cape, Ltd., and *Drama Review*.

lems I face as playwright are practical, working problems, problems I face not before, but during the writing. To be quite accurate about it, these problems usually come up after the writing is done, arising out of a certain curiosity to know how I did it. So what I would like to talk about now are these problems, even though I risk disappointing the general longing for something profound and creating the impression that an amateur is talking. I haven't the faintest notion of how else I should go about it, of how not to talk about art like an amateur. Consequently I speak only to those who fall asleep listening to Heidegger.

What I am concerned with are empirical rules, the possibilities of the theatre. But since we live in an age when literary scholarship and criticism flourish, I can not quite resist the temptation of casting a few side glances at some of the theories of the art and practice of the theatre. The artist indeed has no need of scholarship. Scholarship derives laws from what exists already; otherwise it would not be scholarship. But the laws thus established have no value for the artist, even when they are true. The artist can not accept a law he has not discovered for himself. If he can not find such a law, scholarship can not help him with one it has established; and when the artist does find one, then it does not matter that the same law was also discovered by scholarship. But scholarship, thus denied, stands behind the artist like a threatening ogre, ready to leap forth whenever the artist wants to talk about art. And so it is here. To talk about problems of the theatre is to enter into competition with literary scholarship. I undertake this with some misgivings. Literary scholarship looks on the theatre as an object; for the dramatist it is never something purely objective, something separate from him. He participates in it. It is true that the playwright's activity makes drama into something objective (that is exactly his job), but he destroys the object he has created again and again, forgets it, rejects it, scorns it, overestimates it, all in order to make room for something new. Scholarship sees only the result; the process, which led to this result, is what the playwright can not forget. What he says has to be taken with a grain of salt. What he thinks about his art changes as he creates his art; his thoughts are always subject to his mood and the moment. What alone really counts for him is what he is doing at a given moment; for its sake he can betray what he did just a little while ago. Perhaps a writer should not talk about his art, but once he starts, then it is not altogether a waste of time to listen to him. Literary scholars who have not the faintest notion of the difficulties of writing and of the hidden rocks that force the stream of art into oft unsuspected channels run the danger of merely asserting and stupidly proclaiming laws that do not exist.

Doubtless the unities of time, place and action which Aristotle—so it was supposed for a long time—derived from Greek tragedy constitute the ideal of drama. From a logical and hence also esthetic point of view, this thesis is incontestable, so incontestable indeed, that the question arises if it does not set up the framework once and for all within which each dramatist must work. Aristotle's three unities demand the greatest precision, the greatest economy and the greatest simplicity in the handling of the dramatic material. The unities of time, place and action ought to be a basic dictate put to the dramatist by literary scholarship, and the only reason scholarship does not hold the artist to them is that Aristotle's unities have not been obeyed by anyone for ages. Nor can they be obeyed, for reasons which best illustrate the relationship of the art of writing plays to the theories about that art.

The unities of time, place and action in essence presuppose Greek tragedy. Aristotle's unities do not make Greek tragedy possible; rather, Greek tragedy allows his unities. No matter how abstract an esthetic law may appear to be, the work of art from which it was derived is contained in that law. If I want to set about writing a dramatic action which is to unfold and run its course in the same place inside of two hours, for instance, then this action must have a history behind it, and that history will be the more extensive the fewer the number of stage characters there are at my disposal. This is simply an experience of how the theatre works, an empirical rule. For me a history is the story which took place before the stage action commenced, a story which alone makes the action on the stage possible. Thus the history behind Hamlet is, of course, the murder of his father; the drama lies in the discovery of that murder. As a rule, too, the stage action is much shorter in time than the event depicted; it often starts out right in the middle of the event, or indeed towards the end of it. Before Sophocles' tragedy could begin, Oedipus had to have killed his father and married his mother, activities that take a little time. The stage action must compress an event to the same degree in which it fulfills the demands of Aristotle's unities. And the closer a playwright adheres to the three unities, the more important is the background history of the action.

It is, of course, possible to invent a history and hence a dramatic action that would seem particularly favorable for keeping to Aristotle's unities. But this brings into force the rule that the more invented a story is and the more unknown it is to the audience, the more careful must its exposition, the unfolding of the background be. Greek tragedy was possible only because it did not have to invent its historical background, because it already possessed one. The spectators knew the myths with which each drama dealt; and because these myths were public, ready coin, part of religion, they made the feats of the Greek tragedians possible, feats never to be attained again; they made possible their abbreviations, their straightforwardness, their stichomythy and choruses, and hence also Aristotle's unities. The audience knew what the play was all about; its curiosity was not focused on the story so much as on its treatment. Aristotle's unities presupposed the general appreciation of the subject matter—a genial exception in more recent times is Kleist's *The Broken Jug*—presupposed a religious theatre based on myths. Therefore as soon as the theatre lost its religious, its mythical significance, the unities had to be reinterpreted, or discarded. An audience facing an unknown story will pay more attention to the story than to its treatment, and by necessity then such a play has to be richer in detail and circumstances than one with a known action. The feats of one playwright can not be the feats of another. Each art exploits the chances offered by its time, and it is hard to imagine a time without chances. Like every other form of art, drama creates its world; but not every world can be created in the same fashion. This is the natural limitation of every esthetic rule, no matter how self-evident such a rule may be. This does not mean that Aristotle's unities are obsolete; what was once a rule has become an exception, a case that may occur again at any time. The one-act play obeys the unities still, even though under a different condition. Instead of the history, the situation now dominates the plot, and thus unity is once again achieved.

But what is true for Aristotle's theory of drama, namely its dependency upon a certain world and hence its validity relative to that world, is also true of every other theory of drama. Brecht is consistent only when he incorporates into his dramaturgy that *Weltanschauung*, the communist philosophy, to which he—so he seems to think—is committed; but in doing so he often cuts off his own nose. Sometimes his plays say the very opposite of what they claim they say, but this lack of agreement can not always be blamed on the capitalistic audience. Often it is simply a case where Brecht, the poet, gets the better of Brecht, the dramatic theorist, a situation that is wholly legitimate and ominous only were it not to happen again.

Let us speak plainly. My introducing the audience as a factor in the making of a play may have seemed strange to many. But just as it is impossible to have theatre without spectators, so it is senseless to consider and treat a play as if it were a kind of ode, divided into parts and delivered in a vacuum. A piece written for the theatre becomes living theatre when it is played, when it can be seen, heard, felt, and thus experienced immediately. This immediacy is one of the most essential aspects of the theatre, a fact so often overlooked in those sacred halls where a play by Hofmannsthal counts for more than one by Nestroy, and a Richard Strauss opera more than one by Offenbach. A play is an event, is something that happens. In the theatre everything must be transformed into something immediate, something visible and sensible; the corollary to this thought, however, is that not everything can be translated into something immediate and corporeal. Kafka, for example, really does not belong on the stage. The bread offered there gives no nourishment; it lies undigested in the iron stomachs of the theatre-going public and the regular subscribers. As luck would have it, many think of the heaviness they feel not as a stomach ache, but as the heaviness of soul which Kafka's true works emanate, so that by error all is set aright.

The immediacy sought by every play, the spectacle into which it would be transformed, presupposes an audience, a theatre, a stage. Hence we would also do well to examine the theatres for which we have to write today. We all know these money-losing enterprises. They can, like so many other institutions today, be justified only on an idealistic basis: in reality, not at all. The architecture of our theatres, their seating arrangements and their stages, come down from the court theatre or, to be more precise, never got beyond it. For this reason alone, our so-called contemporary theatre is not really contemporary. In contrast to the primitive Shakespearean stage, in contrast to this "scaffold" where, as Goethe put it, "little was shown, everything signified," the court theatre made every effort to satisfy a craving for naturalness, even though this resulted in much greater unnaturalness. No longer was the audience satisfied to imagine the royal chamber behind the "green curtain"; every attempt was made to show the chamber. Characteristic of such theatre is its tendency to separate audience and stage, by means both of the curtain as well as having the spectators sit in the dark facing a well-lit stage. This latter innovation was perhaps the most treacherous of all, for it alone made possible the solemn atmosphere in which our theatres suffocate. The stage became a peep show. Better lighting was constantly invented, then a revolving stage, and it is said they have even invented a revolving house! The courts went, but the court threatre stayed on. Now to be sure, our time has discovered its own form of theatre, the movies. But no matter how much we may emphasize the differences, and how important it may be to emphasize them, still it must be pointed out that the movies grew out of theatre, and that they can at last achieve what the court theatre with all its machinery, revolving stages and other effects only dreamed of doing: to simulate reality.

The movies, then, are nothing more nor less than the democratic form of the court theatre. They intensify our sense of intimacy immeasurably, so much so that the movies easily risk becoming the genuinely pornographic art. For the spectator is forced into being a "voyeur," and movie stars enjoy their immense popularity because those who see them come also to feel that they have slept with them; that is how well movie stars are photographed. A larger-than-life picture is an indecency.

Just what then is our present-day theatre? If the movies are the modern form of the old court theatre, what is the theatre? There is no use in pretending that the theatre today is anything much more than a museum in which the art treasures of former golden ages of the drama are put on exhibition. There is no way of changing that. It is only too natural, at a time like ours, a time which, always looking toward the past, seems to possess everything but a living present. In Goethe's time the ancients were rarely performed. Schiller occasionally, but mostly Kotzebue and whoever else they were. It is worthwhile to point out that the movies preempt the theatre of its Kotzebues and Birch-Pfeiffers, and it is hard to imagine what sort of plays would have to be put on today, if there were no movies and if all the scriptwriters wrote for the legitimate stage.

If the contemporary theatre is to a large extent a museum, then this has definite effects on the actors which it employs. They have become civil servants, usually even entitled to their pensions, permitted to act in the theatre when not kept busy making movies. The members of this once despised estate have settled down now as solid citizens—a human gain, an artistic loss. And today actors fit into the order of professional rank somewhere between the physicians and small industrialists, surpassed within the realm of art only by the winners of the Nobel prize, by pianists and conductors. Some actors are visiting professors of sorts, or independent scholars, who take their turn appearing in the museums or arranging exhibitions. The management, of course, takes this into account when it arranges its playbill more or less with an eye to its guest stars; says the management: what play should we put on when this or that authority in this or that field is available to us at such and such a date? Moreover actors are forced to move about in many different acting styles, now in a baroque style, now in a classical one, today acting naturalism, tomorrow Claudel. An actor in Molière's day did not have to do that. The director, too, is more important, more dominant than ever, like the conductor of an orchestra. Historical works demand, and ought to demand, proper interpretation; but directors as yet dare not be as true to the works they put on as some conductors are quite naturally to theirs. The classics often are not interpreted but executed, and the curtain falls upon a mutilated corpse. But then, where is the danger in it all? There is always the saving convention by which all classical things are accepted as perfection, as a kind of gold standard in our cultural life, with all things looked upon as gold that shine in Modern Library or Temple classics. The theatre-going public goes to see the classics, whether they be performed well or not; applause is assured, indeed is the duty of the educated man. And thus the public has legitimately been relieved of the task of thinking and of passing judgment other than those learned by rote in school.

Yet there is a good side to the many styles the present-day theatre must master, although it may at first glance appear bad. Every great age of the threatre was possible because of the discovery of a unique form of theatre, of a particular style, which determined the way plays were written. This is easily demonstrable in the English or Spanish theatre, or the Vienna National Theatre, the most remarkable phenomenon in the German-speaking theatre. This alone can explain the astounding number of plays written by Lope de Vega. Stylistically a play was no problem for him. But to the degree that a uniform style of theatre does not exist today, indeed can no longer exist, to that extent is writing for the theatre now a problem and thus more difficult. Therefore our contemporary theatre is two things: on one hand it is a museum, on the other an experimental field, each play confronting the author with new challenges, new questions of style. Yes, style today is no longer a common property, but highly private, even particularized from case to case. We have no style, only styles, which puts the situation in art today in a nutshell. For contemporary art is a series of experiments, nothing more nor less, just like all of our modern world.

If there are only styles, then, too, we have only theories of the art and practice of the theatre, and no longer one dramaturgy. We now have Brecht's and Eliot's, Claudel's and that of Frisch or of Hochwaelder: always a new theory of drama for each dramatic offering. Nevertheless one can conceive of a single theory of drama, a theory that would cover all particular instances, much in the same way that we have worked out a geometry which embraces all dimensions. Aristotle's theory of drama would be only one of many possible theories in this dramaturgy. It would have to be a new *Poetics,* which would examine the possibilities not of a certain stage, but of the stage, a dramaturgy of the experiment itself.

What, finally, might we say about the audience without which, as we have said before, no theatre is possible? The audience has become anonymous, just "the paying public," a matter far worse than first strikes the eye. The modern author no longer knows his public, unless he writes for some village stage or Caux, neither of which is much fun. A playwright has to imagine his audience; but in truth the audience is he himself—and this is a danger which can neither be altered now nor circumvented. All the dubious, well-worn, politically misused notions which attach themselves to the concepts of "a people" and "society," to say nothing of "a community," have perforce also crept into the theatre. What points is an author to make? How is he to find his subjects, what solutions should he reach? All these are questions for which we may perhaps find an answer once we have gained a clearer notion as to what possibilities still exist in the theatre today.

In undertaking to write a play I must first make clear to myself just where it is to take place. At first glance that does not seem like much of a problem. A play takes place in London or Berlin, in the mountains, a hospital or on a battlefield, wherever the action demands. But it does not work out quite that way. A play, after all, takes place upon a stage which in turn must represent London, the mountains or a battlefield. This distinction need not, but can be made. It depends entirely on how much the author takes the stage into account, how strongly he wants to create the illusion without which no theatre can exist, and whether he wants it smeared on thickly with gobs of paint heaped upon the canvas, or transparent, diaphanous and fragile. A playwright can be deadly serious about the place: Madrid, the Ruetli, the Russian steppe, or he can think of it as just a stage, the world, his world.

How the stage is to represent a given place is, of course, the task of the scene designer. Since designing scenes is a form of painting, the developments which have taken place in painting in our time have not failed to touch the theatre. But the theatre can really neither abstract man nor language, which is in itself both abstract and concrete, and scenery, no matter how abstract it would pretend to be, must still represent something concrete to make sense, and for both of these reasons, abstraction in scenic design has essentially failed. Nevertheless the "green curtain" behind which the spectators have to imagine the place, the royal chamber, was reinstituted. The fact was recalled that the dramatic place and the stage were not one and the same, no matter how elaborate, how verisimilar the stage setting might be. The fact is the place has to be created by the play. One word: we are in Venice; another, in the Tower of London. The imagination of the audience needs but little support. Scenery is to suggest, point out, intensify, but not describe the place. Once more it has become transparent, immaterialized. And similarly the place of the drama to be shown on the stage can be made immaterial.

Two fairly recent plays which most clearly illustrate the possibility referred to as immaterializing the scenery and the dramatic place are Wilder's *Our Town* and *The Skin of Our Teeth*. The immaterializing of the stage in *Our Town* consists of this: the stage is nearly empty; only a few objects needed for rehearsals stand about—some chairs, tables, ladders and so on; and out of these everyday objects the place is created, the dramatic place, the town, all out of the world, the play, the wakened imagination of the spectators. In his other play Wilder, this great fanatic of the theatre, immaterializes the dramatic place: where the Antrobus family really lives, in what age and what stage of civilization, is never wholly clear; now it is the ice age, now a world war. This sort of experiment may be met quite often in modern drama; thus it is indefinite where in Frisch's play, *Graf Oederland,* the strange Count Wasteland abides; no man knows where to wait for Godot, and in *The Marriage of Milord Mississippi* (*Die Ehe des Herrn Mississippi*) I expressed the indefiniteness of the locale (in order to give the play its spirit of wit, of comedy) by having the right window of a room look out upon a northern landscape with its Gothic cathedral and apple tree, while the left window of the same room opens on a southern scene with an ancient ruin, a touch of the Mediterranean and a cypress. The really decisive point in all this is that, to quote Max Frisch, the playwright is making poetry with the stage, a possibility which has always entertained and occupied me and which is one of the reasons, if not the main one, why I write plays. But then—and I am thinking of the comedies of Aristophanes and the comic plays of Nestroy—in every age poetry has been written not only *for,* but *with* the stage. . . .

But a play is bound not only to a place, but also to a time. Just as the stage represents a place, so it also represents a time, the time *during* which the action takes place as well as the time *in* which it occurs. If Aristotle had really demanded the unity of time, place and action, he would have limited the duration of a tragedy to the time it took for the action to be carried out (a feat which the Greek tragedians nearly achieved), for which reasons, of course, everything would have to be concentrated upon that action. Time would pass "naturally," everything coming one after the other without breaks. But this does not always have to be the case. In general the actions on the stage follow one another but, to cite an example, in Nestroy's magical farce, *Death on the Wedding Day (Der Tod am Hochzeitstag)*, there are two acts taking place simultaneously and the illusion of simultaneity is skillfully achieved by having the action of the second act form the background noise for the first, and the action of the first act the background noise for the second. Other examples of how time is used as a theatrical device could be easily recalled. Time can be shortened, stretched, intensified, arrested, repeated; the dramatist can, like Joshua, call to his heaven's orbits, "Theatre-Sun, stand thou still upon Gideon! And thou, Theatre-Moon, in the valley of Ajalon!"

It may be noted further that the unities ascribed to Aristotle were not wholly kept in Greek tragedy either. The action is interrupted by the choruses, and by this means time is spaced. When the chorus interrupts the action, it achieves as regards time—to elucidate the obvious like an amateur—the very same thing the curtain does today. The curtain cuts up and spreads out the time of an action. I have nothing against such an honorable device. The good thing about a curtain is that it so clearly defines an act, that it clears the table, so to speak. Moreover it is psychologically often extremely necessary to give the exhausted and frightened audience a rest. But a new way of binding language and time has evolved in our day.

If I cite Wilder's *Our Town* once again, I do so because I assume that this fine play is widely known. You may recall that in it different characters turn toward the audience and talk of the worries and needs of their small town. In this way Wilder is able to dispense with the curtain. The curtain has been replaced by the direct address to the audience. The epic element of description has been added to the drama. For this reason, of course, this form of theatre has been called the epic theatre.

Yet when looked at quite closely, Shakespeare's plays or Schiller's

Goetz von Berlichingen are in a certain sense also epic theatre. Only in a different, less obvious manner. Since Shakespeare's histories often extend over a considerable period of time, this time span is divided into different actions, different episodes, each of which is treated dramatically. *Henry IV, Part I,* consists of nineteen such episodes, while by the end of the fourth act of *Goetz* there already are no less than forty-one tableaux. I stopped counting after that. If one looks at the way the over-all action has been built up, then, with respect to time, it is quite close to the epic, like a movie that is run too slowly, so that the individual frames can be seen. The condensation of everything into a certain time has been given up in favor of an episodic form of drama.

Thus when an author in some of our modern plays turns toward the audience, he attempts to give the play a greater continuity than is otherwise possible in an episodic form. The void between the acts is to be filled; the time gap is to be bridged, not by a pause, but by words, by a description of what has gone on in the meanwhile, or by having some new character introduce himself. In other words, the expositions are handled in an epic manner, not the actions to which these expositions lead. This represents an advance of the word in the theatre, the attempt of the word to reconquer territory lost a long time ago. Let us emphasize that it is but an attempt; for all too often the direct address to the audience is used to explain the play, an undertaking that makes no sense whatever. If the audience is moved by the play, it will not need prodding by explanations; if the audience is not moved, all the prodding in the world will not be of help.

In contrast to the epic, which can describe human beings as they are, the drama unavoidably limits and therefore stylizes them. This limitation is inherent in the art form itself. The human being of the drama is, after all, a talking individual, and speech is his limitation. The action only serves to force this human being on the stage to talk in a certain way. The action is the crucible in which the human being is molten into words, must become words. This of course, means that I, as the playwright, have to get the people in my drama into situations which force them to speak. If I merely show two people sitting together and drinking coffee while they talk about the weather, politics or the latest fashions, then I provide neither a dramatic situation nor dramatic dialogue, no matter how clever their talk. Some other ingredient must be added to their conversation, something to add pique, drama, double meaning. If the audience knows that there is some poison in one of the coffee cups, or perhaps even in both, so that the conversation is really one between two poisoners, then this little coffee-for-two idyl becomes through this artistic device a dramatic situation, out of which and on the basis of which dramatic dialogue can develop. Without the addition of some special tension or special condition, dramatic dialogue can not develop.

Just as dialogue must develop out of a situation, so it must also lead into some situation, that is to say, of course, a new situation. Dramatic dialogue effects some action, some suffering, some new situation, out of which in turn new dialogue can again develop, and so on and so forth.

However, a human being does more than just talk. The fact that a man also thinks, or at least should think, that he feels, yes, more than anything feels, and that he does not always wish to show others what he is thinking or feeling, has led to the use of another artistic device, the monologue. It is true, of course, that a person standing on a stage and carrying on a conversation with himself out loud is not exactly natural; and the same thing can be said, only more so, of an operatic aria. But the monologue (like the aria) proves that an artistic trick, which really ought not be played, can achieve an unexpected effect, to which, and rightly so, the public succumbs time and again; so much so that Hamlet's monologue, "To be or not to be," or Faust's, are among the most beloved and most famous passages in the theatre.

But not everything that sounds like a monologue is monologue. The purpose of dialogue is not only to lead a human being to a point where he must act or suffer, but at times it also leads into a major speech, to the explanation of some point of view. Many people have lost the appreciation of rhetoric since, as Hilpert maintains, some actor who was not sure of his lines discovered naturalism. That loss is rather sad. A speech can win its way across the footlights more effectively than any other artistic device. But many of our critics no longer know what to make of a speech. An author, who today dares a speech, will suffer the same fate as the peasant Dicaeopolis; he will have to lay his head upon the executioner's block. Except that instead of the Acharnians of Aristophanes, it will be the majority of critics who descend on the author—the most normal thing in the world. Nobody is more anxious to bash out someone's brains than those who haven't any.

Moreover, the drama has always embodied some narrative elements; epic drama did not introduce this. So, for instance, the background of an action has always had to be related, or an event announced in the form of a messenger's report. But narration on the stage is not without its dangers for it does not live in the same manner, is not tangible the way an action taking place on the stage is. Attempts have been made to overcome this, as by dramatizing the messenger, by letting him appear at a crucial moment, or by making him a blockhead from whom a report can only be extracted with great difficulties. Yet certain elements of rhetoric must still be present if narration is to succeed on the stage. Stage narratives can not exist without some exaggeration. Observe, for instance, how Shakespeare elaborates on Plutarch's description of Cleopatra's barge. This exaggeration is not just a characteristic of the baroque style, but a means of launching Cleopatra's barge upon the stage, of making it visible there. But while the speech of the theatre can not exist without exaggeration, it is important to know when to exaggerate and above all, how. . . .

These elements and problems of place, time, and action, which are all, of course, interwoven and are but hinted at here, belong to the basic material, to the artistic devices and tools of the craft of the drama. But let me make it clear here and now, that I make war upon the notion of "the craft of the drama." The very idea that anyone who makes a sufficiently diligent and steadfast endeavor to achieve something in that art will succeed in the end or even that this craft can be learned is a notion we thought discarded long ago. Yet it is still frequently met with in critical writings about the art of play-writing. This art is supposed to be a sound-and-solid, respectable and well-mannered affair. Thus, too, the relationship between a playwright and his art is considered by some to be like a marriage in which everything is quite legal when blessed with the sacraments of esthetics. For these reasons, perhaps, critics often refer to the theatre, much more than to any other form of art, as a craft which, depending on the particular case, has been more or less mastered. If we investigate closely what the critics really mean by "the craft of the drama," then it becomes obvious that it is little else but the sum of their prejudices. There is no craft of the theatre; there is only the mastery of the material through language and the stage or, to be more exact, it is an overpowering of the material, for any creative writing is a kind of warfare with its victories, defeats and indecisive battles. Perfect plays do not exist except as a fiction of esthetics in which, as in the movies, perfect heroes may alone be found. Never yet has a playwright left this battle without his wounds; each one has his Achilles' heel, and the playwright's antagonist, his material, never fights fairly. It is cunning stuff, often not to be drawn out of its lair, and it employs highly secret and low-down tricks. This forces the playwright to fight back with every permissible and even non-permissible means, no matter what the wise exhortations, rules and adages of the masters of this craft and their most honored trade may say. Best foot forward won't get an author anywhere in the drama, not even his foot in the doorway. The difficulties in writing for the drama lie where no one suspects them; sometimes it is no more than the problem of how to have two people say hello, or the difficulty in writing an opening sentence. What is sometimes considered to be the craft of the drama can be easily learned inside half an hour. But how difficult it is to divide a given material into five acts and how few subjects there are which can be divided that way, how nearly impossible it is to write today in iambic pentameter, those things are hardly ever suspected by the hack writers who can slap a play together any time and without trouble, who can always divide any subject into five acts, and who have always written and still write with facility in iambic pentameter. They really pick their material and their language in the way some critics think this is done. They are not so much amateurs when they talk about art as when they tailor art to their talk. No matter what the material is like, they always fashion the same bathrobe to be sure the audience will not catch cold and that it will sleep comfortably. There is nothing more idiotic than the opinion that only a genius does not have to obey those rules prescribed for writers of talent. In that case I should like to be counted among the geniuses. What I want to emphasize strongly is that the art of writing a play does not necessarily start out with the planning of a certain child, or however else a eunuch thinks love is made; but it starts out with love making of which a eunuch is incapable. Though really the difficulties, pains and also fortunes of writing do not lie within the realm of things we mean to talk about or even can talk about. We can only talk about the craft of the drama, a craft that exists only when one *talks* of drama, but not when one writes plays. The craft of the drama is an optical illusion. To talk about plays, about art, is a much more utopian undertaking than is ever appreciated by those who talk the most.

Employing this—really non-existent—craft, let us try and give shape to a certain material. Usually there is a central point of reference, the hero. In theories of the drama a difference is made between a tragic hero, the hero of tragedy, and a comic hero, the hero of comedy. The qualities a tragic hero must possess are well known. He must be capable of rousing our sympathy. His guilt and his innocence, his virtues and his vices must be mixed in the most pleasant and yet exact manner, and administered in doses according to well-defined rules. If, for example, I make my tragic hero an evil man, then I must endow him with a portion of intellect equal to his malevolence. As a result of this rule, the most sympathetic stage character in German literature has turned out to be the devil. The role of the hero in the play has not changed. The only thing that has changed is the social position of the character who awakens our sympathy.

In ancient tragedy and in Shakespeare the hero belongs to the highest class in society, to the nobility. The spectators watch a suffering, acting, raving hero who occupies a social position far higher than their own. This continues still to impress audiences today.

Then when Lessing and Schiller introduced the bourgeois drama, the audience saw itself as the suffering hero on the stage. But the evolution of the hero continued. Buechner's Woyzeck is a primitive proletarian who represents far less socially than the average spectator. But it is precisely in this extreme form of human existence, in this last, most miserable form, that the audience is to see the human being also, indeed itself.

And finally we might mention Pirandello, who was the first, as far as I know, to render the hero, the character on the stage, immaterial and transparent just as Wilder did the dramatic place. The audience watching this sort of presentation attends, as it were, its own dissection, its own psychoanalysis, and the stage becomes man's internal milieu, the inner space of the world.

Of course, the theatre has never dealt only with kings and generals; in comedy the hero has always been the peasant, the beggar, the ordinary citizen—but this was always in comedy. Nowhere in Shakespeare do we find a comic king; in his day a ruler could appear as a bloody monster but never as a fool. In Shakespeare the courtiers, the artisans, the working people are comic. Hence, in the evolution of the tragic hero we see a trend towards comedy. Analogously the fool becomes more and more a tragic figure. This fact is by no means without significance. The hero of a play not only propels an action on, he not only suffers a certain fate, but he also represents a world. Therefore we have to ask ourselves how we should present our own questionable world and with what sort of heroes. We have to ask ourselves how the mirrors which catch and reflect this world should be ground and set.

Can our present-day world, to ask a concrete question, be represented by Schiller's dramatic art? Some writers claim it can be, since Schiller still holds audiences in his grip. To be sure, in art everything is possible when the art is right. But the question is if an art valid for its time could possibly be so even for our day. Art can never be repeated. If it were repeatable, it would be foolish not just to write according to the rules of Schiller.

Schiller wrote as he did because the world in which he lived could still be mirrored in the world his writing created, a world he could build as a historian. But just barely. For was not Napoleon perhaps the last hero in the old sense? The world today as it appears to us could hardly be encompassed in the form of the historical drama as Schiller wrote it, for the reason alone that we no longer have any tragic heroes, but only vast tragedies staged by world butchers and produced by slaughtering machines. Hitler and Stalin can not be made into Wallensteins. Their power is so enormous that they themselves are no more than incidental, corporeal and easily replaceable expressions of this power; and the misfortune associated with the former and to a considerable extent also with the latter is too vast, too complex, too horrible, too mechanical and usually simply too devoid of all sense. Wallenstein's power can still be envisioned; power as we know it today can only be seen in its smallest part for, like an iceberg, the largest part is submerged in anonymity and abstraction. Schiller's drama presupposes a world that the eye can take in, that takes for granted genuine actions of state, just as Greek tragedy did. For only what the eye can take in can be made visible in art. The state today, however, can not be envisioned for it is anonymous and bureaucratic; and not only in Moscow and Washington, but also in Berne. Actions of state today have become *post-hoc* satyric dramas which follow the tragedies executed in secret earlier. True representatives of our world are missing; the tragic heroes are nameless. Any small-time crook, petty government official or policeman better represents our world than a senator or president. Today art can only embrace the victims, if it can reach men at all; it can no longer come close to the mighty. Creon's secretaries close Antigone's case. The state has lost its physical reality, and just as physics can now only cope with the world in mathematical formulas, so the state can only be expressed in statistics. Power today becomes visible, material only when it explodes as in the atom bomb, in this marvelous mushroom which rises and spreads immaculate as the sun and in which mass murder and beauty have become one. The atom bomb can not be reproduced artistically since it is mass-produced. In its face all of man's art that would recreate it must fail, since it is itself a creation of man. Two mirrors which reflect one another remain empty.

But the task of art, insofar as art can have a task at all, and hence also the task of drama today, is to create something concrete, something that has form. This can be accomplished best by comedy. Tragedy, the strictest genre in art, presupposes a formed world. Comedy—in so far as it is not just satire of a particular society as in Molière—supposes an unformed world, a world being made and turned upside down, a world about to fold like ours. Tragedy overcomes distance; it can make myths originating in times immemorial seem like the present to the Athenians. But comedy creates distance; the attempt of the Athenians to gain a foothold in Sicily is translated by comedy into the birds undertaking to create their own empire before which the gods and men will have to capitulate. How comedy works can be seen in the most primitive kind of joke, in the dirty story, which, though it is of very dubious value, I bring up only because it is the best illustration of what I mean by creating distance. The subject of the dirty story is the purely sexual, which because it is purely sexual, is formless and without objective distance. To be given form the purely sexual is transmuted, as I have already mentioned, into the dirty joke. Therefore this type of joke is a kind of original comedy, a transposition of the sexual onto the plane of the comical. In this way it is possible, today in a society dominated by John Doe, to talk in an accepted way about the purely sexual. In the dirty story it becomes clear that the comical exists in forming what is formless, in creating order out of chaos.

The means by which comedy creates distance is the conceit. Tragedy is without conceit. Hence there are few tragedies whose subjects were invented. By this I do not mean to imply that the ancient tragedians lacked inventive ideas of the sort that are written today, but the marvel of their art was that they had no need of these inventions, of conceits That makes all the difference. Aristophanes, on the other hand, lives by conceits. The stuff of his plays is not myths but inventions, which take place not in the past but the present. They drop into their world like bomb shells which, by throwing up huge craters of dirt, change the present into the comic and thus scatter the dirt for everyone to see. This, of course, does not mean that drama today can only be comical. Tragedy and comedy are but formal concepts, dramatic attitudes, figments of the esthetic imagination which can embrace one and the same thing. Only the conditions under which each is created are different, and these conditions have their basis only in small part in art.

Tragedy presupposes guilt, despair, moderation, lucidity, vision, a sense of responsibility. In the Punch-and-Judy show of our century, in this back-sliding of the white race, there are no more guilty and also, no responsible men. It is always, "We couldn't help it" and "We didn't really want that to happen." And indeed, things happen without anyone in particular being responsible for them. Everything is dragged along and everyone gets caught somewhere in the sweep of events. We are all collectively guilty, collectively bogged down in the sins of our fathers and of our forefathers. We are the offspring of children. That is our misfortune, but not our guilt: guilt can exist only as a personal achievement, as a religious deed. Comedy alone is suitable for us. Our world has led to the grotesque as well as to the atom bomb, and so it is a world like that of Hieronymus Bosch whose apocalyptic paintings are also grotesque. But the grotesque is only a way of expressing in a tangible manner, of making us perceive physically the paradoxical, the form of the unformed, the face of a world without face; and just as in our thinking today we seem to be unable to do without the concept of the paradox, so also in art, and in our world which at times seems still to exist only because the atom bomb exists: out of fear of the bomb.

But the tragic is still possible even if pure tragedy is not. We can achieve the tragic out of comedy. We can bring it forth as a frightening moment, as an abyss that opens suddenly; indeed many of Shakespeare's tragedies are already really comedies out of which the tragic arises.

After all this the conclusion might easily be drawn that comedy is the expression of despair, but this conclusion is not inevitable. To be sure, whoever realizes the senselessness, the hopelessness of this world might well despair, but this despair is not a result of this world. Rather it is an answer given by an individual to this world; another answer would be not to despair, would be an individual's decision to endure this world in which we live like Gulliver among the giants. He also achieves distance, he also steps back a pace or two who takes measure of his opponent, who prepares himself to fight his opponent or to escape him. It is still possible to show man as a courageous being.

In truth this is a principal concern of mine. The blind man, Romulus, Uebelohe, Akki, are all men of courage. The lost world order, is restored within them; the universal escapes my grasp. I refuse to find the universal in a doctrine. The universal for me is chaos. The world (hence the stage which represents this world) is for me something monstrous, a riddle of misfortunes which must be accepted but before which one must not capitulate. The world is far bigger than any man, and perforce threatens him constantly. If one could but stand outside the world, it would no longer be threatening. But I have neither the right nor the ability to be an outsider to this world. To find solace in poetry can also be all too cheap; it is more honest to retain one's human point of view. Brecht's thesis, that the world is an accident, which he developed in his *Street Scene* where he shows how this accident happened, may yield—as it in fact did—some magnificent theatre; but he did it by concealing most of the evidence! Brecht's thinking is inexorable, because inexorably there are many things he will not think about.

And lastly it is through the conceit, through comedy that the anonymous audience becomes possible as an audience, becomes a reality to be counted on, and also, one to be taken into account. The conceit easily transforms the crowd of theatre-goers into a mass which can be attacked, deceived, outsmarted into listening to things it would otherwise not so readily listen to. Comedy is a mousetrap in which the public is easily caught and in which it will get caught over and over again. Tragedy, on the other hand, predicated a true community, a kind of community whose existence in our day is but an embarrassing fiction. Nothing is more ludicrous, for instance, than to sit and watch the mystery plays of the Anthroposophists when one is not a participant.

Granting all this there is still one more question to be asked: is it permissible to go from a generality to a particular form of art, to do what I just did when I went from my assertion that the world was formless to the particular possibility for writing comedies today. I doubt that this is permissible. Art is something personal, and something personal should never be explained with generalities. The value of a work of art does not depend on whether more or less good reasons for its existence can be found. Hence I have also tried to avoid certain problems, as for example the argument which is quite lively today, whether or not plays ought to be written in verse or in prose. My own answer lies simply in writing prose, without any intentions of thereby deciding the issue. A man has to choose to go one way, after all, and why should one way always be worse than another? As far as my concepts of comedy are concerned, I believe that here, too, personal reasons are more important than more general ones that are always open to argument. What logic in matters of art could not be refuted! One talks best about art when one talks of one's own art. The art one chooses is an expression of freedom without which no art can exist, and at the same time also of necessity without which art can not exist either. The artist always represents his world and himself. If at one time philosophy taught men to arrive at the particular from the general, then unlike Schiller who started out believing in general conclusions, I can not construct a play as he did when I doubt that the particular can ever be reached from the general. But my doubt is mine and only mine, and not the doubt and problems of a Catholic for whom drama holds possibilities non-Catholics do not share. This is so even if, on the other hand, a Catholic who takes his religion seriously is denied those possibilities which other men possess. The danger inherent in this thesis lies in the fact that there are always those artists who for the sake of finding some generalities to believe in accept conversion, taking a step which is the more to be wondered at for the sad fact that it really will not help them. The difficulties experienced by a Protestant in writing a drama are just the same difficulties he has with his faith. Thus it is my way to mistrust what is ordinarily called the building of the drama, and to arrive at my plays from the unique, the sudden idea or conceit, rather than from some general concept or plan. Speaking for myself, I need to write off into the blue, as I like to put it so that I might give critics a catchword to hang onto. They use it often enough, too, without really understanding what I mean by it.

But these matters are my own concerns and hence it is not necessary to invoke the whole world and to make out as if what are my concerns are the concerns of art in general (lest I be like the drunk who goes back to Noah, the Flood, original sin and the beginning of the world to explain what is, after all, only his own weakness). As in everything and everywhere, and not just in the field of art, the rule is: No excuses, please!

Nevertheless the fact remains (always keeping in mind, of course, the reservations just made) that we now stand in a different relationship to what we have called our material. Our unformed amorphous present is characterized by being surrounded by figures and forms that reduce our time into a mere result, even less, into a mere transitional state, and which give excessive weight to the past as something finished and to the future as something possible. This applies equally well to politics. Related to art it means that the artist is surrounded by all sorts of opinions about art and by demands on him which are based not upon his capacities, but upon the historical past and present forms. He is surrounded therefore by materials which are no longer materials, that is possibilities, but by materials which have already taken on shape, that is some definitive form. Caesar is no longer pure subject matter for us; he has become the Caesar whom scholarship made the object of its researches. And so it happened that scholars, having thrown themselves with increasing energy not only upon nature but also upon the intellectual life and upon art, establishing in the process intellectual history, literary scholarship, philosophy and goodness knows what else, have created a body of factual information which can not be ignored (for one can not be conscious of these facts and at the same time pretend to be so naive that one need pay no attention to the results of scholarship). In this way, however, scholars have deprived the artist of materials by doing what was really the artist's task. The mastery of Richard Feller's *History of Berne* precludes the possibility of an historical drama about the city of Berne; the history of Berne was thus given shape before some literary artist could do it. True, it is a scholastic form (and not a mythical one which would leave the way open for a tragedian), a form that severely limits the field for the artist, leaving to art only psychology which, of course, has also become a science. To rewrite such a history in a creative literary manner would now be a tautology, a repetition by means which are not suitable or fitting, a mere illustration of scholarly insights; in short, it would be the very thing science often claims literature to be. It was still possible for Shakespeare to base his Caesar upon Plutarch, for the Roman was not a historian in our sense of the word but a storyteller, the author of biographical sketches. Had Shakespeare read Mommsen he could not have written his Caesar because he would of necessity have lost the supremacy over his materials. And this holds true now in all things, even the myths of the Greeks which, since we no longer live them but only study, evaluate, investigate them, recognizing them to be mere myths and as such destroying them, have become mummies; and these, bound tightly round with philosophy and theology, are all too often substituted for the living thing.

Therefore the artist must reduce the subjects he finds and runs into everywhere if he wants to turn them once more into real materials, hoping always that he will succeed. He parodies his materials, contrasts them consciously with what they have actually been turned into. By this means, by this act of parody, the artist regains his freedom and hence his material; and thus material is no longer found but invented. For every parody presupposes a conceit and an invention. In laughter man's freedom becomes manifest, in crying his necessity. Our task today is to demonstrate freedom. The tyrants of this planet are not moved by the works of the poets. They yawn at a poet's threnodies. For them heroic epics are silly fairy tales and religious poetry puts them to sleep. Tyrants fear only one thing: a poet's mockery. For this reason then parody has crept into all literary genres, into the novel, the drama, into lyrical poetry. Much of painting, even of music, has been conquered by parody, and the grotesque has followed, often well camouflaged, on the heels of parody: all of a sudden the grotesque is there.

But our time, up to every imaginable trick there is, can handle all that and nothing can intimidate it: the public has been educated to see in art something solemn, hallowed and even pathetic. The comic is considered inferior, dubious, unseemly; it is accepted only when it makes people feel as bestially happy as a bunch of pigs. But the very moment people recognize the comic to be dangerous, an art that exposes, demands, moralizes, it is dropped like a hot potato, for art may be everything it wants to be so long as it remains *gemütlich*.

We writers are often accused of art that is nihilistic. Today, of course, there exists a nihilistic art, but not every art that seems nihilistic is so. True nihilistic art does not appear to be nihilistic at all; usually it is considered to be especially humane and supremely worthy of being read by our more mature young people. A man must be a pretty bungling sort of nihilist to be recognized as such by the world at large. People call nihilistic what is merely uncomfortable. Then also people say, the artist is supposed to create, not to talk; to give shape to things, not to preach. To be sure. But it becomes more and more difficult to create "purely" or however people imagine the creative mind should work. Mankind today is like a reckless driver racing ever faster, ever more heedlessly along the highway. And he does not like it when the frightened passengers cry out, "Watch out" and "There's a warning sign! Slow down" or "Don't kill that child!" What is more, the driver hates it even worse when he is asked, "Who is paying for the car?" or "Who's providing the gas and oil for this mad journey?", to say nothing of what happens when he is asked for his driver's license. What unpleasant facts might then come to light! Maybe the car was stolen from some relatives, the gas and oil squeezed from the passengers, and really not gas and oil but the blood and sweat of us all; and most likely he wouldn't even have a driver's license and it would turn out that this was his first time driving. Of course, it would be embarrassing if such personal questions were to be asked. The driver would much prefer the passengers to praise the beauty of the countryside through which they are traveling, the silver of the river and the brilliant reflection of the icecapped mountains in the far distance, would even prefer to have amusing stories whispered into his ear. Today's author, however, can no longer confine himself with good conscience to whispering pleasant stories and praising the beautiful landscape. Unfortunately, too, he can not get out of this mad race in order to sit by the wayside, writing the pure poetry demanded of him by all the non-poets. Fear, worry, and above all anger open his mouth wide.

How very nice it would be if we could end now on this emphatic note. It would be a conclusion that could be considered at least partially safe and not wholly impossible. But in all honesty we must ask ourselves at this point if any of this makes sense today, if it were not better if we practiced silence. I have tried to show that the theatre today is, in the best sense of the word to be sure, in part a museum, and in part a field of experimentation. I have also tried to show here and there what these experiments are. Is the theatre capable of fulfilling this, its latter destiny? Not only has the writing of plays become more difficulty today but also the rehearsing and performing of these plays is harder. The very lack of time results at best in only a decent attempt, a first probing, a slight advance in what might be the right direction. A play that is to be more than a merely conventional piece, that is really to be an experiment, can no longer be solved at the writing desk. Giraudoux's fortune was that he had Jouvet. Unhappily this happens only once or twice. The repertory theatre of Germany can afford less and less to experiment. A new play must be gotten rid of as quickly as possible. The museum's treasures weigh too heavily in the scales. The theatre, our whole culture, lives on the interest of the well invested intellect, to which nothing can happen any more and for which not even royalties have to be paid. Assured of having a Goethe, Schiller or Sophocles at hand, the theatres are willing now and then to put on a modern piece—but preferably only for a premiere performance. Heroically this duty is discharged, and sighs of relief are breathed all around when Shakespeare is performed next time. What can we say or do? Clear the stages completely! Make room for the classics! The world of the museum is growing and bursts with its treasures. The cultures of the cave dwellers have not yet been investigated to the nth degree.

Let the custodians of the future concern themselves with our art when it is our turn. It does not make much difference then if something new is added, something new is written. The demands made of the artist by esthetics increase from day to day. What is wanted is the perfection which is read into the classics. And let the artist even be suspected of having taken one step backwards, of having made a mistake, just watch how quickly he is dropped. Thus a climate is created in which literature can be studied but not made. How can the artist exist in a world of educated and literate people? This question oppresses me, and I know no answer. Perhaps the writer can best exist by writing detective stories, by creating art where it is least suspected. Literature must become so light that it will weigh nothing upon the scale of today's literary criticism: only in this way will it regain its true worth.

ORIGINS

One approach to the problem of defining drama has been to seek its essence in its origins. Thus Nietzsche, in *The Birth of Tragedy,* stressed the germinative influence of music in Greek tragedy, and scholars like Gilbert Murray, Jane Harrison, A. E. Cornford, and Theodor H. Gaster have combined anthropological findings and inferences from the earliest known dramatic specimens to construct theories about the development of drama out of primitive religious rituals. As Aristotle cryptically suggests, drama certainly did not burst full blown from the forehead of Thespis or some other cultural inventor but grew by gradual improvisation, tragedy from the "dithyramb" or choric hymn in honor of Dionysus and comedy from the "phallic songs" that presumably celebrated Dionysus as a fertility god. But Dionysus is merely one of many dying-and-reviving gods who lent themselves as central characters in the ritual year-drama from which drama as an art form may have evolved. Relying on Johan Huizinga's concept of the play-element in culture, Benjamin Hunningher discusses how man's instinct for imitative play was afforded expression in ritual dramas by which he sought to negotiate with mysterious and sacred forces behind nature. And in the third selection, Richard Southern analyzes three specific rites of graduated sophistication in order to suggest the phases through which primitive ritual may pass on its way toward theatrical drama. All of these selections, we need to bear in mind, stress the transformative process *from* ritual *toward* drama. To assume that because it may have originated in primitive rites drama *is* essentially ritualistic is to court the "genetic fallacy."

ARISTOTLE

Poetics

IV

Poetry in general seems to have sprung from two causes, each of them lying deep in our nature. First, the instinct of imitation is implanted in man from childhood, one difference between him and other animals being that he is the most imitative of living creatures, and through imitation he learns his earliest lessons, and no less universal is the pleasure felt in things imitated. We have evidence of this in the facts of experience. Objects which in themselves we view with pain we delight to contemplate when reproduced with minute fidelity, such as the forms of the most ignoble animals and of dead bodies. The cause of this again is that to learn gives the liveliest pleasure, not only to philosophers but to men in general, whose capacity, however, of learning is more limited. Thus the reason why men enjoy seeing a likeness is that in contemplating it they find themselves learning or inferring, and saying perhaps, "Ah, that is he." For if you happen not to have seen the original, the pleasure will be due not to the imitation as such, but to the execution, the coloring, or some such other cause.

Imitation, then, is one instinct of our nature. Next there is the instinct for harmony and rhythm, meters being manifestly sections of rhythm. Persons, therefore, starting with this natural gift developed by degrees their special aptitudes, till their rude improvisations gave birth to poetry.

Poetry now diverged in two directions, according to the individual character of the writers. The graver spirits imitated noble actions and the actions of good men. The more trivial sort imitated the actions of meaner persons, at first composing satires, as the former did hymns to the gods and the praises of famous men. A poem of the satirical kind cannot indeed be put down to any author earlier than Homer, though

Translated by S. H. Butcher, *Aristotle's Poetics,* revised edition, 1911.

many such writers probably there were. But from Homer onward, instances can be cited: his own *Margites*, for example, and other similar compositions. The appropriate meter was also here introduced; hence the measure is still called the iambic or lampooning measure, being that in which people lampooned one another. Thus the older poets were distinguished as writers of heroic or of lampooning verse.

As in the serious style Homer is pre-eminent among poets, for he alone combined dramatic form with excellence of imitation, so he too first laid down the main lines of comedy by dramatizing the ludicrous instead of writing personal satire. His *Margites* bears the same relation to comedy that the *Iliad* and *Odyssey* do to tragedy. But when tragedy and comedy came to light, the two classes of poets still followed their natural bent: the lampooners became writers of comedy, and the epic poets were succeeded by tragedians, since the drama was a larger and higher form of art.

Whether tragedy has as yet perfected its proper types or not and whether it is to be judged in itself or in relation also to the audience, this raises another question. Be that as it may, tragedy—as also comedy—was at first mere improvisation. The one originated with the leaders of the dithyramb, the other with those of the phallic songs, which are still in use in many of our cities. Tragedy advanced by slow degrees; each new element that showed itself was in turn developed. Having passed through many changes, it found its natural form, and there it stopped.

Aeschylus first introduced a second actor; he diminished the importance of the chorus and assigned the leading part to the dialogue. Sophocles raised the number of actors to three and added scene-painting. Moreover, it was not till late that the short plot was discarded for one of greater compass, and the grotesque diction of the earlier satyric form for the stately manner of tragedy. The iambic measure then replaced the trochaic tetrameter which was originally employed when the poetry was of the satyric order and had greater affinities with dancing. Once dialogue had come in, nature herself discovered the appropriate measure. For the iambic is, of all measures, the most colloquial: we see it in the fact that conversational speech runs into iambic form more frequently than into any other kind of verse—rarely into hexameters, and only when we drop the colloquial intonation. The additions to the number of episodes or acts, and the other improvements of which tradition tells, must be taken as already described, for to discuss them in detail would doubtless be a large undertaking.

BENJAMIN HUNNINGHER

The Primitive Phase

Theater is play—which defines it neither as real nor as unreal, neither as wise nor as foolish, neither as good nor as bad. Theater serves no practical purpose if judged by the standards of everyday life. It is uncommon, separate. Exclusively for those who similarly separate themselves from life (its participants) does theater become truthful, important, orderly. This holds true, not only for theater, but for all art. It characterizes to a great extent also another human activity—the rite. Here lies our first and most permanent tie between the theater and art on one hand and religion and rite on the other. Everything which "does not belong," which serves no direct purpose in nature, which knows no function in society, which essentially escapes the intellect, belongs to the other side of life, to the "totally different," [1] that has from primitive times been experienced as a supernatural force, usually leading into religion.

As an idea, "play" may escape the meshes of rational definition, but as phenomenon we see it everywhere, always a satisfaction to the human urge for pleasure and recreation. It is apparent that from it in spiritual activity the metaphor,[2] for example, has developed and with that, the entire potentiality for abstract thought, which in turn indicates that not only religion, but also man's entire spiritual life, is unthinkable and impossible without play. Play releases man from the limits of matter. In stage-play, pleasure lies in imitation, originally of external and tangible existence. By the same metaphoric road,[3] this imitation can reach the entire breadth and depth of human emotion. The theater and the rite meet again in such imitation: in primitive cultures, in fact, they are one, and the same.

Huizinga put the question of whether or not the peculiar relationship between play and beauty is the result of the very form and order created by play. It is true, at any rate, that play fences in an area of the imagination in which it creates absolute order, strictly guarded against anything which might disturb the *in-lusio,* the illusion. In every respect, the order it creates is contrary to the disorder of the imperfect world outside the play area: the contrast is so obvious that it seems willed and purposed. With that observation, play is revealed to serve not only as pleasure but also as protection: it creates order to bring a certain part of the chaotic world under control. Though still far from any practical purpose in everyday life, it acquires with this a certain social or perhaps more psychological function.

Protection manifests itself, for instance, in the play of the children. They play at "getting married," not to imitate what they have seen, but to recreate: in doing this, they organize and arrange things according to their own standard. In some languages, children use a diminutive form for such a situation, as in Dutch *bruiloftje,* "little wedding." Their play establishes some control over the adult world. That the function of play was originally protective is more especially seen in the play of primitive people, who as adults, of course, reflect in their games the problems of their mature life, the struggle for food and the preservation of life.

To them, the order of nature, the regular succession and change of the seasons, is of utmost importance. It makes no difference whether one accepts Frobenius' opinion, that the discovery of nature's succession assailed the emotions of primitive men and "the actual fact of the natural rhythm in growth and decline seized upon their inward understanding and this in its turn led to compulsive and reflex action," [4] or prefers Huizinga's theory that the order of play preceded awareness of natural order which was incorporated into play and portrayed by it. Nearly all primitive people enact the regular changes of nature in their plays,[5] clearly intending to bring under their control elements which they do not dominate and, if necessary, to correct them. In such enactment, the element of play retreats gradually into the background and presentation comes to the fore, to such an extent that we may even speak of vicarious representation in dramatic action. So it coincides with ritual. But there purpose prevails.

Play, however, remains inherent in man, and thus the term *Sacer Ludus* [6] is very appropriate. The joy derived from playing is maintained in ritual and expressed itself as spiritual elevation and exaltation, especially when the *Sacer Ludus* "succeeds" and order is felt to be maintained and protected through the performance of the rite. The degree of emotion, together with the necessary collectivity of the rite and lack of adequate language, forced ritualistic representation into the form of dance.

At this point we must go into greater detail. Primitive man depended upon nothing so much as the order of nature. Although the twentieth century has taught many of us the brutality of bare existence, it is still difficult to imagine the perpetual fear in the primitive's life of endless subjection. Now that we can understand a little of such anxiety, we realize that in archaic times every deviation in the natural order brought with it terror and the bitter struggle for life. The primitive somehow had to overpower the force maintaining or disturbing order in nature and to compel it to regulate time and tide so that man might live another year in the jungle. Existence, life, could not be thought of in terms of decades; men managed from season to season, periodically renewing their lease on life.[7] That lease was never bestowed mercifully; it had to be extorted with every ounce of force at the primitive's disposal.

The individual could not achieve success in such an environment. As a matter of fact, he could not even survive alone in the wilderness. If anything were to be accomplished, the community had to do it; and for this reason, primitive men lived a communal existence [8] in which the individual for his own sake as well as for the tribe's had to subordinate his own interests completely. The community fought for the lease on life and won it: over the whole primitive world, the community strove by collective rites to approach and dominate the force which ruled nature.[9]

The circumstances under which the rites were performed make it clear to us with what fear, what intensity, what concentration of power they were performed. The element of adoration is completely lacking.[10] If we use Frobenius' word "Ergriffenheit," we had best translate it as "awe" of the change and succession in nature. For the primitives, hope was fervent and endless, but security was unobtainable and the threat of destruction and death never ending.

How could this unknown but ever present force be approached and coerced into order? Language could not yet do it; it was too undeveloped. Even for their own uses, the language of primitives did not extend beyond the primary needs of daily life. Was it not far easier for them to portray the course and suspense of the hunt in a mimic dance after it was over than in the still undeveloped and intractable symbol of the word? When we notice that the American Indians, for example, moved that dance from after the hunt to before it, we know that we have reached the next stage of development, of which the purpose is not to relate what has passed but to dominate what is to come. The Supernatural is still too alien and too different to evolve into an individual or a god, but it was certainly thought of as having human qualities. If it could not understand language, it could at any rate understand reality. The minute imitation of that reality, performed by the community on its own behalf, made the desire of the community perfectly clear.

This is the basis for all sympathetic rites, properly called "charms." In the first place, they explain something and express a wish. More than this, the performers themselves enjoy their imitative dance and conceive of the supernatural forces as also deriving pleasure from watching the performance, which pleasure in turn will bring those forces to quicker compliance and concession. The more ardor glowing in the imitative performance, the greater the results on which the tribesmen may count. There was, as we can see, double reason for performing with heart and soul, and the dances had a frenetic character among all primitive peoples.[11]

More than this, nothing so transports a person, so enables him to approach and enter into the Supernatural as the rhythm of a dance. "In song and in dance man exhibits himself as a member of a higher community: he has forgotten how to walk and speak, and is on the point of taking a dancing flight into the air." [12] Nietzsche was speaking of Greek archaic man, but there was no essential difference between him and the archaic man of other periods and regions. "Who knows the power of the dance, lives in God," said the mystic Jeladdin Rum, speaking of his dancing Mewlewidervishes.[13] Primitive man had not conceived of the gods, but what could bring him into closer and more intimate contact with that vaguely human Supernatural force than the winging rhythm of the dance? "It grips the soul, and even the soul of the gods." [14]

Frazer noted and set down many of these sympathetic dances.[15] Well-known, among others, are the rain charms, in use among the Indians of the Plains today. In times of continuous drought, the medicine man leads the adult males in a vigorous and lengthy dance around a sacred hill or tree. When the dance has reached its peak, he himself climbs the hill or tree and repeatedly pours water on the ground or on the dancers' heads.[16] It goes without saying that the spirit who enjoyed the dance realizes that he must give rain. If he fails to do so, the dance will be repeated over and over again, until the spirit understands either that he must in decency repay the tribe for his pleasure, or (more probably) that the force of the dance must press him to fulfill the dancers' desires.

In archaic societies usually the whole community dances, not just the able-bodied males. The dances are exact—a single misstep and the dance must be repeated from the beginning, to prevent the spirit from becoming confused and to preserve the order of the dance itself. The members of the tribe are therefore trained from infancy, and in the complicated dance forms accompanying a growing culture, a leader is needed who through his special relationship with the Supernatural can give detailed instructions concerning the dance. The priests consequently lead the rites, which remain nonetheless expressive of community desire.

Even more important than these incidental rites was the great drama of what, for centuries, we have casually referred to as "the Year." In the archaic world the return of spring meant no less than the escape from death and the return of hope in life. Naturally enough, the community did everything in its power to facilitate and insure spring's return, when a new lease on life could be taken for another cycle of seasons. In or after the solstice—in what we now call December—an early beginning was made to drive out the enemy, winter, death, after which followed the rites of purification, fasting, and lighting of fires. Februarius was in Rome the time of purification and originally the last month of the year.

Through often repeated communal and mimetic dance-ritual, the tribes did everything they could to attract the new life which they longed to receive. As soon as the spring appeared in nature the entire community hurried to welcome it and strengthen its power by an elaborate representation of its victory over winter and summer. The battle between winter and summer is of primary importance in the development of primitive religion as well as of the theater. Frazer's numerous examples demonstrate how, through annual repetition of these rites, the idea of a definite seasonal change retires to the background and winter-in-general gradually opposes summer-in-general, death opposes life.

And slowly an identification was formed between the community leader in the rites of summer and the new life about to break forth, which must afterwards die down completely before hope might be nursed for a new spring. From this concept arose the performance of the year-king or year-priest, known over the whole world, who overcomes death to bring life. With the approach of winter the year-king himself turns into the daemon of death and must perish in a duel with the champion or king of the next year for life to spring forth anew.

This is not the place to enter into a discussion of the secondary developments of this idea, or of the ways they influence theatrical forms still known to us. It was sometimes possible for a king to substitute for himself a slave or captive alien, a mock-king for a day or more, who had to take over the duties of ruler and enjoy all the king's privileges, after which he was sent to his death, burdened with scorn. The fates of Christopher Sly, Krelis Louwen, and Jeppe-of-the-Hill are less tragic, though all are the descendants of those grossly misused substitutes for the year-king. After the execution, the real king came out of hiding to be honored as the reincarnation of life. In other places, the ruler had to be slain and succeeded by his son; in the blood relationship was expressed the continuity of life. Such succession, of course, led to the institution of sacred and venerated dynasties.

Secondary developments are important in the development of the theater for other reasons, since with them arise the myths which eventually change the character of ritual. The interchange of life and death did not remain the subject of ritual dance, but was replaced by the acts and deeds of a certain priest or king or, finally, god. Though his story was still to some extent a reflection of the old year-drama, he himself received a name and became in some degree an individual; the imagination and memory of many generations could add more deeds, more actions to the basic drama of his existence. This development deeply influenced ritual performance, for in the cult of such a hero, the dancer taking his part was no longer himself, a human being reaching out of himself to the Supernatural, but became the very god, or his enemy, or his son: in short, he attempted to present someone else, to play a part.[17]

It is difficult for modern man to realize the enormous importance of this change—indeed, we can hardly imagine the real significance to archaic man of the mimic dance-rite.[18] We must therefore emphasize once more the fact that for him this was no aimless dance but a carefully-planned portrayal, a reflection of observed natural phenomena. For him, life was too difficult to permit art for art's sake alone: the dance-ritual was a means of entering the Unseen by force, of driving one's way into the Power over the world, to capture for oneself some participation in that Power. If the primitive had not been convinced that he could achieve this result through his dance, the rite would have been no rite, but merely dance. But ritual cannot exist without a practical purpose.

Every believer, no matter how simple or how exalted, is tempted by doubt. It should not surprise us, then, that even in the trance of his communal dance-rite, primitive man sometimes had difficulty in accepting the efficacy of those things which he so dearly wished to believe: union with the world-force, his ability to make the Unseen visible to his fellow-believers through the medium of his dance. Therefore he put on a mask: the bigger, the more exalted that mask was, the more the onlookers and other dancers were confirmed in their identification of the wearer with, let us say, the rain-daemon.

Their belief in its turn would work upon him, so that their greater intensity in the performance of the ritual would complete, beyond all doubt, the desired union within himself. The mask was thus a matter of prime importance in the accomplishment of unification with the mighty Power.

Among primitive men the belief was widespread that every living creature manifested itself in dual shape. This held good not only for the visible aspect of nature, but also for the invisible aspect; and in this concept originated, as a sort of safety measure, the frequently used double mask. On the one hand, the mask protected the dual manifestation of the man who wore it; on the other, it captured the daemon he portrayed: an explanation which should make clear why, among some primitive peoples, the mask almost automatically caused the union of its wearer with the daemon.

In the history of the theater the double mask has played but a minor role, at least so far as ancient and western cultures are concerned. The single mask, on the other hand, remained exceptionally important until the end of the classical period and was found in the later period, for example, in the *commedia dell'arte*. It developed from archaic times in the change from nature-rite to myth-cult and finally came to portray an individual: the king, the hero, and at last the god celebrated in the myth. With this, its function changed as well. For the actor, it became an external expedient to characterize the figure he represented; at the same time, it long maintained something of its hieratic character in the eyes of the onlookers and served as a *trait d'union* between cult and stage. For precisely the same reasons, the sacred garments worn in the cult were retained in the Greek theater.

Although the development toward mythical rite implied a far-reaching change, the subject of the portrayal remained more or less the same. Again and again we encounter the struggle between life and death, with destruction on one side and resurrection on the other. When portrayal by representation replaced action *in concreto,* the mimicking rite could gradually adjust itself to the myth's essential miracle. A year-king or year-priest who was slain and lived on in his successor gave way to a hero or demi-god—in the ancient world, for example, Hercules. Finally it was the god himself who died, went to the realm of the dead, to return again for his resurrection. This imagery, indeed, comes closer to the original vegetation-subject than the old rite did, with its protagonist and antagonist. It is understandable that in the development of ritual drama toward the mythical religions, such as those of the Near East, rite and myth merged, and many scholars feel that this is what took place in prehistoric Greece. In any case, with these religions we have definitely passed out of the primitive phase.

In addition to the year-rite and the manifestations of sympathetic magic, the archaic period provided frequent opportunity for the mimic-dance to develop out of the complexities of religious consciousness. Hunting and war dances were designed to bring good luck and were thus to some extent charms. The same does not hold true for the initia-tion rites, performed when youths were inducted into tribal adulthood. The initiators as well as the initiated considered this a turning point in the lives of the young men; more than that, it was for them a departure from an old life and the undertaking of a new one—as many initiation rites clearly indicate, a kind of rebirth.[19]

Introduction into the secrets of life and their meaning belonged, of course, to initiation. Almost always, the mimic-dance took over from a language as yet too little developed to describe all the secrets passed on by the tribe to the young men. The initiation continued to develop itself, too, and in a much later phase the initiation dance was often so lost in conflicting and confusing symbolism that only the priest could explain its ancient meaning. At this point, its original function, that of teaching the inexperienced, had disappeared entirely, and in turn language, now fully developed, was called in to assist; explanation by the initiating priest became the rule.

There is certainly some question as to whether or not these rites, in addition to expressing the urge to mimic, also served as occasions for joy, pleasure, and imitation for its own sake. In any case, they do not compare with the year-play as a propelling force in the development of drama. They are worth considering here, though, because of the influence they exercised and because of the importance some scholars have attached to them.

All these rites, their developments and secondary aspects, may seem remote to us, but Europe is full of relics of similar archaic cults. Its literature may not give much evidence of this, but we must bear in mind that in the history of mankind, literature belongs only to the most recent period. Still, at the beginning of vernacular literature in Europe we have the *Jeu de la feuillée*, by Adam le Bossu, and somewhat later, in the Hulthem Manuscript (conservatively dated about 1375) the *Abel spel vande Winter ende Somer* (Noble play of Winter and Summer), whose close ties—however far their form from archaic rites—with the year-drama cannot be denied. Again, clear traces of rites are to be found in the English mumming-plays, which belong more to folklore than to formal literature.

In his *Golden Bough*, James Frazer collected a treasury of European folk customs that clearly go back to fertility rites; [20] and the results of later researches make it clear that these same rites were customary among the oldest tribes of Europe,[21] and in turn among the generations following them. What else can we expect, after all, since the struggle for life changes so little because of different climates or continents?

A single example should suffice; in various districts of Europe, particularly in southern Germany, at the approach of spring the men (sometimes only the bachelors) customarily carry winter, or death, out of their village in the shape of a monstrous straw doll. With much noise, they throw the doll into the water, sometimes even burn it, but not before its women's clothing has been removed. This execution is always accompanied by a round-dance. The clothes become in turn the symbol of continuity and are put on a maiden, colorfully adorned. Garlands deck her hair, and she is carried in triumph to the village amidst the cheers and shouts of the villagers. This folk custom, apparently so simple and happy, is directly descended from the bloody rites of which we spoke earlier.

We must observe that such customs were not written down and described before the nineteenth century, which indicates that many traditions continued to exist through the years in different forms and disguises, without leaving the slightest trace in writings and archives. The cultural historian particularly must constantly keep this fact in mind.

It is clear from the foregoing survey that in the rites of archaic religion there was plenty of opportunity for the exercise of the human urge to mimetic play. This germ of theater was particularly developed in the year-play, though it was unable to expand into an independent expression and its ritual characteristics never disappeared. Its performance was an action in itself and had a prescribed purpose: it was not a mental commemoration; it was an act of identification carried out in energetic ecstasy by the entire tribe or community. Through this autonomous act, it aimed at obtaining for that group a part in the Supernatural, at extorting demands from the Power-over-Life. With the appearance of myth, that development began which eventually led to the separation of ritual and theater.

NOTES

1. See R. Otto, *Das Heilige. Über das Irrationale in der Idee des Göttlichen und sein Verhältnis zum Rationalen*, 1917, Gotha.
2. See J. Huizinga, *Homo Ludens*, Haarlem, 1938, Ch. I.
3. See Jac. van Ginneken, *Gelaat, Gebaar en Klankexpressie*, Leiden, 1919, ch. V and VI.
4. Leo Frobenius, *Schicksalskunde im Sinne des Kulturwerdens*, Leipzig, 1932, p. 142.
5. Frazer, *op. cit. passim*, esp. chapter "The Killing of the Tree-spirit."
6. G. van der Leeuw, *Wegen en Grenzen*, 2 ed., Amsterdam, 1948, p. 107.
7. Theodor H. Gaster, *Thespis. Ritual, Myth and Drama in the Ancient Near East*, New York, 1950.
8. John Collier, *Indians of the Americas*, New York, 1948, ch. II.
9. W. O. E. Oesterley, *The Sacred Dance. A Study in Comparative Folklore*, Cambridge, 1923, p. 15 seq.
10. Loomis Havemeyer, *The Drama of Savage People*, New Haven, 1916, p. 109.
11. Oesterley, *op. cit.*, p. 19 seq.
12. F. Nietzsche, *The Birth of Tragedy*, transl. Wm. A. Haussmann, Edinburgh-London, 1927, p. 27.
13. Erwin Rohde, *Psyche, Seelenkult und Unsterblichkeitsglaube der Griechen*, 7–9 Aufl., Tübingen, 1921. H. S. Nyberg, *Die Religion des alten Iran*, Leipzig, 1938.
14. G. van der Leeuw, *op. cit.*, p. 87.
15. Frazer, *op. cit.*, ch. "Sympathetic Magic" and "The Magical Control of the Weather."
16. W. Mannhardt, *Wald- und Feldkulte*, I, p. 214 seq. and p. 327 seq. Curt Sachs, *World History of the Dance*, New York, 1937, ch. II.
17. See Th. H. Gaster, *op. cit.*; also Jane E. Harrison, *Ancient Art and Ritual*, New York-London, 1913.
18. Cecil J. Sharp and A. P. Oppé, *The Dance*, London, 1924, p. 4 seq.

19. Jane E. Harrison, *Themis,* 2 ed., Cambridge, 1927. George Thomson, *Aeschylus and Athens,* London, 1941.

20. Frazer, *op. cit.,* v. IV, p. 233 seq., p. 247, p. 249 seq., p. 260, p. 264 seq.; v. IX, p. 404 seq.; v. X, p. 119 seq.

21. O.a. Bertha S. Phillpotts, *The Elder Edda and Ancient Scandinavian Drama,* Cambridge, 1920. Vilhelm Grønbeck, *The Culture of the Teutons,* London, 1931.

RICHARD SOUTHERN

The Costumed Player

THE BAVARIAN WILD MEN

Looking at a West-End theatre, or a theatre on Broadway, or in Paris, or Bombay, or Osaka, at night with the names in lights and the audience going in past the box-office, it is really not believable that this all started out of a 10th-century Christian Church liturgy. It is no more convincing to place its origin on the threshing-floors of Ancient Greece. Would it then be any more satisfying to say that the beginning lies in Primitive Ritual?

Let us take an example of primitive ritual; turning from the lighted theatre let us go into the Bavarian Mountains.

There a fairly simple, ancient ceremony survives. On the eve of St. Nicholas' Day (6 December) certain masked men come out of the snowy woods on skis and approach a village. An atmosphere reigns over the houses. The older, more experienced inhabitants and the children remain indoors, and peer through the windows into the night not without apprehension for what they will see. Horns of elfland blow. The "wild men" wear voluminous distorting costumes of animal skins, and heavy concealing headdresses with horns or antlers (Fig. 1). They knock at doors and windows and claim kisses of the girls or catch them in the street and rub them with snow. The reign of the Wild Men lasts till daybreak.

Now, can we properly call this "theatre"? Can we decide even that the origins of theatre lie here?

It seems to me that we shall have to say that the answer is both Yes and No. There are no words; there is no play. There is no particular place of performance; no stage; no scenery; no playhouse; and no rehearsal. Here there is not even—and this is perhaps the most noticeable lack of all—any assembled audience as such. True, there are many who furtively watch, and a few who brave the elements and the eeriness for, more or less, the devil of it. But what there is, is the masked group of men and the action itself—the thing they do. Resuming in two words we have the *Costumed Player*.

Fig. 1. A Bavarian Wild Man

But how far can this be called theatrical action in the sense of being a prepared performance of something with the intent to make an effect on people? At first one might say, "In no sense at all!" But then there is the putting on of the costumes and masks. There is no rehearsal; but there may be (it is hard to say) a quality of *improvisation*, for not one of these "performers" can know just what will happen or how the night will go. And we shall admit, on reflection, that that very uncertainty is an experience which no player ever escapes even in a modern theatre; that particular quality of the unpredictable, and its accompanying demand for a quick ability to improvise, is a quality of all theatre.

Beyond this it is just possible to see the germ at least of three other things that may grow into positive theatre elements; procession, visitation in disguise, and the animal.

First: we have the notion of *processional theatre* because the Wild

Men go through the streets from house to house. They do this, almost certainly, for the reason that is the original reason for all processional theatre; namely, to spread the magic about a whole community. This may perhaps be an earlier idea even than the public assembly gathered for the same purpose. However, the reason for both the assembly of people at an act of theatre and for the procession from house to house among the people's homes is to effect a communal spreading of the magic of a ritual act.

It is not difficult to see the origin of this. When we realize that much of primitive theatre consists in giving—the distribution of Good Omen —we may well see that a primitive people would wish the omen to be communicated not only to themselves personally but to their flocks, to their crops, to their very hearths and homes for the coming year. And thus it is not surprising to see the act of Good Luck performed at one house and then at another, just as the waits or carol singers pass from door to door at Christmas. Indeed there is more than a similarity, there is an identity of purpose, for the waits travelled to take the Luck to the homes of the community. The waits did not primarily call for coppers. (In many cases where a collection of money is made today, we find that there originally existed a ritual not for receiving but for giving. What the waits bring was once more significant than what they now receive.)

Thus then there is a processional element in early theatre. Not only is something enacted, but the virtue of the enactment is communicated by a led procession to houses, to fields and to flocks. This leads on to the next point.

Second: We shall meet again in our story the idea of a *visitation* by masked men or men *in disguise*. "Mummings" or processions of disguised riders at night to a house with the purpose of bestowing a Gift, constitute the source from which derives the court masque in English theatre history.

Third: We have the animal element present in this ritual in the skins and horns of the Wild Men. This is not the place to trace the significance of this animal element back to see where it came from for that would take us certainly out of the realms of theatre; but we may trace it forward and we shall find that it can take on a significance so great as to become the very centre of certain performances—and it would not be too curious to see its survival even today in the fantastic horse of the pantomime.

But we can scarcely find in all the above any element that could go on the stage of one of those modern theatres we were looking at and hold a modern audience under its spell.

Have we indeed any justification to expect so much of the primitive theatre—namely, that it should hold a modern audience? Strangely enough, I think we have. Given that the audience has an open mind, a piece of great primitive theatre should make as profound an effect today as a piece of great sophisticated theatre: its language is the same.

This is not really surprising. We should all be familiar by now with the idea that art is not a thing that grows nearer to perfection the more civilized society becomes. A cave painting can evoke a similar satisfaction to that offered by the Classic Masters and the Great Moderns; and so also great theatre is great theatre whatever its period, and primitive theatre is neither crude nor ineffectual merely because it is primitive.

But we have not satisfied ourselves that in the Bavarian Mountain ceremony we can claim a true example of full theatre so let us go on to another example.

I take this time a British rite, which will witness that memorials of primitive and savage elements still lurk in the background of the English.

THE PADSTOW HORSE

This ceremony shows a step forward in comparison with the Bavarian, and the step is theatrically a significant one. In it we are again concerned with an animal mask, but one now used in an action capable of that double layer of meaning that we saw was characteristic of a work of art. The action itself expresses something on the manifest level about Death and Birth, but in the doing of the action there is also expressed in concealed language something about the ideal of Living.

The animal signified by the mask is, though it bears no positive resemblance to any living creature, the Horse.

Padstow is a town on the north coast of Cornwall. In the stables of the Golden Lion is kept what Miss Violet Alford speaks of as "an alarming coal-black object crouching against the wall." And her description is very true.

On the evening of 30 April this object is taken out and paraded round the town to the accompaniment of "The Night Song." There is much concerning this, and the ritual that is to follow on the next day, that is lost or disappearing, but let us look at the object.

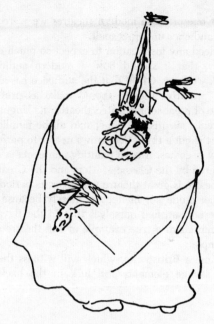

Fig. 2. The Padstow Horse

It is a black mask with a tall, pointed headdress. On the headdress are white lines. White lines encircle the eyes. A bow or knot of hair crowns the point of the headdress. A red tongue hangs from the mouth. There are heavy grey eyebrows and beard of hair. Great "ears" project (Fig. 2). The appearance of the mask is so similar to a mask from the gulf of Papua (Fig. 3) that one is confounded at the glimpse of the primitivity of origins.

When this mask is assumed by a man, there spreads out from its neck a circle of black material some five feet in diameter, stretched horizontally on a hoop at the level of the wearer's shoulders. From the hoop again depends a sort of great skirt, also in black, covering the wearer right down to the ground.

From the front of the hoop projects a small, carved, grotesque horse's head, with a movable jaw and a mane made from a cow's tail. Behind, on the opposite side, is a crude, gay horse-tail. This strange, this "alarming, even diabolical" object is led or cajoled by a Mayer (a May man), or Teaser, with a club. The horse ambles after him. . . .

Fig. 3. A mask from Papua

On Mayday the ceremony begins. In this, at certain moments, and to the accompaniment of accordion, mandoline and drum, the Horse dances (Fig. 4).

It is when the Padstow Horse dances that we see a remarkable example of the fact that the essence of the theatre resides in the effect made on an audience by the way what is done is done. The diabolical, creeping crinoline becomes a completely unrecognizable swirl of shining black magic, for which the words "awe-inspiring" are merely fitting. It creates its own background of primal jungle. It is savage and terrible. It tips its great circle up into a waving disc that transcends any relation to the shape of horse or man. Its skirts swirl round following the wind of its going, and just that particular command that the great player seeks, with his technique, to exert over an audience is imposed on us as we watch, with a tribute untouched by grudge or criticism. This mask, in a ceremony deriving from the springs of civilization, is as potent in theatrical effect today as an enchanting ballerina.

For all that, the ceremony is irrecoverably corrupt. The players can know its original significance only by intuition. It has become the draw of tourists, and the subject of countless modern improvements. Yet it brought a gasp in 1953 even to the Albert Hall. This piece of primitive theatre can go straight on to our stage.

We can include only two further details here. First, at a certain line in the song the Horse must sink to the ground and lie " 'quiet like, dead like.' " At another he must bounce into the air revivified.

Second, his black costume is shiny with tar. In his dancing he occasionally pursues a woman, catches her and throws his skirts over her. She is thus marked with the mark of the Horse; and this is lucky for

Fig. 4. The Padstow Horse dancing, with his "Mayer"

her. It is considered to be more lucky for married women than for unmarried women.

How far, before we go on, are we in a position to try to say what all this "means"? We can make a beginning. Speaking far too briefly we might say that in both the cases above we have been dealing with an "imitative magic" ceremony. It is designed to foreshadow good luck and fertility in the coming year. But notice that even here in these primitive rituals the law of the essence of theatre obtains. It is not what is done that matters—what is done is merely a faded symbol (nowadays at least); and it is not how it is done that matters—for all that is left of the manner is a rough, preferably good-humoured teasing; but it is the effect that is still made on people by the way the Wild Men or the Horse do this strange thing that makes it ultimately significant. That effect is of the eerie and the untellable, and in the eyes of the elders and children watching from a village window, one has no difficulty in seeing the impression made still by the method of performing an act of theatre.

So far then we have two elementary ceremonies. One can be claimed as theatre only with some hesitation, perhaps reckoning it as a sort of proto-theatre; while in the other we may feel justified in seeing the beginnings of a deliberate art, a performing art, having its own field and its own laws—something we may trace, without at any point having to take too abrupt a step, into our theatre performance today. But some steps we shall clearly have to take, for the Padstow ceremony lacks the means for certain developments in expression.

It is not easy to say for what reason a form of theatre develops or comes to suffer change and addition. One supposes that it is because those who use it find it does not offer them sufficient scope, or that it offers scope in a style of expression that is uncongenial to some new outlook of the times. If, in our own age, the move to abolish the proscenium arch meets with realization we shall be faced with precisely such a change. Changes may be sweeping; if so we may have to define a new phase in theatre development, but some do no more than add a facility to an existing phase. What additions does the Padstow Horse make to the Bavarian ceremony? It exemplifies:

(a) the development of a mask into a new and self-sufficing theatrical character, a fantastic animal;

(b) the introduction of significant action performed to convey an idea by imitative magic or by mime (the death and birth ideas);

(c) a separate kind of action, not primarily mimic but rhythmic—a beginning of dance; and

(d) in consequence of the rhythmic dance, music.

But it goes no further; and there is even in this first phase of theatre development one source of expression of major importance to add still, the resource of words. Though on this point we ought to add that in all the above there has been nothing that has denied the use of words: mime is by no means a silent action, it is the expression of an idea by acting it, and the acting may easily contain words—and even simple dialogue. What we are now to be concerned with, however, is the employment of words to carry or to amplify the main meaning of the action—dialogue planned to tell a particular story or event; the play.

THE BRITISH MUMMERS' PLAY

Throughout England there are various versions of the Mummers' Play. It is perhaps remarkable that it should be so widespread. It is not a local custom like the Padstow Horse but occurs from Cumberland to Lincolnshire and down to Dorset. In all the versions there is the same central theme, the conflict of a hero with an adversary, his defeat and death, his cure and return to life. But the surviving versions show almost every type of corruption and patching-up. It will be especially significant to a student to find for instance that in some versions it is not the hero who is vanquished but the adversary, while the hero is left in triumph. What are we in such a case to make of the end, when the players are involved in an odd finale—taking the care to cure and resurrect the Powers of Evil! Or when, as is likely to happen, they drop the concluding incident altogether as a defect, and thus deprive the whole action of its magic essence!

Again, a corruption in Hanoverian times has made the hero in some versions, *King* George. We go back only to find that earlier again he is *Saint* George. But is this, then, a Christian rite? Surely—no. Presumably a more primitive, pre-Christian hero lies still deeper, hidden by the politic imposition of Saint George.

Sir Edmund Chambers and R. J. E. Tiddy have left searching studies of many features of this remarkable survival that we cannot touch here, and The British Folk Dance and Song Society have made a coloured sound-film of a version that comes from the villages of Symondsbury and Eype in Dorset, which has some unusual additions. But we must confine ourselves here to the origin of theatre.

We may picture men in a primitive community before the days of recorded history, reaching an early stage in civilization when they have come to a ceremony like that of the Bavarian Mountains. Possibly in its original, this ceremony would show certain features that are very much graver (even more terrible) than any in this millennia-old survival. But these are not our concern; they would not cause us to change our minds and say, "This is theatre."

Now add a particular action with a mask, and the theatre begins. And this small change is all the difference between the two ceremonies of Bavaria and Cornwall. Then let us take another step and, forgetting the Wild Men and the Horse for the moment, let us suppose that the persons who are attending upon the central mask begin to encourage it with cries. Here is a positive example of such a thing: certain girls who follow the Padstow Horse cry out, when he breaks off to chase a woman, the words "'Oss 'Oss! We, 'Oss!" It is a curious elliptic expression. Some have presumed it to mean, "Horse, Horse, go not to her but to us!" Or, with the south-country reversal of cases, ". . . not to she, but to we—to we, Horse!". If this be true it is a deep injunction that only needs elaboration to turn it into a choral prayer. If such cries now become part of the ceremony then we have but to add responding cries from the central mask, or from an opposite group of participants, and we arrive at a vocal exchange with significant words; and once given vocal exchange we have the possibility of dialogue—and invocation and response.

What other use will primitive man make of the voice in his rituals? One nearly inevitable use will be for a leading participant to use it to proclaim his nature—possibly at first by chanted sounds, but soon by a verbal statement beginning "I am . . ." And what followed had to be originally a great announcement, for the speaker was at that moment the Great Power. It is then not surprising that in primitive ritual (and for a long way into, and beyond, early accepted drama itself) a recurrent feature of opening speeches is what we call *The Vaunt*. For example:

A typical opening line of the Hero in the Mummers' Play is "Here am I, St. George, an Englishman so stout . . ." etc.

And a typical opening line by a character in *The Castle of Perseverance* is "I am Mankind's fair Flesh, flourished in flowers . . ." etc.

Again, frequently in the Cornish Cycle the idea of the vaunting of a character at the opening of his part is enshrined in the most apt stage-direction, *Hic pompabit Salamon*—Here Soloman shall "pomp."

Finally, in Japanese Noh plays we find still such opening lines as "I am Hitomaru. I live in the valley of Kamagaye . . ." etc.

So then, pursuing our thought we see this primitive group developing its technique to allow individual, pre-arranged announcements by certain players of themselves or the roles they play. Let two players now give their vaunts in opposition to each other and the way is prepared for the next element of the drama, *The Strife*. And that is exactly what the Mummers' Play is, a strife between two vaunted heroes before a group of supporting characters—agon and antagonist before a chorus.

Recapitulating now this picture of primitive men embarking on the first steps of the development of theatre, we see them begin by passing out of the Bavarian ritual and developing one of the masks to special and particular significance. We next hear their voices. We are now ready to picture the group taking a further step, and this is the step taken in the Mummers' Play.

The Occasion

The performances are seasonal; they thus partake of that element of the Special Occasion. The season is generally around Christmas, more especially on Boxing Day, on Twelfth Night, or on Plough Monday. The ceremony is thus concerned with the turn of the sun towards the ascendant again, and the inspiring and immense task of resuming work for a new year after the solstice.

Here then is the first of four significant elements. The second is the costume.

The Costume

The men taking part in a Mummers' Play today occasionally wear strange versions of modern or period or nondescript clothes, but this is not ritual. The true Mummer dons "papers" (Fig. 5).

Fig. 5. A Mummer in his papers

A set of "papers" is a strange thing to look at. A genuine example from Marshfield, Gloucestershire, is to be seen at Blaise Castle Museum outside Bristol. It consists of a basis of an overall or old coat, covered with sewn-on strips of newspaper, or ribbons. The headdress is similarly bedecked, and so profusely that the strips hang down and entirely hide the face and head of the wearer. The whole man is transformed into a walking, rustling, white anonymity of fluttering. Only his farm boots betray him.

The effect of this disguised figure is still closely similar to the effect of the Bavarian Wild Men. More than this, it is almost exactly the same effect as certain African medicine figures (as Figs. 5 and 6 will demonstrate).

Fig. 6. A Medicine-man in his costume

Concerning this effect, so unexpected a writer as Kenneth Grahame has left us a brief sketch:

"Twelfth-night had come and gone, and life next morning seemed a trifle flat and purposeless. But yester-eve, and the mummers were here! They had come striding into the old kitchen, powdering the red brick floor with snow from their barbaric bedizenments, and stamping and crossing and declaiming till all was whirl and riot and shout. Harold was frankly afraid; unabashed, he buried himself in the cook's ample bosom. Edward feigned a manly superiority to illusion, and greeted these awful apparitions familiarly, as Dick and Harry and Joe. As for me, I was too big to run, too rapt to resist the magic and surprise. Whence came these outlanders, breaking in on us with song and ordered masque and a terrible clashing of wooden swords? And, after

these, what strange visitants might we not look for any quiet night . . .?

"This morning, house-bound . . . Edward, being violently stage-struck on his first introduction to the real Drama, was striding up and down the floor proclaiming, 'Here be I, King Gearge the Third,' in a strong Berkshire accent . . ."

Here is a very good entrance indeed into primitive theatre—an authentic impression of the solemn mystery of it, retained by an un-questioning small boy. The task of the actor is to retain this same ascendancy throughout all the turns and enshroudings that such a mind takes as it goes on to maturity. For this he will clearly need equipment at every phase of the story. The development of that equipment to match the convolutions of the mind is the history of the theatre.

Thus far the player depends only on his own self, his mystic costume and his grave outlandish dialogue—and by this we are reminded that the same quotation also leads us to the third element significant to us in the Mummers' ritual, the thing we are especially concerned with at this juncture—their play. It gives us a microscopic glimpse of the action, and actually quotes a vital line; what can be added concerning the emergence of these early words in the act of theatre?

The Words

One somewhat remarkable observation rises at once. For some reason that is difficult at first to define, these early words are not introduced fundamentally for the sake of the meaning they might impart. One might have supposed that words came into the theatre to make clear something which without them would not be clear, but this is not so. On reflection one sees a very good theatrical reason for this apparent contradiction. Theatre is a place of action, of the thing *done*, in the Greek sense of "drama." If the thing done is so done that its meaning is not comprehensible without explanatory words, then it is ill done; it is bad drama and poor theatre.

A dramatic action is not a dramatic action if you have to say what it means as you perform it. All good theatre should be comprehensible (though not perhaps as deeply moving) to a deaf man, so far as the action represented goes. The Mummers' Play affords an illustration of how it can be, as I shall soon show.

The purpose of the first use of words in theatre seems rather to have been to add to the means of moving an audience. This opinion is based on two things that otherwise would be inexplicable in the Mummers' Play. The first is that the speeches themselves are often unaccountably obscure. The second is that in no version surviving today are the speeches delivered in a normal style of speaking. They are "singsong," or chanted; they are spoken in a deliberate convention.

It is necessary to beware of being misguided by two over-rationalized explanations here. The first would say that the reason why the speeches are obscure as we now have them is because they have suffered corruption in the process of handing down from mouth to mouth over the generations. The second would say regarding their delivery that it is simply crude; and is crude merely because it is in the mouths of uninstructed speakers who don't know enough about elocution to give a better rendering.

The first explanation would presuppose that formerly, in their primitive state, the speeches were *not* obscure, but were as clear as normal speeches today. The second explanation is seen straightway to be coloured with a certain, not uncommon, preconception; namely that all vocal delivery in the theatre is and always was intended to imitate the delivery of everyday speech—that is to say, to be naturalistic.

It is not impossible that the bases on which these two explanations rest are both fallacies. One reflection suggesting that the first explanation rests on a fallacy is that no reason can be advanced why words in any great mystery *should* be clear in their meaning. To be clear is to be certain, and thus to be limited. Certainty and mysticism cannot live together.

If the leading Mummer were to begin his Vaunt with "I am the Spirit of Living," the whole ceremony collapses in emotional meaning like a house falling down beneath a bomb. Such a remark cannot be accepted as a fiction. It is, for better or for worse, an attempt to state the truth directly, and as such leads us into the risk of every error of which words are capable; even then in the end it cannot succeed because no one can state the Truth.

But if the player says "I am Saint George," that is entirely acceptable. It is untrue, but we do not question it. We know, with him, that he means not that but a mystery, whether our knowledge of that fact is conscious or unconscious.

If then "I am Saint George" is acceptable, there is no reason why "I am King George" (or King William), or "I am Lord George" (or as in one instance "I am Lloyd George") should not be equally acceptable! Or indeed (with qualifications) whatever you will. The meaning is *not* of first importance.

Thus it is true, first, that a ceremony into whose words corruptions have crept is not in any way invalidated as a ceremony, but can live despite them. And second, that this being so it is highly unlikely that even the original ceremony itself was logically *clear*—either in ultimate import or in the immediate words spoken.

Here, then, is a tentative and perhaps revolutionary theory. We cannot, of course, accept it without rigorous testing. The remainder of all the theatrical ceremonies alluded to in this book are available for such a testing. But our conclusion upon examining the essential and inevitable entrance of words into drama is the apparent paradox that, in theatre, understanding the meaning of the words does not greatly matter. What does matter is that they supply yet another channel through which that deeper, or secondary, impression of the performance can be conveyed.

The words accompanying a spell are rarely comprehensible, and early theatrical speech resembled incantations accompanying a rite. The achievement of magic is not explicable; you may analyze the mechanism, but not by that acquire command of it.

The Actions

For the fourth and last point which we can profitably discuss here about the Mummers' Play as an example of developing theatrical art, we leave the new element of words and turn back to the basic, original element, action. What may we learn from the Mummers' Play to help us in forming our idea of the way in which the *act* of theatre developed?

There are three points about the actions here: (*a*) the killing itself, (*b*) the processional element again, and lastly (*c*) a new technical matter especially important for our understanding of the spatial relation between a performance and the audience who watch it.

(*a*) *The Killing*. The centre of the Mummers' Play is an action—the spectacle of the fall of the hero as he dies before the adversary. We have had something of the idea of this ritual death in the dying of the Padstow Horse during his dance. Now the Mummers' Play takes a step further and underlines the mimetic action by making it the culmination of a sword fight.

Here we are offered a transcendent example of the real strength of the theatric art, for the Mummers' Play presents the death almost entirely by means of action alone. The words have virtually no part in it and make but a trifling reference, or none at all, to it. It remains a thing *done,* not said.

This is a demonstration of the true strength of theatre because thereby we can see theatre offering us a medium for evoking emotion that is distinct to it alone. Expressed in any other medium this death is not so seizing: expressed in theatrical action it can grip the spectator with instant, inexplicable clutch.

To draw the action, or to describe it in words, could not convey just the same thing that the falling and lying still of the performer conveys. And this is not because he is a "great actor"; nor because of any deep message in his lines. It is simply in the nature of theatre.

Proof of this can be found in the version of the play from Symondsbury (recorded in the film), where a hobby horse is, somewhat unusually, included. Beside the film, there is also published the script of the performance. To compare these two in respect of one particular passage is highly instructive; and to put that passage in its context, here is a brief synopsis of the whole performance.

The version is unusual in having four parts. The first is orthodox in general, though with unusual details. It consists of a Presentation, the Vaunts, then instead of one Strife we have a succession of four Strifes; first, a separate one between St. Patrick (St. George's ally) and "Captain Bluster"; next, one between St. George himself and "Gracious King"; next, between St. George and—significantly—"Colonel Spring." In this last Strife Colonel Spring, very interestingly, falls only to revive immediately of his own accord and then, after a second Strife, is made to fall again. Next, the traditional "Doctor" enters for the Cure, and in this case he revives all three of the dead men.

The second part of this version is entirely unorthodox and is perhaps an importation from another ceremony. Here St. George does not appear at all, but we see instead two country folk, Jan and Bet his wife (both are played by men, and Jan is played by the same actor who, earlier, introduced the performance in the guise of Father Christmas). A dispute arises between man and wife, swelling to a quarrel and a fight in which the woman (or man-woman) is killed. St. Patrick enters and calls in the Doctor, who is here named Mr. Martin Dennis, and the dead woman is revived with by-play strongly suggestive of fertility ritual.

The third part brings in Jan and Bet again, and also a very special and curious addition—a "Hobby Horse" (called Tommy the pony).

The woman mounts on his back and rides him. Jan attempts to mount and is thrown. He rises enraged . . . And now for the sixth time in this strange conglomeration, the rite of mystic death is performed, but performed with an effect in the action itself that brings us to the essence of theatre.

In the published script of the play there is no more indication of the emotion of this incident than a curt stage-direction and a reference in the next line of dialogue:

> (*Tommy throws Jan off and kicks him. Jan gets up and knocks Tommy down*)
>
> BET: You naughty old rogue. You have killed my pony you have, you old rogue.

There is nothing whatever in this that is not present in the performance, and there is nothing whatever (in the material sense) that is added to this during the performance, yet the lines as written are crude, bare, almost contemptible; while out on the wintry roadway,* with the echoes of the chanting players' voices ringing in the onlookers' ears; with the haunting strangeness; with the effect of that raptness too great "to resist the magic and surprise" that held the child in Kenneth Grahame; and with, perhaps, the relaxed effect following on the low comedy of Bet's revival—in the cold afternoon with all this bustle, to see, suddenly and unexpectedly, Jan lash out with his club at the Hobby-horse's head, to hear the clip of the blow, to "hear" the voices instantly cease, and to see the foolish, gay, cavorting, innocently-malicious, fantastic creature quite sharply stop, fall and lie still in the frosty mud, brings an emotion mysteriously near to tears.

No one can see in the lines of the script alone what could do this thing to an audience. No one could draw the episode to be so moving. But the theatre can take these lines and—merely in terms of action—wrest this thing out of them, with nothing added save its own quality. This is the difference between written drama and theatre in action. The lines of Bet and Jan may be forgotten in an hour, but the spectacle of Tommy inert on the frozen road may be ineffaceable for a lifetime, through the act of theatre.

The rite now continues. The horse is revived and unaccountably

* The Film was unfortunately taken, for photographic reasons, in summer, not in the real winter.

takes part next in a "smelling-out" ceremony among the audience, which may be comic today but which springs from who knows what grim original? And finally Jan himself is smelled-out as "the biggest rogue that is here" and kicked by Tommy "through the door."

Part Four takes a completely unexpected lyrical note. The Warriors of the first part all march in procession round Jan and Bet with a song called "The Singing of the Travels," outlining incidents in a farmer's life of travail. All ends with a traditional request to the Lady of the House to

> . . . tie a bow of ribbon now
> On this our Christmas Holly Bough.

(b) *The Processional Element.* So much for the action of the Mummers' Play. We next come to a development of the processional element.

To begin, both the line about Tommy kicking Jan out *through the door* and the final invocation to the Lady of the House, not to mention Kenneth Grahame's reminiscence, show that such a performance was once at any rate a wandering one and went from house to house. The action implied is clear; a march to a house, entry into that house, the presentation of the play before the assembled household, a final address to the Master or Lady of the house, a general exeunt, and a march to a fresh house to perform again—and so on. One of the most ancient and characteristic exclamations of a player springs from the occasion of these visits to crowded halls; it is the cry that opens so many speeches right down to the days of the Tudor Interludes—the cry:

> Room, a room, brave gallants all,
> Pray give me room to rhyme . . .

Thus they ask the crowd assembled in the houseplace for this ritual occasion, to step back for a while to permit the bringers of the play to come in.

At Marshfield in Gloucestershire, however, there is an example of a variation of this proceeding which may very likely be the basis from which the system of English medieval pageant cars arose.

Marshfield is a small but comparatively elongated town, tending to spread out along either side of a straggling High Street, lined with quiet two-storey buildings mostly in local stone, and with a few side lanes at intervals, turning off towards the surrounding country. The Church and the small triangular market place are at one end of this High Street.

In order to give their annual performance on Boxing-Day morning, the dressed Mummers, in a procession of seven headed by the Town Crier, march into the Market Place from an adjoining street. There they give their first performance which lasts some fifteen or twenty minutes (*see* Fig. 7).

Then they re-form their procession and, again led by the Town Crier, march away along the High Street to a corner farther down and give the second performance. Then they form up and proceed again in the same way to a third station still farther along the High Street. And next to a fourth point near the far end.

Thus the performance is given at either end of the main street of the town and at two stations in between.

They then make a detour on their return to give their final performance (or performances) in the garden before one (or it may have been more) of the local gentry's houses.

Let us for a moment break off to consider the great stream of the development of theatrical presentation. It would appear on the evidence we have that the whole occasion surviving today at Marshfield makes a not unrepresentative picture of an occasion in primitive days of the pagan theatre long ago. How far we are right in making this deduction we cannot, with our present knowledge, say; but the inference drawn in this book is that, since the performance of the Mummers' Play shows a strife, a death of the hero, and a revival by magic means (even if it is today only the magic of a comic doctor—indeed maybe especially because of this) it follows it is a pagan ceremony. Possibly the chief evidence for this is that the means of revival is magic (or nowadays comic; that is, it is maintained now for a reason that is no longer understood and has to be cloaked as "nonsense"). If it is a magic ceremony, it is pre-Christian. If it is pre-Christian, it is at least pre-10th-century A.D. in origin.

This reasoning may be fallacious, but we cannot stand still and wait to be assured; we must try to read the evidence we have with our present knowledge. With this proviso, then, we can say the following:

Provided "primitive" man in Britain did in fact present his theatrical ceremonies in the way described above, it is reasonable to believe that with the introduction of Christianity and the consequent attempt gradually to impose the vast Bible story upon the compact aboriginal myth, the theatrical performance changed in content (giving us the Mystery Plays, as we shall see), but that the form the show took was maintained more or less unaltered.

This now would mean that a primitive community (such as Marshfield once was, but a little larger and living in a somewhat more extensive town with more streets) on suffering the impact of the new Christian belief, and having to stage its "propaganda" with new resources for the players, might develop performances on raised platforms; but such a development would take place *in the tradition of the processional show*—such as we have outlined above from Marshfield.

We have only now to credit the organizers with the sense to put those raised stages on wheels, and we have the origin of the English pageant-waggon system of theatre that we connect with the York, the Towneley and the Chester Mystery Cycles of plays.

The only real variation, besides the use of a raised stage to help more people to see the action better, is the achievement of a much longer play, by making a number of groups of players perform successively at each of the appointed stations in the street or town.

Thus (again, I stress, on the evidence of our present knowledge) the English pageant-waggon show may have had its technical ancestor in the processional repetitions of the Mummers' Play at successive street corners—merely adding a succession of repeated performances, a raised stage on wheels to play each scene upon, and drawing each waggon from station to station for its repetition, exactly as the Mummers move down the High Street at Marshfield for the repetition of their solitary scene.

The processional element in the, apparently stationary, Mummers' Play is noticeably common, once one looks for it. Thus at Symondsbury the players still march in full costume and stirring procession, to the tune of a very haunting traditional air, when they set off to perform their ritual.

All this may grow in time to be a pretty long ritual to take into a farmhouse. We are shortly to see performances on a greater scale still, something certainly exceeding the bounds of four square walls, performances which institute in fact another phase of theatre development; but for all that, these new great shows will still have the origins of their technique in the primitive phase of the Mummers. Especially can we see how true this is when with the performance at Marshfield we notice one last particular element in the development of the primitive players' resources during this first phase of their story.

(c) *The Circle*. This new point is one that is more apt for description by picture than by words. It relates to the spatial relation of the spectators with regard to the performance. It is the use of the shape of the circle (*see* Fig. 7). The circle is the natural shape that an audi-

Fig. 7. The Marshfield Mummers' performance

ence takes up when it assembles round an open space to watch the action of a group of players. It is the gathering-round of a crowd to look at an incident; nothing more formal or more regular than that. At present all we are concerned with is to note that a convenient area to perform any group-action is one that measures much the same one way as another—that is, it is roughly "circular"; and that, to see the action in such an area, the spectators will gather anywhere they choose around) this area to watch; which means—since they do not want to be unsighted by other spectators in front—in a more or less even "ring" round the area. And once that ring is complete, in a thickening of that ring, with more layers of onlookers as more spectators arrive.

Just as the lines of the Mummers' Play gave evidence of the indoor technique in the call for "Room, room!," so other versions give evidence of the circular technique out of doors; thus the "paceakers'" (an Easter variant) from Heptonstall, Yorkshire, begins with a now-corrupt speech:

> Ring a ring I enter the or, to see this merry act begin.
> I'll act it right and act it safe, and act it on a public state:
> And if you can't believe this words I say,
> Step in St. George and clear my way.

Before considering this circle further it is worth while to break off to inquire why its understanding is so important.

It is always important to see the shape of a performance. One thing of the utmost desirability in any record of an unfamiliar style of theatrical occasion is that the record should include sufficient information for us to visualize the whole lay-out—not the actor alone. Our knowledge is hindered when observers report details of an action or ritual, but neglect to help us to form a picture of the immediate surroundings.

Our requirements are very simple. The three items which it is of greatest importance for us to have described are:

(a) the area in which the action takes place;
(b) the way the spectators are situated with regard to that area;
(c) the way, or ways, by which the players enter and leave that area.

Any study of what the players do in the performance itself, however detailed and sympathetic, is weakened if we have not those three details first; and it would bring a new illumination to our understanding of theatrical procedure (especially when in primitive or unfamiliar conditions) if we could prevail upon all observers to take these three points as a formula to head every description.

Many accounts of theatrical performances are invalidated for us because they do not include the means for readers to put the action into any sort of setting. There is in this perhaps an indication of how little we have realized, in the past, the need to see a performance not as an isolated thing, but as an action presented before an audience and in specific surroundings. We tend, when we describe a show, to isolate the centre from the rest with all its vital atmosphere. This may be a consequence of our present picture-frame convention in the theatre of today, where the aim seems to be to cut off the show as independently as possible from any consciousness of the outside world. Such an isolation simply could not take place in any of the early phases of theatre development. All early theatre shows were essentially seen and experienced in the conditions of normal reality—of light and weather and landscape—on the familiar earth, under the everyday sky; or at night in the homely hall of a normal country house, by the usual candle- or torchlight.

Right through all the first five phases of theatre development, the physical surroundings in which the show was given were fully visible and were an inextinguishable part of the spectator's impression of the show. It is essential to realize the fact that, until the phase of "Stage Illusion," they were visually inseparable from the show.

At Marshfield, the description of the above three essentials is simple.

The area of the action is a street corner or the ground of the open market place.

The spectators dispose themselves in regard to this area simply by coming and taking up positions at will round the sides of it.

The entrance to the area for the players is by a side street between the surrounding houses, and through the "ring" of spectators at that point.

The entrance once made, the players separate and spread over the area of the place to form a 60-ft. circle of seven men. There in solitary formality they stand—stations, as it were, of the drama. Each actor can, in his place, declaim a speech when required; or any one of them can leave his station and move round the ring at need, or march into the centre to meet another player or players to take part in some concerted action. "Come in, Bold Prince!" is not exclusively an invitation to the character to enter through a door; but it can be used simply as the cue for that particular player to leave his station at the edge of the circle and *come in* to the centre to take part in some action, or merely to take up the speaking in his turn.

It is sufficient for our purpose at this point to leave the description of the circular arrangement of the Mummers' Play with this comment; here is a large and simple scheme, it is important to notice because it already embodies the basis of one of the most developed theatrical techniques that we shall find in the next phase, a technique which is to run parallel with, and perhaps be more important than, the wheeled pageant system of the medieval Mysteries—that is, the performance in a Round.

Summary

The Mummers' Play, then, is (like our first ceremony) an action; and (like our second ceremony) an action of death and resurrection. But to the action there now are added traditional words. These words have no high poetic meaning, indeed much of what survives today is gibberish. But this makes no difference. Something has been added to the act of theatre, and the opportunity is already created for the introduction of the poet as a specialist in words. Of this we shall say more later.

Concerning these early words, it is curious to learn how many major traditional theatre manifestations of the world do go on without the majority of the audience, or congregation, understanding a word that is said in them. Thus, few but specialists can follow the dialogue of a Noh play in Japan. The greater part of the Tibetan festival dramas is in a court language now out of use. In the Burmese theatre, till some years ago, only courtiers could understand the language of the plays. But we have seen with our approach to the subject in this chapter how much more there is in theatre than depends on the meaning of the words. Even did we doubt the fact, we need only visit a performance in a foreign tongue by a theatrical company that is accomplished at its job, and we shall feel how, even today, this primitive feature of the theatre craft is still at work, and how much of the occasion can still come over to us when the dialogue itself is incomprehensible—and especially is this true when the theme of the play is familiar, as it was in all early theatre.

In addition to these considerations about this new element in the story of developing theatre, the Mummers' Play has given us reason to consider four other items:

First, the element of Special Occasion arising from the time of year of performance, and the significance of the season;

Second, further details about the development of primitive theatrical costume;

Third, the Action considered in the light of the subject for a play;

And fourth, the Action on the one hand presented as a procession (or by repetition at various places in the intervals of a procession), and on the other the Action presented as a stationary performance within a circle.

In every example of theatre so far described the whole dramatic technicology has been confined to one single thing—the Costumed Player.

FORM

From one point of view, all of the elements of drama could be subsumed under the concept of form. The genres discussed in the following section, "Generic Forms," represent different ways of ordering and shaping dramatic material and are hence forms in themselves. Similarly, the classical "rules" discussed in the section called "Form: The Unities" obviously contribute to the form of any play, as we could distinguish the form of, say, Aeschylus' *Agamemnon* from that of *Hamlet* by analyzing how the two plays differ in their use of action, time, and place. Thus the present section should be read in conjunction with the two immediately following it and should be kept in mind when the student reaches those essays later on that stress the formative aspects of plot, imagery, illusion, and language.

As an abstract thing-in-itself, form is exceedingly elusive. Since each play shapes its own dramatic experience, it would seem more logical perhaps to talk about the form of individual plays instead of about form as such. Turning, however, from a vague "universal" to concrete particulars is no solution, since the form of *Hamlet*, for instance, is itself an abstraction from the more particular forms created by each of its parts: imagery, theme, dialogue, characters, locations, times, and so forth. In each of these we may perceive a form—the "curve" of tone, the "symmetry" of themes, the "rise and fall" of action, the "crossing" of characters, and so on. Particularizing even further, we arrive at the point at which each line, phrase, and even word exhibits its own form. "To generalize," Blake said, "is to be an idiot"; but particularizing can be a kind of idiocy too—one that renders us incapable ultimately of saying anything about anything.

We can speak meaningfully, then, about the forms of individual plays and about generic forms (tragedy, comedy, and so on). But there also seems a place for formal concepts that transcend individual plays and genres and apply to drama itself. Thus Kenneth Burke finds in the raising and satisfying of expectations in the audience a principle of form that cuts across generic lines entirely, though different genres will set up different *kinds* of expectation and satisfy them in different ways. Burke's conception of form goes beyond the simple notion of suspense to include expectations about motive, theme, imagery, tone, structure, and style. "Expectation" implies temporal progression in drama, an "after this, then . . ." principle in terms of which the action develops. Marvin Rosenberg, however, finds a distinction between "linear" form, which is based on temporal progression and associated with the conventional plot-oriented drama, and "contextual" form, in which causal sequence is subordinated to or even eliminated in favor of non-progressive exposures of psychological states or explorations of static situations. The consecutive development of action and character has always been merely one way of imparting form to a play. Thus eliminating this kind of "linear" form, as Samuel Beckett does in *Waiting for Godot* (where the expectation implied by "waiting" is never satisfied), does not mean that the play dissolves in formlessness but merely that the burden of form shifts to such "spatial" concepts as symmetry, contrast, and patterned movement. In exploring the relations between drama and religion, Harold Watts also employs the "linear" concept of form, which he associates with tragedy as a "total assertion" about the human condition, and opposes it to the essentially comic concept of "cyclical" form.

KENNETH BURKE

Psychology and Form

It is not until the fourth scene of the first act that Hamlet confronts the ghost of his father. As soon as the situation has been made clear, the audience has been, consciously or unconsciously, waiting for this ghost to appear, while in the fourth scene this moment has been definitely promised. For earlier in the play Hamlet had arranged to come to the platform at night with Horatio to meet the ghost, and it is now night, he is with Horatio and Marcellus, and they are standing on the platform. Hamlet asks Horatio the hour.

> HOR. I think it lacks twelve.
> MAR. No, it is struck.
> HOR. Indeed? I heard it not: then it draws near the season
>   Wherein the spirit held his wont to walk.

Promptly hereafter there is a sound off-stage. "A flourish of trumpets, an ordnance shot off within." Hamlet's friends have established the hour as twelve. It is time for the ghost. Sounds off-stage, and of course it is not the ghost. It is, rather, the sound of the king's carousal, for the king "keeps wassail." A tricky, and useful, detail. We have been waiting for a ghost, and get, startlingly, a blare of trumpets. And, once the trumpets are silent, we feel how desolate are these three men waiting for a ghost, on a bare "platform," feel it by this sudden juxtaposition of an imagined scene of lights and merriment. But the trumpets announcing a carousal have suggested a subject of conversation. In the darkness Hamlet discusses the excessive drinking of his countrymen. He points out that it tends to harm their reputation abroad, since, he argues, this one showy vice makes their virtues "in the general censure take corrup-

Originally published in *Counter-Statement;* Harcourt, Brace and World, Inc., New York, 1931. Second Edition, Revised: Hermes Publications, Los Altos, California, 1953. Reprinted by permission of Hermes Publications and the author.

tion." And for this reason, although he himself is a native of this place, he does not approve of the custom. Indeed, there in the gloom he is talking very intelligently on these matters, and Horatio answers, "Look, my Lord, it comes." All this time we had been waiting for a ghost, and it comes at the one moment which was not pointing towards it. This ghost, so assiduously prepared for, is yet a surprise. And now that the ghost has come, we are waiting for something further. Program: a speech from Hamlet. Hamlet must confront the ghost. Here again Shakespeare can feed well upon the use of contrast for his effects. Hamlet has just been talking in a sober, rather argumentative manner— but now the flood-gates are unloosed:

> Angels and ministers of grace defend us!
> Be thou a spirit of health or goblin damn'd,
> Bring with thee airs from heaven or blasts from hell . . .

and the transition from the matter-of-fact to the grandiose, the full-throated and full-voweled, is a second burst of trumpets, perhaps even more effective than the first, since it is the rich fulfilment of a promise. Yet this satisfaction in turn becomes an allurement, an itch for further developments. At first desiring solely to see Hamlet confront the ghost we now want Hamlet to learn from the ghost the details of the murder —which are, however, with shrewdness and husbandry, reserved for "Scene V.—Another Part of the Platform."

I have gone into this scene at some length, since it illustrates so perfectly the relationship between psychology and form, and so aptly indicates how the one is to be defined in terms of the other. That is, the psychology here is not the psychology of the *hero,* but the psychology of the *audience.* And by that distinction, form would be the psychology of the audience. Or, seen from another angle, form is the creation of an appetite in the mind of the auditor, and the adequate satisfying of that appetite. This satisfaction—so complicated is the human mechanism—at times involves a temporary set of frustrations, but in the end these frustrations prove to be simply a more involved kind of satisfaction, and furthermore serve to make the satisfaction of fulfilment more intense. If, in a work of art, the poet says something, let us say, about a meeting, writes in such a way that we desire to observe that meeting, and then, if he places that meeting before us—that is form. While obviously, that is also the psychology of the audience, since it involves desires and their appeasements.

The seeming breach between form and subject-matter, between technique and psychology, which has taken place in the last century is the result, it seems to me, of scientific criteria being unconsciously introduced into matters of purely aesthetic judgment. The flourishing of science has been so vigorous that we have not yet had time to make a spiritual readjustment adequate to the changes in our resources of material and knowledge. There are disorders of the social system which are caused solely by our undigested wealth (the basic disorder being, perhaps, the phenomenon of overproduction: to remedy this, instead of having all workers employed on half time, we have half working full time and the other half idle, so that whereas overproduction could be the greatest reward of applied science, it has been, up to now, the most menacing condition our modern civilization has had to face). It would be absurd to suppose that such social disorders would not be paralleled by disorders of culture and taste, especially since science is so pronouncedly a spiritual factor. So that we are, owing to the sudden wealth science has thrown upon us, all *nouveaux-riches* in matters of culture, and most poignantly in that field where lack of native firmness is most readily exposed, in matters of aesthetic judgment.

One of the most striking derangements of taste which science has temporarily thrown upon us involves the understanding of psychology in art. Psychology has become a body of information (which is precisely what psychology in science should be, or must be). And similarly, in art, we tend to look for psychology as the purveying of information. Thus, a contemporary writer has objected to Joyce's *Ulysses* on the ground that there are more psychoanalytic data available in Freud. (How much more drastically he might, by the same system, have destroyed Homer's *Odyssey!*) To his objection it was answered that one might, similarly, denounce Cézanne's trees in favor of state forestry bulletins. Yet are not Cézanne's landscapes themselves tainted with the psychology of information? Has he not, by perception, *pointed out* how one object lies against another, *indicated* what takes place between two colors (which is the psychology of science, and is less successful in the medium of art than in that of science, since in art such processes are at best implicit, whereas in science they are so readily made explicit)? Is Cézanne not, to that extent, a state forestry bulletin, except that he tells what goes on in the eye instead of on the tree? And do not the true values of his work lie elsewhere—and precisely in what I distinguish as the psychology of form?

Thus, the great influx of information has led the artist also to lay his emphasis on the giving of information—with the result that art tends more and more to substitute the psychology of the hero (the subject) for the psychology of the audience. Under such an attitude, when form is preserved it is preserved as an annex, a luxury, or, as some feel, a downright affectation. It remains, though sluggish, like the human appendix, for occasional demands are still made upon it; but its true vigor is gone, since it is no longer organically required. Proposition: The hypertrophy of the psychology of information is accompanied by the corresponding atrophy of the psychology of form.

In information, the matter is intrinsically interesting. And by intrinsically interesting I do not necessarily mean intrinsically valuable, as witness the intrinsic interest of backyard gossip or the most casual newspaper items. In art, at least the art of the great ages (Æschylus, Shakespeare, Racine) the matter is interesting by means of an extrinsic use, a function. Consider, for instance, the speech of Mark Antony, the "Brutus is an honourable man." Imagine in the same place a very competently developed thesis on human conduct, with statistics, intelligence tests, definitions; imagine it as the finest thing of the sort ever written, and as really being at the roots of an understanding of Brutus. Obviously, the play would simply stop until Antony had finished. For in the case of Antony's speech, the value lies in the fact that his words are shaping the future of the audience's desires, not the desires of the Roman populace, but the desires of the pit. This is the psychology of form as distinguished from the psychology of information.

The distinction is, of course, absolutely true only in its non-existent extremes. Hamlet's advice to the players, for instance, has little of the quality which distinguishes Antony's speech. It is, rather, intrinsically interesting, although one could very easily prove how the play would benefit by some such delay at this point, and that anything which made delay possible without violating the consistency of the subject would have, in this, its formal justification. It would, furthermore, be absurd to rule intrinsic interest out of literature. I wish simply to have it restored to its properly minor position, seen as merely one out of many possible elements of style. Goethe's prose, often poorly imagined, or neutral, in its line-for-line texture, especially in the treatment of romantic episode—perhaps he felt that the romantic episode in itself was enough?—is strengthened into a style possessing affirmative virtues by his rich use of aphorism. But this is, after all, but one of many possible facets of appeal. In some places, notably in *Wilhelm Meister's Lehrjahre*

when Wilhelm's friends disclose the documents they have been collecting about his life unbeknown to him, the aphorisms are almost rousing
in their efficacy, since they involve the story. But as a rule the appeal of
aphorism is intrinsic: that is, it satisfies without being functionally
related to the context.[1] . . . Also, to return to the matter of Hamlet, it
must be observed that the style in this passage is no mere "information-
giving" style; in its alacrity, its development, it really makes this one
fragment into a kind of miniature plot.

One reason why music can stand repetition so much more sturdily
than correspondingly good prose is that music, of all the arts, is by its
nature least suited to the psychology of information, and has remained
closer to the psychology of form. Here form cannot atrophy. Every dis-
sonant chord cries for its solution, and whether the musician resolves or
refuses to resolve this dissonance into the chord which the body cries
for, he is dealing in human appetites. Correspondingly good prose,
however, more prone to the temptations of pure information, cannot so
much bear repetition since the æsthetic value of information is lost once
that information is imparted. If one returns to such a work again it is
purely because, in the chaos of modern life, he has been able to forget
it. With a desire, on the other hand, its recovery is as agreeable as its
discovery. One can memorize the dialogue between Hamlet and Guildenstern, where Hamlet gives Guildenstern the pipe to play on. For,
once the speech is known, its repetition adds a new element to compensate for the loss of novelty. We cannot take a recurrent pleasure in the
new (in information) but we can in the natural (in form). Already, at the
moment when Hamlet is holding out the pipe to Guildenstern and asking him to play upon it, we "gloat over" Hamlet's triumphal descent
upon Guildenstern, when, after Guildenstern has, under increasing embarrassment, protested three times that he cannot play the instrument,
Hamlet launches the retort for which all this was preparation:

"Why, look you now, how unworthy a thing you make of me. You
would play upon me, you would seem to know my stops; you would
pluck out the heart of my mystery; you would sound me from my lowest
note to the top of my compass; and there is much music, excellent voice,
in this little organ, yet cannot you make it speak. 'Sblood, do you think
I am easier to be played on than a pipe? Call me what instrument you
will, though you can fret me, you cannot play upon me." [2]

In the opening lines we hear the promise of the close, and thus feel
the emotional curve even more keenly than at first reading. Whereas

in most modern art this element is underemphasized. It gives us the gossip of a plot, a plot which too often has for its value the mere fact that we do not know its outcome.[3]

Music, then, fitted less than any other art for imparting information, deals minutely in frustrations and fulfilments of desire,[4] and for that reason more often gives us those curves of emotion which, because they are natural, can bear repetition without loss. It is for this reason that music, like folk tales, is most capable of lulling us to sleep. A lullaby is a melody which comes quickly to rest, where the obstacles are easily overcome—and this is precisely the parallel to those waking dreams of struggle and conquest which (especially during childhood) we permit ourselves when falling asleep or when trying to induce sleep. Folk tales are just such waking dreams. Thus it is right that art should be called a "waking dream." The only difficulty with this definition (indicated by Charles Baudouin in his *Psychoanalysis and Æsthetics,* a very valuable study of Verhaeren) is that today we understand it to mean art as a waking dream for the artist. Modern criticism, and psychoanalysis in particular, is too prone to define the essence of art in terms of the artist's weaknesses. It is, rather, the audience which dreams, while the artist oversees the conditions which determine this dream. He is the manipulator of blood, brains, heart, and bowels which, while we sleep, dictate the mould of our desires. This is, of course, the real meaning of artistic felicity—an exaltation at the correctness of the procedure, so that we enjoy the steady march of doom in a Racinian tragedy with exactly the same equipment as that which produces our delight with Benedick's "Peace! I'll stop your mouth. (*Kisses her*)" which terminates the imbroglio of *Much Ado About Nothing.*

The methods of maintaining interest which are most natural to the psychology of information (as it is applied to works of pure art) are surprise and suspense. The method most natural to the psychology of form is eloquence. For this reason the great ages of Æschylus, Shakespeare, and Racine, dealing as they did with material which was more or less a matter of common knowledge so that the broad outlines of the plot were known in advance (while it is the broad outlines which are usually exploited to secure surprise and suspense) developed formal excellence, or eloquence, as the basis of appeal in their work.

Not that there is any difference in kind between the classic method and the method of the cheapest contemporary melodrama. The drama, more than any other form, must never lose sight of its audience: here the failure to satisfy the proper requirements is most disastrous. And since certain contemporary work is successful, it follows that rudimentary laws of composition are being complied with. The distinction is one of intensity rather than of kind. The contemporary audience hears the lines of a play or novel with the same equipment as it brings to reading the lines of its daily paper. It is content to have facts placed before it in some more or less adequate sequence. Eloquence is the minimizing of this interest in fact, *per se*, so that the "more or less adequate sequence" of their presentation must be relied on to a much greater extent. Thus, those elements of surprise and suspense are subtilized, carried down into the writing of a line or a sentence, until in all its smallest details the work bristles with disclosures, contrasts, restatements with a difference, ellipses, images, aphorism, volume, sound-values, in short all that complex wealth of minutiæ which in their line-for-line aspect we call style and in their broader outlines we call form.

As a striking instance of a modern play with potentialities in which the intensity of eloquence is missing, I might cite a recent success, Capek's *R.U.R.* Here, in a melodrama which was often astonishing in the rightness of its technical procedure, when the author was finished he had written nothing but the scenario for a play by Shakespeare. It was a play in which the author produced time and again the opportunity, the demand, for eloquence, only to move on. (At other times, the most successful moments, he utilized the modern discovery of silence, with moments wherein words could not possibly serve but to detract from the effect: this we might call the "flowering" of information.) The Adam and Eve scene of the last act, a "commission" which the Shakespeare of the comedies would have loved to fill, was in the verbal barrenness of Capek's play something shameless to the point of blushing. The Robot, turned human, prompted by the dawn of love to see his first sunrise, or hear the first bird-call, and forced merely to say "Oh, see the sunrise," or "Hear the pretty birds"—here one could do nothing but wring his hands at the absence of that æsthetic mould which produced the overslung "speeches" of Romeo and Juliet.

Suspense is the concern over the possible outcome of some specific detail of plot rather than for general qualities. Thus, "Will A marry B or C?" is suspense. In *Macbeth*, the turn from the murder scene to the porter scene is a much less literal channel of development. Here the presence of one quality calls forth the demand for another, rather than one tangible incident of plot awaking an interest in some other possible tangible incident of plot. To illustrate more fully, if an author managed over a certain number of his pages to produce a feeling of sultriness or oppression, in the reader, this would unconsciously awaken in the reader the desire for a cold, fresh northwind—and thus some aspect of a northwind would be effective if called forth by some aspect of stuffiness. A good example of this is to be found in a contemporary poem, T. S. Eliot's *The Waste Land,* where the vulgar, oppressively trivial conversation in the public house calls forth in the poet a memory of a line from Shakespeare. These slobs in a public house, after a desolately low-visioned conversation, are now forced by closing time to leave the saloon. They say good-night. And suddenly the poet, feeling his release, drops into another good-night, a good-night with *désinvolture,* a goodnight out of what was, within the conditions of the poem at least, a graceful and irrecoverable past.

> "Well that Sunday Albert was home, they had a hot gammon,
> And they asked me in to dinner, to get the beauty of it hot"—
> [at this point the bartender interrupts: it is closing time]
> "Goonight Bill. Goonight Lou. Goonight May. Goonight. Ta ta.
> Goonight. Goonight.
> Good-night, ladies, good-night, sweet ladies, good-night, good-
> night."

There is much more to be said on these lines, which I have shortened somewhat in quotation to make my issue clearer. But I simply wish to point out here that this transition is a bold juxtaposition of one quality created by another, an association in ideas which, if not logical, is nevertheless emotionally natural. In the case of *Macbeth* similarly, it would be absurd to say that the audience, after the murder scene, wants a porter scene. But the audience does want the quality which this porter particularizes. The dramatist might, conceivably, have introduced some entirely different character or event in this place, provided only that the event produced the same quality of relationship and contrast (grotesque seriousness followed by grotesque buffoonery). . . . One of the most beautiful and satisfactory "forms" of this sort is to be found in Baudelaire's *Femmes Damnées,* where the poet, after describing the business of a Lesbian seduction, turns to the full oratory of his apostrophe:

> *"Descendez, descendez, lamentables victimes,*
> *Descendez le chemin de l'enfer éternel . . ."*

while the stylistic efficacy of this transition contains a richness which transcends all moral (or unmoral) sophistication: the efficacy of appropriateness, of exactly the natural curve in treatment. Here is morality even for the godless, since it is a morality of art, being justified, if for no other reason, by its paralleling of that staleness, that disquieting loss of purpose, which must have followed the procedure of the two characters, the *femmes damnées* themselves, a remorse which, perhaps only physical in its origin, nevertheless becomes psychic.[5]

But to return, we have made three terms synonymous: form, psychology, and eloquence. And eloquence thereby becomes the essence of art, while pity, tragedy, sweetness, humor, in short all the emotions which we experience in life proper, as non-artists, are simply the material on which eloquence may feed. The arousing of pity, for instance, is not the central purpose of art, although it may be an adjunct of artistic effectiveness. One can feel pity much more keenly at the sight of some actual misfortune—and it would be a great mistake to see art merely as a weak representation of some actual experience.[6] That artists today are content to write under such an æsthetic accounts in part for the inferior position which art holds in the community. Art, at least in the great periods when it has flowered, was the conversion, or transcendence, of emotion into eloquence, and was thus a factor added to life. I am reminded of St. Augustine's caricature of the theatre: that whereas we do not dare to wish people unhappy, we do want to feel sorry for them, and therefore turn to plays so that we can feel sorry although no real misery is involved. One might apply the parallel interpretation to the modern delight in happy endings, and say that we turn to art to indulge our humanitarianism in a well-wishing which we do not permit ourselves towards our actual neighbors. Surely the catharsis of art is more complicated than this, and more reputable.

Eloquence itself, as I hope to have established in the instance from *Hamlet* which I have analyzed, is no mere plaster added to a framework of more stable qualities. Eloquence is simply the end of art, and is thus its essence. Even the poorest art is eloquent, but in a poor way, with less intensity, until this aspect is obscured by others fattening upon its leanness. Eloquence is not showiness; it is, rather, the result of that desire in the artist to make a work perfect by adapting it in every minute detail to the racial appetites.

The distinction between the psychology of information and the psychology of form involves a definition of æsthetic truth. It is here precisely, to combat the deflection which the strength of science has caused to our tastes, that we must examine the essential breach between scientific and artistic truth. Truth in art is not the discovery of facts, not an addition to human knowledge in the scientific sense of the word.[7] It is, rather, the exercise of human propriety, the formulation of symbols which rigidify our sense of poise and rhythm. Artistic truth is the externalization of taste.[8] I sometimes wonder, for instance, whether the "artificial" speech of John Lyly might perhaps be "truer" than the revelations of Dostoevsky. Certainly at its best, in its feeling for a statement which returns upon itself, which attempts the systole to a diastole, it *could* be much truer than Dostoevsky.[9] And if it is not, it fails not through a mistake of Lyly's æsthetic, but because Lyly was a man poor in character, whereas Dostoevsky was rich and complex. When Swift, making the women of Brobdingnag enormous, deduces from this discrepancy between their size and Gulliver's that Gulliver could sit astride their nipples, he has written something which is æsthetically true, which is, if I may be pardoned, profoundly "proper," as correct in its Euclidean deduction as any corollary in geometry. Given the companions of Ulysses in the cave of Polyphemus, it is true that they would escape clinging to the bellies of the herd let out to pasture. St. Ambrose, detailing the habits of God's creatures, and drawing from them moral maxims for the good of mankind, St. Ambrose in his limping natural history rich in scientific inaccuracies that are at the very heart of emotional rightness, St. Ambrose writes "Of night-birds, especially of the nightingale which hatches her eggs by song; of the owl, the bat, and the cock at cock-crow; in what wise these may apply to the guidance of our habits," and in the sheer rightness of that program there is the truth of art.

In introducing this talk of night-birds, after many pages devoted to other of God's creatures, he says,

"What now! While we have been talking, you will notice how the birds of night have already started fluttering about you, and, in this same fact of warning us to leave off with our discussion, suggest thereby a further topic"—and this seems to me to contain the best wisdom of which the human frame is capable, an address, a discourse, which can make our material life seem blatant almost to the point of despair. And when the cock crows, and the thief abandons his traps, and the sun lights up, and we are in every way called back to God by the well-meaning admonition of this bird, here the very blindnesses of religion become the deepest truths of art.

NOTES

1. Similarly, the epigram of Racine is "pure art," because it usually serves to formulate or clarify some situation within the play itself. In Goethe the epigram is most often of independent validity, as in *Die Wahlverwandtschaften*, where the ideas of Ottilie's diary are obviously carried over bodily from the author's notebook. In Shakespeare we have the union of extrinsic and intrinsic epigram, the epigram growing out of its context and yet valuable independent of its context.

2. One might indicate still further appropriateness here. As Hamlet finishes his speech, Polonius enters, and Hamlet turns to him, "God bless you, sir!" Thus the plot is continued (for Polonius is always the promise of action) and a full stop is avoided: the embarrassment laid upon Rosencranz and Guildenstern is not laid upon the audience.

3. Yet modern music has gone far in the attempt to renounce this aspect of itself. Its dissonances become static, demanding no particular resolution. And whereas an unfinished modulation by a classic musician occasions positive dissatisfaction, the refusal to resolve a dissonance in modern music does not dissatisfy us, but irritates or stimulates. Thus, "energy" takes the place of style.

4. Suspense is the least complex kind of anticipation, as surprise is the least complex kind of fulfilment.

5. As another aspect of the same subject, I could cite many examples from the fairy tale. Consider, for instance, when the hero is to spend the night in a bewitched castle. Obviously, as darkness descends, weird adventures must befall him. His bed rides him through the castle; two halves of a man challenge him to a game of nine-pins played with thigh bones and skulls. Or entirely different incidents may serve instead of these. The quality comes first, the particularization follows.

6. Could not the Greek public's resistance to Euripides be accounted for in the fact that he, of the three great writers of Greek tragedy, betrayed his art, was guilty of æsthetic impiety, in that he paid more attention to the arousing of emotion *per se* than to the sublimation of emotion into eloquence?

7. One of the most striking examples of the encroachment of scientific truth into art is the doctrine of "truth by distortion," whereby one aspect of an object is suppressed the better to emphasize some other aspect; this is, obviously, an attempt to *indicate* by art some fact of knowledge, to make some implicit aspect of an object as explicit as one can by means of the comparatively dumb method of art (dumb, that is, as compared to the perfect ease with which science can indicate its discoveries). Yet science has already made discoveries in the realm of this "factual truth," this "truth by distortion" which must put to shame any artist who relies on such matter for his effects. Consider, for instance, the motion picture of a man vaulting. By photographing this process very rapidly, and running the reel very slowly, one has upon the screen the most striking set of factual truths to aid in our understanding of an athlete vaulting. Here, at our leisure, we can observe the contortions of four legs, a head and a butt. This squirming thing we saw upon the screen

showed up an infinity of factual truths anent the balances of an athlete vaulting. We can, from this, observe the marvelous system of balancing which the body provides for itself in the adjustments of movement. Yet, so far as the æsthetic truth is concerned, this on the screen was not an athlete, but a squirming thing, a horror, displaying every fact of vaulting except the exhilaration of the act itself.

8. The procedure of science involves the elimination of taste, employing as a substitute the corrective norm of the pragmatic test, the empirical experiment, which is entirely intellectual. Those who oppose the "intellectualism" of critics like Matthew Arnold are involved in an hilarious blunder, for Arnold's entire approach to the appreciation of art is through delicacies of taste intensified to the extent almost of squeamishness.

9. As for instance, the "conceit" of Endymion's awakening, when he forgets his own name, yet recalls that of his beloved.

MARVIN ROSENBERG

A Metaphor for Dramatic Form

I suggest that the form of conventional drama is linear—that, while it takes place in a continuing present, it moves as it were from left to right, from a beginning through a chain of chronological sequences toward an end. This traditional form in modern times has been distorted and shattered by adventuring playwrights trying to hold time at bay, to circumscribe the present, to isolate non-narrative felt life. I propose to develop a metaphor to describe their adventures in form.

In the traditional mode, the line of forward movement organizes the drama. Every important speech or action is an arrow pointing to a next speech or action, all merging into the sequential Aristotelian beginning-middle-end pattern. It is an economical mode, and ideally every element has some significance for the forward progress; nothing is aimless, as it so often is in life. A thousand times in life a man will say, "What a miserable day," and nothing follows, nor do we expect anything; let one in the theatre say, "So foul and fair a day I have not seen," and we sense this to be part of the man's special history and future; it must point forward to a development in mood, character, action. Life is a ground on which random figures momentarily emerge to a threshold of perception, and then fade, coalesce with new figures, or dissolve into the ground as our gestalts change. In conventional drama the gestalt is fixed, the ground is a controlled field for the movement of a clearly defined figure across it.

In the simplest dramatic type, the melodrama, the forward line is the essence of the play. A dead body has been discovered; some two hours later successively linked events will have led to the discovery of the killer. For purposes of tension the flow of the line will be interrupted by titillating reversals, but the momentary blocks will only increase the

From *The Journal of Aesthetics and Art Criticism*, Vol. XVII no. 2, 1958. Reprinted by permission of the author and publisher.

force by which the audience is rushed toward the predestined stop. All dispensable elements—character, language—that slow the line must be stripped away.

The same linear form can be beautifully complex—as in *Oedipus*. Basically the story is the same: the finding of a murderer. The end is known in the beginning; and speeches and action point to the end with a force and directness that melodrama can only envy. Creon, Teiresias, the messenger come pat; the old shepherd is in the wings. The linear pace toward destiny is almost intolerable. But unlike melodrama, and its thin hypnotic line, *Oedipus* moves forward in breadth. What happens is only important because of what happens in Oedipus, what happens in the others, the meaning of what happens, the language and spectacle. These broad scarves braid about the central line of the play, and the whole unrolls in a wide, firm texture that will bear the weight of our full scrutiny, sensual, emotional, intellectual.

Analogically, the simple action melodrama is like a popular melody: it moves thinly from a beginning to an end, setting up little arches of expectation, completing them, bringing them toward a final terminus— a satisfying, unmistakable end we have been led to anticipate. Chords play around the line of melody, but are submerged in it—unless improvising musicians, tired of the thin forward movement, thicken it with complementary themes that often only disguise or destroy the thread of song, which is too light to bear them. Similarly, in pretentious melodrama, heavily laden with pompous language and character, the action line is often smothered, and the play grinds on pointlessly. A musical parallel to the complex progression of *Oedipus* would be a classical symphony—a Beethoven. Musicians themselves call this form "dramatic"; its straightforward line carries the hearer along, arousing expectations, satisfying them, while leading forward to new expectations, all building to a peak of excitement released in the finale. But the musical line is dense with counterpoint; supporting themes, like supporting characters in a play, oppose the main theme or submit to it, and the whole moves on a broad front toward the climactic suspense. The end of a classical symphony is an absolute terminus; few things end so completely: thump crash crash THUMP CRASH *THUMP!* There is no mistake about it: this is the end of the line. Complex plays usually break off less sharply, may leave a suggestion that life goes on; but normally their end, too, is unmistakable, and sometimes close to excessive (as in the repeated fortissimos of death in *Hamlet,* or the long bravura of

Cyrano), since the playwright also has a passion to wring us tight before he lets us go.

There is good reason for the linear form in drama. It promises the precious catharsis that life can rarely offer. The crises of life don't end; as one subsides, another—many another—builds up in the wings. Mortality is inexorably continuous. In drama we can experience the ultimate torment of joy and have done with it, we can participate in the wildest forbidden passions and hostilities, titanic externalizations of the fantasies that shake us privately—and at play's end we are through with them, for the moment purified and free of them, as the expiating curtain scene washes them clean.

The deep satisfactions inherent in this sequential tension-release pattern have made it the dominant dramatic form, so much so that a sensitive modern aesthetician, Susanne Langer, has seen in the "movement toward destiny"—what to me is a manifestation of the "linear pattern"—the *only* form. "It is only a present filled with its own future that is really dramatic. A sheer immediacy, an imperishable direct experience without the ominous forward movement of consequential forward action, would not be so . . . This tension between past and future is what gives to acts, situations, and even such constituent elements as gestures and attitudes and tones the peculiar intensity known as dramatic quality . . ."

Tragedy is an advance toward destiny, a self-consummation, Mrs. Langer says; and these phrases have themselves the lure of the cathartic terminal form, of the act committed, punished, and eternally expiated. A great trouble must be met, a great crisis against which the spirit hurls itself, and discovers its fate and final end. Herein lies a technical secret of the linear form: an advance toward tragic fate is always over a rocky road, guarded by one or more great obstacles or enemies, and the more truly fearful the course, the more the audience is enlisted emotionally in its champion's journey. Forward action develops more friction if it must beat down counter-action; and so we have the beguiling Hegelian theories that drama is conflict, that purposeful will must drive ahead against anti-will, and out of the clash will come synthesis—in other equations recognition or rebirth.

But to many modern artists, in all art forms, the easy hypnotic power of the neat linear form has seemed insufficient to convey the raggedness of existence. They are trying to break from the representation of smooth, unlifelike, closed experience, and suggest the incompleteness, the discontinuous continuity, the confused emotional tone of living. In the linear form, as mind follows movement, there is often—to use Sypher's phrase about narrative painting—"shallow-seeing," a gliding across surfaces. A strong current of modern painting, non-representational, tries to hold the mind on intensity rather than carry it along a line, to set up a system of tensions within the frame, so the mind does not follow a familiar image but instead acquaints itself with a complex, subtle experience. Other modern paintings convey an image enriched by many perspectives, instead of the single conventional perspective. Experimental music gives up the "dramatic" horizontal, contrapuntal line of a classical symphony in favor—sometimes in Schoenberg, for instance—of a series of verticals, moments of chorded experience; and the whole forms in the mind as a texture, rather than a line. This modern music does not regularly build to a finish with a clashing peroration; it sometimes hardly "ends" at all, but only stops, as if the composition is a segment of a greater patternless continuity.

Similarly modern drama, poetry, and the novel have been trying to escape the tyranny of time progression, to catch the myriad dimensions of the present.[1] This has meant, for drama, a radical change of perspective, particularly toward character. When action is linear, characterization must be narrowed to justify selected arrow-acts leading to an end. But human motivation is never simple enough to fit into the stripped down line of melodrama; even in the great linear plays, even in *Hamlet*, say, with the extra dimension of the soliloquy, there is room only to suggest barely the complex of motives that usher in a tragic act—which is why we must search our own consciences for Hamlet's full motivation. Non-linear drama set out to recognize the ambiguity of all human behavior, rather than the chain-link effects of isolated acts.[2]

Thus Strindberg, reaching toward this form in introducing *Miss Julie:* "A character came to signify a man fixed and finished: one who invariably appeared either drunk or jocular or melancholy, and characterizations required nothing more than a physical defect such as a club-foot, a wooden leg, or a red nose . . . This simple way of regarding human beings still survives in the great Molière. Harpagon is nothing but a miser, although Harpagon might have been not only a miser, but also a first-rate financier, an excellent father, and a good citizen. I do not believe in simple stage characters; and the summary judgments of authors —this man is stupid, that one brutal, this jealous, that stingy, and so forth—should be challenged by the Naturalists who know the richness of the soul-complex and realize that vice has a reverse side very much

like virtue . . . I have drawn my characters vacillating, disinte-
grating . . ."

Strindberg's first step, in this play, was to give dimension to his character by suggesting lifelike qualities of inconsistency—vacillation, disintegration—that could as easily impede the linear progress as expedite
it. But given the traditional form he used, the characters had to be subdued to the movement toward destiny, and Strindberg learned that no
forward story line could contain the ambiguity of human behavior. So
he tried to circumscribe a moment of it, tried as did other expressionists
to turn from the linear to a more pliable dramatic form—a form I will
call "contextual." The tensions of context, rather than direction, of
vertical depth, rather than horizontal movement, became important—as
they did for the experimental artist, musician, novelist. Hence a drama
like *The Dream Play*—a montage of scenes that follow each other without progressing, rich in symbol and association, meaningful not in
sequence or suspense, but in the reflection of a discontinuous psychic
activity.[3] The way of another pioneer, Pirandello, was to concentrate
on a narrow area of mortality—a dilemma in illusion and reality—and go
deeply behind it, layer after layer, trying to bare it to infinity.[4] As the
point of view shifts from character to character, new contexts assert
themselves, and we discover in art, as in life, that gestalts depend on
perspectives, which are many, various, impermanent.

The contextual form is a tremendous challenge to the playwright.
Here the ready tension of linear action-counteraction drama is difficult
to match, because the materials of the contextual mode are strange and
obstinate—they reside in the aimless, unclimactic multiplicity of emotional life. A tenacious idiom is needed to catch and hold this fluidity
on the stage, a kind of free association is needed, of the sort Joyce developed—*free* only in its mercurial spread, splendidly controlled and
integrated and exciting in its linkages of words, emotions, thoughts. To
absorb a theater audience in tensions of context rather than sequence,
the linkages must be made visual—but not *only* visual, as they are in the
liquid, implicit symbolism of the ballet; in the theater, except for brief
interludes, verbal and visual imagery must function together.

Contextual drama has taken two general directions. In the first, character is treated as in the traditional form: made to seem "real," with
a life direction, but providing a minimum of linear movement. From this
central focus, the characters are extended in dimension instead of being
developed in a direction. This form inherits from Chekov's technique
of examining many planes of human surface opposed in tension, and

suggesting the forces struggling beneath them. There are many moments in Chekov when life is stopped, non-sequential, timeless; when his several characters speak thoughts and feelings that have almost nothing to do with each other, or with a forward action; they speak past each other, dreaming away their own lives, sounding their separate notes. The effect is not of a contrapuntal, horizontal advance, but rather of a series of sad, exquisite harmonics—vertical, time-stopped chords. So skilful is the playwright in suggesting the tension and depth of the moment rather than of sequence that his dramas sometimes leave the impression of being all mood, all lingering present when in fact they are firmly threaded on a forward line.

A modern example of the contextual character drama is *Death of a Salesman*. Its time is interior, in Eric Auerbach's phrase: it moves from a central situation back and forth in fantasy and memory to widen and deepen a present emotional moment.[5] A linear ending is tagged on to the play, but it is neither necessary nor inevitable.

The second, more difficult form is a more purely contextual drama, a theater image of a mental state. Of course, all drama is an image of our mental states; but in the traditional form, a "real" character does the hard experiencing for us, stands between us and ourselves, while in this second kind of drama we come face to face with our own inner processes. But not as explicitly as in the old, overt Moralities, or in the simple simile form as in Evreinov's brief *Theatre of the Soul*, with its personified characters Rational Entity, Emotional Entity, etc. Instead, in this modern experimental drama, the characters are "people" in the usual theatrical sense: the two bums in *Waiting for Godot*, Kilroy in *Camino Real*, Joseph K. in *The Trial*. They have conventional passions and hurts; but their identity is sunk in their passions and hurts, of which they become the transparent images (rather than intermediate symbols) and we recognize the passions and hurts as our own.

Waiting for Godot is a good recent example. It ends exactly where it began, though there are bits of movement within it, because it is not a story of the life of its characters but of a condition of living, and that is timeless. What we see is waitingness, a chronic, anonymous waitingness, relieved as it is in life by contrasts of kindness and cruelty and quiet and noise and biological function and poetic dream—but always in the context of the long now. At the other extreme from *Godot* is *Camino Real*. In *Godot*, the frame is not crowded: the strokes are broad, the colors mainly somber, and the large design is relatively easy to grasp. In *Camino Real*, the frame is alive with the ceaseless business of the mind: fantasy, passion, cliché, regression, aggression, vanity. Almost the complete spectrum is projected, and projected nearly simultaneously, rather than sequentially; at any one moment we can almost catch a glimpse of the whole shifting mosaic.

The shape of contextual drama is elusive because its matter is shapelessness. It tries to convey the content of experience before a form has been impressed on it by thought. Form in art and life is limiting, inhibitory, it is a pattern imposed on the anarchic human matrix—call it the id—by the individual and the collective conscious—call it the superego. Humanity is almost defined by its compulsion to make such patterns. Civilizations are collective designs to channel or contain impulses in the interest of tolerable group living; the individual ego survives by projecting a hypothetical order on the unorder of psychic existence. But the psyche knows no order, it is fluid, and rebels against containment. Behind the imposed patterns of conscious, time-regulated routine, the dream-life of our waking existence goes on untamed. This is what contextual drama seeks to surround and exhibit. It is a reality which the tidy linear form cannot cope with. So, like modern mathematicians who, unable to find a pattern in the interaction of multiple sky bodies, have come to hypothesize a "regular disorder," the contextual playwright has given up the linear vision of order for a form that seeks to enclose the loose mesh of experience. "Dream-like" as it is, this material has generally been regarded as "non-representational" on the stage, has been dramatized in the framework of a dream, and usually treated with the resources of fantasy: dream music, wraithlike figures, balletic movement; or with the phantasmagoric scenic imagery Strindberg used in *The Dream Play,* and Gide partly in his stage adaptation of Kafka's contexual novel *The Trial.*[6] *Camino Real* and *Godot* are remarkable for avoiding this; [7] they depend essentially on the conventional, representational means of apparently real characters interacting through the usual stage techniques which are often ironically juxtaposed with startling effect: a lyric moment on the heels of violence, soliloquy after stichomythia, tears after frank slapstick. Their sudden, comforting moments of humor save them—as life is saved—from nightmare: from such a nightmare as Per Lagerkvist's chilling play in this mode, *The Secret of Heaven.*

These plays reached toward Maeterlinck's dream of pure drama of being. Maeterlinck himself had learned to create a suffused mood for such drama; but he never achieved a texture palpable enough, crosshatched enough, to continuously excite sense, feeling, and thought.

Modern contextual drama effects this by translating the restless intensity of inner life into busy, loaded symbolic action. Many perspectives
of the same perception are brought together; many intense, momentary
chorded experiences poise side by side in tension; and the dynamic context conveys a sense of the ever-dissolving gestalts of existence. There
is no easy terminal release from this kind of artistic experience. The
audience is confronted with its passions, not forgiven them. This drama's
form is flux; as if the playwrights are reaching, in the second part of the
usual linear equation, "Life is————", for a statement so vast and ambiguous and disturbing that it seems, indeed, they are bent on discard-
ing limiting terms altogether in favor of a simple declarative sentence:
"Life is."

NOTES

1. Brecht, who also tried to shatter the spell of sequential drama, did so for
a different reason. Essentially a propagandist, he would deliberately break
the thread of an "epic" play to recall to audiences the social meaning of what
they were seeing. He thought of such drama as discursive, conveying its
impact through the accumulation of intellectual impressions, rather than
through a hypnotic engagement of the emotions. But even in Brechtian drama,
his didactic interruptions are usually forgotten by an audience as soon as
they are finished and the action advances. (Thus Eric Bentley, in *The Playwright as Thinker,* notes the triumph of Brecht's practice over his theory.)
Our submission to the linear form is similarly apparent in "flashback" dramas
which usually vary from the norm only in explicitly stating the inevitable
destiny in the beginning. So powerful is the linear spell that once an audience
is "flashed back," it usually promptly suspends its memory of the known
destiny, and moves forward with the action as if from a fresh beginning. It
will make this adjustment once (as in *The Diary of Anne Frank*), or many
times (as in *The Lark*).
2. In this discussion, I don't want to seem to suggest that one form is better
than another. Both will survive; each will use the other when it serves. What
I am trying to do here is project an image of their functions.
3. Though even here Strindberg did not completely free himself from the
beginning-end pattern. He might as well have. The framework about the
divine princess who learns that life is hell only states explicitly the experience
which the center of the play conveys much better, dramatically.
   Eugene Ionesco, in the same tradition, has so revolted against "form" that
he makes its absence in his works obtrusive. He too externalizes man's inner
fears; thus the press of inanimate things is likely to overwhelm his heroes
physically as well as psychically: in one play, furniture suddenly proliferates,
in another coffee cups multiply, in a third a corpse grows—all eventually
burying the human characters. Ionesco writes of his deliberately anti-linear

style: "(My own plays originate) from a state of soul, not from an ideology, from an impulse and not a program; the cohesion that gives a structure to emotions in their pure state corresponds to an inner necessity, and not to a logic of construction imposed from outside; there is no subjection to a predetermined action, but exteriorization of a psychic dynamism, projection upon the stage of internal conflicts, of the inner universe." (*Theatre Arts*, June 1958, 10.)

4. Genet's *The Maids* is a recent play in this multi-layered mode.

5. Laurents' *A Clearing in the Woods* is a more recent attempt to dramatize being similarly.

6. *The Trial* conveys the confused condition of being by combining the tensions of context with some of the suspense of progression toward a destiny—but a destiny of the psyche.

7. However, *Camino Real* uses—unnecessarily—a dream framework.

HAROLD H. WATTS

Myth and Drama

I

Every century—perhaps every decade—has its topics. In one sense, the effort to state the essence of tragedy and of comedy is one of our topics. This, unlike other topics that obsess us, is certainly not ours alone. Very nearly as long as men have possessed comedies and tragedies, they have labored to explain to each other what it was they possessed; it has never seemed "good enough" simply to luxuriate in the immediate pleasure which either tragedy or comedy affords. Thus, speculation on the natures of comedy and tragedy is a permanent as well as a twentieth century topic. But our accent, as we discuss these problems, is not the accent of other centuries. We are not very deeply impressed by the useful distinctions between the mechanics of the two forms; nor does the insight that one form moves us to tears and the other stirs us to laughter seem to take us to the heart of the question.

That the insights of earlier men into tragedy and comedy do not satisfy us may be an oblique reflection of a parlous condition; so be it. We have not the soundness and health to rest satisfied with the perceptions of difference that other men have found clarifying. With us, the tragedy-comedy difference has become not a question of dramaturgy or of surface-level psychology. It has become closely entwined with the religious question as it too is debated among us. Indeed, one of our recurrent suspicions is that the tragedy-comedy question is in fact the religious question. (This suspicion, I shall show, is part-right, part-wrong.) Such a suspicion once would have been termed sacrilegious since it mingles sacred and profane. It is a suspicion that now is inacceptable to some parties to the tragedy-comedy discussion for very dif-

From *Cross Currents*, Vol. V (1955), pp. 154–70. Reprinted by permission of the author and the publisher.

ferent reasons; for it hints that there persists, for man, an area apart, an area of the sacred, on which tragedy and comedy impinge.

It is strange but true that to say that drama is closely allied with the sacred stirs, in our times, resistance not from the clergy, who now draw freely on terms proper to dramatic discussion to cast light on religious mysteries; the resistance comes from hard-headed students of the drama who want to peg the discussion at a level that reflects Aristotle or that records "actual practice" or that traces the better-known and more obvious human responses to both tragedy and comedy. But these hard-headed efforts but prolong the confidence that drama is an utterly secular activity, one that has no tangential relations with religion—one that, in consequence, will be in no way illuminated by an association with religion, with myth and cult. This resistance, as it persists among us, is chiefly useful as astringent to all sorts of discussion of drama that hints or announces that the play and the theatre constitute one of the few sacred activities left to us. Criticism that refuses to trace analogies between drama and myth is certainly limiting, but it is certainly less misleading than an interpretation of the drama that finds it a valid surrogate for all that used to go under the name of religion.

Our relation to the drama, the drama's possible goods for us in this century, are described correctly by neither of the extremes just mentioned. A fair account of the situation of nineteenth and twentieth century man in relation to the drama is this: By the unfolding "logic" of Western intellectual growth, the forms of the sacred that seemed real and compulsive in many centuries—that indeed enabled earlier men to treat drama and other forms of art as manifestly secular—lost their power to stir the majority of cultivated minds. Thus, the present sense of many persons that drama, at least, is sacred and is in clear opposition to the emptiness of modern life is a sense which records an interesting shift in the meaning of the words *sacred* and *secular*. *Sacred* once referred to the portion of human life in which revealed truth, offered us by a church, made specific demands on us and gave us specific aids, and the secular was just that portion of life that seemed free of those demands and not dependent on those aids. This traditional division—once drama had reached the inn-yard or princely halls—definitely regarded both comedy and tragedy as secular creations. The drama was an amusement, a distraction, an activity on which the church did not "move in" except when stirred by excess of indecency or atheism. To us, this assignment of the drama to a secular realm seems less obvious. We partake of a general intellectual atmosphere in which the sacred (to put the matter mildly) is not hedged securely against the secular; the secular so occupies our waking thoughts that we may even regard the realm of the sacred as a pious fiction rather than as a going reality. And some of us find that the real sacred (if indeed it does exist) flourishes in an activity that men used confidently to regard as secular; we find the sacred in music or art or—as here—the drama with its power to light up our existence, to criticize or transform our secular boredom.

Those who find that drama is, for modern man, a locus of the sacred are a rather mixed company. Skeptics, workers in depth psychology, liturgists, ordinarily devout persons—these unlikely companions share what I have called a twentieth-century topical debate, the degree of sacredness in drama, and find they respond to the effects of drama— effects that they find peculiar and haunting. The traditional sacred is gone or—we suspect with varying emotions—is on the point of leaving us. We discover with relief that what we are about to lose is "really" available to us elsewhere—in the drama, for example.

Before we accept this discovery as fact, we ought to ask whether the relation between drama and religion, drama and myth, is one of essential identity or one of similarity. It is my feeling that the relation is one of similarity: a similarity that must be studied since it is deep, persistent, and illuminating to both drama and religion. Drama is no surrogate for myth and cult, but what it offers us finds partial explanation in what myth and cult have offered men.

II

So long as drama had, for its undoubted locus, the region of the secular, questions about tragedy and comedy, about their common root and their differences, were debated in what one must now regard as a dry, bright atmosphere. There is something cold as well as competent, insensitive as well as clear, in the treatment Aristotle and others accorded the tragedy they knew. It is plain that many modern persons, skeptics as well as believers, find a more tremendous, more "sacred" import in tragedy than Aristotle found. (By extension, we find the same sort of import in comedy.) Rightly or wrongly, we are drawn by the dark uncertainties which drama embodies; and if this is our taste, we will experience no satisfaction when we read critics who wrote in other centuries and could reduce both tragedy and comedy to bright certainties, who looked to the playhouse for mechanically clever vehicles that enforced the moral platitudes of an era. Yet if both comedy and tragedy

indeed do more, if they constantly draw us back toward their two Western sources of origin—the church chancel or the sacred grove—this
covert filiation is a source of irritation to students who are willing to
concede that drama is powerful and yet maintain that drama's "real"
climate is certainly the climate of secular life: life untouched in any way
by the sacred. Persons who feel that the "real" locus of drama has always been the sacred—or, the contention here, displays a close similarity
to the sacred—turn from matters of construction, turn from the rise and
fall of fashion in dramatic form, to the *effects* of viewed drama that
pass beyond amusement and such superficial categories of criticism as
realism, naturalism, and romanticism.

Yet is not this latter interest in drama, if uncritically followed, but a
pursuit of surrogates for the conventional forms of the sacred: the
church, its ritual, its body of organized dogma? Doubtless. We would
not be impelled to isolate the sacred in drama did we not have some
qualms about the conventional locus of the sacred. If we are devout,
our study of drama is probably an attempt to win intellectual confirmation for truths that we still believe but which we find no longer self-
confirming. And if we are skeptical, our study of drama proceeds with
more passion still; drama does not just explain and validate the sacred
—a religion that we persist in believing. Instead, drama *is* the sacred.

Both these approaches to the sacred—or, as I believe, the *resemblance*
to the sacred—in the drama are partisan approaches. What is the
sacred if we define it (as we now try to) not in terms of a church or a
lapsed tradition? One ought to be able to define the sacred in terms of
human action, or at least attempt to. The sacred is "created"—exists for
us and probably becomes available to other persons who are in any way
like us—by any gesture or word which makes a total assertion. Any word
or gesture which offers, to our own awareness and the awarenesses that
we are able to reach, some insight about what existence collectively *is*
—this is a sacred word or announcement rather than a secular one. In
contrast, a secular utterance concerns itself with some smaller portion
of experience; neither actually nor by implication does it describe some
aspect of the total act of existing. It is concerned with conveying facts,
practical procedures under certain explicit circumstances, or—at its most
ambitious—short-range predictions.

This distinction between what is sacred and what is secular does not
rest on the authority of a particular revelation or the encrusted, poly-
chrome prestige of a religious tradition. Rather do all churches and
traditions rest on such a distinction; and all revolts against church and

tradition are in essence (whatever they are accidentally, as *specific* protests) denials that the distinction between sacred and secular, between total assertion and what we may call partial assertion is a valid one. (The revolts usually express an understandable bitterness with some of the applications of the sacred, of total assertions; they do not usually envisage their own result: a denial that any total assertion whatever is valid. Yet this is the uneasy course that, in part, has created our present question.)

The peculiar twentieth century attitude toward drama, whether it is developed in a skeptic or a believer, is testimony that the distinction between total assertion, the sacred, and partial assertion, the secular, is one that, at least, haunts us. It is felt that one sort of gesture and assertion—here, drama—has an impact and validity different from another kind of gesture and assertion—say, a radio commercial praising a dentifrice.

So viewed, the contrast between the sacred and the secular makes little reference to church and tradition; the contrast rests on a juxta-position of two sorts of direct experience. A sacred assertion—whether it be couched in myth, performed in rite, codified in dogma or (as some of us seem to suspect) enacted in significant drama—is a total assertion. It asserts what man's life is, and it cannot be demonstrated as true; it can be only accepted or rejected as true. A secular assertion is an observation of fact. It is a reference to a physical fact that can readily be checked; it makes—less clearly, we will admit if we are at all reflective —some observation about comparatively small phases of society, and offers us ways of seeming to manage "small" areas of human social and moral relations. When we are secularized, when we congratulate ourselves (if that is our mood) that the sacred has been driven from our lives, we believe that we are freed of the burden and the nonsense of making total assertions or of listening to discourses based on the total assertions that men "like us" have made in the past.

There are many reasons why such freedom is to be desired. For many decades, secular evangelists, working in the spirit of Lucretius, have impellingly pled with us to give up a frustrating taste for total assertion; man can (the evangel runs) live better by partial assertions. We can always check partial assertions, whether they be scientific laws or the little useful rules of thumb by which "actually" we conduct our societies and personal affairs. Yet we should never cease to observe—and this is what drives us back to drama or art or music as possible loci of the sacred—that secular evangelists offer us at least one total assertion, at

least one *sacred* statement: that man *ought* to be willing to live by partial or secular assertions. Whether this one unavoidable, irreducible total
assertion—the assertion that makes possible the cancellation of the
sacred—is true, right, and correct we cannot say; faced with it, we are
in as much doubt as we are when we face any of the other total, sacred
assertions about man and his destiny. Perhaps we do well when we
hesitate to accept it as bindingly true. At least, the current plunge into
the depths harbored by comedy and tragedy may indicate that the
sacred resembles proverbial truth: crushed to earth at a particular point,
it rises vigorously elsewhere. But what would St. Augustine and other
foes of secular spectacle think if they were to learn that a quasi-sacred
light shines behind the theatrical proscenium?

III

Despite resemblances, it is stupid—it is, I believe, indefensible—to maintain that drama proffers to man *all* the effects of the sacred. Likewise,
it is misleading to press too far the analogy between full religious
activity, "pegged" to a myth, and the public performance of a play.
Church-harbored rite and theatre-harbored drama have their rich similarities, similarities which I shall explore. But it is useless to wring
final drops from perceived similarities that, say, draw *Oedipus Rex* and
a religious rite toward each other. Music and art and drama and
church-harbored rite may be akin since, in our terms, they all make
inclusive rather than partial statements about life. But not all inclusive
statements are the same statement. These various "statements," moreover, exist within unlike media, which make possible effects that are
different although they may supplement each other intimately. Beethoven's Ninth may give us a feeling of transcendence (indeed, it
does); it may give us the feeling that our ears have now listened to the
music of the spheres and that our minds, for once, encompass the universe. But all this encompassing is not the precise encompassing that
religious rite makes possible, when at a gesture from the priest we come
forward to drink from a cup rather than—in response to Beethoven's
invitation as celebrant—to immerse ourselves in a wonderful sea of harmony. Likewise, a retablo in a well-lighted art gallery is not a retablo
in the Cathedral at Seville. A changed context has altered a powerful
religious object into a powerful work of art; on the gallery wall, it has
become something new, for, cut off from the gestures of the priest, the
imprecision of cathedral light, and the mélange of cathedral odors

pleasant and nauseous, the retablo addresses us in a different way. The way is still sacred since the effect the art-object, the retablo, creates is an inclusive one; it makes a total assertion. But it is not the inclusive effect to which it once contributed an essential note in a Spanish chapel.

The retablo's history can be our clue to the limitations we ought to impose on any discussion of the sacred in drama. Drama, let us concede, abounds in the sacred as here defined; it is indeed a sacred that can be studied in relation to the sacred of rite and myth. Modern criticism of drama abounds in over-assertions on this point; and these over-assertions but testify to a slightly frantic desire to offset religious *accidie*. No less than the Ninth Symphony and the Spanish retablo on the gallery wall does drama make total assertions. But they can never be identical with the assertions mediated to man by the complex of myth, rite, and dogma that makes up any "church." Consider the retablo on the gallery wall. It does not cease to make some of the total assertions it made in a chapel. But its assertions become involved in a different context of effect. The new context, let me insist, is not an unworthy one. (What is more essential to a full, even a sacred, existence than comprehension of the nuances and the mergings of styles of visual assertion that the skillfully displayed retablo offers us?) But it is not the same context. Vision is the "faculty" that the retablo always appealed to and always will appeal to. But a changed context—museum rather than chapel—has certainly altered the assertion that is mediated. In the chapel we "saw" this assertion: Existence finds its sum and center in a figure extended on several pieces of wood. In the gallery we "see" something like this: Existence finds its meaning in the competence of a creative and ingenious mind that is able to fuse—completely and for eternity—shades of color, given "real" objects (a body and a cross), and the lines that reproduce on a flat surface the colors and shapes of nature. This is not a contemptible fusion; it is, in my sense, sacred. But it is not the still more complex fusion that once took place in the Spanish chapel.

The analogy provided by the two states of the retablo is clear. Drama has great power, like the retablo in the museum, to remind us of what was, for many centuries, regarded as the sole locus of the sacred: the church, the temple-cave, the sacred grove. Drama rests on narrative, just as religious ceremonial rests on narrative (or myth). But we are too quick to say that drama gives to us—because of this and other resemblances—the essential of what has been, for "historical reasons," lost to us: the assertions that came to man in church or cave or grove. To insist on this perception of difference is not to attempt to discredit drama; it is the first step toward a precise definition of what drama does indeed make available to us.

If drama gives the sacred, it does not give the complete sacred assertion if our standard is (as it should be) the experience of the religious person rather than (as it often is) the experience of the person who feels religious while he is in the theatre. When this is the emphasis, it is drama that is teaching us (if we are interested) what religion is. Nor does it do this badly if we do not posit an identity between the two, if we do not suppose that one of the two (here religion) is expendable. (This is Cromwell's heresy toward drama in reverse.) At the present stage of our scrutiny of the topic (What is drama? What are the relations between tragedy and comedy?), there may be profit in sending drama to school to religion instead of religion to school to drama. (It is this latter relation that is set up when we say that the viable elements of religion "live on" in drama. It is the thesis of this essay that, whatever the resemblances, neither activity can hope to "live on" in the other.)

What do these two vehicles of total assertion have in common? Most strikingly, gesture and costume. Gesture and costume alike set the priest apart from his congregation and the personages of a drama from *their* congregations. Also in common, the two vehicles have a story. But the differences are at once apparent. How soon costume and gesture become inalterable in a "church," and how quickly the abundance of story that human fancy can supply becomes only one or two stories! And in drama—whatever its roots in old rite—how comparatively free is the range of costume and gesture, and how endlessly abundant—though this lies only on the surface—is the combination of represented event!

There are, however, differences just as immediate and striking. Religion "aspires" toward a state of fixity; drama exists—survives even—only by displaying a *superficial* ferment of change and innovation. How can we say that drama and religion are the same? A drama that does not produce new formulas dies, and a religion that lives in an unceasing ferment of innovation is (we usually judge) on its way to death. Let these differences be acknowledged then. For it is an acknowledgment that should make us quite humble about theories that "explain" the origin of the drama in religion; how could that which had to be conservative to survive (religion) "beget" that which has to be innovating to survive (drama)? Is not the history of Greek drama, conservative though it be by our standards, a series of innovations? Is not the failure of Greek religion, its tendency to respond to novel modes of thought, a negative testimony to the root-fixity of that sacred which we call religion?

But over and above this difference and beyond the similarity of gesture and costume that does not take our understanding very far, there is this resemblance that, first, casts a light on drama in general and, second, casts a most startling light on what has always been a key-question: the difference between comedy and tragedy. The resemblance is this: *Religion and drama both rest on narrative.*

What narrative is in drama we presume we know. That we may presume too much—that we may be too sure that we know what narrative "does" in a play—will not be clear to us until we make an attempt to be more precise about its religious analogue, myth. A myth is simply a narrative that a cult *happens* to employ for the purpose of making an overall assertion about man's experience of existing. Further, religion makes not one but two distinct uses of narrative material, uses that we will presently be explicit about. These two distinct uses are a sure clue to the two distinct sorts of drama, tragedy and comedy. This correspondence once perceived, we are far on our way to answering two questions: How are we to explain the coexistence of tragedy and comedy? (Answer: the coexistence is explained *by analogy* to the two uses made of narrative by cult.) How are we to explain the effects—often contradictory—of tragedy and comedy on us? How—to rephrase this second question—may we state, in some approximation to rational assertion, the permanently moving power of the logically contradictory all-over assertions that drama provides us with?

It is plain that in answering the question about the coexistence of comedy and tragedy we shall be explaining an effect in terms of its origin (an origin resembling if not identical with the two sorts of use of myth by religion that we shall identify). It is also plain that an explanation of the permanently moving power of the logical opposites, tragedy and comedy, must be a psychological explanation, an explanation that draws on one's insight into human reactions *now*. Yet the two answers are finally identical if one assumes—as I do—that there has been no great change in man himself—that the men whose expectations in a sense "created" the two forms, tragedy and comedy, are not altogether unlike the men who, in this century, continue to "demand" (if only in debased forms) both the laughable and the frightening.

IV

Let us, as lovers of drama or as esteemers of the *effects* of drama, seek to be instructed by the two uses of myth that we can observe in developed religions. For in these two uses are both the roots of comedy and tragedy and the rationale of their persisting appeal.

If religion has any distinguishing mark, it is this: it is an all-over assertion about the existence in which man is involved. (Magic is no such all-over assertion. It is not so much science before science as pragmatics before pragmatics.) Logically, one would expect that there would be, in religion, only one all-over assertion. But logic is a minor though not utterly absent element in religion and in drama; whatever their differences, both religion and drama must be faithful to existence first and only secondarily faithful to a pursuit of order. Thus, from the point of view of logic, a religious statement about the complete nature of reality, a statement made in terms of myth and cherished by cult, "ought" to make other statements of a similar nature impossible of assertion. Logic would suggest this question: if existence "at its heart" is thus and so, is it likely that the very same existence is "at its heart" something quite different? Yet developed religions make two such assertions, not one—assertions logically opposed to each other and cancelling.

One must, however, insist that religion does not proliferate uselessly contradictory statements about what is the total existence (its nature, its place for man) which we experience. But most developed religions find place for the following two (and contradictory) statements about existence. Logic would cancel one or the other, and we indeed find that systematizers of religion and secular systematizers of insights that have a religious origin if not at present a religious context struggle to cancel one of the two all-over statements as false or as an obscure form of the other statement. But these efforts overlook this truth: that both religion and drama are primarily records of man existing rather than of man trying to put his existence into comprehensible order. Religion and drama share this function; they enable man to *endure* existing, whereas philosophy and (in an often delusive way) science offer man the prospect of *comprehending* existence. Religion and drama are not interchangeable, despite certain present hopes. But one of the signs that they address themselves to the same task is that both are involved in advancing, at the same time, contradictory assertions about man and his existence.

(That is, portions of a religious ritual make assertions that later portions cancel, logically. Comedy makes assertions about existence which tragedy always casts doubt on.)

Religion rests on a narrative. From the narrative may be drawn doctrines exceedingly abstract and indeed opposed to an esteem for narrative, for time-contained event, as the primary means of revelation (e.g., Buddhism). But what religion latterly becomes (and not all developed religions become the same thing) is not our interest here. Our interest must concern itself with how religion "began"—at least, "began" when it reached a point at which it supplemented its direct perceptions of numen—the wonderful, the pervasively compulsive—with narrative. The contrast between Greek religion, which richly supplemented its perceptions of the numinous with narrative and Latin religion which simply preserved, for several historical centuries, the perception of numen suggests that man did—at some unrecorded time in some civilizations—build into the structure of religion key-narratives that came to bear the great weight of religious superstructure—the weight of cult, rite, and dogma.

What were the two uses to which narrative was put at this point in the growth of religion—a point early, real, but mostly unrecoverable? They are sharply contrasting uses. They are uses that record two logically opposed insights which man came to have about his position in the world. Both insights are valid and real; they may be incompatible with each other, but they are not, by that circumstance, either to be disregarded or discredited. Man created and used mythological narrative for these two purposes: he asserted that existence, in its root organization, was *cyclic;* he asserted that existence—and this was an unconscious criticism of his cyclic assertion—was not what he had at first thought it but was, instead, *linear.*

We shall presently define and distinguish these two assertions. Let us grant at once the logical contradiction—indeed, to many, the puerility —involved in entertaining these two assertions simultaneously. It is plain that once the opposition between these two assertions is clearly perceived, many persons will judge that they have one more reason to dismiss the authority of religious experience. One may concede that such persons move in intellectual regions that are less demanding on the sympathetic imagination—regions that have their own sort of profit. But such persons are cut off from the profit that is the gift to man of religion and myth, and they are also in a poor position to measure the conflicting endowments, to man, of tragedy and comedy. These persons are not likely to see the significance of the likewise perplexing fact that tragedy and comedy are also logical incompatibles that coexist and that are intimately related in ways that vex and elude. Both tragedy and comedy are representations of experience; both mediate comprehension of experience. Are these two acts of comprehension so opposed to each other as to coexist only senselessly, as do random acts? Or do they have a supplementing function as they present their opposed visions of the universe? One form gives us the universe as a place suffused with laughter (*sustained* by laughter, we shall see); the other gives us the universe as a place falling in pieces, all props awry, "all coherence gone." Tragedy and comedy—the preliminary answer must be—constitute an uneasy unity: drama. But their coexistence *is* a unity and not an accident, not "random" coexistence, as above. And we can best understand the supplementary functions of these humanly contrived narratives—narratives that constantly vary on the surface—by seeking the analogy that links them with the two *uses* of myth that we discover in many developed religions.

As noted, what we present is an analogy only. Yet it is an analogy that (I believe) puts our ideas about comedy and tragedy in better order. Yet it is an analogy valid at only one point; it concerns only the two contrasting *uses* to which myth is put in religion and the two contrasting trains of reaction, of sensibility and induced comment, which the two forms of drama can stir in man. To make no mystery: comedy has its religious analogue in the *cyclic* assertions that myth enables religion to make, and tragedy finds its analogue in the non-cyclic, *linear* assertions that myth sometimes supports. I would deny utterly the truth or usefulness of the analogy were it pushed beyond this point—were it argued that the myth that "asserts cycle" is comic *in substance* and the myth that asserts the linear perception tragic in substance. There is no comedy-tragedy contrast by which one can divide the abundance of myth. The *story* of Osiris and the *story* of Jesus—it has often been observed—resemble each other. Certainly the story of Osiris, a story that is the vehicle of a cyclic assertion, is not comic; it is quite as grim as the story of Jesus which, I judge, mediates a linear assertion. The story of Osiris "happened" to be "captured" by a religion which, at a particular time, needed to "assert cycle"; and the story of Jesus happened to be put to use as a narrative support to a linear, non-cyclic insight about existence. (The bulk of myth—of narrative that exists and functions to some degree in a religious context—asserts cycle. But the normal is not a binding norm; there is nothing abnormal about a story that a religion uses to express a linear insight about man's life. To my mind, the story of the "white god" Quetzalcoatl—the god who abandons his people *once* and promises a single return—asserts the linear almost as forcefully as does the narrative about Jesus.)

Deeper in drama, then—if the analogy I am drawing has real power to cast light—than the contrast between the laughable and the "weepable" is this one: comedy is a representation of life that asserts cycle (as does the bulk of myth), and tragedy is that representation of life that asserts the linear, the non-cyclic. The laughter that, rightly, we associate with comedy is important but surface testimony to the fact that we have cause to rejoice when we contemplate the totality of existence as cycle; the tears that we shed for tragedy, the qualm that tragedy is said to stir, is a natural by-product of the perception that total existence is not cyclic at all—at least, not cyclic when it concerns us most intimately.

Comedy and tragedy, then, are secular purveyors—I mean no disrespect by the word—of two all-over assertions about the root-nature of existence as man must experience it. (In *one* of these two ways he must experience it; he has no further choice.) The *materials* of comedy and tragedy do often differ much more than do the narrative materials that constitute the two sorts of myth. But, as often observed, what really distinguishes comedy from tragedy is the treatment accorded the materials that come to hand. It would not be impossible to alter *Oedipus Rex* into a knock-about farce, nor would it be difficult to transform Malvolio into a figure of devastating import, particularly were one writing a naturalistic or sociological tragedy. The imperfect religious analogue to all this is what we have already noted: that the narrative that becomes myth does not automatically proclaim whether it will be cyclic or linear; *that* is determined by the kind of existence it takes on in a specific religious context.

V

What are the distinguishing marks of these two all-over assertions, the cyclic and the linear?

Let us begin their precise definition thus. When we say that myth asserts two all-over insights into existence, we are concerned with existence collectively perceived and *not* discriminated. "Early man" had many of the powers of discriminatory judgment that we have; that is, he could look sensibly at *portions* of existence. Aspects of his arts, the bulk of his "civil law," and the conduct of his economy are sufficient records of this. But he—no more than we—could not escape making a collective or all-over assertion about the world in which he was immersed. Nor is the "advance of human thought"—as modern drama, for one, obliquely testifies—from collective assertions to assertions that are more modest, more discriminated. Indeed, without a collective assertion of some kind, discrimination itself ceases; and this is just as true in a secular context as in a religious one. What we regard as the "advance of human thought" is simply a substitution of a later and more logically defensible collective assertion for an earlier one. The later assertion may be more valid, more soundly based. But that is not the point here. What we must perceive is that our "advance" has not freed our thought from the task of making total assertions not completely unlike the early religious cyclic and linear assertions.

Respect for them established, one may attempt a genetic explanation of the two mythological assertions that (I believe) casts great light on the way tragedy and comedy still function for us. A genetic explanation is not exhaustive; and, in this instance, it involves this bold hypothesis: that we can reproduce the intellectual and emotional growth of early man. What we say firmly on such a topic, we should also say modestly. But we need not abandon the effort; it is no more bold than the genetic efforts of literary scholars who speak of the formative attention of "Shakespeare's audience"—it is no more risky than the discourses on medieval piety that "explain" certain beautiful tensions at Chartres.

Man was first aware—and to this ancient scriptures are witness—of that which bore in on him from outside. He was aware of the great forces of nature as he saw them in wind and wave and weather; he was aware of his terrible dependence on the fertility of grass-land and arable field. And he was just as deeply impressed by the social forces that weighed on him: his family, his tribe, his tribal enemies. To assume as early man did that these outside forces—nature and the collective groups —made up each man's existence is to assume truly; it is also to assume incompletely, as religion after religion discovered at some point in its course.

Yet this incomplete assumption—that man's existence is composed of the awful natural and social forces that toss man about—"created" as its corollary an assertion made in terms of myth rather than, as here, in terms of abstract concept. Man employed myth for this reason: man must be more than the victim of the forces that are outside him; he must be their *imaginative* master. It is not enough to discriminate these external forces and come to a competent control of *some* of them. The nascent arts of agriculture did not free man from the need of myths about the forces of growth; the early and perhaps relatively satisfactory codes of law did not obviate the preservation of myths about the "origin" of law; and successful magic and medicine was never a threat to the inclusive assertions of religion. In short, all the practical control and knowledge of what bore in on man had to be supplemented by assertions that provided man *imaginative* all-over control. This control was provided by myths that, whatever their variety, were put to one task, the task of asserting cycle; they were man's warrant over and above his own observation for the recurrence of season and crop and for the persistence (despite the aging of all men and the death of leaders) of a given and experienced social form. It was myth and rite that could assure men that what man could not control was, in the long run, as much to be depended on as what he could control; natural and social phenomena would be exactly what man already knew them to be. Nature and society, myth testified, would always come full circle, would offer apprehensive man familiarity and not novelty. Man used, for example, the myth of Osiris to give himself this cyclic assurance. Osiris, we know, dies not once but many times; his scattered members are gathered by Isis in a basket again and again—in fact, year after year, so long as the society that uses the myth of Osiris persists. Mr. Joseph Campbell, in *The Hero with a Thousand Faces*, has revealed to us the impressive and yet monotonous use to which certain narrative materials were once put; the "thousand faces" are really the face of one hero. Beneath surface variety, the hero offers man the assurance of a *recurrent* salvation, of security in nature and in society that can never be really threatened by natural catastrophe or military invasion. The myth always repeats itself and is *cyclic*. If Osiris eternally dies and eternally is brought back to life, each man can feel secure: his plot of land will bear again, and the tribe or society to which he belongs will survive any temporary perils. Thanks to the myth, man is in calm imaginative control of what actually is beyond his just-nascent science and his nonexistent sociology.

Is Christ Osiris? Is he too a vegetation god, a supporter of cycle? Not to those who cherished his story. Yet the bold outlines of his story are similar to the Osiris narrative; for this, some persons call him the last and most triumphant of the Asia Minor vegetation deities. On the basis of narrative materials, there is no utterly conclusive way of repudiating the similarity. But what one may deny—concerning Christ, concerning Quetzalcoatl as well—is that the Christ-story was put to the use the Osiris story was put to. A central Christian phrase refers to Christ as "our sacrifice once offered"; whatever the contradictory implications of certain Christian rituals, a sense that Christ did indeed die only once and rise only once remains at the heart of the Christian assertion and is opposed to the sense that lies at the heart of the Osiris mystery and similar mysteries.

Genetically speaking, what "begot" the Christian assertion? It was a second total perception of what existence was. After he had gained imaginative control of what lay outside him, man became aware of himself. He could express this awareness of himself only by uttering—with the aid of some myth—a total assertion that, logically but not actually, cancelled the cyclic assertion. (There are few developed religions in which the two assertions do not persist as peers.) When man turns to himself, he "knows" that what myth and cult have, to that point, told him either is not true or is very incompletely true. Nature and society are eternally dying and eternally reborn: let that stand. But man himself—man apart from the great processes that very nearly have him at their utter mercy—man is eternally dying and he never will be reborn.*

What is this second total assertion which the story of Christ, as well as other stories, implements? The assertion that man's existence is in time, historical. The assertion that to man *as man* (as opposed to man when he is plainly the creature of natural and social forces) the same event, the same choice, never comes round again. Man as man makes a choice among a series of events that follow each other in a non-repeating sequence; he has only one chance to make a certain choice since the time for a certain choice comes only once. As man, his experience is basically linear however much he may be, as an object, subject

---

* It is beside the point to appeal to the developed dogma of Eastern religions which "work" this non-cyclic insight into the continuing assertion of cycle by elaborating theories of reincarnation and karma—and then absorb both the awareness of cycle and the "illusion" of linear existence into a superior awareness: Nirvana. That these complex adjustments had to be made is at least testimony to the existence and power, over man's will, of the insights that we now reconstitute. The synthesis called Nirvana is a witness to the painful tension created by the coexistence, in religious life, of the two ancient assertions that concern us. And Nirvana, as a theory, does not concern us, for it casts little light on either comedy or tragedy.

to the effects of natural and social cycle. As a cyclically oriented creature, man plants a crop at a certain time of the year and rethatches his
house against the monsoons, and also prepares himself for the public
fasts and the public rejoicings peculiar to his society. These come round
again and again. But man comes to see that such preparations are not
all his destiny or even a finally distinguishing part. He is, at the center
of his nature, a creature of time, of *line;* and he and his forebears were,
at the least, misled when they found the clue to human nature in
what, in some sense, lay outside each separate man: in nature and the
social group. The essential lies inside each man, in his experience of
choice, of sequence; hence, the second total assertion, the one we have
called the *linear* one.

The essential—we should observe when we watch *Hamlet* or *Oedipus*
as well as when we savor the impact of the Christ-story—lies inside each
man; it lies in man's experience of a horrid, sheerly linear necessity
which no man, once he is aware of it, is ever able to evade. This is the
necessity of choice; it is a necessity that gets no comforting "moral support" from the phases of the moon or the return of a season. Each human
choice, at a certain time in a non-repetitive sequence of events, projects
into future time only a certain portion of the past; each choice denies to
the future significant developments of other portions of the past. This
is human choice; it is also existence conceived in a linear fashion.

This all-over perception sought—and, of course, found—an august
warrant. Not just the Jesus-myth itself but the whole body of what used
to be called "sacred history" constituted a widely embracing myth that
detached itself from the bulk of ancient myth and its cyclic assertions.
The bulk of story that we may call the Christian myth—as well as groups
of story that have some resemblance to it—braced man for the assertion
that is just as essential to his health as is the earlier assertion of cycle.
The linear assertion is, I believe, a record of a later, a more subtle, and
certainly a more intimate reading of man's position in the world since
it sees that man as a person, an individual, has an "economy" for which
there are very few clues and models outside man. Why was this insight
comparatively late in coming? Because what was outside man first
rushed in on human awareness promising inclusive instruction. (And
the cyclic instruction is one that man has never been able to dispense
with.) But insofar as man has discovered individuality and personality,
he has involved himself in myths that limit if they do not cancel the
assurances of cyclic legend. A god that dies only once "answers" to

man's more subtle analysis of the conditions of human action (as opposed to the conditions of natural event to which man was first eager to assimilate human action.) A god that dies only once, a god that does not enjoy the easy luxury of dying again and again, a god that traces the arc of choice only once—that god is a human god. His myth is a warrant for our most painful perceptions about what it is to be a human being rather than a tide that rushes up the shore or a society that persists even though its members unimportantly perish.

VI

The point of the analogy between cyclic and linear myth on the one hand and comedy and tragedy on the other now shapes up. Comedy, on a non-religious level, offers man the assurance that he can bank on the universe and its laws and, more importantly, on society and its structure. As does the myth that asserts cycle, comedy offers the individual the illusion that he exists and moves in a universe he can count on. This illusion, when it is effectively held, is a cause for rejoicing; it is a cause for *laughter*. It was in this sense that Dante wrote a *Comedy;* his poem was, at the last, an assurance of order—to be sure, an order of a complex kind. Even more ordinary comedy makes available to man some of the comforts that early man drew from religiously "asserting cycle." The comic narrative—in materials gulfs apart from the Osiris legend but in effect quite close to it—must, like *all* narratives, embody an upset, a threat to our sense of certainty. Farce or high comedy—the effect is the same. What is the archetypical plot? A shift of forces, a social realignment, threatens the security of the chief persons on the stage—threatens *our* security. Comedy, it appears, has its qualm as well as tragedy. But the qualm is allayed by a combination of strategies that dissociates comedy from tragedy. For it is soon clear that the threat is neither serious nor permanently effective. It is a trivial threat, no more, to the status quo—to what we would call in religious terms the continuance of cycle. And it is also soon clear that the persons involved are not full, real persons like ourselves. They are "comic"; in religious language, they have only that degree of reality that marks a cyclic interpretation of man's experience—they are not sufficiently alive to qualify or even shatter that view. Since the characters in a comedy are incomplete, they easily loom before us as quasi-ritual figures who march through the events of the comic play as unconcernedly as did the King of Egypt when he performed his yearly role of Osiris in the New Year festivals.

What is all that comedy offers us? It is certainly not a contemptible "all." It is simply an "all" that is inferior to the "all" that tragedy offers us, just as the "all" of Egyptian religion is at once valid and yet distinctly inferior to the gifts of a religion that has strong linear marks. In fact, all that comedy offers us is *a sense of regain*. The comic "qualm" —the "situation," the misunderstanding, the threat of someone's security —threatens the status quo in a way that is sometimes playful and sometimes serious. But very few comedies leave us with anything but a sense that the status quo has been essentially re-established. The happy ending reasserts the security of the important characters; much more important, their individual security amounts to a promise that well-known social forms will persist. The effect of cycle, put slightly in doubt, has, with the descent of the last curtain, been established more firmly than ever.

And as audience we have *regained* the security, personal and social, that the initial dramatic situation playfully threatened. We are, as characters, where we were at the commencement of the play, or where we deserved to be. The society to which we, as audience, imaginatively belong has been "established" more firmly than ever. In a popular farce, it is the most obvious sort of conventional standards which have been threatened by (say) adultery or sharp business practice and which are, in the last insincere minutes of the play, refounded; in a play of Shaw's like *Candida* it is the society of the Shavian elect. The differences are there, but they do not, in our connection, count. *Parlor, Bedroom, and Bath* and *Candida* function for their different audiences in exactly the same way. They mediate—in an obscure secular way, I admit—a counterpart of the cyclic religious assurance. They tell us that there is a secure, predictable, and even recurrent place provided for man in the universe. Further, they tell us that man can exercise imaginative control over this universe. The threats to this control—the situation that troubles Act I—always turn out to be delusive; and the comic drama always terminates with man more in imaginative command of his universe than before.

Not so tragedy. Tragedy, like the linear total assertion which it resembles, is no play for imaginative control of the world; it is a confession, sometimes noble and sometimes desponding, that man's "game" —the "game" utterly proper to him—lies somewhere else. It is a perception that, for man, imaginative control of the world that is distinctly external to him is beside the point. And when we regard comedy from the vantage-point of tragedy, we see that what it offers man is not so much a sense of regain as an *illusion* of regain. Comedy keeps man domiciled—and fairly securely domiciled—in a world that he does not live in properly unless he wills to live in a contradictory world at the same time. Comedy offers man an illusory paradise: the paradise of imaginative control of what is outside man. But man is driven from this paradise by his dismaying discovery that he does not entirely belong there. He is driven out not by any flaming sword but by his own nature whose destiny it is to exercise choice and thus deny or qualify all cyclically-based perceptions. For the reassuring continuum of cycle external to man, tragedy puts before us a discontinuity: man that chooses not to repeat, man that by his choice wills the unknown. Such a being is, from the cyclic point of view, a *lusus naturae*, one that taints and distorts the secure universe for which both Osiris and comedy stand. Were we to pair phrases, we might say that tragedy offers us a gift as permanent and pervasive as the comic sense of regain; it is a sense of loss, an awareness that man, in his most intimate activities, follows a line that leads only to darkness and an enigma—a line that will never curve back upon itself and so in the future confirm what it has been. The characteristic human act—that of choice—is closely allied with loss, even though we seem to choose to win something, to gain something. Choice, the specific linear activity, the activity that we see brought to sharp focus in Gethsemane and in the palace at Elsinore, always has for its ground-bass the note of loss. We turn our back on the joys we are certain of and might like to repeat, and we put ourselves in the trust of the future: a moment or an hour that we do not know but yet must count on—and we have willed to lose, if we must, the profit that can come to us from past moments: moments we have savored and could—did not choice intervene with its crucial break—still count on. Agony and death at some future time are but incidental marks of tragedy. The real agony, the real death, come at the moment when we choose; when, willing loss, we trust ourselves to an enigma; when we abandon the comic vein and cease counting on limited certainties. Not only is the crucifixion "a sacrifice once offered"; each crucial choice that marks a tragic drama is such a sacrifice, for it is loss of the world that the cyclic temper would preserve as man's great comfort and support. Whatever the upshot of tragic choice, whatever temporary palliatives and patent compensations may move toward us, the fact persists: we have given up or, at least, qualified a very useful insight into man's experience, the comic insight, the insight that we have compared with the cyclic assertions certain myths have made. In comedy the world we inhabit is but playfully threatened; by the end of the play, it is refounded more firmly than before. But in tragedy, as if in accord with its linear, non-reversible nature, choice threatens the world, the status quo, in deadly earnest. In choice, we do not know with much confidence what it is we shall create; we know with grim certainty what it is that we destroy: our happiness, our security—in short, our confidence in a future that follows—or seems to follow—cyclic laws.

Both tragic insight and the religious assertion that we call linear are not easy to endure, whether we arrogate to them exclusive truth or confess sadly that the comic or the cyclic insights are true also. Christians have permitted themselves the alleviation of encrusting their linear faith with recurrent ritual that prolongs, throughout the "Christian year," a necessary minimum of cyclic illusion. And, when we draw back from the blank that is choice and act in time, in linear succession, we may turn back to comedy which, in its way, represents our human lot if not our essential human lot. One way to endure tragedy, on the stage and off, is to listen to some of the things that comedy tells us when it speaks of "fundamental decency" and the recurrence of events and their correspondence to an understandable, definable order.

It is plain that there is nothing "wrong" with a penchant for comedy; tragedy is "truer" than comedy (it is a more penetrating comment on our lot) but it is less endurable. This relation between the truth of the two dramatic forms also gains light from the comparable religious tension. There is nothing "wrong" about the persistence of cyclic insights in a religion basically linear (e.g., the Christian). A perception that, at the centers of our being, we exist linear-wise can never cancel the truth that in relation to external forces we live under a cyclic dispensation. What is perhaps "wrong" is a reworking of the two religious insights that deprives either of its proper authority. This is the chief heresy that Western eyes find in Buddhism: the denial that both recurrence and unique event have high significance in man's life.

Finally, all that tragedy offers us in the audience is loss or deprivation: the possibility of becoming something that we have not yet been. If tragedy offers us a gain, it is a gain that is, unlike the comic gain, incalculable. If the tragedy we watch is real tragedy and not deterministic tragedy, which has the *events of tragedy* but the *certainty* of comedy, we live for a while lives from which the cyclic effects have fallen away or have receded into the background. Comedy occurs at any moment (it has the effect, if not the actuality, of being repeatable); tragedy occurs at only one moment: a moment that has come *this time* and that will never come again. It presents us with the spectacle of ourselves urged by the logic inherent in once-occurring events to make a choice. We cannot escape choice and responsibility for the choice which we make. Yet we make the choice without a full knowledge of the consequences. How can we, in a universe conceived in a linear way, have such knowledge? It is only in a cyclically conceived universe that we seem to have such knowledge. It is a knowledge which the other sort of drama strips from us.

For this reason, the tragic qualm—however purgation be explained —is never really purged. When we watch the acts of Oedipus and Hamlet and the results of those acts, the only comfort we draw is analogous to that which we get from a myth aligned with linear perceptions. Christ on the cross or Quetzalcoatl on his raft of serpents wrenches our eyes from a flattering and comforting view of our destinies as men. As men, we are apart from mountain and stream, we are apart from society collectively considered; we are—in all conventional or comic sense—apart from each other. We can find union only in the insight given to us by linear myth or by its analogue in tragic drama: that every moment is a crucifixion if we face it seriously. To do this we are most of the time incompetent. We would like to deny that we are Prince Hamlet. We would rather, along with Eliot's Prufrock, go to swell a crowd and there take refuge in sententious and (in our sense) "comic" remarks.

If we are correct, if the similarities between drama and religion are indeed striking, are we correct to oppose those who, directly or covertly, treat drama as a full surrogate for religious assertion? I think we are. The basic dissimilarity persists although it is not our duty here to study it. The religious context provides fixity and hence authority as the companions of the opposed total assertions, and drama provides a context of constant variety and change. This latter context will seem the correct and perhaps the only one to those who doubt that even the most sensitive and analytical attention to experience can win to binding answers. Such doubt is not hampering provided the doubter does not take the final step and observe that religion is really about the same thing as that which drama treats in two logically opposed ways.

Religion, we should repeat, is "about" that which is sensed as permanently true; drama handles the permanently uncertain in what we see and recollect. All that the similarities we have traced here support is this observation: there are two sovereign ways of naming the impermanent and the fixed. Since these ways belong to both religion and drama, we are tempted to identify religion and drama. This we must refuse to do, for when we say "the same" we offer up, in the name of system and simplicity, discriminations rich, suggestive, and illogical that are a large part of the treasure that has been put into our hands.

GENERIC FORMS

In the previous section certain conceptions of "form" drifted into the region of "genre" with the association (in Watts's essay) of "linear" and "cyclical" movements with tragedy and comedy respectively. As we mentioned in the headnote to that section, "form" is an elusive notion. We *experience* form temporally, as spectators or readers of a play, but afterwards, when we reflect upon the play as a completed activity, form seems to resolve itself into spatial concepts, into a matter of curves, cones, pyramids, rises and falls, etc. Generic form is not a matter of visualizable shapes (though we may call upon such shapes as metaphors to express complex relations) but of conceptual categories that unite certain plays and distinguish them from others. The possible categories are almost unlimited. We might group plays by their length, subject-matter, historical period, sexual gender of characters, scenic locations, etc. The criteria of the major dramatic categories are considerably more difficult to formulate and apply than these. But complexity is the price of significance.

Genre study does not deny the individuality of plays; it merely assumes that likeness is as important as unlikeness. Indeed, the individuality of a play, like that of a person, is perhaps most meaningfully established by differentiation, not by isolation. We can perceive the distinctive "Lear-ness" of *King Lear* best by comparing it to other tragedies instead of trying to treat it as if it existed in a literary vacuum. Nor does genre study assume that there are fixed and final categories to which every play must submit or else suffer critical banishment. Genres come into existence historically and are modified, combined, and sometimes abandoned. Not all dramatic genres are discussed in detail in the following selections, but the essay by Northrop Frye offers a sweeping, full-circle view of the various ways in which tragedy, comedy, irony, and masque can merge into even more specific dramatic forms under the general influence of such concepts as action, visual imitation, significance, and vision. The essays by Robert B. Heilman and the editors deal with the enduring forms of tragedy and comedy, and those by Ellen D. Leyburn and Martin Esslin suggest modern developments and departures that may lead into new generic territories.

NORTHROP FRYE

Specific Forms of Drama

We have now to see whether this expansion of perspective, which enables us to consider the relation of the *lexis* or verbal pattern to music and spectacle, gives us any new light on the traditional classifications within the genres. The division of dramas into tragedies and comedies, for instance, is a conception based entirely on verbal drama, and does not include or account for types of drama, such as the opera or masque, in which music and scenery have a more organic place. Yet verbal drama, whether tragic or comic, has clearly developed a long way from the primitive idea of drama, which is to present a powerful sensational focus for a community. The scriptural plays of the Middle Ages are primitive in this sense: they present to the audience a myth already familiar to and significant for that audience, and they are designed to remind the audience of their communal possession of this myth.

The scriptural play is a form of a spectacular dramatic genre which we may provisionally call a "myth-play." It is a somewhat negative and receptive form, and takes on the mood of the myth it represents. The crucifixion play in the Towneley cycle is tragic because the Crucifixion is; but it is not a tragedy in the sense that *Othello* is a tragedy. It does not, that is, make a tragic *point;* it simply presents the story because it is familiar and significant. It would be nonsense to apply such tragic conceptions as hybris to the figure of Christ in that play, and while pity and terror are raised, they remain attached to the subject, and there is no catharsis of them. The characteristic mood and resolution of the myth-play are pensive, and pensiveness, in this context, implies a continuing imaginative subjection to the story. The myth-play emphasizes dramatically the symbol of spiritual and corporeal communion. The scriptural plays themselves were associated with the festival of Corpus

Christi, and Calderon's religious plays are explicitly *autos sacramentales* or Eucharist plays. The appeal of the myth-play is a curious mixture of the popular and the esoteric; it is popular for its immediate audience, but those outside its circle have to make a conscious effort to appreciate it. In a controversial atmosphere it disappears, as it cannot deal with controversial issues unless it selects its audience. In view of the ambiguities attaching to the word myth, we shall speak of this genre as the *auto*.

When there is no clear-cut distinction between gods and heroes in a society's mythology, or between the ideals of the nobility and the priesthood, the *auto* may present a legend which is secular and sacred at once. An example is the No drama of Japan, which with its unification of chivalric and otherworldly symbols and its dreamy un-tragic, un-comic mood so strongly attracted Yeats. It is interesting to see how Yeats, both in his theory of the *anima mundi* and in his desire to get his plays as physically close to the audience as possible, reverts to the archaic idea of corporeal communion. In Greek drama, too, there is no sharp boundary line between the divine and the heroic protagonist. But in Christian societies we can see glimpses of a secular *auto*, a romantic drama presenting the exploits of a hero, which is closely related to tragedy, the end of a hero's exploit being eventually his death, but which in itself is neither tragic nor comic, being primarily spectacular.

Tamburlaine is such a play: there the relation between the hero's hybris and his death is more casual than causal. This genre has had varying luck: more in Spain, for instance, than in France, where the establishing of tragedy was part of an intellectual revolution. The two attempts in France to move tragedy back towards heroic romance, *Le Cid* and *Hernani*, each precipitated a big row. In Germany, on the other hand, it is clear that the actual genre of many plays by Goethe and Schiller is the heroic romance, however much affected they have been by the prestige of tragedy. In Wagner, who expands the heroic form all the way back to a sacramental drama of gods, the symbol of communion again occupies a conspicuous place, negatively in *Tristan*, positively in *Parsifal*. In proportion as it moves closer to tragedy and further from the sacred *auto*, drama tends to make less use of music. If we look at the earliest extant play of Aeschylus, *The Suppliants*, we can see that close behind it is a predominantly musical structure of which the modern counterpart would normally be the oratorio—it is perhaps possible to describe Wagner's operas as fermented oratorios.

In Renaissance England the audience was too bourgeois for a

chivalric drama to get firmly established, and the Elizabethan secular *auto* eventually became the history play. With the history play we move from spectacle to a more purely verbal drama, and the symbols of communion become much attenuated, although they are still there. The central theme of Elizabethan history is the unifying of the nation and the binding of the audience into the myth as the inheritors of that unity, set over against the disasters of civil war and weak leadership. One may even recognize a secular Eucharist symbol in the red and white rose, just as one may recognize in the plays that end by pointing to Elizabeth, like Peele's *Arraignment of Paris,* a secular counterpart of a mystery play of the Virgin. But the emphasis and characteristic resolution of the history play are in terms of continuity and the closing up both of tragic catastrophe and (as in the case of Falstaff) of the comic festival. One may compare Shaw's "chronicle play" of *Saint Joan,* where the end of the play is a tragedy, followed by an epilogue in which the rejection of Joan is, like the rejection of Falstaff, historical, suggesting continuity rather than a rounded finish.

The history merges so gradually into tragedy that we often cannot be sure when communion has turned into catharsis. *Richard II* and *Richard III* are tragedies insofar as they resolve on those defeated kings; they are histories insofar as they resolve on Bolingbroke and Richmond, and the most one can say is that they lean toward history. *Hamlet* and *Macbeth* lean toward tragedy, but Fortinbras and Malcolm, the continuing characters, indicate the historical element in the tragic resolution. There seems to be a far less direct connection between history and comedy: the comic scenes in the histories are, so to speak, subversive. *Henry V* ends in triumph and marriage, but an action that kills Falstaff, hangs Bardolph and debases Pistol is not related to comedy in the way that *Richard II* is related to tragedy.

We are here concerned only with tragedy as a species of drama. Tragic drama derives from the *auto* its central heroic figure, but the association of heroism with downfall is due to the simultaneous presence of irony. The nearer the tragedy is to *auto,* the more closely associated the hero is with divinity; the nearer to irony, the more human the hero is, and the more the catastrophe appears to be social rather than a cosmological event. Elizabethan tragedy shows a historical development from Marlowe, who presents his heroes more or less as demigods moving in a kind of social ether, to Webster, whose tragedies are almost clinical analyses of a sick society. Greek tragedy never broke completely from the *auto,* and so never developed a social form, though there are tendencies to it in Euripides. But whatever the proportions of heroism and irony, tragedy shows itself to be primarily a vision of the supremacy of the event or *mythos*. The response to tragedy is "this must be," or, perhaps more accurately, "this does happen": the event is primary; the explanation of it secondary and variable.

As tragedy moves over towards irony, the sense of inevitable event begins to fade out, and the sources of catastrophe come into view. In irony catastrophe is either arbitrary and meaningless, the impact of an unconscious (or, in the pathetic fallacy, malignant) world on conscious man, or the result of more or less definable social and psychological forces. Tragedy's "this must be" becomes irony's "this at least is," a concentration on foreground facts and a rejection of mythical superstructures. Thus the ironic drama is a vision of what in theology is called the fallen world, of simple humanity, man as natural man and in conflict with both human and non-human nature. In nineteenth-century drama the tragic vision is often identical with the ironic one, hence nineteenth-century tragedies tend to be either *Schicksal* dramas dealing with the arbitrary ironies of fate, or (clearly the more rewarding form) studies of the frustrating and smothering of human activity by the combined pressure of a reactionary society without and disorganized soul within. Such irony is difficult to sustain in the theatre because it tends toward a stasis of action. In those parts of Chekhov, notably the last act of *Three Sisters*, where the characters one by one withdraw from each other into their subjective prison-cells, we are coming about as close to pure irony as the stage can get.

The ironic play passes through a dead center of complete realism, a pure mime representing human life without comment and without imposing any sort of dramatic form beyond what is required for simple exhibition. This idolatrous form of mimesis is rare, but the thin line of its tradition can be traced from Classical mime-writers like Herodas to their *tranche-de-vie* descendants in recent times. The mime is somewhat commoner as an individual performance, and, outside the theatre, the Browning monodrama is a logical development of the isolating and soliloquizing tendencies of ironic conflict. In the theatre we usually find that the spectacle of "all too human" life is either oppressive or ridiculous, and that it tends to pass directly from one to the other. Irony, then, as it moves away from tragedy, begins to merge into comedy.

Ironic comedy presents us of course with "the way of the world," but as soon as we find sympathetic or even neutral characters in a comedy, we move into the more familiar comic area where we have a group of humors outwitted by the opposing group. Just as tragedy is a vision of the supremacy of *mythos* or thing done, and just as irony is a vision of *ethos*, or character individualized against environment, so comedy is a vision of *dianoia*, a significance which is ultimately social significance, the establishing of a desirable society. As an imitation of life, drama is, in terms of *mythos*, conflict; in terms of *ethos*, a representative image; in terms of *dianoia*, the final harmonic chord revealing the tonality under the narrative movement, it is community. The further comedy moves from irony, the more it becomes what we here call ideal comedy, the vision not of the way of the world, but of what you will, life as you like it. Shakespeare's main interest is in getting away from the son-father conflict of ironic comedy towards a vision of a serene community, a vision most prominent in *The Tempest*. Here the action is polarized around a younger and an older man working in harmony together, a lover and a benevolent teacher.

The next step brings us to the extreme limit of social comedy, the symposium, the structure of which is, as we should expect, clearest in Plato, whose Socrates is both teacher and lover, and whose vision moves toward an integration of society in a form like that of the symposium itself, the dialectic festivity which, as is explained in the opening of the *Laws*, is the controlling force that holds society together. It is easy to see that Plato's dialogue form is dramatic and has affinities with comedy and mime; and while there is much in Plato's thought that contradicts the spirit of comedy as we have outlined it, it is significant that he contradicts it directly, tries to kidnap it, so he speak. It seems almost a rule that the more he does this, the further he moves into pure exposition or dictatorial monologue and away from drama. The most dramatic of his dialogues, such as *Euthydemus*, are regularly the most indecisive in philosophic "position."

In our own day Bernard Shaw has tried hard to keep the symposium in the theatre. His early manifesto, *The Quintessence of Ibsenism*, states that a play should be an intelligent discussion of a serious problem, and in his preface to *Getting Married* he remarks approvingly on the fact that it observes the unities of time and place. For comedy of Shaw's type tends to a symposium form which occupies the same amount of time in its action that the audience consumes in watching it. However, Shaw discovered in practice that what emerges from the theatrical symposium is not a dialectic that compels to a course of action or thought, but one that emancipates from formulated principles of conduct. The shape of such a comedy is very clear in the bright little sketch *In Good*

King Charles's Golden Days, where even the most highly developed human types, the saintly Fox and the philosophical Newton, are shown to be comic humors by the mere presence of other types of people. Yet the central symposium figure of the haranguing lover bulks formidably in *Man and Superman,* and even the renunciation of love for mathematics at the end of *Back to Methuselah* is consistent with the symposium spirit.

The view of poetry which sees it as intermediate between history and philosophy, its images combining the temporal events of the one with the timeless ideas of the other, seems to be still involved in this exposition of dramatic forms. We can now see a mimetic or verbal drama stretching from the history-play to the philosophy-play (the act-play and the scene-play), with the mime, the pure image, halfway between. These three are specialized forms, cardinal points of drama rather than generic areas. But the whole mimetic area is only a part, a semicircle, let us say, of all drama. In the misty and unexplored region of the other semicircle of spectacular drama we have identified a quadrant that we have called the *auto,* and we have now to chart the fourth quadrant that lies between the *auto* and comedy, and establish the fourth cardinal point where it meets the *auto* again. When we think of the clutter of forms that belong here, we are strongly tempted to call our fourth area "miscellaneous" and let it go; but it is precisely here that new generic criticism is needed.

The further comedy moves from irony, and the more it rejoices in the free movement of its happy society, the more readily it takes to music and dancing. As music and scenery increase in importance, the ideal comedy crosses the boundary line of spectacular drama and becomes the masque. In Shakespeare's ideal comedies, especially *A Midsummer Night's Dream* and *The Tempest,* the close affinity with the masque is not hard to see. The masque—or at least the kind of masque that is nearest to comedy, and which we shall here call the ideal masque—is still in the area of *dianoia:* it is usually a compliment to the audience, or an important member of it, and leads up to an idealization of the society represented by that audience. Its plots and characters are fairly stock, as they exist only in relation to the significance of the occasion.

It thus differs from comedy in its more intimate attitude to the audience: there is more insistence on the connection between the audience and the community on the stage. The members of a masque are ordinarily disguised members of the audience, and there is a final gesture of surrender when the actors unmask and join the audience in a dance. The ideal masque is in fact a myth-play like the *auto*, to which it is related much as comedy is to tragedy. It is designed to emphasize, not the ideals to be achieved by discipline or faith, but ideals which are desired or considered to be already possessed. Its settings are seldom remote from magic and fairyland, from Arcadias and visions of earthly Paradise. It uses gods freely, like the *auto*, but possessively, and without imaginative subjection. In Western drama, from the Renaissance to the end of the eighteenth century, masque and ideal comedy make great use of Classical mythology, which the audience is not obliged to accept as "true."

The rather limited masque throws some light on the structure and characteristics of its two far more important and versatile neighbors. For the masque is flanked on one side by the musically organized drama which we call opera, and on the other by a scenically organized drama, which has now settled in the movie. Puppet-plays and the vast Chinese romances where, as in the movie, the audience enters and leaves unpredictably, are examples of pre-camera scenic masques. Both opera and movie are, like the masque, proverbial for lavish display, and part of the reason for it in the movie is that many movies are actually bourgeois myth-plays, as half a dozen critics suddenly and almost simultaneously discovered a few years ago. The predominance of the private life of the actor in the imaginations of many movie-goers may perhaps have some analogy with the consciously assumed disguise of the masque.

Opera and movie possess, unlike the masque, the power of producing spectacular imitations of mimetic drama. The opera can only do this by simplifying its musical organization, otherwise its dramatic structure will be blurred by the distortion of acting which the highly repetitive structure of music makes necessary. The movie similarly must simplify its spectacle. In proportion as it follows its natural bent for scenic organization, the movie reveals its affinities with other forms of scenic masque: with the puppet-play in Chaplin and others, with the *commedia dell'arte* in recent Italian films, with the ballet and pantomime in musical comedies. When the movie succeeds in imitating a mimetic drama, the distinction between the two forms is not worth making, but the generic difference shows itself in other ways. Mimetic drama works towards an end which illuminates, by being logically connected with, the beginning: hence the parabola shape of the typical five-act mimetic structure, and hence the teleological quality in drama expressed by the term discovery. Spectacular drama, on the other hand, is by nature processional, and tends to episodic and piecemeal discovery, as we can see in all forms of pure spectacle, from the circus parade to the revue. In the *auto* too, on the other side of spectacular drama, the same processional structure appears in the long continued stories of Shakespearean history and scriptural pageant. In the rotating performance and casual attendance of the movie, and the sequence of arias forcibly linked to dramatic structure by recitative in the opera, one can see the strong native tendency to linear movement in spectacular forms. In Shakespeare's first experimental romance, *Pericles,* the movement toward processional structure, a sequence of scenes "dispersedly in various countries," is very clear.

The essential feature of the ideal masque is the exaltation of the audience, who form the goal of its procession. In the *auto,* drama is at its most objective; the audience's part is to accept the story without judgement. In tragedy there is judgement, but the source of the tragic discovery is on the other side of the stage; and whatever it is, it is stronger than the audience. In the ironic play, audience and drama confront each other directly: in the comedy the source of the discovery has moved across to the audience itself. The ideal masque places the audience in a position of superiority to discovery. The verbal action of *Figaro* is comic and that of *Don Giovanni* tragic; but in both cases the audience is exalted by the music above the reach of tragedy and comedy, and though as profoundly moved as ever, is not emotionally involved with the discovery of plot or characters. It looks at the downfall of Don Juan as spectacular entertainment, much as the gods are supposed to look at the downfall of Ajax or Darius. The same sense of viewing the dramatic mimesis through a haze of spectacular exhilaration is also of central importance in the movie, as it is even more obviously in the puppet-play from which the movie is chiefly descended. We move from ironic to ideal comedy through the symposium, and we note that at the conclusion of Plato's *Symposium* the prophecy is made that the same poet should be able to write both tragedy and comedy, though the ones who have done so most successfully are those who, like Shakespeare and Mozart, have had a strong interest in spectacular forms.

For our next step we must return to the masque proper. The further comedy moves from irony, the less social power is allowed to the humors. In the masque, where the ideal society is still more in the ascendant, the humors become degraded into the uncouth figures of the

Jonsonian antimasque, who are said to be descended from a dramatic form far older than the rest of the masque. Farce, being a non-mimetic form of comedy, has a natural place in the masque, though in the ideal masque its natural place is that of a rigorously controlled interlude. In *The Tempest*, a comedy so profound that it seems to draw the whole masque into itself, Stephano and Trinculo are comic humors and Caliban an antimasque figure, and the group shows the transition very clearly. The main theme of the masque involves gods, fairies, and personifications of virtues; the figures of the antimasque thus tend to become demonic, and dramatic characterization begins to split into an antithesis of virtue and vice, god and devil, fairy and monster. The tension between them partly accounts for the importance of the theme of magic in the masque. At the comic end this magic is held by the benevolent side, as in *The Tempest;* but as we move further away from comedy, the conflict becomes increasingly serious, and the antimasque figures less ridiculous and more sinister, possessed in their turn of powers of enchantment. This is the stage represented by *Comus*, which is very close to the open conflict of good and evil in the morality play. With the morality play we pass into another area of masque which we shall here call the archetypal masque, the prevailing form of most twentieth-century highbrow drama, at least in continental Europe, as well as of many experimental operas and unpopular movies.

The ideal masque tends to individualize its audience by pointing to the central member of it: even the movie audience, sitting in the dark in small units (usually of two), is a relatively individualized one. A growing sense of loneliness is noticeable as we move away from comedy. The archetypal masque, like all forms of spectacular drama, tends to detach its settings from time and space, but instead of the Arcadias of the ideal masque, we find ourselves frequently in a sinister limbo, like the threshold of death in *Everyman*, the sealed underworld crypts of Maeterlinck, or the nightmares of the future in expressionist plays. As we get nearer the rationale of the form, we see that the *auto* symbol of communion in one body is reappearing, but in a psychological and subjective form, and without gods. The action of the archetypal masque takes place in a world of human types, which at its most concentrated becomes the interior of the human mind. This is explicit even in the old moralities, like *Mankynd* and *The Castell of Perseveraunce*, and at least implicit in a good deal of Maeterlinck, Pirandello, Andreyev, and Strindberg.

Naturally, with such a setting, characterization has to break down into elements and fragments of personality. This is why I call the form the archetypal masque, the word archetype being in this context used in Jung's sense of an aspect of the personality capable of dramatic projection. Jung's persona and anima and counsellor and shadow throw a great deal of light on the characterization of modern allegorical, psychic, and expressionist dramas, with their circus barkers and wraith-like females and inscrutable sages and obsessed demons. The abstract entities of the morality play and the stock types of the *commedia dell'arte* (this latter representing one of the primitive roots of the genre) are similar constructions.

A sense of confusion and fear accompanies the sense of loneliness: Maeterlinck's early plays are almost dedicated to fear, and the constant undermining of the distinction between illusion and reality, as mental projections become physical bodies and vice versa, splits the action up into a kaleidoscopic chaos of reflecting mirrors. The mob scenes of German expressionist plays and the mechanical fantasies of the Čapeks show the same disintegration at work in a social context. From the generic point of view, one of the most interesting archetypal plays is Andreyev's powerful *The Black Maskers,* in which its author saw re-flected not only the destruction of an individual's *nobile castello,* which is its explicit theme, but the whole social collapse of modern Russia. This play distinguishes two groups of dissociative elements of person-ality, one group connected with self-accusation and the other with the death-wish, and it exhibits the human soul as a castle possessed by a legion of demons. It is evident that the further the archetypal masque gets from the ideal masque, the more clearly it reveals itself as the emancipated antimasque, a revel of satyrs who have got out of control. The progress of sophisticated drama appears to be towards an *anag-norisis* or recognition of the most primitive of all dramatic forms.

At the far end of the archetypal masque, where it joins the *auto,* we reach the point indicated by Nietzsche as the point of the birth of tragedy, where the revel of satyrs impinges on the appearance of a commanding god, and Dionysos is brought into line with Apollo. We may call this fourth cardinal point of drama the epiphany, the dramatic apocalypse or separation of the divine and the demonic, a point directly opposite the mime, which presents the simply human mixture. This point is the dramatic form of the point of epiphany, most familiar as the point at which the Book of Job, after describing a complete circuit from tragedy through symposium, finally ends. Here the two monsters Behemoth and Leviathan replace the more frequent demonic animals.

The Classical critics, from Aristotle to Horace, were puzzled to understand why a disorganized ribald farce like the satyr-play should be the source of tragedy, though they were clear that it was. In medieval drama, where the progression through sacred and heroic *auto* to tragedy is so much less foreshortened, the development is plainer. The most clearly epiphanic form of scriptural drama is the Harrowing of Hell play, which depicts the triumph of a divine redeemer over demonic resistance. The devils of that play are the Christian forms of figures very like the Greek satyrs, and dramatic groups generically very close to the satyrs are never far from any scriptural play that deals directly with Christ, whether tamed and awed as in the *Secunda Pastorum,* or triumphantly villainous, as in the crucifixion and Herod plays. And just as Greek tragedy retained and developed the satyr-play, so Elizabethan tragedy retains a satyric counterpoint in its clown scenes and the farcical under-plots of *Faustus* and many later tragedies. The same element provides those superb episodes of the porter in *Macbeth,* the grave-diggers in *Hamlet,* and the serpent-bearer in *Antony and Cleopatra,* which so baffled Classically-minded critics who had forgotten about the satyr-play. Perhaps we could make more dramatic sense out of *Titus Andronicus* if we could see it as an unharrowed hell, a satyr-play of obscene and gibbering demons.

The two nodes of the scriptural play are Christmas and Easter: the latter presents the triumphant god, the former the quiet virgin mother who gathers to herself the processional masque of the kings and shepherds. This figure is at the opposite end of the masque from the watching queen or peeress of an ideal masque, with the virtuous but paralyzed Lady of *Comus* halfway between. A female figure symbolizing some kind of reconciling unity and order appears dimly at the end of the great panoramic masques of *Faust* and *Peer Gynt,* the "eternal feminine" of the former having some of its traditional links. Modern examples of the same epiphanic form range from Claudel's Annunciation play to Yeats's *Countess Cathleen,* where the heroine is really a female and Irish Jesus, sacrificing herself for her people and then cheating the devils by the purity of her nature, very much as in the pre-Anselm theory of the atonement. As Yeats remarks in a note, the story represents one of the supreme parables of the world.

ROBERT B. HEILMAN

Tragedy and Melodrama: Speculations on Generic Form

I

This essay grows out of my sense of a persistent confusion in the use of the word *tragedy*. As critics, of course, we know that we can never expect to agree on final definitions that will make possible a consistent criticism. But the discrepancies which we can never finally eliminate, even in professional usage, have got completely out of hand in popular usage. This fact is my starting point, and in this sense, literary criticism merges with social criticism. The word *tragedy* means not only plays of a certain kind but almost all kinds of painful experiences: an early death, an unexpected death by disease, a financial failure, a suicide, a murder, an automobile accident, a train accident, an airplane accident, a successful military movement by a hostile power, a sadistic act, a government error, almost any act of violence. I recall an accident in which a small plane, whose pilot had bailed out, crashed into a building; the newspaper I was then reading headlined the story, "Tragedy to Plane and Factory." This seemed to stretch the idea of tragedy pretty far. The strain was increased by the fact, which was soon revealed, that the factory was a cheese factory, for to many people cheese will not seem the likeliest of tragic materials.

What I want to explore is the possibility of finding distinctions among the host of disagreeable events lumped under the word *tragedy*. Note my word *explore*. Such criticism is not logical demonstration; it is at best a form of rhetoric. That is, it succeeds in so far as it persuades anyone else that it is useful. The most the critic can hope for is to be partially persuasive.

An experiment in making distinctions should justify itself. However, I

From *Texas Quarterly*, Summer 1960, pp. 36–50. Reprinted by permission of the author and publisher.

want to note what seems to me to be an especial danger in that loose use of the word *tragedy* that penetrates our whole society. I do not think we can simply rest in our knowledge that we have wide areas of bad usage. We need to make some effort to counter bad usage. For when a word is a catchall for many meanings only loosely related, it loses character. It tends to be used only for simple or wholesale or lump meanings. In fact, we can propose it as a law of language that when one word gains several meanings, the inferior meaning will tend to force the superior meaning out of circulation: I mean that the rougher, more general, looser, or lazier meaning will win out over the more exact or precise or demanding meaning. This is Gresham's law of semantic currency. When *tragedy* means the whole world of misfortune we cannot distinguish particular misfortunes in terms of their cause, nature, and meaningfulness. We lack the words for this; what is worse, we lack the concepts. What we do not distinguish, we do not understand; I will go a step further and suggest that if experiences are not understood, there is a sense in which they are not even experienced. This confusion extends beyond verbal haziness and begins to interfere with fundamental clarity of mind and therefore, I think, with sense of reality.

II

I believe that the word *tragedy* may suitably be applied to one form of catastrophic experience, and that this can be differentiated from all others. For a start, we may use Aristotle's definition of the tragic hero as the good man who gets into trouble through some error or shortcoming for which the standard term has become the tragic flaw. This I take to be a central, irreducible truth about tragic reality.

This assumption of mine has a number of consequences. The first is that the tragic character is essentially a divided character, and I shall regularly use *divided, dividedness,* and *division* as key words. The idea of goodness and the idea of the flaw suggest different incentives and different directions, a pulling apart, though not of pathological intensity, within the personality. The division in the hero may be of different sorts. In the first place, it may reflect the kind of division that seems inseparable from human community—from the fact that, in the ordering of life, we maintain different imperatives that correspond to different and perhaps irreconcilable needs. Hamlet and Orestes, those heroes so different from each other in time and place and yet so incredibly alike in the trials that visit them, cannot avenge their fathers, the victims of evil deeds, without themselves committing evil deeds. Antigone cannot be true to family duty and love, and to religious obligation, without contravening civil law; and Creon—who in some ways is really a better tragic hero than Antigone—cannot or at least does not maintain civil order without punitive decrees that profoundly violate human feelings and sense of justice. Yet none of these heroes could refrain from the course that leads to guilt without feeling intolerably acquiescent in a public evil.

Such heroes and heroines, if I do not misread them, incorporate the dividedness of a humanity whose values, because they naturally elude the confines of formal logic, create an apparently insoluble situation. In this situation the crucial actions of heroes, though they are exacted by a powerful sense of moral obligation, nevertheless become infused with guilt. For these heroes the two counterimperatives have so much authority that no observer can say with assurance, "It would be better if Hamlet or Antigone or Cordelia had done so and so." Nor could a fully aware person, caught between injunctions that are apparently incompatible, come out of such situations without damage; he could be safe only by canceling part of his awareness. This canceling would surely threaten the common order more than the ambiguous act does. Suppose Hamlet had decided that the ghostly exhortations that he heard were simply the product of tensions within himself, that he was worrying too much, that his best step was to get adjusted to the existent order and to stop brooding about evils which he couldn't help anyway and which might well be only imaginary. Or that Orestes had decided that his father deserved his fate, or Cordelia that she might just as well follow her sisters in apple-polishing an eccentric elder. Maybe these would be safe courses, at least temporarily. But what diminished persons we would have, and what a shrunken sense of reality.

Of characters caught in the Hamlet and Orestes situation we may say that they are divided between "imperatives," that is, different injunctions, each with its own validity, but apparently irreconcilable. With another type of tragic hero the division may be said to be between "imperative" and "impulse," between the moral ordinance and the unruly passion, between mandate and desire, between law and lust. Tradition and community give an ordinance, but egotism drives one away from it. Macbeth seeks power through politics, Faustus through intellect; what makes them tragic, as ordinary power-grabbers are not, is that neither of them can ever, in yielding to impulse, force out of consciousness the imperatives that he runs against. Oedipus has the same division, but with a different alignment of forces: he wants to obey the imperative but is betrayed by the riotous impulse. Finally, there is a third representative tragic dividedness—the split between impulse and impulse, which I believe to be a characteristic situation in Ibsen. Rebecca West and Rosmersholm, for instance, are divided between what I will call the impulses of the old order and those of rationalist enlightenment, in a peculiarly modern tragic situation.

I have used the term *imperative* to denote the obligation of general validity, the discipline of self that cannot be rejected without penalty, whether it is felt as divine law or moral law or civil law, or, in a less codified but no less prescriptive way, as tradition or duty or honor. Imperative reflects a communal consciousness. By *impulse* I refer to the force that originates in or is rooted in or identified with the individual personality and is of an almost biological sort; though the specific feelings that impel the individual may be of the widest occurrence in humanity, they are felt as a need, or as a satisfaction, or as an aggrandizement of the individual, in almost a bodily way. Imperative tends toward the self-abnegatory, impulse toward the self-assertive. But I do not wish to labor this distinction. I have made it, and I have suggested three basic patterns of division, as a way of trying to make concrete the idea of dividedness in the tragic hero.

There are two other consequences of the idea of tragedy as the experience of the good man with the flaw. The first of these is that division means choice: there are alternatives, and man must select one or another. This idea is so familiar that I will limit myself to this bare statement of it. The second is that choice implies consciousness: alternatives are not really alternatives, at least in the dramatic substance, if they do not in some way, however indirectly or however tardily, live in the consciousness of the hero. The drama is a lesser one—it has less range—if the hero simply does not know what it is all about or never comes to know what it is all about. Willie Loman is a hero of such limited consciousness that, for many readers, he pushes *Death of a Salesman* into a lower order of excellence. Division, finally, is not only the occasion of self-awareness or self-knowledge, but the very material of self-knowing. It is the inconsistent and the contradictory that require the studious intelligence; the unified, the coherent, the harmonious dissolve the world of alternatives and render the customary strivings of self-understanding irrelevant.

III

To sum up: *tragedy* should be used only to describe the situation in which the divided human being faces basic conflicts, perhaps rationally insoluble, of obligations and passions; makes choices, for good or for evil; errs knowingly or involuntarily; accepts consequences; comes into a new, larger awareness; suffers or dies, yet with a larger wisdom.

Now this is quite different from popular or journalistic tragedy (here we come to the social dimension of the problem): young man drives fast, hits truck that drives out in front of him, and he and his fiancée are killed. This will almost invariably be called, "Tragedy on Highway 90," and for many people this is *all* of tragedy. The death-dealing truck might be a disease or a careless engineer or a defective airplane wing or an assailant; the essence of it is the shock of unprogrammed death. This is a rather long way from the tragic pattern that we are able to discern in the practice of the Greeks and Elizabethans and at least in the intuitions of some moderns. Even in the most skillful journalism we would hardly be able to get inside the victims and see them as divided between options or struggling in a cloudy dilemma of imperative and impulse; they do not choose but are chosen; something just happens to them; consequences are mechanical, not moral; and most of all they do not grow into that deeper understanding, of themselves and of their fate, which is the dramatic heart of the experience. For in that sudden death there is little to understand; consciousness is not sharpened but is bluntly ended.

To use the term *tragedy* indiscriminately for what Oedipus does and experiences and learns, and for what happens to a car driver through his own or someone else's carelessness, I submit, is not a casual slip of the tongue or a laughable folk error, but a real confusion that can have undesirable consequences for our grasp of reality. For by our Gresham's law of semantic currency, the cheaper meaning forces out the meaning of precise value. Tragedy comes to mean *only* accidents and sudden death or anachronistic death. As a result we tend to lose touch with certain ideas that are an indispensable means of contemplating human catastrophe: the idea that calamity may come from divisions within human nature and within the ordering of life. The idea that man may choose evil. The idea that potential evil within him may overcome him despite resolution or flight. The idea that brutal events may come out of the normal logic of character. The idea that man is never safe from himself. The idea that the knowledge of such ideas is essential to the salvation of the individual and to the health of institutions. All these ideas are implicitly discarded if the word *tragedy* conveys to us only such a thing as a smashup on Highway 90. And what do we put in place of what is lost? The idea that the worst that can happen to us is an unexpected shortening of life. The idea that this cutting short is the work of causes outside ourselves. The idea that we are innocent victims. This is a fantastic loss of tools of understanding and, implicitly, an unhealthy oversimplification of reality.

Here you may want to argue that in using such a phrase as "only unhappy accidents" I am minimizing the extent, the influence, and the force of such events. Not at all. I do not deny the reality of accidents, the pain and anguish they cause, or their power to move us either in daily experience or in literary representation. I do not suppose that we can eliminate unhappy accidents, ignore them, forget them, deny their power over our actions and feelings, or discontinue making literature of them. All I am troubled by is calling them "tragedy," which I am hoping to persuade you is no trivial error. I have the greatest respect for the rare news editor who, instead of announcing "Tragedy on Highway 90," will say "Accident on Highway 90: Two Dead." There is the crux of the matter: putting experience into the right category. Now, for the category of event which is so widely called "Tragedy on Highway 90" the proper term, I suggest, is *disaster*. It is a sufficiently capacious term to include all kinds of fatal accidents, the mortal illnesses that strike (we think) ahead of time, the destructive blows of a nature not yet quite tamed, and all the murderous violence that comes directly or by ricochet from the envious, the hostile, and the mad. Its very etymology makes *disaster* an appropriate term: it implies an undoing by action of the stars, and thus it is a fitting metaphor for all the unhappinesses that seem to come from without, to have no meaningful causes, and to let us feel guiltless. From now on, then, instead of speaking of the two meanings of *tragedy*—the meaning implied in the literary examples that remain always alive, and the contemporary journalistic meaning that pervades all our speech—I shall use the terms *tragedy* and *disaster* to denote these areas of experience that may always be theoretically distinguished.

However much they may be interwoven in the concrete event, tragedy and disaster are two fundamentally different structures of experience; to confuse them will involve errors of three kinds—intellectual, emotional, moral. The intellectual error I have already described or implied: it is to seek the causes of evil always outside ourselves, to whitewash ourselves, to be always without responsibility for calamities. The loose use of the word *tragedy* also leads us to a concomitant error of feeling. For if tragedy is simply what happens to us, we are all victims; victims must be pitied; and we can soon ooze into a rich morass of self-pity. Obviously we don't want to pity ourselves, if we are well people; but the universalization of the disaster principle sneaks pity in the back door. Sometimes we can pity ourselves simply by pitying others: Othello is a case in point. Or, in glorifying the man who pities, we may reveal a desire to cuddle up under that sympathetic wing. The word *compassionate* has become a cliché of book reviewing; in our time it is almost an ultimate term of praise for a writer. It has become embarrassing. Is *compassion* the word that comes to mind when we think of Shakespeare's treatment of Lear or Sophocles' portrayal of Oedipus? Is it not rather completeness of understanding, insight into human division, a full sense of both excellence and flaw? Compare the Christopher Fry character who says, "I'm still remembering/I can give pain, and that in itself is loss/Of liberty." When we shift from feeling sorry for pain received to fear of pain given, we move from the sense of disaster toward the tragic sense.

The third error in taking disaster for tragedy is the moral one of adopting a single-standard quantitative view of life. Disaster centers in death: we are getting less life than we have coming to us. It is not necessary to quarrel with a universal disinclination to die, especially ahead of what looks like sound scheduling; but as a matter of clarity we should observe that in our day the quest for longevity is both more extensive and more passionate than it has ever been before. This appears in our obsession with disaster, the most forceful reminder of mortality. Disaster is the realm of quantity of life; tragedy, of quality of life. The inevitable fear of disaster can grow until it eliminates all issues of quality. I do not complain about fear of death, which is a fact of life; my point is only that the ending of life is not the sole imperfection of life, and that to act as though it is, is not healthful.

IV

In disaster, what happens comes from without; in tragedy, from within. In disaster, we are victims; in tragedy, we make victims, of ourselves or others. In disaster, our moral quality is secondary; in tragedy, it is primary, the very source of action.

In literature, the problem is that of distinguishing between tragedy and what I will call, for the time being, the literature of disaster, which is often called tragedy. I regard the two forms as generically different, though they look alike because they both depict suffering. The literature of disaster comprises all those pages in which we record what has been done to us by fire, famine, the sword, and unjust men; in which our role is that of Job, plagued by our own kind, by machines, and by nature. In tragedy, as an art form, we contemplate our own errors; in the literature of disaster we mark the errors of others and the imperfections of circumstance. In tragedy we act; in the literature of disaster we are acted upon.

In the literature of disaster we find victims of situations that range from very simple to very complex. Though I want to avoid little catalogues that are too neat, I will suggest that we can identify several basic types of the victims that artists have discerned—the victims of nature, the victims of society, the victims of evil individuals, and those who are victims of themselves. This last, of course, sounds very much like tragedy, and the distinction will have to be clarified later.

Since I do not have space for analysis of plays, I will have to be like the Oriental geometrician who stated a theorem, drew an illustrative figure, and substituted, for the steps of demonstration leading to a formal conclusion, simply the word *Behold!* I use Synge's *Riders to the Sea* as an example of the literature of disaster dealing with the victim of nature; this play is generally called a tragedy, but its core is pathos; we remain serene observers, sympathetic, sharing the sadness of death, but never drawn into the experience of division and of self-knowledge, for there is none. The victim of society, a familiar figure in post-Romantic sensibility, appears archetypally in Dr. Stockmann in Ibsen's *Enemy of the People*—an embarrassingly simple picture of a noble reformer done in by a crass community. Our emotional involvement here hardly approaches the adult level. The drama of disaster that deals with the victim of society is managed somewhat more complexly in Friedrich Duerrenmatt's *The Visit* (1955). In this play the townspeople, to gain a vengeful woman's gift of a billion marks, informally sentence to death and execute one of the town's leading citizens, the original seducer of the woman who gives the billion marks. Like various dramas of disaster, *The Visit* has a powerful impact because it devotes itself exclusively to demonstrating the infinitude of human venality. It gains power at the expense of depth and complication; it simply excludes any other human characteristic but vengefulness and corruptibility. It denies the division which is at the heart of tragedy; and so, I submit, it not only narrows the aesthetic experience but reduces us to shocked spectators of a crime. This is one of the two representative risks of the literature of disaster: at the popular extreme it may entice us into a stereotyped situation, ready-made for emotional wear; or, as in *The Visit*, it may lock us out of a situation by making it so eccentric that to enter it would be suicide. That, too, is always a risk of expressionist drama, to which *The Visit* belongs: in such difficulties, as well as in other matters, we realize postrealist expressionism is very much like prerealist allegory.

The victim of the politically disordered society appears in *The Diary of Anne Frank*. Here again is a drama of disaster that offers simple and easy emotional experience, pity for victims; only at one point does it approach tragedy—at the point at which Mr. Frank says, of the tensions among the hiding victims of the Nazis, "We don't need the Nazi to destroy us. We're destroying ourselves." The victim of the evil individual is found in one of the great dramas of disaster in English—Webster's *The Duchess of Malfi*, in which a charming and innocent woman is tortured and destroyed by her cruel brothers. She is not presented tragically; she does not, like great tragic heroes, "earn" her fate. Her honorable conduct simply happens to run afoul of the purposes of her vicious brothers. Lear, on the contrary, has made Goneril and Regan efficacious in the world; they are projections of a part of his own divided nature. Lear has made his world in a way that the Duchess has not. Webster presents the evil brothers as autonomous—like a flood or holocaust that destroys. This is not to deny the existence of autonomous evil; it is simply to say that it is not the world of tragedy.

Finally in Gorki's *Lower Depths* and O'Neill's *The Iceman Cometh* (two works with extraordinary similarities of plot and structure), we find plays that are concerned with the disaster of personality: that is, with that kind of collapse which makes the individual incapable of normal adult life. When we speak of the disaster of the self, however, we remember that the origin of the tragic situation is also within the self. At the risk of too epigrammatic a contrast we may say that the disaster of self has its origin in weakness, the tragedy of self in strength. In disaster, individuals are not up to traditional requirements; in tragedy, they are not held down by traditional requirements and eventually find themselves not up to the special rules they propose for themselves. One aesthetic leads to Mr. Zero, the other to Dr. Faustus; one character says, "Pity me," the other says, "I have sinned."

In *The Duchess of Malfi* Bosola sums up the action with the phrase

"Oh this gloomy world." In *Riders to the Sea* Maurya says, ". . . there isn't anything else the sea can do to me." In *The Iceman Cometh* Larry Slade concludes, "By God, there's no hope! . . . Life is too much for me." "This gloomy world"—what is done to me—what is too much for me: this is the realm of disaster—of what happens to the victims of nature, of societal power or war, of weakness before the exigencies of life, of disillusionment, of corruption, of evil men. The realm of actual disaster that is the raw material of literary art is a large one. We do not underestimate the immediacy or anguish of that realm, or fail in sympathy with those injured or betrayed by such events, if we say, once again, that such fates are something other than tragic, and that the drama portraying such fates is not of the tragic order.

For many things that are terrible are not tragic.

V

The term *literature of disaster* which I have so far used is a cumbersome term and a limiting term. I propose, as my final point, that the literature of disaster is really a subdivision of a larger literary type. To that type, I will give the term *melodrama*.

I am aware that to take *melodrama*, which in casual contemporary usage is a derogatory term designating popular machine-made entertainments, and to apply it to a wide range of literature that includes sober work and somber tones may seem capricious to the point of scandal. I hasten to deny caprice and to explain that I use melodrama as a neutral descriptive term. I use it because I believe that what we call "popular melodrama" has reduced to stereotypes and thus has trivialized the basic structural characteristics of a form that can be serious as well as silly.

Let us look first at the popular sense of *melodrama*. Its nature is suggested by phrases such as these: pursuit and capture, imprisonment and escape, false accusation, cold-blooded villain, innocence beleaguered, virtue triumphant, eternal fidelity, mysterious identity, lovers reconciled, fraudulence revealed, enemies foiled; the whole realm of adventure; the realm of mystery from the supernatural to the whodunit; the realm of vice and crime from horror to detection to reform. It is the world of shock and thrill, of what is regularly called "gripping" and "poignant." But it is rarely devoid of ideas, however flat and hackneyed these may be. In a century and a half its color has been variously revolutionary, democratic, patriotic, antitotalitarian, reformist (anti-gambling, slavery, drinking, dope addiction, etc.). The form is represented with delightful amplitude in an early example, Thomas Merton's *Speed the Plough* (1798), which, along with various popular comic effects, contains upper-class injustice, *nouveau riche* snobbery, poor man's integrity, a lover who almost gives up the poor girl for the rich one, bigamy, economic threats, secret grief, irrational enmity, mysterious identity, old villainy disclosed in a bloodcurdling confessional, a castle fire and a rescue, and garnishings of patriotic sentiment.

When we are still not free from totalitarianism it may seem blasphemous to suggest that Lilliam Hellman's *Watch on the Rhine*, an anti-Nazi play of 1941, offers us, even if a little more sophisticatedly, the same fare as *Speed the Plough*. There is a simple villain-hero structure: we have no choice but to hate the Nazi sympathizer and love everyone else, and everyone is mostly delightful Americans.

Speed the Plough and *Watch on the Rhine* both have the stock devices of entertainment popular in their day. But beneath the standardized appeals there is a basic plot form—the conflict of villains and heroes, of what we nowadays laughingly call good guys and bad guys. Yet such a pattern of action should not be dismissed as the especial property of the simple-minded. For however dull or trite or grotesque the actions of these good and bad competitors may be, the plots are simply a debased popular form of a stable central structure that appears in all times and in trivial and sober plays alike: in this structure, man is pitted against some force outside of himself—a compact enemy, a hostile group, a social pressure, a natural event, an accident, or a coincidence. This is one of the persistent fundamental structures of literature, whether it appear in a silly or meretricious form in a cinema or television thriller or be elaborated with dignity and power in *The Trojan Women* or *Romeo and Juliet*. It draws upon permanent human attitudes, some perilous and some preserving, whether we disavow these when they become ludicrous in a Western or scarcely recognize them in some extraordinary struggle into which we have been drawn by artistic skill—the story of Annapurna, *Nigger of the Narcissus, War and Peace, Richard III*.

In the structure of melodrama, I suggest, man is essentially "whole"; this key word implies neither greatness nor moral perfection, but rather an absence of the kind of inner conflict that is so significant that it *must* claim our first attention. He is not troubled by motives that would distract him from the conflict outside himself. He may, in fact, be humanly incomplete; but his incompleteness is not the issue. In tragedy, man is divided; in melodrama, he has at least a quasi wholeness against besetting problems. In tragedy, the conflict is within man, in melodrama, it is between men, or between men and things.

We can find virtually "whole" or undivided characters in Ibsen's Dr. Stockmann, fighting community greed, and Lillian Hellman's Kurt Müller, fighting against Nazis. They are created by the same conception of character that appears in popular heroes pitted against cattle rustlers, holdup men, or racketeers. I say this not to disparage but to note the neutral fact of identity of character structure. If we rarely inspect the characters of heroes, we inspect those of victims even less. We find a virtually unified nature in Synge's Maurya, whose family is cut down by the sea; in the Franks, cut down by Nazi malice; in the Duchess of Malfi, cut down by her sadistic brothers. Villains are whole characters too—for instance, Duerrenmatt's citizenry that murders for money, and the Duchess of Malfi's murderous brothers. Even the wretched characters depicted by Gorki and O'Neill have a kind of wholeness: the wholeness of half-beings really cut off from any counter-impulses that would leave them split between retreat and participation. Wholeness, in other words, is a technical structure of character and personality; it is morally neutral; in goodness or badness, strength or weakness, the protagonist is in the main free from divergent impulses.

When we speak of the structure of a form we refer not only to its system of characterization and arrangements of characters but to its dynamics, or, in other terms, the structure of its action. We have seen how the popular thriller and the serious problem play, as we usually call it, are organized alike—on some variation of the villain-hero conflict. The final problem is to see how the drama of disaster also belongs to this pattern. In all these cases we have an essentially undivided protagonist facing an outer conflict. In this kind of situation only several types of outcome are possible—victory, or defeat, or perhaps a stalemate or compromise. Here is the *key* point. Disaster and the popular happy-ending play are not different formal entities but are simply the opposite extremes of the spectrum of melodrama: at one end, man, essentially whole, is beaten down by his antagonist; at the other, also essentially whole, he comes out on top. At the one end, man is victim; at the other, victor. The nature of the conflict is the same, the central structure is the same, but the artist chooses one point of view or another. He may see man vs. nature or political forces or society or other individuals, and he may see him as lost or as triumphant; there are scores of plays doing it one way or the other. The identifying mark of the melodramatic structure is not the particular outcome of the plot, but the conception of character and the alignment of forces. This identity we can always find beneath a considerable diversity of arrangements of action.

Finally, the melodramatic organization of experience has a psychological structure. It puts us into a certain posture which we find agreeable and that within limits has a certain utility. In most general terms, what it affords is the pleasure of experiencing wholeness—not the troubling, uneasy wholeness that exists when all the divergent elements of personality remain within the field of consciousness, or the rare integration of powers that may be earned by long discipline, but the sensation of wholeness that is created when one responds with a single impulse or potential and lets this function as a surrogate for the whole personality. In this quasi wholeness he is freed from the anguish of choice and from the pain of struggling with counterimpulses that inhibit and distort his single direct "action." If there is danger he is courageous; he is not distracted by fear, expediency, or the profit motive. Or he can be serene in adversity, unhampered by self-seeking, by impatience with the frailties of others, or by doubt about ends. Thus Kurt Müller in *Watch on the Rhine* and the stage version of Anne Frank's father: through them, melodrama affords a unity of desirable feeling—of the wisdom to bear troubles, of practical competence against evil. One is untroubled by psychic or physical fumbling, by indecisiveness, by weak muscles or strong counterimperatives. One is under the pleasant yoke of what I will call a monopathy: that single strong feeling that excludes all others and thus renders one whole. It may be a monopathy of hope or, for that matter, a monopathy of hopelessness; a monopathy of contempt for the petty, discontent with destiny, indignation at evil doing, or castigation of the guilt of others. Even in defeat and disaster, in being overwhelmed and victimized, I am convinced, the human being is able to find certain monopathic advantages.

Melodrama, in sum, includes the whole range of conflicts undergone by characters who are presented as undivided or at least without divisions of such magnitude that they *must* be at the dramatic center; hence melodrama includes a range of actions that extend from disaster to success, from defeat to victory, and a range of effects from the strongest conviction of frustration and failure that serious art can dramatize to the most frivolous assurance of triumph that a mass-circulation writer can confect. The issue here is not the reordering of the self, but the reordering of one's relations with others, with the world of people or things; not the knowledge of self, but the maintenance of self, in its assumption of wholeness, until conflicts are won or lost. There is a continuous spectrum of possibilities from the popular play in which the hostile force is always beatable to the drama of disaster in which the hostile force is unbeatable; at one extreme we view man in his strength, at the other, in his weakness. In structure of feeling the form is monopathic.

But the tragic hero is divided; he is in some way split between different forces or motives or values. His nature is dual or even multifold; the different elements are always present and dramatically operative; they are always realities that have to be reckoned with. In structure of feeling we may call tragedy "polypathic." The monopathic concentration may actually make melodrama in some ways more overwhelming, as in *The Duchess of Malfi*, where everything enlarges the sense of ruin; but tragedy, where impulses and options are double and multifold, where we are drawn now this way and now that, exacts a very much more complex and troubling awareness. One example: the spectacle of the aged Lear in the storm is overwhelming, too. But it cannot inspire simply a monopathic pity, since we do not forget that in a sense Lear has created this storm himself. Profound pity for the victim, yes, but also acknowledgment of the paradoxical presence of justice, and sense of irony—all are present in a disturbing polypathic experience.

In melodrama, man is seen in his strength or in his weakness; in tragedy, in both his strength and his weakness at once. In melodrama, he is victorious or he is defeated; in tragedy, he experiences defeat in victory, or victory in defeat. In melodrama, man is simply guilty or simply innocent; in tragedy, his guilt and his innocence coexist. In melodrama, man's will is broken, or it conquers; in tragedy, it is tempered in the suffering that comes with, or brings about, new knowledge.

The pathological extreme of the tragic condition is schizophrenia—where normal dividedness is magnified into the split that is illness. The pathological extreme of the melodramatic condition is paranoia—in one phase, the sense of a hostile "they" who will make one their victim, and, in another phase, the sense of one's own grandeur and, implicitly, of the downfall of others. Melodrama has affinities with politics; tragedy, with religion. Pragmatic politics appears as a competition for power between good and evil; our side is "good," and the other side, "evil." In the religious view of man is a sense of his dividedness, of the co-presence of counterimpulses always striving for dominance, of the fact that throughout his life he is a dual creature with equal possibilities of coming to salvation or damnation. Melodrama leans toward the timely, tragedy toward the timeless; on the one hand we have the world of protest and problem plays; on the other, the world of meditation and myth.

So much for the efforts to pile up distinctions between two basic sets of habits and attitudes. We have described melodrama as monopathic, presenting man in defeat or victory, in guilt or innocence; as having affiliations with politics and history, drawn to the topics that change with time. We have described tragedy as polypathic, showing man's victory in defeat, his mingling of guilt and innocence; as having affiliations with religion and myth, seeking the constants that transcend change. I have meant to suggest rather than to insist. It would not be helpful to make absolute, unvarying boundary lines; in life and literature, as they exist, there are not many instances of pure types. The literary work or the human personality *leans* in one direction or the other; it rarely *plunges* toward an extreme. But one cannot judge the individual work, or the person's way of confronting reality—one cannot say that here is a melodramatic style with some moments of the tragic or that here is a tragic cast of mind that includes something of the melodramatic—without first distinguishing the theoretical poles of attraction. The test of these theoretical constructions is their helpfulness in identifying actual literary structures or in understanding the strategies of spirit that men devise to face an imperfect world.

JAMES L. CALDERWOOD
HAROLD E. TOLIVER

Introduction to Comedy

Like tragedy, comedy has suffered from the infiltration of popular meanings into a literary context. Since the comic in ordinary experience is roughly synonymous with "funny" and "laughable," it is only natural to think of laughter as the distinctive feature of dramatic comedy. But defining any genre by its effects upon us—laughter, tears, spiritual uplift, and so on—is risky. What a work does and what it is are different things, and we do not establish the latter by exploring the former. Nevertheless, comic theory from Plato to Arthur Koestler has been regularly seduced away from the objective properties of comedy —structure, themes, styles, characterization—to pursue the elusive nature of laughter. More recent criticism has come to recognize that not every funny play is a comedy (for instance, Harold Pinter's *The Dumbwaiter*) nor every comedy a funny play (Shakespeare's *Measure for Measure*). Still, the persistence of affective theories reminds us that comedy does have an enduring affiliation to laughter that we need to take account of, however glancingly.

What laughter actually is, whether a "sudden glory," a "surge of vital feeling," a catharsis of psychic tension, or something else, is less to the point here than its pattern of development. One generally acknowledged cause of laughter is the incongruous, which implies a forced linkage of disparate categories. The clown's distended nose, the motley fool in court, the pompous strut leading to a pratfall, verbal devices like hyperbole, understatement, and pun: all accord in being somehow discordant. The incongruous in space is the disproportionate or asymmetrical, in time the unexpected. Thus Kant says that humor consists of a "strained expectation being suddenly reduced to nothing." Anticipation set up and then reversed, or fulfilled explosively, characterizes physical slapstick no less than the witty joke; even disastrous reversals can sometimes seem funny after the initial dismay has worn off. (At the end of the movie *The Treasure of Sierra Madre* when the gold dust for which three men have suffered and nearly died is blown away by the wind, their "expectations being suddenly reduced to nothing," they slump to the ground and then gradually commence laughing.) In humor as in magic the false lead prepares the way for the irrational effect; and hence our bafflement at the magical act can easily pass on into bemused laughter. As the analogy to magic suggests, there is a certain freedom to the comic; it is an open society where any association (or dissociation) is permissible and everything is more or less than it seems. The banana peel and the punchline both disclose to us that a prior situation contained undreamed of potentials, that our bondage to the appearances of things was itself only apparent.

If we take a kind of "a, b, c, X!" sequence as typical of humor, then in structure at least, much comedy is a joke writ large. For the comic plot normally puts its major characters, usually young lovers, on a path toward frustration, but then intercepts this development with a "punchline" reversal in which victory and a happy ending are wrested out of apparent defeat. Tragic plots unfold the probabilities of a given situation, showing us a world harnessed to the irreversibility of cause and effect, action and reaction. Comedy, on the other hand, like humor, specializes in the improbable, the reversible, the redemption that comes from nowhere (*deus ex machina*). Nothing in *Tartuffe* prepares us for the officer of a suddenly omniscient king, or in *Arms and the Man* for Bluntschli's inheriting, just in time to qualify him as a suitor to Raina, 200 horses, 70 carriages, 4000 tablecloths, 9600 sheets and blankets, and so on. In looking back over them, tragic plots, like some dice, seem "loaded" in that, given *that* starting point, this ending seems unavoidable. Comic plots are also "loaded," but rather in the sense of being fertile, capable of multiplying in all directions. They do not exhaust possibilities but escape them, liberating their characters from the laws of action and reaction. That does not mean, however, that comedy is less realistic than tragedy, since reality does not noticeably prefer logic to illogic or causality to coincidence; it means merely that each genre sets its own ground rules in the process of transforming reality.

COMEDY AND RITUAL

Like tragedy, comedy may have had its origins in ritual—the same fertility rituals in which the dying and reviving god of nature (Dionysus, Attis, Osiris, and others) was imitatively worshipped. Tragedy is believed to reflect the phase of the ritual in which the god-king-scapegoat suffers and dies; comedy, it is held, passes beyond this to a final phase in which the god's rebirth and sacred marriage to the earth goddess are celebrated, in part by a festive procession called the *komos* (hence, *komedia*). Comedy thus completes a pattern begun by tragedy, moving around or beyond death to events suggestive of ongoing life. Not that specific comedies in moving around death to life are slavishly adhering to ancient ritual formuli. A potential death phase may appear in comedies by authors totally unaware of such rituals merely because the traditional happy ending of comedy becomes "happy" by evading potential unhappiness, and unhappiness in the intensified realm of dramatic action normally figures as death: the ending of Christopher Fry's *The Lady's Not for Burning*, for instance, is happy at least partly in virtue of the fact that the lady might have been *for* burning.

Though a melodramatic Renaissance comedy like Peele's *Mucedorus* may kill off half the cast en route to a happy ending, for survivors "death" is encountered only symbolically. The ritual combat of a young man with an old man (summer against winter, life against death, fertility against sterility) is sometimes suggested in comedy by the conflict between a son and his father over the issue of marriage. If life is to continue, youth must be served, which means that old age must be not literally killed but transformed somehow. If the "senex," or old man, is cast as the hero, as in the early Greek comedies of Aristophanes, we may encounter a miraculous regeneration. In *The Knights*, for instance, the old man Demos grows young again through the ministrations of a sausage-selling magician-cook, perhaps thus reflecting, as F. M. Cornford argues, the resurrection of the slain god-king in fertility rituals. In Shakespeare, a pseudo-death and subsequent revival is frequently accorded the heroine—for example, Hero in *Much Ado About Nothing*, Helena in *All's Well That Ends Well*, Imogen in *Cymbeline*, Hermione and Perdita in *The Winter's Tale*. Nearly everyone qualifies for the role in *The Tempest*, where a senex figure, Prospero, manipulates the action in the interests of youth, to which he graciously gives way at the end. Normally, however, young lovers are at the center of the comic action, and repressive father figures must be converted to paternal permissiveness, often by harassments and humiliations of a nearly fatal sort. Thus the misanthropic father in Menander's *The Grouch* (c. 317 B.C.) is obliged by comic necessity to fall into a well so that a young man can earn both his gratitude and his daughter by fetching him out again. In Synge's *The Playboy of the Western World* (1907) the young hero becomes a center of sexual attraction because he is thought to have killed his father (for trying to marry him off to an elderly widow). When the father reappears, alive and crusty as ever, the son flattens him once again with a spade, and though he rises yet again he is now willing to pass the mantle of family authority to the son. The convention of symbolically killing off the senex is evidently as indestructible as most of the senex figures themselves. A recent British play of Joe Orton, *Entertaining Mr. Sloane* (1964), blandly exploits the implication of the convention by having the young Mr. Sloane actually murder the old and moralistic Kemp so that he is free to be "entertained," in the cyclic fashion of fertility gods like Adonis, half a year by one lover and half a year by another. Even in extreme cases when death does occur in comedy, it is by no means the all-absorbing, conclusive death of tragedy but merely one phase of an over-all comic movement.

The ritual origins of comedy appear to have left an imprint upon its endings also. Most fertility rituals begin on a note of inhibition as the worshippers abstain from sex and food—thus imitating the suspension of life and time during the transition period between the god's death and his rebirth, between winter and spring, the old and the new year—and then work towards a final release of such inhibitions in sexual promiscuity and feasting suggestive of the rejuvenation of life. The feast, probably once the eating of an animal symbolizing the god (the Dionysiac bull or goat, for instance), brought the worshippers into a state of communion both with the god and with one another. Comedy too, whether directly indebted to ritual in given cases or not, fosters a sense of the continuity and community of life. Whereas tragedy, with the death of a hero who has been the focal point of his society, ends with an old order breaking up or greatly devitalized, comedy goes on to form a new society around the young couple whose wedding usually marks the play's conclusion. In less decorous comedies like Machiavelli's *Mandragola* and Wycherley's *The Country Wife*, the wedding is supplanted by a youth's success in seducing an old man's wife or daughter. The idea of social communion behind the ritual feast also helps account for the large number of comedies that end with some suggestion of eating, whether it be formal feasting as in Aristophanes' *The Wasps*, a simple invitation to dinner as in Plautus' *The Rope*, or merely routine preparations for breakfast as in Peele's *The Old Wives' Tale*. In any event, comedy is traditionally dedicated to bringing together at its close a happy society liberated from such restraints upon human impulse as age, law, sterility, and guilt, and surrounded by images of abundant and continuing life.

KINDS OF COMEDY: ROMANCE AND SATIRE

Judging from the descriptive terms that have been applied to it, nothing multiplies and mutates so rapidly as comedy. Critics have identified such classes as Old and New Comedy, classical and medieval comedy, high and low comedy, sweet and bitter, dark, farcical, pastoral, sentimental, laughing, comedy of manners, of humors, of ideas, of intrigue, and so on. Almost, it would seem a genre for every play; which suggests that shaping such a clutter into a reasonably coherent or manageable form is difficult. Nevertheless, some guidelines are necessary, if only as general boundaries within which individual plays can exhibit their specialness.

Perhaps most useful here is Northrop Frye's argument that comedy lies between satire and romance. This means, not that comedy *is* satire or romance, each a legitimate genre in its own right, but that it is influenced by them. The earliest surviving Greek comedy, the Old Comedy of Aristophanes, is indeed satiric: a tightly structured but loosely plotted sort of musical revue drama which gives the dramatist maximum freedom to attack either individuals, like Socrates in *The Clouds*, or social, political, and moral abuses in general. In the line of satiric descent from Old Comedy would appear the plays of Machiavelli, Ben Jonson, Molière, Congreve, Sheridan, and Shaw, to mention merely a few. New Comedy, on the other hand, as represented by Menander of Athens and the Roman dramatists Plautus and Terence, though not exclusively romantic, contains enough in the way of shipwrecks, separated lovers, lost children, concealed identities, and other such improbabilities, all leading to a final recognition and reconciliation scene, to suggest its affinities to romance. Romantic comedy, it should be stressed, does not mean merely plays concerned with love or courtship, which, while normally present in romantic comedy, may also be the concern of essentially satiric comedies like Congreve's *The Way of the World*. What is meant, rather, is a kind of comedy that reflects the literary genre of romance in a light but on the whole sympathetic manner, as, for instance, in Plautus' *The Rope* or in the comedies of Lyly, Peele, Greene, and, for the most part, Shakespeare.

Satire usually represents human experience as degraded, romance as elevated. Comedies animated by a satiric spirit may present us with characters like Jonson's Volpone or Molière's Tartuffe, whose greed, cunning, and hypocrisy enable them to dominate societies composed of the hopelessly foolish and the helplessly virtuous. Romantic comedy, on the other hand, may give us a world in which both nature and society accede to the benevolent magic of a Prospero, and viciousness is rendered either harmless or humorous. Romance normally affirms the saving graces of life, depicting the human condition from a perspective of charity. Thus *The Tempest* concludes upon images of a redeemed world, even potentially dangerous characters being absorbed into an atmosphere of forgiveness. But in *Volpone* and *Tartuffe*, though certain characters are redeemed, it is at the expense of other characters, and the stress is not on charity but punishment. All ends well, perhaps, but not convincingly so: Tartuffe is restrained less by moral than by theatrical means, and as the major characters in *Volpone* line up for sentencing we do not feel that the organized processes of social order have succeeded but that depravity has failed—just barely.

The structure of comedy no less than its view of human experience is varyingly affected by romance and satire. Satiric comedy naturally centers in characters who are somehow ridiculous—misers, misanthropes, hypocrites, braggarts, who in one way or another violate the canons of common sense or deviate from conventional standards. The normal way of structuring such a play is to make the traditional happy ending contingent upon the defeat of the ridiculous characters. Defeat means primarily exposure, the stripping away of delusions and pretense. This sort of exposure is most effective, of course, after the success of the ridiculous seems assured. Absurdities are given free rein and then at some crowning moment brought up short—while Tartuffe stands greedily surveying his spoils or when Mosca in *Volpone* thinks he has maneuvered Volpone into a corner and himself into a fortune. The movement here, then, is through freedom (or license) to frustration and restraint. In romantic comedy, on the other hand, since the focus is upon sympathetic characters, like Rosalind and Orlando in *As*

You Like It, the happy ending arises not from restraining the ridiculous characters but from liberating the hero and heroine. The movement here tends to be through frustration to freedom: hence the standard plot in which boy and girl, after meeting, are kept apart by various restraints from which they finally disengage themselves.

One way of viewing this structural distinction is in terms of movements to or away from "law." Continuing with the examples of *Volpone* and *Tartuffe,* for instance, we note that both plays end on climactic scenes in which the law suddenly clamps down on transgressors, whereas romantic comedies tend to begin with a stress upon a rule of law that is subsequently circumvented or relaxed. *A Midsummer Night's Dream* begins with an entire society in bondage to the Athenian law requiring a daughter to marry a husband of her father's choosing; at the end of the play Duke Theseus simply sets the law aside. In *The Merchant of Venice* Portia reveals that, if it is subjected to closer scrutiny, the law apparently guaranteeing Shylock his pound of Antonio's flesh can become in itself an avenue to freedom. Thus romantic and satiric comedy define "law" in different ways. In the latter, it stands for norms of good sense and general experience that have been violated and need to be reinstated if life is to be conducted on a fairly reasonable basis. The violators, of course, need not be persons; they may as easily be ideas, such as the idea of war as a glorious enterprise, which it is the aim of Shaw's *Arms and the Man* to deflate. Nor need "law" be taken literally: in Shaw's play the law that reasserts itself at the end is simply the standard of practical reason and straightforward fact. In romantic comedy, however, "law," if it is of the statutory sort, is less a curb upon excesses than excessive itself, like the law of slavery in Roman comedies or the repressive rule of Duke Frederick in *As You Like It.* Here again we need to consider law figuratively as a symbol of blighting influences in general: the economic injustices harped on at the opening of *The Second Shepherd's Play,* the puritanism of *Malvolio* in *Twelfth Night,* the rigid sense of honor that causes Bertram to reject Helena in *All's Well That Ends Well.* So inherent in the structure of comedy is this movement through restraint to release that even a benign parent like Prospero is obliged to sentence Ferdinand to a period of "wooden slavery," his log-carrying chores, if only, as he explains, to make his subsequent release the more attractive. In either event, however, whether society is freed of tyranny through imposing the law or freed from the tyranny of law itself, the result is an elimination of extremes and a return to a sane and liberal normality.

TRAGEDY AND COMEDY

Speaking of an elimination of extremes may well remind us of tragedy and its tendency to expel by banishment or death the exceptional individual. No doubt there are points at which comedy and tragedy touch, however tentatively. The tragic hero is often an extremist, an over-reacher like Faustus or Macbeth, and yet it is in a comedy by Massinger that we find a dominating figure called Sir Giles Overreach, whose comic fate is to suffer madness upon discovering that his grasp has exceeded the length of his arm. Characters like Sir Giles, Shylock, Volpone, Tartuffe, and Alceste (in Molière's *The Misanthrope*) have their scapegoat functions no less than tragic heroes like Oedipus or Samson; and in their uncompromising commitment to particular vices they may even achieve a kind of largeness in folly that is comically analogous to tragic grandeur. The analogy, however, is more a matter of burlesque or parody than of equation, and hence criticism since Aristotle has been busier to contrast than to compare the two genres.

By way of contrast, then, we might remind ourselves that although both forms originated in fertility rituals, they reflect defferent phases of those rituals. Tragedy, centering in the suffering and death of the god-hero, partially develops a ritual whose full cycle is completed by comedy. Thus Northrop Frye speaks of tragedy as "uncompleted comedy" and of comedy as containing tragedy implicitly within itself. On the surface of it, the death with which tragedy normally ends would certainly seem complete enough, but death is "complete" only when it terminates a cycle of youth, maturity, and age: the premature deaths of tragic heroes are curtailments, not completions. The tragic hero moves down a linear path that breaks off in a chasm; he "falls." But the pattern of ritual is cyclical rather than linear, tracing as it does the cycle of the seasons. The rebirth and marriage of the god that conclude fertility rituals do not represent progress, which is a linear conception; they represent a *return,* of the god to life, of nature from the sterile winter to the fertile spring, of society to the state it occupied "before." Everything returns to its beginnings, and this cyclic pattern of ritual is carried over into comedy, the "return to before" being a temporal expression of what we referred to in spatial terms as comedy's re-establishment of a balance or norm at its conclusion.

As this cyclical "return to before" suggests, comedy is a more conservative genre than tragedy, more self-protective. It does not venture everything at the risk of great losses or in the expectation of large gains but conserves what it has in the interests of continuity. Tragedy presents us with heroes who take up extreme positions on the ledges and limbs of human experience and risk everything in remaining there. Its most recurrent feature is thus a sense of loss, most commonly the loss of life. And yet in the process of losing, tragic heroes also gain a great deal in the qualitative refinement of consciousness we have called *anagnorisis*. Comedy, too, deals in losses, but unlike those of tragedy they are temporary, for the full comic sequence is actually loss-and-recovery. Prospero's dukedom and Alonzo's son, Orgon's peace of mind and possessions, Millamant's fortune, hosts of heroines: all are lost only as a preliminary to being triumphantly found again. The stress here is not upon achievement, an improving movement beyond the present, but upon a recapturing of the past. And from this vantage point we can see that the theme of loss-and-recovery subsumes the motif of death and rebirth discussed earlier. In dying, Mr. Roberts is not really lost; the play "finds" him again in the form of Ensign Pulver, who will hurl the Captain's palm tree overboard and restore the ship to its earlier "norm" of quasi-mutiny.

Thus though comedy is more complete than tragedy, it is less final. As Lear says of Cordelia after her death,

> Thou'lt come no more,
> Never, never, never, never, never!

Nor will any of the tragic heroes; the Lear or Oedipus or Phaedra experience at its end is over, a unique and final action. But comedy is recurrent, always coming around, like ritual, to where it was and ought to be, where we want it to be. Its endings are always beginnings, or re-beginnings. The Callimachos, Ferdinands, Mirabels, and Bluntschlis are sufficiently non-unique to be always with us, and there is no guarantee that even prison can permanently contain the Tartuffian spirit.

The tragic sequence is from *praxis* (action) through *pathos* (suffering) to *anagnorisis* (recognition). Comedy also concludes with recognition scenes but of a different sort from those in tragedy. For one thing, in tragedy the *anagnorisis* is usually experienced by the hero alone, while in comedy it is generalized, in the proper spirit of comic community, to include as many characters as possible. What Samson thinks and feels during the moment of inwardness before he turns his strength upon the pillars, only he knows; and though Hamlet tries to convey to Horatio his sense of expanded awareness after his ocean voyage, his words fly out but his thoughts, if we are to judge from Horatio's monosyllabic replies, apparently remain behind. Shakespearean comedy, on the other hand—and comedy in general—typically concludes with scenes in which most of the characters troop forward in a state of headshaking mystification to be enlightened by a Portia or a Rosalind or a Prospero. Thus the comic *anagnorisis* is often a kind of unearned dividend of information—such as the fact that Cesario is really Viola in *Twelfth Night* or that Mirabel in *The Way of the World* has all along held a secret deed of conveyance—that is gratuitously distributed by a character who throughout the play has gratuitously withheld it from circulation. This revealing of something that has been present but concealed all along is in marked contrast to the tragic *anagnorisis* as something not present to begin with but created by the action of the play and the ordeal of the hero.

The *anagnorisis* in either comedy or tragedy may be a discovery of identity, as it is for Oedipus in *Oedipus Tyrannos* and for Jack Worthing in *The Importance of Being Earnest*. The tragic hero, however, discovers not merely his real identity but the quality and substance of it, what he has been and done, and what, therefore, he now is. The stress is upon the constricting effects of time as the hero's past catches up with his present, subjecting him to a moral redefinition, the innocent Oedipus becoming the polluted Oedipus. But Jack Worthing's discovery that he is actually Ernest Moncrieff is a liberation of the present by the past, an opening up of certain future opportunities, such as marriage to Gwendolyn. Oedipus is compelled to revise his view of himself in radical fashion, recognizing that he has changed not merely in surface identity or in his external relations to others, but in essence. Thus the action of Sophocles' play *redefines* Oedipus while that of Wilde's play simply *renames* Jack Worthing.

This renaming as distinguished from redefining is typical of comedy in that comic identities are often shifted about like counters over a surface of unvarying essences. This is true not only in cases of misplaced identity, such as Jack Worthing's, but in cases of disguised identity as well, Viola-as-Cesario being no different in essence from Viola-as-Viola in *Twelfth Night*. Nor on the whole do comic characters develop. By the end of her play Viola is neither better nor worse than she was at the beginning, despite the fact that a good deal has happened to her. By the same token, Volpone is Volpone is Volpone; he is led off finally, not chastened, merely foiled, his unregeneracy and incapacity for change appropriately figured in his being confined to a hospital for "incurables."

So, too, at the end of Menander's *The Grouch,* where the confirmed misanthrope Cnemon, like his descendants Jaques in *As You Like It* and Alceste in Molière's *The Misanthrope,* sets out to achieve permanent petrifaction of character as a hermit.

It is true that remarkable character changes sometimes occur in comedy. At the end of Plautus' *The Rope,* for instance, a villainous slave-trader whose evil schemes are disastrously undermined suddenly turns all smiles and graciousness as he goes jovially off to dine with a man he has good cause to hate. But such changes are usually unconvincing. They nearly always occur at the end of a comedy where the demands of plot and the convention of the happy ending provoke an arbitrary substitution of one mask for another instead of an authentic evolution of inner impulses and convictions.

Unlike tragedy, then, comedy tends to register the impact of experience upon character quantitatively rather than qualitatively. Experience and character do not, as they do in tragedy, interpenetrate. Happenings multiply in the life of the comic character but do not modify him.

Thus comedy specializes in two-dimensional, flat, or surface characterization. The profound individuality of tragic heroes is embodied even in the titles of their plays: *Prometheus, Agamemnon, Antigone, Oedipus Tyrannos, Medea, Doctor Faustus, Hamlet, Othello, Phaedra,* to name a few. If, as a sort of index of the difference in focus, we compare these with the titles of comedies, the individual coloring of tragic titles bleaches out into a generic blankness in comedy—for example, Menander's *Double Deceiver, Hero, Hated Man, Selfish Person,* and others, Molière's *The Miser, The Intellectual Ladies,* or *The Misanthrope,* Wycherley's *The Country Wife,* Goldsmith's *The Good Natured Gentleman,* Somerset Maugham's *The Constant Wife,* and so on. It is equally suggestive that there has occurred in each period of great comedy an efflorescence of the "character" as a minor literary genre (New Comedy and the "characters" of Theophrastus, Elizabethan-Jacobean comedy and the "characters" of Joseph Hall and Sir Thomas Overbury, neoclassic French comedy and the "characters" of La Bruyère, and early eighteenth-century English comedy and the "characters" of Addison and Steele). We need to add, of course, that tragedy too has its full quota of stock characters; but the function of such characters in tragedy seems in part to provide an environment in which the tragic hero's individuality is fortified by contrast. The individuality of Hamlet, for instance, is framed by such stock types as the sententious

Polonius, the innocent maiden Ophelia, the soldier Fortinbras, the fop Osric, and the faithful friend Horatio.

There are various reasons for the presence of stock characters in comedy. For one thing, repetition is a great source of humor, the clown who gets flattened by a swinging door becoming funnier each time it happens; and repetition is the essence of the stock character. The reason, in fact, that we can type such a character in the first place is that from situation to situation he keeps repeating himself, just as from play to play he is repeated by dramatists. The complex character is unique because he registers the differences between situations and hence responds to each with stylistic appropriateness, or at least discloses a potential for varying responses. In contrast, the stock character suffers from situation-deafness: all occasions register alike to him, their differences lying outside the restricted tonal range of his mind and conduct. In Thomas Love Peacock's *Nightmare Abbey* a character called Mr. Toobad channels every situation through a filter of religious paranoia, and responds on all occasions, whatever the context, by crying in alarm, "The devil is come among us, having great wrath!" To the fop, both dining rooms and desert islands are appropriate scenes for a flourishing of fashions; and to the *miles gloriosus*, or braggart warrior, all places are substitute battlefields calling as insistently as Pavlov's bells for verbal foamings at the mouth.

By virtue of his constricted, repetitive style of mind and action, the stock character carries his own "alienation effect" which serves the comic cause. A certain emotional distance on the part of the audience seems a prerequisite for laughter, familiarity in this respect breeding not contempt but concern, as when our amusement at the stumbling drunk turns to something else when we learn that he drinks, say, out of grief for a child's death. The perpetual smile on the clown's painted face serves this distancing requirement of humor by keeping us from perceiving any real winces of pain when he takes a header. So with the stock character, whose unalterable oversimplicity, *idée fixe* mentality, and repetitious style of conduct constitute a kind of character-mask preventing us from seeing anything beneath that could lay claim to our feelings. Even a character like Falstaff, who is infinitely variable in his responses to the world and hence by no means two-dimensional in either character or physique, is given a painted smile of witty invulnerability to wear on all occasions. It is at the end of 2 *Henry IV*, when Shakespeare momentarily erases that smile and discloses the face beneath, that Falstaff becomes other than funny.

INVULNERABILITY AND COMIC DETACHMENT

The mask of invulnerability covers not merely comic characters but comedy itself, which specializes in the art of remaining unmarked by experience. If we consider the prevalence of funny stories about "The Time the Drains Plugged Up" or "Our Trip Through Paris During the Rush Hour," it is evident that humor capitalizes on trouble. Or perhaps we should say "on troubles survived," for surviving trouble or escaping potential injury seems to provide the sort of relief that in itself borders on humor. The humor of the drains or the drive through Paris, however, is not in the experience itself, when our feelings, of frustration, annoyance, dismay, are too immediately involved, but after the fact, in the retelling of the experience. Temporal distance in this case supplies the invulnerability that enables us, having survived, to laugh with a sense of detachment. But temporal distance is not available in drama, where the action is primarily in the present tense, so detachment, and the invulnerability of characters that helps produce it, must be bought in other ways. In the ramshackle world of farce, where everything from suspenders to suspension bridges collapses, where mountains disintegrate, trains collide, and human bodies reverberate like kettledrums under a constant rain of blows, characters like Laurel and Hardy or the Three Stooges are invulnerable by convention. After the first brain-addling, spine-curling, head-on smash-up has produced no more than a ripple of annoyance among the victims, we can sit back and watch them fall out second story windows, off speeding cars, and down precipices, assured that they will have only our laughter to show for it. In sophisticated comedies like *The Tempest*, the same convention is in effect, though handled differently. We quickly gather that compassionate feelings are unnecessary when Prospero's magic arches its protective rainbow over the tempests of human affairs.

In *The Tempest* we view the action over Prospero's shoulder. He is a kind of "interior dramatist," stationing the players, ordering the plot, creating with his magical "art" the comic spectacle; and through him we become conscious of Shakespeare the controlling dramatist "outside" the play, who, in fidelity to the comic form, is maneuvering everything toward desired ends. Shakespeare used many such "interior dramatists" —Oberon, Rosalind, Viola, the Duke in *Measure for Measure*. They know something the other characters are unaware of, and when they produce their knowledge everything resolves into harmony. In this, Shakespeare is only personifying within his comedies a fact of comedy in general: that the maneuvering hand of the playwright is more obvious here than in other genres. Compare, for instance, two crucial bits of action, the murder of Duncan in *Macbeth* and the assumption of a disguise by Viola in *Twelfth Night*. Shakespeare wants both actions to occur; his plots demand that they occur. But in the tragedy, he lets the action issue from the character of Macbeth. Macbeth is ambitious, therefore he kills Duncan. Viola's action, however, does not arise from her character. She does not assume a boy's disguise because, say, she is guileful, cowardly, latently homosexual, or something else. Virtually no reason is given, nor are any inferences about her character appropriate. She assumes the disguise because Shakespeare's comic plot hinges upon her doing so. In tragedy, the plot dances to the tune of the characters, in comedy the characters dance to the tune of the plot. The effect of this arbitrariness of action is to keep the audience emotionally removed from the dramatic experience, wary of investing affective capital in events that may turn inside out in an instant.

From another angle, comedy's maneuvering us into a state of emotional detachment can be seen as an enabling of intellectual engagement. Horace Walpole said that life is a tragedy to the man who feels, a comedy to the man who thinks. That is oversimple, but it is true that as spectators of tragedy we tend to register experience through the consciousness of the tragic hero, inevitably absorbing some of the emotional impact of his ordeal, whereas in comedy we are spared the pain of vicarious injuries and forego the comforts of uncritical involvement because we have been led away from individual perspectives to an intellectual overview analogous to that of the playwright. From that altitude, we look down upon a world of mortal foolishness and redeeming vitality from which our own world, we begin uneasily to realize, is separated only by the thin line of artistic illusion.

ELLEN DOUGLASS LEYBURN

Comedy and Tragedy Transposed

The remark of Socrates at the end of the *Symposium* that the genius of tragedy and comedy are the same has usually been taken as a joking paradox meant to round off gaily a night of talking and drinking. Yet its measure of truth has haunted responses to the supreme achievements in drama. The heightening of the tragedy of Lear by the Fool, "who labours to outjest his heart-struck injuries," on the one hand, and the deepening of the comedy of *Le Misanthrope* through the suffering of Alceste, on the other, are enough to make us pause before dismissing the remark of Socrates. Plato's jest, if indeed it be jest, seems nearer to the truth of what we find in postclassical drama than does Aristotle's strict separation of tragedy and comedy.

Nevertheless, we have had the feeling until recently that when we used the terms, we knew at least vaguely what they meant and could be understood by others when we used them to distinguish kinds of drama which were distinct even when they appeared in the same play. The assumption that tragedy is one dramatic mode and comedy another has been the foundation of all the varied and elaborate structures of definition of both genres. And the same assumption persists in the proliferation of analyses of the death of tragedy which have followed Joseph Wood Krutch's lament over the paralysis of tragic power in modern man in his much-quoted chapter called "The Tragic Fallacy," which appeared as long ago as the Twenties and fits the whole thesis of his book *The Modern Temper*. The very force of Krutch's indictment grows from his knowing so clearly what he thinks the demands of tragedy are and wherein modern drama is deficient. This clarity of conviction about the nature of tragedy is equally marked in more recent

From *The Yale Review*, Vol. LIII, no. 4. Copyright 1964 by Yale University. Reprinted by permission of the publisher.

treatments of the same theme, such as William Van O'Connor's *Climates of Tragedy,* which appeared during the Second World War, and George Steiner's *The Death of Tragedy,* which has appeared still more recently. The same assurance marks criticism of comedy. However varied their definitions, the critics resemble each other in seeming to know what it is they are defining.

What I should like to suggest is that in modern drama comedy has so far invaded tragedy—and tragedy, comedy—that the terms have lost their old distinctness. Whereas comedy has for centuries displayed man's weakness, this now seems to be the function of tragedy—or of drama which is intended to arouse the emotions commonly called tragic, whatever new name we try to find for the plays of Tennessee Williams or Arthur Miller or John Osborne. Whereas tragedy has in earlier eras looked at man in "boundary situations," it is now the comedies of Beckett and Ionesco which show man in extremity; and the equally terrifying plays of Pinter and Duerrenmatt make use of grotesque comedy to reveal the precariousness of life and the condition of man confronted with pervasive evil. Duerrenmatt's note on *The Visit* ends: "*The Visit of the Old Lady* is a wicked play, yet for this very reason it must not be presented wickedly, but most humanely, with sadness, not with anger, but also with humor, for nothing harms this comedy—which ends tragically—more than brutal seriousness." Tragedy and comedy seem to have shifted not only in perspective and in substance, but also in effect. Our responses are almost the reverse of what used to be the conventional attitudes to tragedy and comedy. We resist tragic identi- fication with the miserable characters of most of our serious drama and look at them with the detachment which has hitherto seemed appro- priate to critical comedy. Conversely, the comedies that end tragically compel us into a strange and unwilling empathy rather than into comic judgment: in the seemingly odd characters we recognize our most familiar selves, and in their fantastic plights, the very situations in which we are involved.

The dramatists of the absurd are clearly conscious of this interpene- tration of tragedy and comedy and deliberately exploit its disturbing imaginative effect. Ionesco makes the illuminating statement: "Person- ally, I have never understood the distinctions that are made between the comic and the tragic. Since the comic is the intuition of the absurd, it seems to me more hopeless than the tragic. . . . The comic offers no escape . . . the comical is tragic, and the tragedy of man, derisory." Ionesco's assertion is highly characteristic not just of his own attitude, repeatedly expressed in comments on his plays and manifested in the plays themselves, but also of the mood of much of the drama of the absurd besides his own. The writers of serious plays, on the contrary, seem unaware of the intrusion of comic elements into their pathetic worlds. They solemnly present their small characters and seem to demand for them the large emotional response aroused by tragedy. This unawareness confuses the artistic effect of their plays; but it is in itself an impressive demonstration of the pervasiveness of the interpenetration of tragedy and comedy which marks the drama of our time. The shifts in the nature of both tragedy and comedy reflect the convulsion of society and of man's sense of himself which characterizes the world which the dramatists inhabit.

Arthur Miller and Tennessee Williams are perhaps the most striking examples of contemporary dramatists who consider themselves writers of tragedies and yet have produced plays in which the themes and characters resemble those of earlier critical comedy. There are almost as many contradictions as theories among definitions of tragedy; but two criteria which are consistently used by critics with otherwise extremely diverse theories are that tragedy should have a hero with stature enough to make his suffering significant and that its course of action should produce enlightenment. Neither of these criteria is fulfilled, I think, by the plays of Williams and Miller. The protagonists arouse pity, but little admiration and little of the identification necessary for tragic terror; and in the rhythm of the plays the emphasis is largely on passion rather than on purpose and perception. On the other hand, both dramatists focus their plays on the very kind of human weakness which has hitherto been the subject of critical or realistic comedy. The self-deception of their leading characters is of the sort which earlier dramatists have held up to ridicule. It is the anomaly of a pathetic view of characters formerly seen as objects of satire which makes the difficulty for the traditionalist in responding to such plays according to the authors' intentions. The contradictory feelings which the characters evoke seem to me more important than their sheer inadequacy as tragic heroes so much stressed by Krutch and his followers. The discrepancy between expectation and event for such characters lacks the kind of irony which has been thought of as tragic; and of enlightenment there is little or none. *Death of a Salesman* and *A Streetcar Named Desire*, each the most successful play of its author, well illustrate all of these points.

It was in answer to the criticism of Willy Loman as a tragic hero that Miller wrote "Tragedy and the Common Man" to serve as introduction to a Viking Press edition of *Death of a Salesman*. His contention is that "the common man is as apt a subject for tragedy in its highest sense as kings were," a judgment with which in our day few would quarrel. It is not Willy's low station, but his low intelligence (or if intelligence seems too narrow a word, his lack of sheer force of being) which keeps his woes from affecting us as do those of Orestes, Hamlet, Medea, and Macbeth—the tragic figures of the past whom Miller cites. "Ineffectual" is the word which seems to characterize Willy both as salesman and as father. His constant need of bolstering from both Linda and Charley and his pitiful efforts to win the respect of Biff in order to feed his own self-esteem make it strange for Miller to say in reference to him that "the tragic hero is intent upon claiming his whole due as a personality," though Willy's personality is so small that the comment has a kind of unintentional irony. Even apart from the hallucinated scenes with Ben and the suggestions of actual insanity, Willy's characteristic state is bewilderment. He enters the play puzzled by his fruitless effort to reach his territory, and he leaves it persuading himself that Biff will be "magnificent . . . with twenty thousand dollars in his pocket." The lack of integrity which has made him teach Biff to steal seems to be the result of inability to distinguish truth from falsehood rather than of deliberate dishonesty. Biff, who for all his limitations comes much nearer to self-realization than his father does, tries to open Willy's eyes: "The man don't know who we are! The man is gonna know! (*To Willy*) We never told the truth for ten minutes in this house! . . . Pop! I'm a dime a dozen, and so are you!" But Biff's tears simply send Willy into a new "phony dream"; and the son's comment at his father's grave is: "Charley, the man didn't know who he was." This hardly fits Miller's conception of tragedy as "a man's total compulsion to evaluate himself justly." Rather, Willy's self-deception, although Miller treats it so as to win compassion, is of exactly the sort which has regularly marked the comic figure. Even his physical defects of fatness and flabbiness which make the salesmen laugh at him and call him "walrus" and his loudmouthed over-heartiness of manner identify him with a long line of aging comic butts who have tried to convince an unbelieving world and themselves that they are "well liked." It is worth notice in passing that *A View from the Bridge* again depicts a man past middle age who has no power to "evaluate himself justly" and that in the later play sexual jealousy over a young girl brings the pathetic protagonist even nearer to one of the stereotypes of comedy.

The counterpart to the amorous old fool in traditional comedy has been the woman who tries to trade upon fading sexual attractiveness; and it is this formula which Willliams transmutes into the heartrending character of Blanche DuBois. Like Willy, she seeks and is given bolstering from the other characters; and Stella, like Linda in *Salesman,* not only gives the needed compliments but urges the other characters to tell Blanche how pretty her finery is and how fresh and attractive she looks. But Williams is more willing than Miller is to let harsh judgment of his weakling have expression in the play. Willy hears the voice of reality largely through the kindly tones of Charley, who does tell him to grow up, but endures his insults and gives him money under the fiction of weekly loans, whereas Blanche has to listen to the taunts of Stella's husband, whom she regards as "subhuman." Miller depends primarily on Willy's own self-revelation to show the audience the discrepancies between Willy as he is and Willy as he thinks he is. Williams, in contrast, uses the harsh judgment of Stanley not only to add to Blanche's misery, but also to enlighten the audience about her "lies and conceit and tricks." The conflict between the dream and the grim reality is thus accentuated through the hostility of the character who reveals the ugly truth. By giving Blanche a personal antagonist when she is already incapable of coping with her inner plight and has "run for protection . . . from under one leaky roof—to another leaky roof—because it was storm—all storm, and [she] was—caught in the center," Williams intensifies her woe and provides the bitter irony of her seeking shelter under the roof of her sharpest critic. At the same time, the audience is made to see her partly through Stanley's eyes. He becomes a kind of satiric chorus within the play, which heightens the anomaly of our being asked to respond with tragic emotions to so wretched a figure as Blanche. But Stanley is far more than simply an interpreter. It is he who, through his cruel disillusioning of Mitch, makes Blanche lose what tenuous hold on reality she has had and brings about her final desolate departure to the mental hospital, still trying to enact the part of the gracious lady, depending on "the kindness of strangers."

Both of these plays are full of irony, even of the irony of fate; but we miss the grandeur which pits the tragic hero against his fate and leads to tragic irony. There is a strong element of the ludicrous which makes the plights of both Willy and Blanche more painful. Fate, in the form of the social order, does seem to have played a cruel joke on the simple-minded and well-meaning Willy Loman in giving him the false goals of success through personality and of getting away with whatever can be filched. In his refusal to be enlightened by Biff, he does seem to go off to his useless suicide as the dupe of a power he cannot combat. Blanche is equally the victim of a hideous practical joke. She is ridiculous in her effort to charm the naïve Mitch with her pretense of innocence. And in her case, the fate which finally tricks her takes the very palpable form of Stanley, though the state to which she has been reduced before the play begins can be called a joke played on her by fate in the form of the social order, just as society has largely represented fate for Willy. But both are too weak to achieve a tragic protest. Since they are simply victims, the irony leaves us uncomfortable at the advantage taken of weakness rather than filled with awe at heroic man confronting mysterious forces within him and without. The ambivalence of the response to both plays comes from the fact that the protagonists are self-deluded enough to seem appropriate objects of mockery; but they are too miserable and too sympathetically viewed by their creators to allow the audience to feel as comic the irony in what happens to them. Consequently, the plays present a seemingly double vision on the part of the playwrights and have a disconcertingly mixed effect.

This kind of apparently unintentional doubleness marks a great number of contemporary plays. It would be easy to link many other soberly treated characters, such as the disagreeable ones of John Osborne or the sentimentalized ones of William Inge, with the traditional figures of critical comedy. The plays of Williams and Miller seem more impressive demonstrations of the penetration of serious drama by comic types only because Williams and Miller seem to make larger tragic claims.

Since the writers of absurd comedy are highly conscious of the doubleness of their plays and use it with full artistic awareness and often with great artistic skill, their plays are much more profoundly disturbing than are those of the humorless writers of serious plays with weak heroes. The contradictions of pain and amusement in the best comedies of the absurd are evoked with clear intention and the most deliberate finesse. Ionesco is the playwright who has been most explicit about his conception of the theatre as the mirror of the contradictions of life: "I try to project on the stage my inner conflict (incomprehensible to myself) telling myself always that, the microcosm being the image of the macrocosm, it can be that this interior world, broken, disarticulated, is in some way the mirror or the symbol of universal contradictions." It is the absurdity, the tragic comedy, of life itself of which these dramatists seek to make their plays the image. The surface effect of most of their plays is comic; but the vision which informs it is largely tragic. Martin Esslin in *The Theatre of the Absurd* quotes Pinter's comment:

"The point about tragedy is that it is *no longer* funny." The writers of the "funny" plays of our time are concerned with the same ultimate questions about man's identity and his destiny which in earlier periods have led to the writing of tragedy. One after another of the plays of Beckett and Ionesco, of Pinter and Duerrenmatt, show man in extremity and posing ultimate questions about his very existence: who he is, why he lives, and why he suffers. Yet these plays which reach no comic resolution and raise ultimate rather than temporal questions are clearly comic in the sense of being outrageously funny. The farcical element in the dramaturgy, with its dependence on mime and music-hall slapstick devices, has been much discussed. My concern here is not with the arts the playwrights use to evoke laughter; but with the fact that the plays do evoke it and use it exactly to sharpen the terror. Comedy is an essential part of the situations presented and makes their desperateness more real. The seemingly meaningless repetitions of the dialogue—as skillful a use of language as the most florid passages in heroic drama, the clowning and dependence on farcical gesture, the monopolizing of the stage by objects, bear an organic relation to the absurd situations and are the very means by which the dramatists produce the feeling (to quote Ionesco again) that "in a space without space, all seems to be volatilized, all is *menaced* [my italics] . . . by an imminent, silent engulfment, in I know not what abyss, beyond day and beyond night." The plays as wholes present comic incongruity raised to tragic proportions and effecting in the audience tragic involvement and the tragic feelings of pity and terror. Because of the intense reality of these dramas and because they do raise more fundamental questions, the mixture of feelings they produce is nearer to the old tragic emotion than that of contemporary plays of solely tragic intention. Again, two very familiar plays offer proof of all the points suggested. *Waiting for Godot* and *The Chairs* are both funny and terrible.

The two tramps in Beckett's play are preoccupied with the question which confronts all men and has lately been asked more insistently perhaps than ever before: why live at all? Indeed, their recurrent attempts at suicide make one of the unifying repetitions in the circular motion of the play, if their painfully funny frustrations of action can be called motion. They debate the question of *The Myth of Sisyphus* and seem to stumble upon a measure of Camus's answer. For if they do not decide to live and protest, their very persistence in waiting constitutes a kind of protest. They differ from Camus, of course, in not **being sure** that Godot will *not* come in spite of their continually baffled hopes. This refusal quite to accept the logic of their own experience is part of what makes us enter into their situation with the kind of identification we accord to tragic characters. It does not require the constant reminders Beckett puts into their mouths that "We are all humanity," to make us recognize ourselves in their already battered state and in the beatings and subjection to physical infirmity within the play. We are drawn to them not just by their clowning and by our amusement at the brisk turns of stichomythia with which they try to amuse themselves. They are irresistibly appealing in their uneasy need of each other, in their very endurance of what we must endure. And we give them the kind of empathy which we withhold from Willy Loman and Blanche DuBois.

The old couple in *The Chairs* ask the still more elementary question of who we are. They show man not just at the limits of his being as man, but beyond identity; and yet in their need to affirm their identity, to leave some message, they too compel us to ally ourselves with them. The frenzy of their attempts to establish connection with the "real" invisible characters and their being crowded apart even from each other by the oppressive multiplication of chairs make vivid their inability to exist even before their suicide in the dank waters that surround their island. Their own progressive loss of the power of articulate speech and the inane babblings of the dumb orator whom they leave as their surrogate are the audible counterpart of the visual image. The laughter which Ionesco evokes by the farcical movement and by the ridiculous echoing "orphan-dworfan" speech, which finally becomes the "Arf . . . arf . . . arf" of helpless barking, makes the tragic effect much deeper than could a direct appeal to the pity and terror in which the search for identity involves us.

The shifting of ground in the realms of tragedy and comedy poses for contemporary critics an awkward problem of terminology. The old phrases like "mixed drama" and "tragicomedy," which sufficed to describe the combination in one play of known and recognizable modes, have little relevance to the strange new genres which seem to be evolving. Furthermore, while the serious plays with weak characters and the comic plays which move us tragically seem to be opposite and complementary parts of the same phenomenon, the dramatic rendering of the dislocation of our times, they are so different in substance and in effect that no one term could conceivably embrace both. The rather cumbersome phrase "Theatre of the Absurd," to which Esslin's book with that title has given wider currency, is useful for the funny plays of tragic import; *The Dark Comedy,* the title of the valuable study by J. L. Styan, which has appeared since this essay was first written, supplies another usable designation; but no new term seems to have been invented for the corresponding and opposite kind of plays which treat ridiculous characters pathetically. As we grope toward nomenclature and definition (a groping perhaps not unrelated to the struggles of Ionesco's characters with language) we come back broodingly to Plato's joke at the end of the *Symposium:* "the chief thing which he remembered was Socrates compelling the other two to acknowledge that the genius of comedy was the same with that of tragedy, and that the true artist in tragedy was an artist in comedy also. To this they were constrained to assent, being drowsy, and not quite following the argument."

MARTIN ESSLIN

The Theatre of the Absurd

The plays of Samuel Beckett, Arthur Adamov, and Eugène Ionesco have been performed with astonishing success in France, Germany, Scandinavia, and the English-speaking countries. This reception is all the more puzzling when one considers that the audiences concerned were amused by and applauded these plays fully aware that they could not understand what they meant or what their authors were driving at.

At first sight these plays do, indeed, confront their public with a bewildering experience, a veritable barrage of wildly irrational, often nonsensical goings-on that seem to go counter to all accepted standards of stage convention. In these plays, some of which are labeled "anti-plays," neither the time nor the place of the action are ever clearly stated. (At the beginning of Ionesco's *The Bald Soprano* the clock strikes seventeen.) The characters hardly have any individuality and often even lack a name; moreover, halfway through the action they tend to change their nature completely. Pozzo and Lucky in Beckett's *Waiting for Godot,* for example, appear as master and slave at one moment only to return after a while with their respective positions mysteriously reversed. The laws of probability as well as those of physics are suspended when we meet young ladies with two or even three noses (Ionesco's *Jack or the Submission*), or a corpse that has been hidden in the next room that suddenly begins to grow to monstrous size until a giant foot crashes through the door onto the stage (Ionesco's *Amédée*). As a result, it is often unclear whether the action is meant to represent a dream world of nightmares or real happenings. Within the same scene the action may switch from the nightmarish poetry of high emotions to pure knock-about farce or cabaret, and above all, the dialogue tends to get out of hand so that at times the words

From *Tulane Drama Review,* IV (May 1960), copyright © 1960 by *The Drama Review*. Reprinted by permission of the author and *The Drama Review*.

seem to go counter to the actions of the characters on the stage, to degenerate into lists of words and phrases from a dictionary or traveler's conversation book, or to get bogged down in endless repetitions like a phonograph record stuck in one groove. Only in this kind of demented world can strangers meet and discover, after a long and polite conversation and close cross-questioning, that, to their immense surprise, they must be man and wife as they are living on the same street, in the same house, apartment, room, and bed (Ionesco's *The Bald Soprano*). Only here can the whole life of a group of characters revolve around the passionate discussion of the aesthetics and economics of pinball machines (Adamov's *Ping-Pong*). Above all, everything that happens seems to be beyond rational motivation, happening at random or through the demented caprice of an unaccountable idiot fate. Yet, these wildly extravagant tragic farces and farcical tragedies, although they have suffered their share of protests and scandals, do arouse interest and are received with laughter and thoughtful respect. What is the explanation for this curious phenomenon?

The most obvious, but perhaps too facile answer that suggests itself is that these plays are prime examples of "pure theatre." They are living proof that the magic of the stage can persist even outside, and divorced from, any framework of conceptual rationality. They prove that exits and entrances, light and shadow, contrasts in costume, voice, gait and behavior, pratfalls and embraces, all the manifold mechanical interactions of human puppets in groupings that suggest tension, conflict, or the relaxation of tensions, can arouse laughter or gloom and conjure up an atmosphere of poetry even if devoid of logical motivation and unrelated to recognizable human characters, emotions, and objectives.

But this is only a partial explanation. While the elements of "pure theatre" and abstract stagecraft are certainly at work in the plays concerned, they also have a much more substantial content and meaning. Not only *do* all these plays make sense, though perhaps not obvious or conventional sense, they also give expression to some of the basic issues and problems of our age, in a uniquely efficient and meaningful manner, so that they meet some of the deepest needs and unexpressed yearnings of their audience.

The three dramatists that have been grouped together here would probably most energetically deny that they form anything like a school or movement. Each of them, in fact, has his own roots and sources, his own very personal approach to both form and subject matter. Yet they also clearly have a good deal in common. This common denominator that characterizes their works might well be described as the element of *the absurd*. "Est absurde ce qui n'a pas de but . . ." ("Absurd is that which has no purpose, or goal, or objective"), the definition given by Ionesco in a note on Kafka,[1] certainly applies to the plays of Beckett and Ionesco as well as those of Arthur Adamov up to his latest play, *Paolo Paoli*, when he returned to a more traditional form of social drama.

Each of these writers, however, has his own special type of absurdity: in Beckett it is melancholic, colored by a feeling of futility born from the disillusionment of old age and chronic hopelessness; Adamov's is more active, aggressive, earthy, and tinged with social and political overtones; while Ionesco's absurdity has its own fantastic knock-about flavor of tragical clowning. But they all share the same deep sense of human isolation and of the irremediable character of the human condition.

As Arthur Adamov put it in describing how he came to write his first play, *La Parodie* (1947):

> I began to discover stage scenes in the most common-place everyday events. [One day I saw] a blind man begging; two girls went by without seeing him, singing: "I closed my eyes; it was marvelous!" This gave me the idea of showing on stage, as crudely and as visibly as possible, the loneliness of man, the absence of communication among human beings.[2]

Looking back at his earliest effort (which he now regards as unsuccessful) Adamov defines his basic idea in it, and a number of subsequent plays, as the idea "that the destinies of all human beings are of equal futility, that the refusal to live (of the character called N.) and the joyful acceptance of life (by the employee) both lead, by the same path, to inevitable failure, total destruction." [3] It is the same futility and pointlessness of human effort, the same impossibility of human communication which Ionesco expresses in ever new and ingenious variations. The two old people making conversation with the empty air and living in the expectation of an orator who is to pronounce profound truths about life, but turns out to be deaf and dumb (*The Chairs*), are as sardonically cruel a symbol of this fundamentally tragic view of human existence as Jack (*Jack or the Submission*), who stubbornly resists the concerted urgings of his entire family to subscribe to the most sacred principle of his clan—which, when his resistance finally yields to their entreaties, turns out to be the profound truth: "I love potatoes with bacon" ("J'adore les pommes de terre au lard").

The Theatre of the Absurd shows the world as an incomprehensible place. The spectators see the happenings on the stage entirely from the outside, without ever understanding the full meaning of these strange patterns of events, as newly arrived visitors might watch life in a country of which they have not yet mastered the language.[4] The confrontation of the audience with characters and happenings which they are not quite able to comprehend makes it impossible for them to share the aspirations and emotions depicted in the play. Brecht's famous "Verfremdungseffekt" (alienation effect), the inhibition of any identification between spectator and actor, which Brecht could never successfully achieve in his own highly rational theatre, really comes into its own in the Theatre of the Absurd. It is impossible to identify oneself with characters one does not understand or whose motives remain a closed book, and so the distance between the public and the happenings on the stage can be maintained. Emotional identification with the characters is replaced by a puzzled, critical attention. For while the happenings on the stage are absurd, they yet remain recognizable as somehow related to real life with *its* absurdity, so that eventually the spectators are brought face to face with the irrational side of their existence. Thus, the absurd and fantastic goings-on of the Theatre of the Absurd will, in the end, be found to reveal the irrationality of the human condition and the illusion of what we thought was its apparent logical structure.

If the dialogue in these plays consists of meaningless clichés and the mechanical, circular repetition of stereotyped phrases—how many meaningless clichés and stereotyped phrases do we use in our day-to-day conversation? If the characters change their personality halfway through the action, how consistent and truly integrated are the people we meet in our real life? And if people in these plays appear as mere marionettes, helpless puppets without any will of their own, passively at the mercy of blind fate and meaningless circumstance, do we, in fact, in our overorganized world, still possess any genuine initiative or power to decide our own destiny? The spectators of the Theatre of the Absurd are thus confronted with a grotesquely heightened picture of their own world: a world without faith, meaning, and genuine freedom of will. In this sense, the Theatre of the Absurd is the true theatre of our time.

The theatre of most previous epochs reflected an accepted moral order, a world whose aims and objectives were clearly present to the minds of all its public, whether it was the audience of the medieval mystery plays with their solidly accepted faith in the Christian world order or the audience of the drama of Ibsen, Shaw, or Hauptmann with their unquestioned belief in evolution and progress. To such audiences, right and wrong were never in doubt, nor did they question the then accepted goals of human endeavor. Our own time, at least in the Western world, wholly lacks such a generally accepted and completely integrated world picture. The decline of religious faith, the destruction of the belief in automatic social and biological progress, the discovery of vast areas or irrational and unconscious forces within the human psyche, the loss of a sense of control over rational human development in an age of totalitarianism and weapons of mass destruction, have all contributed to the erosion of the basis for a dramatic convention in which the action proceeds within a fixed and self-evident framework of generally accepted values. Faced with the vacuum left by the destruction of a universally accepted and unified set of beliefs, most serious playwrights have felt the need to fit their work into the frame of values and objectives expressed in one of the contemporary ideologies: Marxism, psychoanalysis, aestheticism, or nature worship. But these, in the eyes of a writer like Adamov, are nothing but superficial rationalizations which try to hide the depth of man's predicament, his loneliness and his anxiety. Or, as Ionesco puts it:

> As far as I am concerned, I believe sincerely in the poverty of the poor, I deplore it; it is real; it can become a subject for the theatre; I also believe in the anxieties and serious troubles the rich may suffer from; but it is neither in the misery of the former nor in the melancholia of the latter, that I, for one, find my dramatic subject matter. Theatre is for me the outward projection onto the stage of an inner world; it is in my dreams, in my anxieties, in my obscure desires, in my internal contradictions that I, for one, reserve for myself the right of finding my dramatic subject matter. As I am not alone in the world, as each of us, in the depth of his being, is at the same time part and parcel of all others, my dreams, my desires, my anxieties, my obsessions do not belong to me alone. They form part of an ancestral heritage, a very ancient storehouse which is a portion of the common property of all mankind.

> It is this, which, transcending their outward diversity, reunites
> all human beings and constitutes our profound common patri-
> mony, the universal language. . . .[5]

In other words, the commonly acceptable framework of beliefs and
values of former epochs which has now been shattered is to be replaced
by the community of dreams and desires of a collective unconscious.
And, to quote Ionesco again:

> . . . the new dramatist is one . . . who tries to link up
> with what is most ancient: new language and subject matter in
> a dramatic structure which aims at being clearer, more stripped
> of inessentials and more purely theatrical; the rejection of
> traditionalism to rediscover tradition; a synthesis of knowledge
> and invention, of the real and imaginary, of the particular and
> the universal, or as they say now, of the individual and the
> collective . . . By expressing my deepest obsessions, I express
> my deepest humanity. I become one with all others, sponta-
> neously, over and above all the barriers of caste and different
> psychologies. I express my solitude and become one with all
> other solitudes. . . .[6]

What is the tradition with which the Theatre of the Absurd—at first
sight the most revolutionary and radically new movement—is trying to
link itself? It is in fact a very ancient and a very rich tradition, nourished
from many and varied sources: the verbal exuberance and extravagant
inventions of Rabelais, the age-old clowning of the Roman mimes and
the Italian *Commedia dell'Arte*, the knock-about humor of circus clowns
like Grock; the wild, archetypal symbolism of English nonsense verse,
the baroque horror of Jacobean dramatists like Webster or Tourneur, the
harsh, incisive and often brutal tones of the German drama of Grabbe,
Büchner, Kleist, and Wedekind with its delirious language and grotesque inventiveness; and the Nordic paranoia of the dreams and per-
secution fantasies of Strindberg.

All these streams, however, first came together and crystallized in
the more direct ancestors of the present Theatre of the Absurd. Of these,
undoubtedly the first and foremost is Alfred Jarry (1873–1907), the
creator of *Ubu Roi*, the first play which clearly belongs in the category
of the Theatre of the Absurd. *Ubu Roi*, first performed in Paris on December 10, 1896, is a Rabelaisian nonsense drama about the fantastic

adventures of a fat, cowardly, and brutal figure, *le père* Ubu, who makes himself King of Poland, fights a series of Falstaffian battles, and is finally routed. As if to challenge all accepted codes of propriety and thus to open a new era of irreverence, the play opens with the defiant expletive, *"Merde!"* which immediately provoked a scandal. This, of course, was what Jarry had intended. *Ubu*, in its rollicking Rabelaisian parody of a Shakespearean history play, was meant to confront the Parisian bourgeois with a monstrous portrait of his own greed, selfishness, and philistinism: "As the curtain went up I wanted to confront the public with a theatre in which, as in the magic mirror . . . of the fairy tales . . . the vicious man sees his reflection with bulls' horns and the body of a dragon, the projections of his viciousness. . . ." [7] But Ubu is more than a mere monstrous exaggeration of the selfishness and crude sensuality of the French bourgeois. He is at the same time the personification of the grossness of human nature, an enormous belly walking on two legs. That is why Jarry put him on the stage as a monstrous potbellied figure in a highly stylized costume and mask—a mythical, archetypal externalization of human instincts of the lowest kind. Thus, Ubu, the false king of Poland, pretended doctor of the pseudoscience of Pataphysics, clearly anticipates one of the main characteristics of the Theatre of the Absurd, its tendency to externalize and project outwards what is happening in the deeper recesses of the mind. Examples of this tendency are: the disembodied voices of "monitors" shouting commands at the hero of Adamov's *La Grande et la Petite Manoeuvre* which concretizes his neurotic compulsions; the mutilated trunks of the parents in Beckett's *Endgame* emerging from ashcans— the ashcans of the main character's subconscious to which he has banished his past and his conscience; or the proliferations of fungi that invade the married couple's apartment in Ionesco's *Amédée* and express the rottenness and decay of their relationship. All these psychological factors are not only projected outwards, they are also, as in Jarry's *Ubu Roi*, grotesquely magnified and exaggerated. This scornful rejection of all subtleties is a reaction against the supposed *finesse* of the psychology of the naturalistic theatre in which everything was to be inferred between the lines. The Theatre of the Absurd, from Jarry onwards, stands for explicitness as against implicit psychology, and in this resembles the highly explicit theatre of the Expressionists or the political theatre of Piscator or Brecht.

To be larger and more real than life was also the aim of Guillaume Apollinaire (1880–1918), the great poet who was one of the seminal forces in the rise of Cubism and who had close personal and artistic links with Jarry. If Apollinaire labeled his play *Les Mamelles de Tiresias* a *"drame surrealiste,"* he did not intend that term, of which he was one of the earliest users, in the sense in which it later became famous. He wanted it to describe a play in which everything was *larger than life,* for he believed in an art which was to be "modern, simple, rapid, with the shortcuts and enlargements that are needed to shock the spectator." [8] In the prologue to *Les Mamelles de Tiresias,* a grotesque pamphlet purportedly advocating an immense rise in the French birthrate, Apollinaire makes the Director of the Company of Actors who perform the play, define his ideas:

> For the theatre should not be an imitation of reality
> It is right that the dramatist should use
> All the illusions at his disposal . . .
> It is right that he should let crowds speak, or inanimate objects
> If he so pleases
> And that he no longer has to reckon
> With time and space
> His universe is the play
> Within which he is God the Creator
> Who disposes at will
> Of sounds gestures movements masses colors
> Not merely in order
> To photograph what is called a slice of life
> But to bring forth life itself and all its truth . . .

Accordingly, in *Les Mamelles de Tiresias* the whole population of Zanzibar, where the scene is laid, is represented by a single actor; and the heroine, Thérèse, changes herself into a man by letting her breasts float upwards like a pair of toy balloons. Although *Les Mamelles de Tiresias* was not a surrealist work in the strictest sense of the term, it clearly foreshadowed the ideas of the movement led by André Breton. Surrealism in that narrower, technical sense found little expression in the theatre. But Antonin Artaud (1896–1948), another major influence in the development of the Theatre of the Absurd, did at one time belong to the Surrealist group, although his main activity in the theatre took place after he had broken with Breton. Artaud was one of the most unhappy men of genius of his age, an artist consumed by the most intense passions; poet, actor, director, designer, immensely fertile and original in his inventions and ideas, yet always living on the borders of sanity and never able to realize his ambitions, plans, and projects.

Artaud, who had been an actor in Charles Dullin's company at the Atelier, began his venture into the realm of experimental theatre in a series of productions characteristically sailing under the label *Théâtre Alfred Jarry* (1927–29). But his theories of a new and revolutionary theatre only crystallized after he had been deeply stirred by a performance of Balinese dancers at the Colonial Exhibition of 1941. He formulated his ideas in a series of impassioned manifestoes later collected in the volume *The Theatre and Its Double* (1938), which continues to exercise an important influence on the contemporary French theatre. Artaud named the theatre of his dreams *Théâtre de la Cruauté,* a theatre of cruelty, which he said, "means a theatre difficult and cruel above all for myself." "Everything that is really active is cruelty. It is around this idea of action carried to the extreme that the theatre must renew itself." Here too the idea of action larger and more real than life is the dominant theme. "Every performance will contain a physical and objective element that will be felt by all. Cries, Wails, Apparitions, Surprises, *Coups de Théâtre* of all kinds, the magical beauty of costumes inspired by the model of certain rituals. . . ." The language of the drama must also undergo a change: "It is not a matter of suppressing articulate speech but of giving to the words something like the importance they have in dreams." In Artaud's new theatre "not only the obverse side of man will appear but also the reverse side of the coin: the reality of imagination and of dreams will here be seen on an equal footing with everyday life."

Artaud's only attempt at putting these theories to the test on the stage took place on May 6, 1935, at the Folies-Wagram. Artaud had made his own adaptation ("after Shelley and Stendhal") of the story of the Cenci, that sombre Renaissance story of incest and patricide. It was in many ways a beautiful and memorable performance, but full of imperfections and a financial disaster which marked the beginning of Artaud's eventual descent into despair, insanity, and abject poverty. Jean-Louis Barrault had some small part in this venture and Roger Blin, the actor and director who later played an important part in bringing Adamov, Beckett, and Ionesco to the stage, appeared in the small role of one of the hired assassins.

Jean-Louis Barrault, one of the most creative figures in the theatre of our time, was in turn, responsible for another venture which played an important part in the development of the Theatre of the Absurd. He staged André Gide's adaptation of Franz Kafka's novel, *The Trial,* in 1947 and played the part of the hero K. himself. Undoubtedly this performance which brought the dreamworld of Kafka to a triumphant unfolding on the stage and demonstrated the effectiveness of this particular brand of fantasy in practical theatrical terms exercised a profound influence on the practitioners of the new movement. For here, too, they saw the externalization of mental processes, the acting out of nightmarish dreams by schematized figures in a world of torment and absurdity.

The dream element in the Theatre of the Absurd can also be traced, in the case of Adamov, to Strindberg, acknowledged by him as his inspiration at the time when he began to think of writing for the theatre. This is the Strindberg of *The Ghost Sonata, The Dream Play* and of *To Damascus.* (Adamov is the author of an excellent brief monograph on Strindberg.)

But if Jarry, Artaud, Kafka, and Strindberg can be regarded as the decisive influences in the development of the Theatre of the Absurd, there is another giant of European literature that must not be omitted from the list—James Joyce, for whom Beckett at one time is supposed to have acted as helper and secretary. Not only is the Nightgown episode of *Ulysses* one of the earliest examples of the Theatre of the Absurd—with its exuberant mingling of the real and the nightmarish, its wild fantasies and externalizations of subconscious yearnings and fears, but Joyce's experimentation with language, his attempt to smash the limitations of conventional vocabulary and syntax has probably exercised an even more powerful impact on all the writers concerned.

It is in its attitude to language that the Theatre of the Absurd is most revolutionary. It deliberately attempts to renew the language of drama and to expose the barrenness of conventional stage dialogue. Ionesco once described how he came to write his first play. (Cf. his "The Tragedy of Language," *TDR,* Spring, 1960.) He had decided to take English lessons and began to study at the Berlitz school. When he read and repeated the sentences in his phrase book, those petrified corpses of once living speech, he was suddenly overcome by their tragic quality. From them he composed his first play, *The Bald Soprano.* The absurdity of its dialogue and its fantastic quality springs directly from its basic ordinariness. It exposes the emptiness of sterotyped language; "what is sometimes labeled the absurd," Ionesco says, "is only the denunciation of the ridiculous nature of a language which is empty of substance, made up of clichés and slogans. . . ." [9] Such a language has atrophied;

it has ceased to be the expression of anything alive or vital and has been degraded into a mere conventional token of human intercourse, a mask for genuine meaning and emotion. That is why so often in the Theatre of the Absurd the dialogue becomes divorced from the real happenings in the play and is even put into direct contradiction with the action. The Professor and the Pupil in Ionesco's *The Lesson* "seem" to be going through a repetition of conventional school book phrases, but behind this smoke screen of language the *real* action of the play pursues an entirely different course with the Professor, vampire-like, draining the vitality from the young girl up to the final moment when he plunges his knife into her body. In Beckett's *Waiting for Godot* Lucky's much vaunted philosophical wisdom is revealed to be a flood of completely meaningless gibberish that vaguely resembles the language of philosophical argument. And in Adamov's remarkable play, *Ping-Pong,* a good deal of the dramatic power lies in the contrapuntal contrast between the triviality of the theme—the improvement of pinball machines —and the almost religious fervor with which it is discussed. Here, in order to bring out the full meaning of the play, the actors have to act *against* the dialogue rather than with it, the fervor of the delivery must stand in a dialectical contrast to the pointlessness of the meaning of the lines. In the same way, the author implies that most of the fervent and passionate discussion of real life (of political controversy, to give but one example) also turns around empty and meaningless clichés. Or, as Ionesco says in an essay on Antonin Artaud:

> As our knowledge becomes increasingly divorced from real life, our culture no longer contains ourselves (or only contains an insignificant part of ourselves) and forms a "social" context in which we are not integrated. The problem thus becomes that of again reconciling our culture with our life by making our culture a living culture once more. But to achieve this end we shall first have to kill the "respect for that which is written" . . . it becomes necessary to break up our language so that it may become possible to put it together again and to reëstablish contact with the absolute, or as I should prefer to call it, with multiple reality.[10]

This quest for the multiple reality of the world which is real *because* it exists on many planes simultaneously and is more than a mere unidirectional abstraction is not only in itself a search for a reëstablished *poetical* reality (poetry in its essence expressing reality in its ambiguity and multidimensional depth); it is also in close accord with important movements of our age in what appear to be entirely different fields: psychology and philosophy. The dissolution, devaluation, and relativization of language is, after all, also the theme of much of present-day depth-psychology, which has shown what in former times was regarded as a rational expression of logically arrived at conclusions to be the mere rationalization of subconscious emotional impulses. Not everything we say means what we intend it to mean. And likewise, in present-day Logical Positivism a large proportion of all statements is regarded as devoid of conceptual meaning and merely emotive. A philosopher like Ludwig Wittgenstein, in his later phases, even tried to break through what he regarded as the opacity, the misleading nature of language and grammar; for if all our thinking is in terms of language, and language obeys what after all are the arbitrary conventions of grammar, we must strive to penetrate to the real content of thought that is masked by grammatical rules and conventions. Here, too, then is a matter of getting behind the surface of linguistic clichés and of finding reality through the break-up of language.

In the Theatre of the Absurd, therefore, the real content of the play lies in the action. Language may be discarded altogether, as in Beckett's *Act Without Words* or in Ionesco's *The New Tenant,* in which the whole sense of the play is contained in the incessant arrival of more and more furniture so that the occupant of the room is, in the end, literally drowned in it. Here the movement of objects alone carries the dramatic action, the language has become purely incidental, less important than the contribution of the property department. In this, the Theatre of the Absurd also reveals its anti-literary character, its endeavor to link up with the pre-literary strata of stage history: the circus, the performances of itinerant jugglers and mountebanks, the music hall, fairground barkers, acrobats, and also the robust world of the silent film. Ionesco, in particular, clearly owes a great deal to Chaplin, Buster Keaton, the Keystone Cops, Laurel and Hardy, and the Marx Brothers. And it is surely significant that so much of successful popular entertainment in our age shows affinities with the subject matter and preoccupation of the avant-garde Theatre of the Absurd. A sophisticated, but nevertheless highly popular, film comedian like Jacques Tati uses dialogue merely as a barely comprehensible babble of noises, and also dwells on the loneliness of man in our age, the horror of overmechanization and overorganization gone mad. Danny Kaye excels in streams of gibberish closely akin to Lucky's oration in *Waiting for Godot*. The brilliant and greatly liked team of British radio (and occasionally television) comedians, the Goons, have a sense of the absurd that resembles Kafka's or Ionesco's and a team of grotesque singers like "Les Frères Jacques" seems more closely in line with the Theatre of the Absurd than with the conventional cabaret.

Yet the defiant rejection of language as the main vehicle of the dramatic action, the onslaught on conventional logic and unilinear conceptual thinking in the Theatre of the Absurd is by no means equivalent to a total rejection of all meaning. On the contrary, it constitutes an earnest endeavor to penetrate to deeper layers of meaning and to give a truer, because more complex, picture of reality in avoiding the simplification which results from leaving out all the undertones, overtones, and inherent absurdities and contradictions of any human situation. In the conventional drama every word means what it says, the situations are clearcut, and at the end all conflicts are tidily resolved. But reality, as Ionesco points out in the passage we have quoted, is never like that; it is multiple, complex, many-dimensional and exists on a number of different levels at one and the same time. Language is far too straightforward an instrument to express all this by itself. Reality can only be conveyed by being *acted out* in all its complexity. Hence, it is the theatre, which is multidimensional and more than merely language or literature, which is the only instrument to express the bewildering complexity of the human condition. The human condition being what it is, with man small, helpless, insecure, and unable ever to fathom the world in all its hopelessness, death, and absurdity, the theatre has to confront him with the bitter truth that most human endeavor is irrational and senseless, that communication between human beings is well-nigh impossible, and that the world will forever remain an impenetrable mystery. At the same time, the recognition of all these bitter truths will have a liberating effect: if we realize the basic absurdity of most of our objectives we are freed from being obsessed with them and this release expresses itself in laughter.

Moreover, while the world is being shown as complex, harsh, and absurd and as difficult to interpret as reality itself, the audience is yet spurred on to attempt their own interpretation, to wonder what it is all about. In that sense they are being invited to school their critical faculties, to train themselves in adjusting to reality. As the world is being represented as highly complex and devoid of a clear-cut purpose or design, there will always be an infinite number of possible interpretations. As Apollinaire points out in his Preface to *Les Mamelles de Tiresias:* "None of the symbols in my play is very clear, but one is at liberty to see in it all the symbols one desires and to find in it a thousand senses—as in the Sybilline oracles." Thus, it may be that the pinball machines in Adamov's *Ping-Pong* and the ideology which is developed around them stand for the futility of political or religious ideologies that are pursued with equal fervor and equal futility in the final result. Others have interpreted the play as a parable on the greed and sordidness of the profit motive. Others again may give it quite different meanings. The mysterious transformation of human beings into rhinos in Ionesco's latest play, *The Rhinoceros,* was felt by the audience of its world premier at Duesseldorf (November 6, 1959) to depict the transformation of human beings into Nazis. It is known that Ionesco himself intended the play to express his feelings at the time when more and more of his friends in Rumania joined the Fascist Iron Guard and, in effect, left the ranks of thin-skinned humans to turn themselves into moral pachyderms. But to spectators less intimately aware of the moral climate of such a situation than the German audience, other interpretations might impose themselves: if the hero, Bérenger, is at the end left alone as the only human being in his native town, now entirely inhabited by rhinos, they might regard this as a poetic symbol of the gradual isolation of man growing old and imprisoned in the strait jacket of his own habits and memories. Does Godot, so fervently and vainly awaited by Vladimir and Estragon, stand for God? Or does he merely represent the ever elusive tomorrow, man's hope that one day something will happen that will render his existence meaningful? The force and poetic power of the play lie precisely in the impossibility of ever reaching a conclusive answer to this question.

Here we touch the essential point of difference between the conventional theatre and the Theatre of the Absurd. The former, based as it is on a known framework of accepted values and a rational view of life, always starts out by indicating a fixed objective towards which the action will be moving or by posing a definite problem to which it will supply an answer. Will Hamlet revenge the murder of his father? Will Iago succeed in destroying Othello? Will Nora leave her husband? In the conventional theatre the action always proceeds towards a definable end. The spectators do not know whether that end will be reached and how it will be reached. Hence, they are in suspense, eager to find out *what* will happen. In the Theatre of the Absurd, on the other hand, the action does not proceed in the manner of a logical syllogism. It does not go from A to B but travels from an unknown premise X towards an un-knowable conclusion Y. The spectators, not knowing what their author is driving at, cannot be in suspense as to how or whether an expected objective is going to be reached. They are not, therefore, so much in suspense as to *what* is going to happen *next* (although the most unex-pected and unpredictable things do happen) as they are in suspense about what the next event to take place will add to their understanding of *what is happening*. The action supplies an increasing number of con-tradictory and bewildering clues on a number of different levels, but the final question is never wholly answered. Thus, instead of being in suspense as to what will happen next, the spectators are, in the Theatre of the Absurd, put into suspense as to *what* the play *may mean*. This suspense continues even after the curtain has come down. Here again the Theatre of the Absurd fulfills Brecht's postulate of a critical, de-tached audience, who will have to sharpen their wits on the play and be stimulated by it to think for themselves, far more effectively than Brecht's own theatre. Not only are the members of the audience unable to identify with the characters, they are compelled to puzzle out the meaning of what they have seen. Each of them will probably find his own, personal meaning, which will differ from the solution found by most others. But he will have been forced to make a mental effort and to evaluate an experience he has undergone. In this sense, the Theatre of the Absurd is the most demanding, the most intellectual theatre. It may be riotously funny, wildly exaggerated and oversimplified, vulgar and garish, but it will always confront the spectator with a genuine intellectual problem, a philosophical paradox, which he will have to try to solve even if he knows that it is most probably insoluble.

In this respect, the Theatre of the Absurd links up with an older tradition which has almost completely disappeared from Western cul-ture: the tradition of allegory and the symbolical representation of abstract concepts personified by characters whose costumes and ac-coutrements subtly suggested whether they represented Time, Chastity, Winter, Fortune, the World, etc. This is the tradition which stretches from the Italian *Trionfo* of the Renaissance to the English Masque, the elaborate allegorical constructions of the Spanish *Auto sacramental* down to Goethe's allegorical processions and masques written for the court of Weimar at the turn of the eighteenth century. Although the living riddles the characters represented in these entertainments were by no means difficult to solve, as everyone knew that a character with a scythe and an hourglass represented Time, and although the characters soon revealed their identity and explained their attributes, there was an element of intellectual challenge which stimulated the audience in the moments between the appearance of the riddle and its solution and which provided them with the pleasure of having solved a puzzle. And what is more, in the elaborate allegorical dramas like Calderón's *El Gran Teatro del Mundo* the subtle interplay of allegorical characters itself presented the audience with a great deal to think out for themselves. They had, as it were, to translate the abstractly presented action into terms of their everyday experience; they could ponder on the deeper meaning of such facts as death having taken the characters representing Riches or Poverty in a Dance of Death equally quickly and equally harshly, or that Mammon had deserted his master Everyman in the hour of death. The dramatic riddles of our time present no such clear-cut solutions. All they can show is that while the solutions have evaporated the riddle of our existence remains—complex, unfathomable, and paradoxical.

NOTES

1. Ionesco, "Dans les Armes de la Ville," *Cahiers de la Compagnie Madeleine Renaud–Jean-Louis Barrault*, No. 20 (October, 1957).
2. Adamov, "Note Préliminaire," *Théâtre II*, Paris, 1955.
3. *Ibid.*
4. It may be significant that the three writers concerned, although they now all live in France and write in French have all come to live there from outside and must have experienced a period of adjustment to the country and its language. Samuel Beckett (b. 1906) came from Ireland; Arthur Adamov (b. 1908) from Russia, and Eugène Ionesco (b. 1912) from Rumania.
5. Ionesco, "L'Impromptu de l'Alma," *Théâtre II*, Paris, 1958.
6. Ionesco, "The Avant-Garde Theatre," *World Theatre*, VIII, No. 3 (Autumn, 1959).
7. Jarry, "Questions de Théâtre," in *Ubu Roi, Ubu Enchaîné*, and other Ubuesque writings. Ed. Rene Massat, Lausanne, 1948.
8. Apollinaire, *Les Mamelles de Tiresias*, Preface.
9. Ionesco, "The Avant-Garde Theatre."
10. Ionesco, "Ni un Dieu, ni un Demon," *Cahiers de la Compagnie Madeleine Renaud–Jean-Louis Barrault*, No. 22–23 (May, 1958).

FORM: THE UNITIES

How a dramatist controls action, time, and location obviously exercizes a shaping influence upon his play. Thus the following essays and excerpts are closely related to the foregoing sections on "Form" and "Generic Forms." However, the prolonged critical debate over the "unities" deserves a separate section because of its peculiar place in the history of dramatic theory. The essays included here represent the turning points of that debate, or, to put it dramatically, the key acts in a critical "play" based on the theme of the unities.

The concept of the dramatic "unities" derives ultimately but distortedly from Aristotle's *Poetics*, in which he says that the action of tragedy should be complete and whole, that is, a "unity," and that it should take place roughly within a day. Aristotle's remark about time is offered casually, by no means as an unalterable dramatic law; however, neoclassic critics of the Renaissance, especially in Italy, converted his remark into a "rule" requiring the action of a play to be confined to twenty-four hours or, as some held, to twelve hours, or, more stringent yet, to the two or three hours in which the play could be staged. From this came the "unity of place," the notion (unmentioned by Aristotle) that all the action should occur in one location. And finally, Aristotle's idea that tragic action should be unified, that

it should proceed on a causal basis without the introduction of extraneous episodes or improbable coincidences, degenerated into the
notion that subplots were forbidden.

Ironically, the three unities, especially those of time and place,
were formulated in the interests of realism; it was not "realistic" for
a play of two hours' duration to represent events that would actually
take years or to show characters in, say, Athens when only ten minutes
ago (according to the theater clocks) they were in Troy. So strictly
adhered to, a desire for realism or lifelikeness runs afoul of what is
sometimes called the "imitative fallacy," that is, the attempt to imitate
a subject with such total fidelity that the qualities of the subject are
embodied in the reproduction (as though to paint a stupid man one
must paint a stupid picture). Absolute realism of this sort, when codified into laws, paradoxically produced plays that were often models
of artificiality—prudent, stiff, and unnatural.

Although much of Sidney's "Apologie for Poetrie" is a defense of the
poetic imagination, which he is anxious to liberate from the shackles of
scientific or historical assertions of "truth," his remarks on drama
printed below confine the playwright's imagination within the narrow
compass of the unities. Writing around 1583, Sidney was unfortunate
in that the finest literature of the Elizabethan age had yet to appear.
Perhaps his excessive respect for classical authorities and his prescriptive view of genre, convention, and decorum might have moder-
ated somewhat had he lived long enough to compare the "proper" but
infirm Gorboduc to Shakespeare's "incorrect" but magnificent King
Lear.

Whereas Sidney, a poet but not a playwright, insisted on classical
standards in the theater, Corneille, the seventeenth-century playwright,
was acutely conscious of the practical difficulties of squeezing the intractable stuff of drama into the precise molds of Aristotle as interpreted
by neoclassic critics. Thus he argues, a bit nervously in the face of the
"authorities," for a liberalization of the unities in the interests of a more
genuinely realistic representation of human actions.

Corneille's restiveness under the rules is intensified in Dryden's

"Essay," which, through the medium of four discussants, explores a variety of approaches to poetic drama. In the earlier part of the essay, Crites (Sir Robert Howard) argues the virtues of classical drama and Eugenius (Dryden's patron, Lord Buckhurst) those of modern (i.e. seventeenth-century) drama. Our selection tunes in at the point in the discussion where Lisideius (Sir Charles Sedley) praises modern French neoclassic drama at the expense of the native English tradition, which has been remiss in adhering to the unities, in a concern for generic purity, and in an observance of stage decorum. In reply, Neander (Dryden himself) grants the charges made against the English but denies that Lisideius' criteria are the only valid ones for the theater. Instead, he advocates variety over purity, vitality over correctness, and truth to Nature over obedience to artistic precepts. In the remainder of the "Essay" (not included here), Dryden analyzes Ben Jonson's *The Silent Woman* to demonstrate that regularity of form is possible even in plays that do not hew strictly to neoclassic practices, and concludes with a defense of rhyme in tragedy.

In his *Preface to Shakespeare,* Samuel Johnson completes the job begun by Corneille and Dryden, going over the head of neoclassical theories to appeal to life and experience. Shakespeare, he argues, went to "general nature" for his dramatic instruction, not to Aristotle's interpreters, and the best measure of his success is not his faithfulness to rules but his continued popularity among discriminating audiences. Why Shakespeare should have remained popular despite his disregard of rules, Johnson says, is simply a matter of common sense: drama does not reproduce reality on a stage but represents it, and these representations operate quite outside the boundaries of time and space, as any audience is instinctively aware.

SIR PHILIP SIDNEY

"Rules of Drama"

Our Tragedies and Comedies (not without cause cried out against), observing rules neither of honest civility nor of skilful Poetry, excepting *Gorboduc* [1] (again, I say, of those that I have seen), which notwithstanding, as it is full of stately speeches and well-sounding phrases, climbing to the height of Seneca's style, and as full of notable morality, which it doth most delightfully teach, and so obtain the very end of Poesy, yet in truth it is very defectious in the circumstances, which grieveth me, because it might not remain as an exact model of all Tragedies. For it is faulty both in place and time, the two necessary companions of all corporal actions. For where the stage should always represent but one place, and the uttermost time presupposed in it should be, both by Aristotle's precept and common reason, but one day, there is both many days, and many places, inartificially imagined. But if it be so in *Gorboduc*, how much more in all the rest, where you shall have Asia of the one side, and Afric of the other, and so many other under-kingdoms, that the player, when he cometh in, must ever begin with telling where he is, or else the tale will not be conceived? Now ye shall have three ladies walk to gather flowers and then we must believe the stage to be a garden. By and by we hear news of shipwreck in the same place, and then we are to blame if we accept it not for a rock.

Upon the back of that comes out a hideous monster, with fire and smoke, and then the miserable beholders are bound to take it for a cave. While in the meantime two armies fly in, represented with four swords and bucklers, and then what hard heart will not receive it for a pitched field? Now, of time they are much more liberal, for ordinary it is that two young princes fall in love. After many traverses, she is

From *The Apologie for Poetrie*, 1595.

got with child, delivered of a fair boy; he is lost, groweth a man, falls in love, and is ready to get another child; and all this in two hours, space: which, how absurd it is in sense, even sense may imagine, and Art hath taught, and all ancient examples justified, and, at this day, the ordinary players in Italy will not err in. Yet will some bring in an example of *Eunuchus* in Terence, that containeth matter of two days, yet far short of twenty years. True it is, and so was it to be played in two days, and so fitted to the time it set forth. And though Plautus hath in one place done amiss, let us hit with him, and not miss with him. But they will say, How then shall we set forth a story, which containeth both many places and many times? And do they not know that a Tragedy is tied to the laws of Poesy, and not of History; not bound to follow the story, but, having liberty, either to feign a quite new matter, or to frame the history to the most tragical conveniency? Again, many things may be told which cannot be showed, if they know the difference betwixt reporting and representing. As, for example, I may speak (though I am here) of Peru, and in speech digress from that to the description of Calicut; but in action I cannot represent it without Pacolet's horse.[2] And so was the manner the ancients took, by some Nuncius [3] to recount things done in former time or other place. Lastly, if they will represent an history, they must not (as Horace saith) begin *ab ovo*,[4] but they must come to the principal point of that one action which they will represent. By example this will be best expressed. I have a story of young Polydorus, delivered for safety's sake, with great riches, by his father Priam to Polymnestor, king of Thrace, in the Trojan war time. He, after some years, hearing the overthrow of Priam, for to make the treasure his own, murdereth the child. The body of the child is taken up by Hecuba. She, the same day, findeth a slight to be revenged most cruelly of the tyrant. Where now would one of our tragedy writers begin, but with the delivery of the child? Then should he sail over into Thrace, and so spend I know not how many years, and travel numbers of places. But where doth Euripides? Even with the finding of the body, leaving the rest to be told by the spirit of Polydorus. This need no further to be enlarged; the dullest wit may conceive it. But besides these gross absurdities, how all their plays be neither right tragedies, nor right comedies, mingling kings and clowns, not because the matter so carrieth it, but thrust in clowns by head and shoulders, to play a part in majestical matters, with neither decency nor discretion, so as neither the admiration and commiseration, nor the right sportfulness, is by their mongrel tragi-comedy obtained. I know

Apuleius [5] did somewhat so, but that is a thing recounted with space of time, not represented in one moment: and I know the ancients have one or two examples of tragi-comedies, as Plautus hath *Amphitrio*. But, if we mark them well, we shall find, that they never, or very daintily, match hornpipes and funerals. So falleth it out that, having indeed no right comedy, in that comical part of our tragedy we have nothing but scurrility, unworthy of any chaste ears, or some extreme show of doltishness, indeed fit to lift up a loud laughter, and nothing else: where the whole tract of a comedy should be full of delight, as the tragedy should be still maintained in a well-raised admiration. But our comedians think there is no delight without laughter; which is very wrong, for though laughter may come with delight, yet cometh it not of delight, as though delight should be the cause of laughter; but well may one thing breed both together. Nay, rather in themselves they have, as it were, a kind of contrariety: for delight we scarcely do but in things that have a conveniency to ourselves or to the general nature: laughter almost ever cometh of things most disproportioned to ourselves and nature. Delight hath a joy in it, either permanent or present. Laughter hath only a scornful tickling.

For example, we are ravished with delight to see a fair woman, and yet are far from being moved to laughter. We laugh at deformed creatures, wherein certainly we cannot delight. We delight in good chances, we laugh at mischances; we delight to hear the happiness of our friends, or country, at which he were worthy to be laughed at that would laugh. We shall, contrarily, laugh sometimes to find a matter quite mistaken and go down the hill against the bias, in the mouth of some such men, as for the respect of them one shall be heartily sorry, yet he cannot choose but laugh; and so is rather pained than delighted with laughter. Yet deny I not but that they may go well together. For as in Alexander's picture well set out we delight without laughter, and in twenty mad antics we laugh without delight, so in Hercules, painted with his great beard and furious countenance, in woman's attire, spinning at Omphale's commandment, it breedeth both delight and laughter. For the representing of so strange a power in love procureth delight: and the scornfulness of the action stirreth laughter. But I speak to this purpose, that all the end of the comical part be not upon such scornful matters as stirreth laughter only, but, mixed with it, that delightful teaching which is the end of Poesy. And the great fault even in that point of laughter, and forbidden plainly by Aristotle,[6] is that they stir laughter in sinful things, which are rather execrable than ridiculous; or in miserable, which are rather to be pitied than scorned. For what is it to make folks gape at a wretched beggar, or a beggarly clown; or, against the law of hospitality, to jest at strangers, because they speak not English so well as we do? What do we learn, since it is certain

> *Nil habet infelix paupertas durius in se,*
> *Quam quod ridiculos homines facit?* [7]

But rather a busy loving courtier, a heartless threatening Thraso, a self-wise-seeming schoolmaster, an awry-transformed traveller—these if we saw walk in stage names, which we play naturally, therein were delightful laughter, and teaching delightfulness: as in the other, the tragedies of Buchanan do justly bring forth a divine admiration. But I have lavished out too many words of this play matter. I do it it because, as they are excelling parts of Poesy, so is there none so much used in England, and none can be more pitifully abused; which, like an unmannerly daughter showing a bad education, causeth her mother Poesy's honesty to be called in question.

NOTES

1. By Thomas Sackville (Lord Buckhurst, 1536–1608) and Thomas Norton (1532–84), published in 1565.
2. A magic horse in the romance, *Valentine and Orson.*
3. Messenger.
4. From the egg (beginning); Horace's *Ars Poetica,* line 147.
5. Roman writer (Second Century) most commonly known for his prose romance, *Metamorphoses* or *Golden Ass.*
6. *The Poetics,* chapter 5.
7. "Unhappy poverty has nothing worse than its ability to make men ridiculous" (Juvenal, *Satires,* III, 152–3).

PIERRE CORNEILLE

Discourse on the Three Unities (1660)

I contend then, and have already stated it, that the unity of action, in comedy, consists in a unity of *intrigue*, or in obstacles to the designs of the main characters; and, in tragedy, it consists in a unity of *danger*, whether the hero succumbs to it or escapes from it. I do not say that one cannot admit several intrigues and obstacles into the former, and several dangers into the latter, provided each necessarily winds into the other. For then the disappearance of the first danger does not render the action complete, since it leads into a second one; and the clearing up of one intrigue does not leave the actors idle, since it encumbers them with another intrigue. . . .

In the second place, this term "unity of action" does not mean that there should be only one action in the play. What the poet selects for his subject ought to have a beginning, a middle, and an end; and these three parts are not only so many actions coming to a center in the principal action; but each of them, moreover, can contain several parts in a similar subordination. There ought only to be a *complete* action, which leaves the mind of the spectator composed. But it can only result through several incomplete parts, which contribute to the progress of the whole, and maintain the spectator in an agreeable suspension. It is necessary that the writer contrive at the end of each act to make the action continuous.

The *liaison des scènes* * which unites all the particular actions of

* According to this rule of French neoclassic drama, the various scenes of a play should be connected by having present, at the start of a scene, an actor who had been on the stage at the end of the preceding scene. The hope of giving an illusion of unity by this means created obvious difficulties. Amusing attempts were made to interpret the rule more elastically without abandoning it. The French critic, D'Aubignac, for example, was willing to permit a connection by having an actor appear at the start of a scene who was "looking for" a character present in the previous one, or who had heard a noise made then.

From *Criticism: The Major Texts*, translated and edited by Walter Jackson Bate, Copyright, 1952, by Harcourt, Brace & World, Inc., and reprinted with their permission.

each act, the one with the other, and of which I have spoken in the *examen* to the *Suivante,* is an important ornament to a poem, and greatly helps to form a continuity of action by giving a continuity of representation. But, in the last analysis, it is only an ornament, and not a rule. The ancients have not always submitted to it, even though most of their acts are filled with two or three scenes; this makes it much easier for them than for us, who sometimes have nine or ten. . . .

Although the action of a dramatic poem ought to have unity, it must be regarded as having two elements: the knotting together, or complication, and the *dénouement,* or unravelling. "The complication," according to Aristotle, "is composed in part what has passed outside the theater before the commencement of the action . . . the rest belongs to the *dénouement* . . ." The complication depends entirely on the choice and illustrious imagination of the poet; and one cannot give for it any rules except that everything ought to be arranged according to probability or necessity . . .

In the *dénouement* I find two things to avoid—a simple change of heart in the character, and the use of the *deus ex machina.* There is no great skill in finishing a poem when that which comprizes an obstacle to the designs of the principal characters, during four acts, simply ceases to exist in the fifth act, without any notable event to make it that way . . . Nor does the use of the machine show any more skill when it only serves to have a god descend in order to conclude everything when the actors no longer know how to settle matters. . . .

From the subject of the action I turn to that of the division of a play into acts, which ought each to contain a part, but not so equal that one does not reserve more for the last act than for the others, and offer less in the first than in the remaining ones. . . . Aristotle does not prescribe the number of acts. Horace limits the number to five . . .

The number of scenes in each act is not subject to any rule. But as every act ought to have a certain number of verses, which keeps its duration equal to that of the others, one can insert more or fewer scenes according as they are shorter or longer, in order to fill out the time that every complete act ought to consume. . . .

The rule for the unity of time has its basis in the statement of Aristotle that "tragedy ought to confine the length of its action within one revolution of the sun, or try not to exceed it very much." This remark gives rise to that famous dispute whether it applies to a natural day of twenty-four hours, or an artificial day of twelve . . . I, for my own part, find there are subjects so hard to enclose in so little time that I will not only accord them the entire twenty-four hours, but I will even avail myself of the license given by the philosopher to exceed them a bit, and without scruple push them up to thirty hours. . . .

Many declaim against this rule, whch they call tyrannical; and they would have reason if it was founded only on the authority of Aristotle. But what ought to make it accepted is the natural reason that gives it support. A dramatic poem is an imitation, or, to put it better, a portrait of men's actions; and without doubt the portraits are more excellent to the degree that they resemble the original. The representation lasts two hours; and it would resemble the original perfectly if the action it represents did not demand any longer in the imitation itself. Thus let us not at all stop at twelve or at twenty-four hours. But let us confine the action of the poem in the least time that we can, so that the representation resembles more closely and is more perfect. . . .

So far as the unity of place is concerned, I do not find any rule about it in Aristotle or Horace. This is why some are led to believe that the rule was established only as a result of the unity of time, and accordingly to persuade themselves that one can extend it to include whatever place one can go to and return in twenty-four hours. This opinion is a bit licentious; and if one had an actor ride past, the two sides of the theater could represent Paris and Rouen. . . .

Our ancients, who have their kings speak in a public place, give this rigorous unity of place rather easily to their tragedies. Sophocles, however, has not observed it in his *Ajax*, who leaves the theater in order to find a lonely place in which to kill himself, and kills himself before the spectators. . . . We cannot take the same liberty of drawing kings and princesses from their apartments. And as the difference and opposition of interests of those who are lodged in the same palace often permit them to make their confidences and disclose their secrets only in their own chambers, it is necessary to look for some other way of arranging for the unity of place if we wish to preserve it in all our poems. . . .

I contend, then, that one should expect this unity to be as exact as possible. But as it does not adapt itself to every sort of subject, I should very willingly admit that whatever took place in a single city would have unity of place. It is not that I wish the theater to represent the city as a whole; that would be too spacious a scene; but the stage might present merely two or three particular places enclosed within its walls. . . . In order to rectify in some fashion this changing of place, when it is inevitable, I should wish to suggest two things. The first is that one should never change the scene in the same act, but solely from one act to another, as is done in the first three acts of *Cinna*. The second suggestion is that the two places should not need to have different scenery, and that neither should be named specifically, but simply be the general place in which the two places are included, such as Paris, Rome, Lyons, Constantinople, and the like. This will help to beguile the spectator, who, not seeing anything that marks the difference in place, does not become aware of it; at least he will not note the difference in a malicious and critical spirit (of which there are a few quite capable), the majority of them attaching themselves with warmth to the action they see represented. . . .

Many of my works will be lacking if one does not wish to admit a modification [of the unity of place], of which I shall content myself in the future when I cannot satisfy the utmost rigor of the rule. . . . It is easy for theoretical critics to be severe. But if they wished to offer ten or twelve poems of this sort to the public, they perhaps would enlarge the rules still more than I have done as soon as they recognized, by experience, how much restraint there is in abiding by them exactly and how many beautiful things are thereby banished from the theater. Be that as it may, these are my opinions, or, if you wish, my heresies touching the principal points of the art. . . .

JOHN DRYDEN

An Essay on Dramatic Poesy

. . . This moderation of Crites, as it was pleasing to all the company, so it put an end to that dispute; which Eugenius, who seemed to have the better of the argument, would urge no farther: but Lisideius, after he had acknowledged himself of Eugenius his opinion concerning the Ancients, yet told him, he had forborne, till his discourse were ended, to ask him why he preferred the English plays above those of other nations? and whether we ought not to submit our stage to the exactness of our next neighbours?

"Though," said Eugenius, "I am at all times ready to defend the honour of my country against the French, and to maintain, we are as well able to vanquish them with our pens, as our ancestors have been with their swords; yet, if you please," added he, looking upon Neander, "I will commit this cause to my friend's management; his opinion of our plays is the same with mine, and besides, there is no reason, that Crites and I, who have now left the stage, should re-enter so suddenly upon it; which is against the laws of comedy."

"If the question had been stated," replied Lisideius, "who had writ best, the French or English, forty years ago, I should have been of your opinion, and adjudged the honour to own own nation; but since that time" (said he, turning towards Neander), "we have been so long together bad Englishmen that we had not leisure to be good poets. Beaumont, Fletcher, and Jonson (who were only capable of bringing us to that degree of perfection which we have), were just then leaving the world; as if in an age of so much horror, wit, and those milder studies of humanity, had no farther business among us. But the Muses, who ever follow peace, went to plant in another country: it was then that the great Cardinal Richelieu began to take them into his protec-

From *Essay on Dramatic Poesie*, 1668; revised edition, 1684.

tion; and that, by his encouragement, Corneille, and some other French-men, reformed their theater (which before was as much below ours, as it now surpasses it and the rest of Europe). But because Crites in his discourse for the Ancients has prevented me, by observing many rules of the stage which the Moderns have borrowed from them, I shall only in short, demand of you, whether you are not convinced that of all nations the French have best observed them? In the Unity of Time you find them so scrupulous that it yet remains a dispute among their poets, whether the artificial day of twelve hours, more or less, be not meant by Aristotle, rather than the natural one of twenty-four; and conse-quently, whether all plays ought not to be reduced into that compass. This I can testify, that in all their dramas writ within these last twenty years and upwards, I have not observed any that have extended the time to thirty hours: in the Unity of Place they are full as scrupulous; for many of their critics limit it to that very spot of ground where the play is supposed to begin; none of them exceed the compass of the same town or city. The Unity of Action in all plays is yet more con-spicuous; for they do not burden them with under-plots, as the English do: which is the reason why many scenes of our tragi-comedians carry on a design that is nothing of kin to the main plot; and that we see two distinct webs in a play, like those in ill-wrought stuffs; and two actions, that is, two plays, carried on together, to the confounding of the audi-ence; who, before they are warm in their concernments for one part, are diverted to another; and by that means espouse the interest of neither. From hence likewise it arises that the one half of our actors are not known to the other. They keep their distances, as if they were Montagues and Capulets, and seldom begin an acquaintance till the last scene of the fifth act, when they are all to meet upon the stage. There is no theatre in the world has anything so absurd as the English tragi-comedy; 'tis a drama of our own invention, and the fashion of it is enough to proclaim it so; here a course of mirth, there another of sadness and passion, and a third of honour and a duel: thus, in two hours and a half, we run through all the fits of Bedlam. The French affords you as much variety on the same day, but they do it not so unseasonably, or *mal à propos,* as we: our poets present you the play and the farce together; and our stages still retain somewhat of the original civility of the Red Bull:

Atque ursum et pugiles media inter carmina poscunt.[1]

The end of tragedies or serious plays, says Aristotle, is to beget admiration, compassion, or concernment; but are not mirth and compassion things incompatible? and is it not evident that the poet must of necessity destroy the former by intermingling of the latter? that is, he must ruin the sole end and object of his tragedy, to introduce somewhat that is forced into it, and is not of the body of it. Would you not think that physician mad, who, having prescribed a purge, should immediately order you to take restringents?

"But to leave our plays, and return to theirs. I have noted one great advantage they have had in the plotting of their tragedies; that is, they are always grounded upon some known history: according to that of Horace, *Ex noto fictum carmen sequar;* [2] and in that they have so imitated the Ancients that they have surpassed them. For the Ancients, as was observed before, took for the foundation of their plays some poetical fiction, such as under that consideration could move but little concernment in the audience, because they already knew the event of it. But the French goes farther:

> *Atque ita mentitur, sic veris falsa remiscet*
> *Primo ne medium, medio ne discrepet imum.* [3]

He so interweaves truth with probable fiction that he puts a pleasing fallacy upon us; mends the intrigues of fate, and dispenses with the severity of history, to reward that virtue which has been rendered to us there unfortunate. Sometimes the story has left the success so doubtful that the writer is free, by the privilege of a poet, to take that which of two or more relations will best suit with his design: as for example, in the death of Cyrus, whom Justin and some others report to have perished in the Scythian war, but Xenophon affirms to have died in his bed of extreme old age. Nay more, when the event is past dispute, even then we are willing to be deceived, and the poet, if he contrives it with appearance of truth, has all the audience of his party; at least during the time his play is acting: so naturally we are kind to virtue, when our own interest is not in question, that we take it up as the general concernment of mankind. On the other side, if you consider the historical plays of Shakespeare, they are rather so many chronicles of kings, or the business many times of thirty or forty years, cramped into a representation of two hours and a half; which is not to imitate or paint Nature, but rather to draw her in miniature, to take her in little; to look upon her through the wrong end of a perspective, and receive her images not only much less, but infinitely more imperfect than the life: this, instead of making a play delightful, renders it ridiculous:

Quodcunque ostendis mihi sic, incredulus odi.[4]

For the spirit of man cannot be satisfied but with truth, or at least verisimility; and a poem is to contain, if not τὰ ἔτυμα, yet ἐτύμοισν ὁμοῖα,[5] as one of the Greek poets has expressed it.

"Another thing in which the French differ from us and from the Spaniards, is that they do not embarrass, or cumber themselves with too much plot; they only represent so much of a story as will constitute one whole and great action sufficient for a play; we, who undertake more, do but multiply adventures which, not being produced from one another, as effects from causes, but rarely following, constitute many actions in the drama, and consequently make it many plays.

"But by pursuing closely one argument, which is not cloyed with many turns, the French have gained more liberty for verse, in which they write; they have leisure to dwell on a subject which deserves it; and to represent the passions (which we have acknowledged to be the poet's work), without being hurried from one thing to another, as we are in the plays of Calderón, which we have seen lately upon our theatres under the name of Spanish plots. I have taken notice but of one tragedy of ours whose plot has that uniformity and unity of design in it, which I have commended in the French; and that is *Rollo*, or rather, under the name of Rollo, the Story of Bassianus and Geta in Herodian: there indeed the plot is neither large nor intricate, but just enough to fill the minds of the audience, not to cloy them. Besides, you see it founded upon the truth of history,—only the time of the action is not reduceable to the strictness of the rules; and you see in some places a little farce mingled, which is below the dignity of the other parts, and in this all our poets are extremely peccant: even Ben Jonson himself, in *Sejanus* and *Catiline*, has given us this oleo of a play, this unnatural mixture of comedy and tragedy; which to me sounds just as ridiculously as the history of David with the merry humours of Golias. In *Sejanus* you may take notice of the scene betwixt Livia and the physician which is a pleasant satire upon the artificial helps of beauty: in *Catiline* you may see the parliament of women; the little envies of of them to one another; and all that passes betwixt Curio and Fulvia: scenes admirable in their kind, but of an ill mingle with the rest.

"But I return again to the French writers, who, as I have said, do not burden themselves too much with plot, which has been reproached to them by an *ingenious person* of our nation as a fault; for, he says, they commonly make but one person considerable in a play; they dwell on him, and his concernments, while the rest of the persons are only subservient to set him off. If he intends this by it,—that there is one person in the play who is of greater dignity than the rest, he must tax, not only theirs, but those of the Ancients, and which he would be loth to do, the best of ours; for it is impossible but that one person must be more conspicuous in it than any other, and consequently the greatest share in the action must devolve on him. We see it so in the management of all affairs; even in the most equal aristocracy, the balance cannot be so justly poised but some one will be superior to the rest, either in parts, fortune, interest, or the consideration of some glorious exploit; which will reduce the greatest part of business into his hands.

"But, if he would have us to imagine, that in exalting one character the rest of them are neglected, and that all of them have not some share or other in the action of the play, I desire him to produce any of Corneille's tragedies, wherein every person, like so many servants in in a well-governed family, has not some employment, and who is not necessary to the carrying on of the plot, or at least to your understanding it.

"There are indeed some protatic persons in the Ancients, whom they make use of in their plays, either to hear or give the relation; but the French avoid this with great address, making their narrations only to, or by such, who are some way interested in the main design. And now I am speaking of relations, I cannot take a fitter opportunity to add this in favour of the French, that they often use them with better judgment and more *à propos* than the English do. Not that I commend narrations in general,—but there are two sorts of them. One, of those things which are antecedent to the play, and are related to make the conduct of it more clear to us. But 'tis a fault to choose such subjects for the stage as will force us on that rock because we see they are seldom listened to by the audience and that is many times the ruin of the play; for, being once let pass without attention, the audience can never recover themselves to understand the plot: and indeed it is somewhat unreasonable that they should be put to so much trouble, as that, to comprehend what passes in their sight, they must have recourse to what was done, perhaps, ten or twenty years ago.

"But there is another sort of relations, that is, of things happening in the action of the play and supposed to be done behind the scenes;

and this is many times both convenient and beautiful; for by it the French avoid the tumult to which we are subject in England, by representing duels, battles, and the like; which renders our stage too like the theatres where they fight prizes. For what is more ridiculous than to represent an army with a drum and five men behind it; all which the hero of the other side is to drive in before him; or to see a duel fought and one slain with two or three thrusts of the foils, which we know are so blunted that we might give a man an hour to kill another in good earnest with them.

"I have observed that in all our tragedies, the audience cannot forbear laughing when the actors are to die; it is the most comic part of the whole play. All *passions* may be lively represented on the stage, if to the well-writing of them the actor supplies a good commanded voice, and limbs that move easily, and without stiffness; but there are many *actions* which can never be imitated to a just height: dying especially is a thing which none but a Roman gladiator could naturally perform on the stage, when he did not imitate or represent, but do it; and therefore it is better to omit the representation of it.

"The words of a good writer, which describe it lively, will make a deeper impression of belief in us than all the actor can insinuate into us, when he seems to fall dead before us; as a poet in the description of a beautiful garden, or a meadow, will please our imagination more than the place itself can please our sight. When we see death represented, we are convinced it is but fiction; but when we hear it related, our eyes, the strongest witnesses, are wanting, which might have undeceived us; and we are all willing to favour the sleight, when the poet does not too grossly impose on us. They therefore who imagine these relations would make no concernment in the audience, are deceived, by confounding them with the other, which are of things antecedent to the play: those are made often in cold blood, as I may say, to the audience; but these are warmed with our concernments, which were before awakened in the play. What the philosophers say of motion, that, when it is once begun, it continues of itself, and will do so to eternity, without some stop put to it, is clearly true on this occasion: the soul being already moved with the characters and fortunes of those imaginary persons, continues going of its own accord; and we are no more weary to hear what becomes of them when they are not on the stage, than we are to listen to the news of an absent mistress. But it is objected, that if one part of the play may be related, then why not all? I answer, some parts of the action are more fit to be represented, some to be related. Corneille says judiciously that the poet is not obliged to expose to view all particular actions which conduce to the principal: he ought to select such of them to be seen, which will appear with the greatest beauty, either by the magnificence of the show, or the vehemence of passions which they produce, or some other charm which they have in them; and let the rest arrive to the audience by narration. 'Tis a great mistake in us to believe the French present no part of the action on the stage; every alteration or crossing of a design, every new-sprung passion, and turn of it, is a part of the action, and much the noblest, except we conceive nothing to be action till the players come to blows; as if the painting of the hero's mind were not more properly the poet's work than the strength of his body. Nor does this anything contradict the opinion of Horace, where he tells us,

> Segnius irritant animos demissa per aurem,
> Quam quae sunt oculis subjecta fidelibus.[6]

"For he says immediately after,

> Non tamen intus
> Digna geri promes in scenam; multaq; tolles
> Ex oculis, quae mox narret facundia praesens.

"Among which many he recounts some:

> Nec pueros coram populo Medea trucidet,
> Aut in avem Procne mutetur, Cadmus in anguem, etc.

That is, those actions which by reason of their cruelty, will cause aversion in us, or by reason of their impossibility, unbelief, ought either wholly to be avoided by a poet, or only delivered by narration. To which we may have leave to add, such as, to avoid tumult (as was before hinted), or to reduce the plot into a more reasonable compass of time, or for defect of beauty in them, are rather to be related than presented to the eye. Examples of all these kinds are frequent, not only among all the Ancients, but in the best received of our English poets. We find Ben Jonson using them in his *Magnetic Lady*, where one comes out from dinner, and relates the quarrels and disorders of it, to save the undecent appearance of them on the stage, and to abbreviate the story; and this in express imitation of Terence, who had done the same before him in his *Eunuch*, where Pythias makes the like relation of what had happened within at the Soldier's entertainment. The relations likewise of Sejanus's death, and the prodigies before it, are remarkable; the one of which was hid from sight, to avoid the horror and tumult of the representation; the other, to shun the introducing of things impossible to be believed. In that excellent play, *The King and no King*, Fletcher goes yet farther; for the whole unravelling of the plot is done by narration in the fifth act, after the manner of the Ancients; and it moves great concernment in the audience, though it be only a relation of what was done many years before the play. I could multiply other instances, but these are sufficient to prove that there is no error in choosing a subject which requires this sort of narrations; in the ill management of them, there may.

"But I find I have been too long in this discourse, since the French have many other excellencies not common to us; as that you never see any of their plays end with a conversion, or simple change of will, which is the ordinary way which our poets use to end theirs. It shows little art in the conclusion of a dramatic poem, when they who have hindered the felicity during the four acts, desist from it in the fifth, without some powerful cause to take them off their design; and though I deny not but such reasons may be found, yet it is a path that is cautiously to be trod, and the poet is to be sure he convinces the audience that the motive is strong enough. As for example, the conversion of the Usurer in *The Scornful Lady* seems to me a little forced; for, being an Usurer, which implies a lover of money to the highest degree of covetousness,—and such the poet has represented him,—the account he gives for the sudden change is, that he has been duped by the wild young fellow; which in reason might render him more wary another time, and make him punish himself with harder fare and coarser clothes, to get up again what he had lost: but that he should look on it as a judgment, and so repent, we may expect to hear in a sermon, but I should never endure it in a play.

"I pass by this; neither will I insist on the care they take that no person after his first entrance shall ever appear, but the business which brings him upon the stage shall be evident; which rule, if observed, must needs render all the events in the play more natural; for there you see the probability of every accident, in the cause that produced it; and that which appears chance in the play, will seem so reasonable to you, that you will there find it almost necessary: so that in the exit of the actor you have a clear account of his purpose and design in the next entrance (though, if the scene be well wrought, the event will commonly deceive you); for there is nothing so absurd, says Corneille, as for an actor to leave the stage only because he has no more to say.

"I should now speak of the beauty of their rhyme, and the just reason I have to prefer that way of writing in tragedies before ours in blank verse; but because it is partly received by us, and therefore not altogether peculiar to them, I will say no more of it in relation to their plays. For our own, I doubt not but it will exceedingly beautify them; and I can see but one reason why it should not generally obtain, that is, because our poets write so ill in it. This indeed may prove a more prevailing argument than all others which are used to destroy it, and therefore I am only troubled when great and judicious poets, and those who are acknowledged such, have writ or spoke against it: as for others, they are to be answered by that one sentence of an ancient author:—*Sed ut primo ad consequendos eos quos priores ducimus, accendimur, ita ubi aut proeteriri, aut aequari eos posse desperavimus, studium cum spe senescit: quod, scilicet, assequi non potest, sequi desinit; . . . praeteritoque eo in quo eminere non possumus, aliquid in quo nitamur, conquirimus.*" [7]

Lisideius concluded in this manner; and Neander, after a little pause, thus answered him:

"I shall grant Lisideius, without much dispute, a great part of what he has urged against us; for I acknowledge that the French contrive their plots more regularly, and observe the laws of comedy, and decorum of the stage (to speak generally), with more exactness than the English. Farther, I deny not but he has taxed us justly in some irregularities of ours, which he has mentioned; yet, after all, I am of opinion that neither our faults nor their virtues are considerable enough to place them above us.

"For the lively imitation of Nature being in the definition of a play, those which best fulfil that law ought to be esteemed superior to the others. 'Tis true, those beauties of the French poesy are such as will raise perfection higher where it is, but are not sufficient to give it where it is not: they are indeed the beauties of a statue, but not of a man, because not animated with the soul of Poesy, which is imitation of humour and passions: and this Lisideius himself, or any other, however biassed to their party, cannot but acknowledge, if he will either compare the humours of our comedies, or the characters of our serious plays, with theirs. He who will look upon theirs which have been written till these last ten years, or thereabouts, will find it a hard matter to pick out two or three passable humours amongst them. Corneille himself, their arch-poet, what has he produced except *The Liar*, and you know how it was cried up in France; but when it came upon the English stage, though well translated, and that part of Dorant acted to so much advantage as I am confident it never received in its own country, the most favourable to it would not put it in competition with many of Fletcher's or Ben Jonson's. In the rest of Corneille's comedies you have little humour; he tells you himself, his way is, first to show two lovers in good intelligence with each other; in the working up of the play to embroil them by some mistake, and in the latter end to clear it, and reconcile them.

"But of late years Molière, the younger Corneille, Quinault, and some others, have been imitating afar off the quick turns and graces of the English stage. They have mixed their serious plays with mirth, like our tragi-comedies, since the death of Cardinal Richelieu; which Lisideius and many others not observing, have commended that in them for a virtue which they themselves no longer practise. Most of their new plays are, like some of ours, derived from the Spanish novels. There is scarce one of them without a veil, and a trusty Diego, who drolls much after the rate of *The Adventures*. But their humours, if I may grace them with that name, are so thin sown, that never above one of them comes up in any play. I dare take upon me to find more variety of them in some one play of Ben Johnson's than in all theirs together; as he who has seen *The Alchemist*, *The Silent Woman*, or *Bartholomew-Fair*, cannot but acknowledge with me.

"I grant the French have performed what was possible on the ground-work of the Spanish plays; what was pleasant before, they have made regular: but there is not above one good play to be writ on all those plots; they are too much alike to please often; which we need not the experience of our own stage to justify. As for their new way of mingling mirth with serious plot, I do not, with Lisideius, condemn the thing, though I cannot approve their manner of doing it. He tells us, we cannot so speedily recollect ourselves after a scene of great passion and concernment, as to pass to another of mirth and humour, and to enjoy it with any relish: but why should he imagine the soul of man more heavy than his senses? Does not the eye pass from an unpleasant object to a pleasant in a much shorter time than is required to this? and does not the unpleasantness of the first commend the beauty of the latter? The old rule of logic might have convinced him, that contraries, when placed near, set off each other. A continued gravity keeps the spirit too much bent; we must refresh it sometimes, as we bait in a journey that we may go on with greater ease. A scene of mirth, mixed with tragedy, has the same effect upon us which our music has betwixt the acts; which we find a relief to us from the best plots and language of the stage, if the discourses have been long. I must therefore have stronger arguments, ere I am convinced that compassion and mirth in the same subject destroy each other; and in the meantime cannot but conclude, to the honour of our nation, that we have invented, increased, and perfected a more pleasant way of writing for the stage, than was ever known to the ancients or moderns of any nation, which is tragi-comedy.

"And this leads me to wonder why Lisideius and many others should cry up the barrenness of the French plots above the variety and copiousness of the English. Their plots are single; they carry on one design, which is pushed forward by all the actors, every scene in the play contributing and moving towards it. Our plays, besides the main design, have under-plots or by-concernments, of less considerable persons and intrigues, which are carried on with the motion of the main plot: as they say the orb of the fixed stars, and those of the planets, though they have motions of their own, are whirled about by the motion of the *primum mobile*, in which they are contained. That similitude expresses much of the English stage; for if contrary motions may be found in nature to agree; if a planet can go east and west at the same time;—one way by virtue of his own motion, the other by the force of the First Mover;—it will not be difficult to imagine how the under-plot, which is only different, not contrary to the great design, may naturally be conducted along with it.

"Eugenius has already shown us, from the confession of the French poets, that the Unity of Action is sufficiently preserved, if all the imperfect actions of the play are conducing to the main design; but when those petty intrigues of a play are so ill ordered, that they have no coherence with the other, I must grant that Lisideius has reason to tax that want of due connection; for co-ordination in a play is as dangerous and unnatural as in a state. In the meantime he must acknowledge, our variety, if well ordered, will afford a greater pleasure to the audience.

"As for his other argument, that by pursuing one single theme they gain an advantage to express and work up the passions, I wish any example he could bring from them would make it good; for I confess their verses are to me the coldest I have ever read. Neither, indeed, is it possible for them, in the way they take, so to express passion, as that the effects of it should appear in the concernment of an audience, their speeches being so many declamations, which tire us with the length; so that instead of persuading us to grieve for their imaginary heroes, we are concerned for our own trouble, as we are in tedious visits of bad company; we are in pain till they are gone. When the French stage came to be reformed by Cardinal Richelieu, those long harangues were introduced to comply with the gravity of a churchman. Look upon the *Cinna* and the *Pompey;* they are not so properly to be called plays, as long discourses of reason of state; and *Polieucte* in matters of religion is as solemn as the long stops upon our organs. Since that time it is grown into a custom, and their actors speak by the hour-glass, like our parsons; nay, they account it the grace of their parts, and think themselves disparaged by the poet, if they may not twice or thrice in a play entertain the audience with a speech of an hundred lines. I deny not but this may suit well enough with the French; for as we, who are a more sullen people, come to be diverted at our plays, so they, who are of an airy and gay temper, come thither to make themselves more serious: and this I conceive to be one reason why comedies are more pleasing to us, and tragedies to them. But to speak generally: it cannot be denied that short speeches and replies are more apt to move the passions and beget concernment in us, then the other; for it is unnatural for any one in a gust of passion to speak long together, or for another in the same condition to suffer him, without interruption. Grief and passion are like floods raised in little brooks by a sudden rain: they are quickly up; and if the concernment be poured unexpectedly in upon us, it overflows us: but a long sober shower gives them leisure to run out as they came in, without troubling the ordinary current. As for Comedy, repartee is one of its chiefest graces; the greatest pleasure of the audience is a chase of wit, kept up on both sides, and swiftly managed. And this our forefathers, if not we, have had in Fletcher's plays, to a much higher degree of perfection than the French poets can reasonably hope to reach.

"There is another part of Lisideius his discourse, in which he rather excused our neighbours than commended them; that is, for aiming only to make one person considerable in their plays. 'Tis very true what he has urged, that one character in all plays, even without the poet's care, will have advantage of all the others; and that the design of the whole drama will chiefly depend on it. But this hinders not that there may be more shining characters in the play: many persons of a second magnitude, nay, some so very near, so almost equal to the first, that greatness may be opposed to greatness, and all the persons be made considerable, not only by their quality, but their action. 'Tis evident that the more the persons are, the greater will be the variety of the plot. If then the parts are managed so regularly, that the beauty of the whole be kept entire, and that the variety become not a perplexed and confused mass of accidents, you will find it infinitely pleasing to be led in a labyrinth of design, where you see some of your way before you, yet discern not the end till you arrive at it. And that all this is practicable, I can produce for examples many of our English plays: as *The Maid's Tragedy, The Alchemist, The Silent Woman:* I was going to have named *The Fox,* but that the unity of design seems not exactly observed in it; for there appear two actions in the play; the first naturally ending with the fourth act; the second forced from it in the fifth; which yet is the less to be condemned in him, because the disguise of Volpone, though it suited not with his character as a crafty or covetous person, agreed well enough with that of a voluptuary; and by it the poet gained the end at which he aimed, the punishment of vice, and the reward of virtue, both which that disguise produced. So that to judge equally of it, it was an excellent fifth act, but not so naturally proceeding from the former.

"But to leave this, and pass to the latter part of Lisideius his discourse, which concerns relations: I must acknowledge with him, that the French have reason to hide that part of the action which would occasion too much tumult on the stage, and to choose rather to have it made known by narration to the audience. Farther, I think it very convenient, for the reasons he has given, that all incredible actions were removed; but whether custom has so insinuated itself into our countrymen, or nature has so formed them to fierceness, I know not; but they will scarcely suffer combats and other objects of horror to be taken from them. And indeed, the indecency of tumults is all which can be objected against fighting: for why may not our imagination as well suffer itself to be deluded with the probability of it, as with any other thing in the play? For my part, I can with as great ease persuade myself that the blows are given in good earnest, as I can that they who strike them are kings or princes, or those persons which they represent. For objects of incredibility,—I would be satisfied from Lisideius, whether we have any so removed from all appearance of truth, as are those of Corneille's *Andromède;* a play which has been frequented the most of any he has writ. If the Perseus, or the son of a heathen god, the Pegasus, and the Monster, were not capable to choke a strong belief, let him blame any representation of ours hereafter. Those indeed were objects of delight; yet the reason is the same as to the probability: for he makes it not a Ballette or masque, but a play, which is to resemble truth. But for death, that it ought not to be represented, I have, besides the arguments alleged by Lisideius, the authority of Ben Jonson, who has forborne it in his tragedies; for both the death of Sejanus and Catiline are related: though in the latter I cannot but observe one irregularity of that great poet; he has removed the scene in the same act from Rome to Catiline's army, and from thence again to Rome; and besides, has allowed a very inconsiderable time, after Catiline's speech, for the striking of the battle, and the return of Petreius, who is to relate the event of it to the senate: which I should not animadvert on him, who was otherwise a painful observer of τὸ πρέπον, or the *decorum* of the stage, if he had not used extreme severity in his judgment on the incomparable Shakespeare for the same fault.—To conclude on this subject of relations; if we are to be blamed for showing too much of the action, the French are as faulty for discovering too little of it: a mean betwixt both should be observed by every judicious writer, so as the audience may neither be left unsatisfied by not seeing what is beautiful, or shocked by beholding what is either incredible or undecent. I hope I have already proved in this discourse, that though we are not altogether so punctual as the French in observing the laws of Comedy, yet our errors are so few, and little, and those things wherein we excel them so considerable, that we ought of right to be preferred before them. But what will Lisideius say, if they themselves acknowledge they are too strictly bounded by those laws, for breaking which he has blamed the English? I will allege Corneille's words, as I find them in the end of his Discourse of the Three Unities: *Il est facile aux speculatifs d'estre severes, etc.* ' 'Tis easy for speculative persons to judge severely; but if they would produce to public view ten or twelve pieces of this nature, they would perhaps give more latitude to the rules than I have done, when by experience they had known how much we are limited and constrained by them, and how many beauties of the stage they banished from it.' To illustrate a little what he has said: By their servile observations of the Unities of Time and Place, and integrity of scenes, they have brought on themselves that dearth of plot, and narrowness of imagination, which may be observed in all their plays. How many beautiful accidents might naturally happen in two or three days, which cannot arrive with any probability in the compass of twenty-four hours? There is time to be allowed also for maturity of design, which, amongst great and prudent persons, such as are often represented in Tragedy, cannot, with any likelihood of truth, be brought to pass at so short a warning. Farther; by tying themselves strictly to the Unity of Place, and unbroken scenes, they are forced many times to omit some beauties which cannot be shown where the act began; but might, if the scene were interrupted, and the stage cleared for the persons to enter in another place; and therefore the French poets are often forced upon absurdities; for if the act begins in a chamber, all the persons in the play must have some business or other to come thither, or else they are not to be shown that act; and sometimes their characters are very unfitting to appear there: as, suppose it were the king's bed-chamber; yet the meanest man in the tragedy must come and dispatch his business there, rather than in the lobby or courtyard (which is fitter for him), for fear the stage should be cleared, and the scenes broken. Many times they fall by it in a greater inconvenience; for they keep their scenes unbroken, and yet change the place; as in one of their newest plays, where the act begins in the street. There a gentleman is to meet his friend; he sees him with his man, coming out from his father's house; they talk together, and the first goes out: the second, who is a lover, has made an appointment with his mistress; she appears at the window, and then we are to imagine the scene lies under it. This gentleman is called away, and leaves his servant with his mistress; presently her father is heard from within; the young lady is afraid the serving-man should be discovered, and thrusts him into a place of safety, which is supposed to be her closet. After this, the father enters to the daughter, and now the scene is in a house; for he is seeking from one room to another for this poor Philipin, or French Diego, who is heard from within, drolling and breaking many a miserable conceit on the subject of his sad condition. In this ridiculous manner the play goes forward, the stage being never empty all the while: so that the street, the window, the houses, and the closet, are made to walk about, and the persons to stand still. Now what, I beseech you, is more easy than to write a regular French play, or more difficult than to write an irregular English one, like those of Fletcher, or of Shakespeare?

"If they content themselves, as Corneille did, with some flat design, which, like an ill riddle, is found out ere it be half proposed, such plots we can make every way regular, as easily as they; but whenever they endeavour to rise to any quick turns and counterturns of plot, as some of them have attempted, since Corneille's plays have been less in vogue, you see they write as irregularly as we, though they cover it more speciously. Hence the reason is perspicuous why no French plays, when translated, have, or ever can succeed on the English stage. For, if you consider the plots, our own are fuller of variety; if the writing, ours are more quick and fuller of spirit; and therefore 'tis a strange mistake in those who decry the way of writing plays in verse, as if the English therein imitated the French. We have borrowed nothing from them; our plots are weaved in English looms: we endeavour therein to follow the variety and greatness of characters which are derived to us from Shakespeare and Fletcher; the copiousness and well-knitting of the intrigues we have from Jonson; and for the verse itself we have English precedents of elder date than any of Corneille's plays. . . .

NOTES

1. "In the middle of plays they ask for a bear and pugilist."
2. "I should write a poem from a familiar story" (*Art of Poetry*, l. 240).
3. "He so lies, and mixes the true and false, that you cannot tell the beginning, middle, or end apart" (*Ibid.*, l. 151).
4. "Whatever you show me in that way I find incredible and disgusting" (*Ibid.*, l. 188).
5. "True things," yet "things like the truth."
6. This and the next two quotations translate as follows: "What we hear through our ears affects us less strongly than what we see through our eyes." "You should not bring onto the stage what should be done off it: some things should be kept from view and told instead with vivid immediacy." "Medea should not cut up her children in view of the audience; Procne should not be transformed into a bird there, nor Cadmus into a snake" (*Art of Poetry*).
7. "Just as we are inspired to follow those we consider most worthy, so— when we despair of excelling or equalling them—our enthusiasm and hope diminish. For what it cannot attain, it ceases to follow. . . . When that we cannot excel is over, we look for something else for which to strive" (Velleius Paterculus, I, 17).

SAMUEL JOHNSON

Preface to Shakespeare

It will be thought strange, that, in enumerating the defects of this writer, I have not yet mentioned his neglect of the unities; his violation of those laws which have been instituted and established by the joint authority of poets and criticks.

For his other deviations from the art of writing I resign him to critical justice, without making any other demand in his favour, than that which must be indulged to all human excellence: that his virtues be rated with his failings: But, from the censure which this irregularity may bring upon him, I shall, with due reverence to that learning which I must oppose, adventure to try how I can defend him.

His histories, being neither tragedies nor comedies are not subject to any of their laws; nothing more is necessary to all the praise which they expect, than that the changes of action be so prepared as to be understood, that the incidents be various and affecting, and the characters consistent, natural, and distinct. No other unity is intended, and therefore none is to be sought.

In his other works he has well enough preserved the unity of action. He has not, indeed, an intrigue regularly perplexed and regularly unravelled: he does not endeavour to hide his design only to discover it, for this is seldom the order of real events, and *Shakespeare* is the poet of nature: But his plan has commonly what *Aristotle* requires, a beginning, a middle, and an end; one event is concatenated with another, and the conclusion follows by easy consequence. There are perhaps some incidents that might be spared, as in other poets there is much talk that only fills up time upon the stage; but the general system makes gradual advances, and the end of the play is the end of expectation.

From *Preface to Shakespeare*, 1765.

To the unities of time and place he has shewn no regard; and perhaps a nearer view of the principles on which they stand will diminish their value, and withdraw from them the veneration which, from the time of *Corneille*, they have generally received, by discovering that they have given more trouble to the poet, than pleasure to the auditor.

The necessity of observing the unities of time and place arises from the supposed necessity of making the drama credible. The criticks hold it impossible, that an action of months or years can be possibly believed to pass in three hours; or that the spectator can suppose himself to sit in the theatre, while ambassadors go and return between distant kings, while armies are levied and towns besieged, while an exile wanders and returns, or till he whom they saw courting his mistress, shall lament the untimely fall of his son. The mind revolts from evident falsehood, and fiction loses its force when it departs from the resemblance of reality.

From the narrow limitation of time necessarily arises the contraction of place. The spectator, who knows that he saw the first act at *Alexandria*, cannot suppose that he sees the next at *Rome*, at a distance to which not the dragons of *Medea* could, in so short a time, have transported him; he knows with certainty that he has not changed his place, and he knows that place cannot change itself; that what was a house cannot become a plain; that what was *Thebes* can never be *Persepolis*.

Such is the triumphant language with which a critick exults over the misery of an irregular poet, and exults commonly without resistance or reply. It is time therefore to tell him by the authority of *Shakespeare*, that he assumes, as an unquestionable principle, a position, which, while his breath is forming it into words, his understanding pronounces to be false. It is false, that any representation is mistaken for reality; that any dramatick fable in its materiality was ever credible, or, for a single moment, was ever credited.

The objection arising from the impossibility of passing the first hour at *Alexandria*, and the next at *Rome*, supposes, that when the play opens, the spectator really imagines himself at *Alexandria*, and believes that his walk to the theatre has been a voyage to *Egypt*, and that he lives in the days of *Antony* and *Cleopatra*. Surely he that imagines this may imagine more. He that can take the stage at one time for the palace of the *Ptolemies*, may take it in half an hour for the promontory of *Actium*. Delusion, if delusion be admitted, has no certain limitation; if the spectator can be once persuaded, that his old acquaintance are

Alexander and *Caesar*, that a room illuminated with candles is the plain of *Pharsalia*, or the bank of *Granicus*, he is in a state of elevation above the reach of reason, or of truth, and from the heights of empyrean poetry, may despise the circumscriptions of terrestrial nature. There is no reason why a mind thus wandering in extasy should count the clock, or why an hour should not be a century in that calenture of the brains that can make the stage a field.

The truth is, that the spectators are always in their senses, and know, from the first act to the last, that the stage is only a stage, and that the players are only players. They came to hear a certain number of lines recited with just gesture and elegant modulation. The lines relate to some action, and an action must be in some place; but the different actions that complete a story may be in places very remote from each other; and where is the absurdity of allowing that space to represent first *Athens*, and then *Sicily*, which was always known to be neither *Sicily* nor *Athens*, but a modern theatre?

By supposition, as place is introduced, time may be extended; the time required by the fable elapses for the most part between the acts; for, of so much of the action as is represented, the real and poetical duration is the same. If, in the first act, preparations for war against *Mithridates* are represented to be made in *Rome*, the event of the war may, without absurdity, be represented, in the catastrophe, as happening in *Pontus;* we know that there is neither war, nor preparation for war; we know that we are neither in *Rome* nor *Pontus;* that neither *Mithridates* nor *Lucullus* are before us. The drama exhibits successive imitations of successive actions; and why may not the second imitation represent an action that happened years after the first, if it be so connected with it, that nothing but time can be supposed to intervene? Time is, of all modes of existence, most obsequious to the imagination; a lapse of years is as easily conceived as a passage of hours. In contemplation we easily contract the time of real actions, and therefore willingly permit it to be contracted when we only see their imitation.

It will be asked, how the drama moves, if it is not credited. It is credited with all the credit due to a drama. It is credited, whenever it moves, as a just picture of a real original; as representing to the auditor what he would himself feel, if he were to do or suffer what is there feigned to be suffered or to be done. The reflection that strikes the heart is not, that the evils before us are real evils, but that they are evils to which we ourselves may be exposed. If there be any fallacy, it is not that we fancy the players, but that we fancy ourselves unhappy for a moment; but we rather lament the possibility than suppose the presence of misery, as a mother weeps over her babe, when she remembers that death may take it from her. The delight of tragedy proceeds from our consciousness of fiction; if we thought murders and treasons real, they would please no more.

Imitations produce pain or pleasure, not because they are mistaken for realities, but because they bring realities to mind. When the imagination is recreated by a painted landscape, the trees are not supposed capable to give us shade, or the fountains coolness; but we consider, how we should be pleased with such fountains playing beside us, and such woods waving over us. We are agitated in reading the history of *Henry* the Fifth, yet no man takes his book for the field of *Agencourt*. A dramatick exhibition is a book recited with concomitants that encrease or diminish its effect. Familiar comedy is often more powerful in the theatre, than in the page; imperial tragedy is always less. The humour of *Petruchio* may be heightened by grimace; but what voice or what gesture can hope to add dignity or force to the soliloquy of *Cato*.

A play read, affects the mind like a play acted. It is therefore evident, that the action is not supposed to be real; and it follows, that between the acts a longer or shorter time may be allowed to pass, and that no more account of space or duration is to be taken by the auditor of a drama, than by the reader of a narrative, before whom may pass in an hour the life of a hero, or the revolutions of an empire.

Whether *Shakespeare* knew the unities, and rejected them by design, or deviated from them by happy ignorance, it is, I think, impossible to decide, and useless to enquire. We may reasonably suppose, that, when he rose to notice, he did not want the counsels and admonitions of scholars and cricks, and that he at last deliberately persisted in a practice, which he might have begun by chance. As nothing is essential to the fable, but unity of action, and as the unities of time and place arise evidently from false assumptions, and, by circumscribing the extent of the drama, lessen its variety, I cannot think it much to be lamented, that they were not known by him, or not observed: Nor, if such another poet could arise, should I very vehemently reproach him, that his first act passed at *Venice*, and his next in *Cyprus*. Such violations of rules merely positive, become the comprehensive genius of *Shakespeare*, and such censures are suitable to the minute and slender criticism of *Voltaire*:

> *Non usque adeo permiscuit imis*
> *Longus summa dies, ut non, si voce Metelli*
> *Serventur leges, malint a Caesare tolli.* *

Yet when I speak thus slightly of dramatick rules, I cannot but recollect how much wit and learning may be produced against me; before such authorities I am afraid to stand, not that I think the present question one of those that are to be decided by mere authority, but because it is to be suspected, that these precepts have not been so easily received but for better reasons than I have yet been able to find. The result of my enquiries, in which it would be ludicrous to boast of impartiality, is, that the unities of time and place are not essential to a just drama, that though they may sometimes conduce to pleasure, they are always to be sacrificed to the nobler beauties of variety and instruction; and that a play, written with nice observation of critical rules, is to be contemplated as an elaborate curiosity, as the product of superfluous and ostentatious art, by which is shewn, rather what is possible, than what is necessary.

He that, without diminution of any other excellence, shall preserve all the unities unbroken, deserves the like applause with the architect, who shall display all the orders of architecture in a citadel, without any deduction from its strength; but the principal beauty of a citadel is to exclude the enemy; and the greatest graces of a play, are to copy nature and instruct life.

---

* "A long time does not so confuse the highest with the lowest but that laws made by Metellus may wish to be abolished by Caesar."

ELEMENTS OF DRAMA

Illusion

More than any other literary form, drama, because it presents characters and events immediately to its audience, without the distancing influences of the printed page or the narrative voice, seems to urge the reality of its illusion. Yet that word "seems" can never quite disappear from any theatergoer's consciousness. In fact, in the previous section, Samuel Johnson dismisses the neoclassical demands for verisimilitude in the theater by pointing out that audiences quite easily accept unrealistic shifts of time and place in drama precisely because they know that they are watching not real human experiences but artistically ordered ones, an "illusion" of reality, not reality itself. But if the audience knows that it is accepting an illusion, it accepts it nevertheless, engaging in what the romantic poet and critic S. T. Coleridge called "that willing suspension of disbelief for the moment, which constitutes poetic faith." This willingness of the audience to share in the artistic illusion corresponds, Arthur Koestler suggests, to the dramatist's original impulse to share his subjective imaginings by transforming them into works of dramatic art that are publicly available. For the audience, the acceptance of illusion is, in its most primitive form, escapist, a shuffling off of the dreary concerns of everyday, but also an ennobling transcendence of the self in which one participates disinterestedly in the experiences of fictional people.

Like Harry Hotspur in Shakespeare's *Henry IV*, Tennessee Williams is acutely conscious that life is, unfortunately, time's fool. In drama, however, even time must have a stop, or at least a literary suspension. Unobscured for once by the insistent urgings of schedules, calendars, timetables, and clocks, the form and significance of human experience emerge for our unhurried contemplation.

Susanne Langer's searching analysis of dramatic illusion gradually develops into a theory of the nature of drama itself, which she regards as poetry, or "virtual history," in the mode of action. Narrative literature is experienced as a completed past, what Achilles or Aeneas "did," but drama is experienced as a continuous present evolving before us in the theater, what Hamlet or Phaedra "does." In drama, however, the present implicitly contains the future, so that the verbs of dramatic action, we might say, are not so much in the present indicative (Hamlet "goes") as in the present participial form (Hamlet "is going"), with the sense that has of a continuity issuing from the past and leading into the future. Purified of the randomness of real actions, drama's illusion is of Destiny, a consecutive convergence of acts upon an end. Dramatic illusion, or form-in-suspension, is what we experience while the play is in progress; dramatic *form,* or completed illusion, is what we afterwards perceive. Thus an experience in time gradually becomes in retrospect a configuration in space. Dealing in "virtual" instead of in "real" acts, drama remains like all art distinct from life, and in doing so requires of its audiences varying degrees of aesthetic distance.

Certain modern dramatists, especially Bertolt Brecht, have rebelled against the Coleridgean notion of a "willing suspension of disbelief" and against Koestler's concept of participation. Illusion, they have felt, is merely "delusion," a mindless acceptance. Instead, the theater should foster extreme forms of aesthetic distancing or, in Brecht's term, "alienation," which would keep the audience sufficiently detached from the actions of a play to perceive, not the "destiny" that Susanne Langer finds implicit in them, but their arbitrariness. Rebelling against the play's ordering of events, intellectually taking over instead of being emotionally taken in by the dramatic illusion, the audience is encouraged to adopt a revolutionary ardor that will carry over into social and political spheres outside the theater as well. Fortunately, Brecht's plays transcend the limitations of his theory, which would convert the theater into a classroom and drama into a glamorized editorial.

ARTHUR KOESTLER

Illusion

THE POWER OF ILLUSION

Literature begins with the telling of a tale. The tale represents certain events by means of auditory and visual signs. The events thus represented are mental events in the narrator's mind. His motive is the urge to communicate these events to others, to make them relive his thoughts and emotions; the urge to *share*. The audience may be physically present, or an imagined one; the narrator may address himself to a single person or to his god alone, but his basic need remains the same: he must share his experiences, make others participate in them, and thus overcome the isolation of the self.

To achieve this aim, the narrator must provide patterns of stimuli as substitutes for the original stimuli which caused the experience to occur. This, obviously, is not an easy task, for he is asking his audience to react to things which are not there, such as the smell of grass on a summer morning. Since the dawn of civilization, bards and storytellers have produced bags of tricks to provide such *Ersatz*-stimuli. The sum of these tricks is called the art of literature.

The oldest and most fundamental of all tricks is to disguise people in costumes and to put them on a stage with masks or paint on their faces; the audience is thereby given the impression that the events represented are happening *here* and *now,* regardless of how distant they really are in space and time. The effect of this procedure is to induce a very lively bisociated condition in the minds of the audience. The spectator knows, in one compartment of his mind, that the people on the stage are actors, whose names are familiar to him; and he knows that they are "acting" for the express purpose of creating an illusion in him, the spectator. Yet in another compartment of his mind he experi-

Reprinted by permission of Macmillan & Co. & Hutchinson & Co., Ltd. from *The Act of Creation* by Arthur Koestler, pp. 301–10. Copyright © Arthur Koeslter 1964.

ences fear, hope, pity, accompanied by palpitations, arrested breathing, or tears—all induced by events which he knows to be pure make-believe. It is indeed a remarkable phenomenon that a grown-up person, knowing all the time that he faces a screen onto which shadows are projected by a machine, and knowing furthermore quite well what is going to happen at the end—for instance, that the police will arrive just in the nick of time to save the hero—should nevertheless go through agonies of suspense, and display the corresponding bodily symptoms. It is even more remarkable that this capacity for living in two universes at once, one real, one imaginary, should be accepted without wonder as a commonplace phenomenon. The following extract from a London newspaper report may help to restore our sense of wonder: [1]

> Twice a week, with a haunting, trumpeted signature tune and a view of terraced roofs stretching away into infinity, *Coronation Street*, Granada Television's serial of North Country life, goes on the air. It has now had 200 issues and is coming up to its second birthday next week. It is one of Britain's most popular television programmes. Enthusiasts call it a major sociological phenomenon. In fact, all marathon TV serials with fixed settings and regular characters are cunningly designed to turn the viewer into an addict. *Coronation Street* eschews glamour and sensational curtains and concentrates on trapping the rugged smug ambience on North Country working and lower middle-class life. It will follow a local event like a council election or an amateur theatrical through instalment after instalment with the tenacity of a parish magazine. Its characters provide parts that actors can sink their teeth into and digest and assimilate. They have become deeply planted, like the permanent set of seven terraced houses, the shop on the corner, the Mission Hall, and the pub.
>
> The characters have devotees who insist on believing in their reality. When the buxom Elsie Tanner was involved with a sailor who, unknown to her, was married, she got scores of letters warning her of the danger. Jack Watson, the actor who played the sailor, was stopped outside the studio by one gallant mechanic who threatened to give him a hiding if he didn't leave Elsie alone.
>
> The strongest personality of them all, the sturdy old bulldog bitch, Ena Sharples, has a huge following. When she was sacked from the Mission Hall of which she was caretaker, viewers from all over the country wrote offering her jobs.

> When she was in hospital temporarily bereft of speech, a fight broke out in Salford between a gang of her fans and an Irish detractor who said he hoped the old bag would stay dumb till Kingdom come.

Moreover, when one of the seven houses on the set became "vacant" because its owner was said to have moved—in fact because the actor in question had been dropped from the programme—there were several applications for renting the house; and when at a dramatic moment of the serial the barmaid in the "Rover's Return" smashed an ornamental plate, several viewers sent in replacements to comfort her.

Of course, these people know that they are watching actors. Do they nevertheless believe that the characters are real? The answer is neither yes nor no, but yes and no. The so-called law of contradiction in logic —that a thing is either A or not-A but cannot be both—is a late acquisition in the growth of individuals and cultures. The unconscious mind, the mind of the child and the primitive, are indifferent to it. So are the Eastern philosophies which teach the unity of opposites, as well as Western theologians and quantum physicists. The addicts of *Coronation Street* who insist on believing in the reality of Ena Sharples have merely carried one step further the momentary split-mindedness experienced by a sophisticated movie-audience at the climax of a Hitchcock thriller; they live in a more or less permanently bisociated world.

THE VALUE OF ILLUSION

But where does beauty, aesthetic value, or "art" enter into the process? The answer requires several steps. The first is to recognize the *intrinsic value* of illusion in itself. It derives from the transfer of attention from the "Now and Here" to the "Then and There"—that is, to a plane remote from self-interest. Self-assertive behaviour is focussed on the Here and Now; the transfer of interest and emotion to a different time and location is in itself an act of self-transcendence in the literal sense. It is achieved through the lure of heroes and victims on the stage who attract the spectator's sympathy, with whom he partially identifies himself, and for whose sake he temporarily renounces his preoccupations with his own worries and desires. Thus the act of participating in an illusion has an inhibiting effect on the self-asserting tendencies, and facilitates the unfolding of the self-transcending tendencies. In other words illusion has a cathartic effect—as all ancient and modern civilizations recognized by incorporating various forms of magic into their purification-rites and abreaction therapies.

It is true that illusion, from Greek tragedy to horror comics, is also capable of generating fear and anger, palpitations and cold sweat, which seems to contradict its cathartic function. But the emotions thus generated are *vicarious* emotions derived from the spectator's participation in another person's existence, which is a self-transcending act. Consequently, however exciting the action on the stage, the anger or fear which it generates will always carry a component of sympathy, an irradiation of unselfish generosity, which facilitates catharsis—just as a varying amount of high-voltage current is always transformed into heat. At a later stage, when the climax of the drama is passed, and the tension ebbs away, the whole amount of the current is consumed in a gentle inner glow.

THE DYNAMICS OF ILLUSION

In the comedy, the accumulation of suspense, and its subsequent annihilation in laughter take place at distinctly separate stages (although the two may overlap in the smiling, anticipated pleasure of the joke to come). In the tragedy, on the other hand, excitation and catharsis are continuous. Laughter explodes emotion; weeping is its gentle overflow; there is no break in the continuity of mood, and no separation of emotion from reason. The hero, with whom the spectator has identified himself, cannot be debunked by slipping on a banana-skin or by any suden incongruity in his behaviour. The gods of the Greek and Hindu pantheon might change into any shape—a swan, a bull, a monkey, a shower of coins—and yet their paramours would lovingly surrender to them. On the bas-reliefs of Indian temples Shiva is often seen making love to Parvati while standing on his head, without appearing ridiculous. When the events in epic or drama take an unexpected turn— Odysseus's companions transformed into swine or chaste Ophelia singing obscene songs—emotion, if aggressively tainted, refuses to perform the jump and explodes in laughter; if sympathetic, it will follow the hero through all vicissitudes. The abrupt change of situation which required an equally quick reorientation of the mind to a different associative context, led in the first case to a rupture between emotion and reason, in the second to a transfer of emotion to the new context whereby its harmonious co-ordination with reason is preserved.

Thus incongruity—the confrontation of incompatible matrices—will be experienced as ridiculous, pathetic, or intellectually challenging, according to whether aggression, identification, or the well-balanced blend of scientific curiosity prevails in the spectator's mind. Don Quixote is a comic or a tragic figure, or a case-history of incipient paranoia, depending on the panel of the tryptich in which he is placed. In all three cases the matrices of reality and delusion—of windmills and phantom-knights—confront each other in the reader's mind. In the first case they collide, and malice is spilled in laughter. In the second, the two universes remain juxtaposed, reason oscillates to and fro between them, compassion remains attached to it and is easily transferred from one matrix to the other. In the third case, the two merge in a synthesis: the (emotionally "neutral") diagnosis of the clinician.

Thus compassion, and the other varieties of the participatory emotions, attach themselves to the narrative told on the stage or in print, like faithful dogs, and follow it whatever the surprises, twists, and incongruities the narrator has in store for them. By contrast, hostility, malice, and contempt tend to persist in a straight course, impervious to the subtleties of intellect; to them a spade is a spade, a windmill a windmill, and a Picasso nude with three breasts an object to leer at. The self-transcending emotions seem to be guided by the maxim *tout comprendre c'est tout pardonner;* the self-asserting emotions are designed for assertion, not comprehension. Hence, when attention is suddenly displaced from one frame of reference to another, the self-asserting impulses, deprived of their *raison d'être,* are spilled in the process, whereas the participatory emotions are transferred to the new matrix.

The physiological considerations which lend support to this view I have already discussed. Anger and fear owe their persistence and momentum to the sympathico-adrenal machinery, which causes them to become occasionally dissociated from reasoning. The self-transcending emotions, on the other hand, are accompanied by parasympathetic reactions which are in every respect the opposite of the former; since they are devoid of massiveness and momentum, there is no cause for their falling out of step with the higher mental activities, and the normal co-ordination of thought and emotion will prevail. If your mind has the nimbleness of migrating, at a moment's notice, into Romeo's in sixteenth-century Verona, then you will also be capable of shedding tears at Juliet's death.

We must remember, however, that emotions are complex mixtures; our amusement at Charlie Chaplin's adventures is full of compassion.

All that is required for a mildly comic effect is that an aggressive factor should be present of sufficient strength to provide a certain inertia of feeling—or anaesthesia of the heart.

ESCAPISM AND CATHARSIS

Illusion, then, is the simultaneous presence and interaction in the mind of two universes, one real, one imaginary. It transports the spectator from the trivial present to a plane remote from self-interest and makes him forget his own preoccupations and anxieties; in other words, it facilitates the unfolding of his participatory emotions, and inhibits or neutralizes his self-asserting tendencies.

This sounds like an escapist theory of art; and in spite of its derogatory connotations, the expression contains a grain of truth—though no more than a grain. The analysis of any aesthetic experience requires, as said before, a series of steps; and the escape offered by transporting the spectator from his bed-sitter in Bayswater to the Castle of Elsinore is merely the bottom step of the ladder. But, nevertheless, it should not be under-estimated. In the first place, if illusion offers escape it is escape of a particular kind, sharply distinguished from other distractions such as playing tennis or bingo. It teaches us to live on two planes at once. Children and primitive audiences who, forgetting the present, completely accept the reality of the events on the stage, are experiencing not an aesthetic thrill, but a kind of hypnotic trance; and addiction to it may lead to various degrees of estrangement from reality. The aesthetic experience depends on that delicate balance arising from the presence of *both* matrices in the mind; on perceiving the hero as Laurence Olivier and Prince Hamlet of Denmark at one and the same time; on the lightning oscillations of attention from one to the other, like sparks between charged electrodes. It is this precarious suspension of awareness between the two planes which facilitates the continuous flux of emotion from the Now and Here to the remoter worlds of Then and There, and the cathartic effects resulting from it. For when interest is deflected from the self it will attach itself to something else; when the level of self-assertive tension falls, the self-transcending impulses become almost automatically dominant. Thus the creation of illusion is in itself of cathartic value—even if the product, judged by more sophisticated standards, is of cheap quality; for it helps the subject to actualize his potential of self-transcending emotions thwarted by the dreary routines of existence. Liberated from his frustrations and anxieties, man can turn into a rather nice and dreamy creature; when he changes into a dark suit and sits in a theatre, he at once shows himself capable of taking a strong and entirely unselfish interest in the destinies of the personae on the stage. He participates in their hopes and sufferings; his frustrated cravings for communion find their primeval outlet in the magic of identification.

To revert to Aristotle, the cathartic function of the tragedy is "through incidents arousing horror and pity to accomplish the purgation of such emotions." In cruder terms, a good cry, like a good laugh, has a more lasting after-effect than the occasion seems to warrant. Taking the Aristotelian definition at face value, it would seem that the aesthetic experience could purge the mind only of those emotions which the stage-play has created; that it would merely take out of the nervous system what it has just put in, leaving the mind in the same state as before. But this is not so. The emotion is not created, but merely stimulated by the actors; it must be "worked up" by the spectator. The work of art does not provide the current, like an electricity company, but merely the installations; the current has to be generated by the consumer. Although this is obvious once we remember it, we tend to fall into the mistake of taking a metaphor at face value and believing that the stage "provides" us with a thrill against cash payment for a seat in the stalls. What we buy, however, is not emotion, but a sequence of stimuli cunningly designed to trigger off our latent participatory emotions which otherwise would remain frustrated or look for coarser outlets, and to assure their ultimate consummation. Life constantly generates tensions which run through the mind like stray eddies and erratic currents. The aesthetic experience inhibits some, canalizes others, but above all, it draws on unconscious sources of emotion which otherwise are only active in the games of the underground.

Thus the concept of catharsis assumes a twofold meaning. Firstly, it signifies that concentation on the illusory events on the stage rids the mind of the dross of its self-centred trival preoccupations; in the second place it arouses its dormant self-transcendent potentials and provides them with an outlet, until they peacefully ebb away. Peaceful, of course, does not necessarily mean a happy ending. It may mean the "earthing" of an individual tragedy in the universal tragedy of the human condition—as the scientist resolves a problem by showing that a particular phenomenon is an instance of a general law. It may dissolve the bitterness of personal sorrow in the vastness of the oceanic feeling; and redeem horror by pity. Tragedy, in the Greek sense, is the school of self-transcendence.

IDENTIFICATION AND MAGIC

The projections of a single cine-camera with its rotating Maltese cross arouse anger, terror, and righteous indignation in up to five successive audiences on a single day, as if it were a machine designed for the wholesale manufacture of adrenalin. Yet the emotions aroused even by a cheap thriller-film are vicarious emotions derived from one of the primordial games of the underground: the transformation of one person or object into another. The fear and anger experienced by the audience is experienced on behalf of another person; the adrenalin secreted into their bloodstream is secreted to provide another person with excess energy for fight or flight; the magic of identification is at work.

It enters into illusion in two stages. The first is the partial identification, in the spectator's mind, of the actor with the character he is meant to represent; the second is the partial identification of the spectator with one or several of the characters. In both cases the identification is only partial, but nevertheless the magic is powerful enough to provide the palpitations and activate the supra-renal glands. And when I speak of magic, I am not speaking metaphorically; the "magic of the stage" is a cliché which originates in the sympathetic magic practised by all primitive and not-so-primitive cultures, rooted in the belief in the substantial identity of the masked dancer with the demon he mines; of the impersonator with the power he impersonates. The unconscious self, manifested in the beliefs of the child and the dreams of the adult, is, as we saw, immune to contradiction, unsure of its identity, and prone to merging it with others. ' "In the collective representations of primitive mentality, objects, beings, events can be, though in a way incomprehensible to us, both themselves and something other than themselves." [2] This description of tribal mentality by a Victorian anthropologist could be applied almost without qualifications to the audiences of *Coronation Street*.

I have taken a short-cut from primitive to contemporary magic, but the development is in fact historically continuous: the latter is a direct descendant of the former. Dramatic art has its origin in ceremonial rites—dances, songs, and mime—which enacted important past or desired future events: rain, a successful hunt, an abundant harvest. The gods, demons, ancestors and animals participating in the event were impersonated with the aid of masks, costumes, tattooings and make-up. The shaman who danced the part of the rain-god *was* the rain-god, and yet remained the shaman at the same time. From the stag dances of the Huichol Indians or the serpent dances of the Zuñi, there is only one step to the goat dance of the Achaeans, the precursor of Greek drama. "Tragedy" means "goat-song" (*tragos*—he goat, *oide*—song); it probably originated in the ceremonial rites in honour of Dyonysius, where the performers were disguised in goat-skins as satyrs, and in the related ceremonies in honour of Apollo and Demeter. Indian and Chinese stage-craft have similarly religious origins. Etruscan drama derived from funeral rites; modern European drama evolved from the medieval mystery plays performed on the occasion of the main church festivals. But though the modern theatre hardly betrays its religious ancestry, the magic of illusion still serves essentially the same emotional needs: it enables the spectator to transcend the narrow confines of his personal identity, and to participate in other forms of existence. For—to quote for a last time the unfashionable Lévy-Bruhl, to whom Freud, Jung, and others owe so much:

> The need of participation remains something more imperious and intense, even among people like ourselves, than the thirst for knowledge and the desire for conformity with the claims of reason. It lies deeper in us and its source is more remote. During the long prehistoric ages, when the claims of reason were scarcely realized or even perceived, it was no doubt all-powerful in all human aggregates. Even today the mental activity which, by virtue of an intimate participation, possesses its object, gives it life and lives through it—finds entire satisfaction in this possession.[3]

THE DAWN OF LITERATURE

The dawn of literature, too, was bathed in the twilight of mysticism and mythology. "The recitation of the Homeric poems on the Panathanaea corresponds to the recitation elsewhere of the sacred texts in the temple; the statement of Phemios that a god inspired his soul with all the varied ways of song expresses the ordinary belief of early historical times." [4] But the earliest *literati*—priests, prophets, rhapsodes, bards—had less direct means to impress their audiences than their older colleagues, the masked and painted illusion-mongers. They had to "dramatize" their tales, by techniques which we can only infer from hints. The dramatization of an epic recital aims, like stage-craft from which it is derived, at creating, to some extent at least, the illusion that the events told are happening now and here. Perhaps the oldest of these techniques is the use of direct speech, to make the audience believe that it is listening not to the narrator but to the characters themselves; its use is still as frequent in the modern novel as it was in the Homeric epos. In the ancient forms of oral recital it was supplemented by imitation of voice and gesture—another tradition still alive in the nursery room. The minstrels and troubadours, the joculators or jugglers, the scôps and the *chansonniers de geste*, were direct descendants of the Roman mimes—actors who, having lost their livelihood when the Roman theatre decayed, became vagabonds and diverted their patrons with dancing, tumbling, juggling and recitals as much acted as told. The early minstrels were called *histriones,* stage-players; the bard Taillefer, who sang the *Chanson de Roland* during the battle of Hastings, is described as a *histrion* or *mimus.*

There is hardly a novelist who had not wished at times that he were a *histrion,* and could convey by direct voice, grimace, and gesture what his characters look like and feel. But writers have evolved other techniques to create the illusion that their characters are alive, and to make their audience fall in love with a heroine who exists only as printer's ink on paper. The real tears shed over Anna Karenina or Emma Bovary are the ultimate triumph of sympathetic magic.

NOTES

1. Compressed from *The Observer,* London, 2.12.62.
2. Lévy-Bruhl (1926), p. 76.
3. Ibid. p. 385
4. J. Fitzmaurice Kelly, article on "Literature" in *Enc. Brit.,* 13th ed.

TENNESSEE WILLIAMS

The Timeless World of a Play

Carson McCullers concludes one of her lyric poems with the line:
"Time, the endless idiot, runs screaming 'round the world." It is this
continual rush of time, so violent that it appears to be screaming, that
deprives our actual lives of so much dignity and meaning, and it is,
perhaps more than anything else, the *arrest of time* which has taken
place in a completed work of art that gives to certain plays their feeling
of death and significance. In the London notices of *Death of a Salesman*
a certain notoriously skeptical critic made the remark that Willy Loman
was the sort of man that almost any member of the audience would have
kicked out of an office had he applied for a job or detained one for conversation about his troubles. The remark itself possibly holds some truth.
But the implication that Willy Loman is consequently a character with
whom we have no reason to concern ourselves in drama, reveals a
strikingly false conception of what plays are. Contemplation is something that exists outside of time, and so is the tragic sense. Even in the
actual world of commerce, there exists in some persons a sensibility to
the unfortunate situations of others, a capacity for concern and compassion, surviving from a more tender period of life outside the present
whirling wire-cage of business activity. Facing Willy Loman across an
office desk, meeting his nervous glance and hearing his querulous voice,
we would be very likely to glance at our wrist watch and our schedule
of other appointments. We would not kick him out of the office, no, but
we would certainly *ease* him out with more expedition than Willy had
feebly hoped for. But suppose there had been no wrist watch or office
clock and suppose there had *not* been the schedule of pressing appointments, and suppose that we were not actually facing Willy across a
desk—and facing a person is *not* the best way to *see* him!—suppose, in

other words, that the meeting with Willy Loman had somehow occurred in a world *outside* of time. Then I think we would receive him with concern and kindness and even with respect. If the world of a play did not offer us this occasion to view its characters under that special condition of a *world without time,* then, indeed, the characters and occurrences of drama would become equally pointless, equally trivial, as corresponding meetings and happenings in life.

The classic tragedies of Greece had tremendous nobility. The actors wore great masks, movements were formal, dance-like, and the speeches had an epic quality which doubtless were as removed from the normal conversation of their contemporary society as they seem today. Yet they did not seem false to the Greek audiences: the magnitude of the events and the passions aroused by them did not seem ridiculously out of proportion to common experience. And I wonder if this was not because the Greek audiences knew, instinctively or by training, that the created world of a play is removed from that element which makes people *little* and their emotions fairly inconsequential.

Great sculpture often follows the lines of the human body: yet the repose of great sculpture suddenly transmutes those human lines to something that has an absoluteness, a purity, a beauty, which would not be possible in a living mobile form.

A play may be violent, full of motion: yet it has that special kind of repose which allows contemplation and produces the climate in which tragic importance is a possible thing, provided that certain modern conditions are met.

In actual existence the moments of love are succeeded by the moments of satiety and sleep. The sincere remark is followed by a cynical distrust. Truth is fragmentary, at best we love and betray each other not in quite the same breath but in two breaths that occur in fairly close sequence. But the fact that passion occurred in *passing,* that it then declined into a more familiar sense of indifference, should not be regarded as proof of its inconsequence. And this is the very truth that drama wishes to bring us. . . .

Whether or not we admit it to ourselves, we are all haunted by a truly awful sense of impermanence. I have always had a particularly keen sense of this at New York cocktail parties, and perhaps that is why I drink the martinis almost as fast as I can snatch them from the tray. This sense is the febrile thing that hangs in the air. Horror of insincerity, of *not meaning,* overhangs these affairs like the cloud of cigarette smoke and the hectic chatter. This horror is the only thing, almost, that is left unsaid at such functions. All social functions involving a group of people not intimately known to each other are always under this shadow. They are almost always (in an unconscious way) like that last dinner of the condemned: where steak or turkey, whatever the doomed man wants, is served in his cell as a mockingly cruel reminder of what the great-big-little-transitory world had to offer.

In a play, time is arrested in the sense of being confined. By a sort of legerdemain, events are made to remain *events*, rather than being reduced so quickly to mere *occurrences*. The audience can sit back in a comforting dusk to watch a world which is flooded with light and in which emotion and action have a dimension and dignity that they would likewise have in real existence, if only the shattering intrusion of time could be locked out.

About their lives people ought to remember that when they are finished, everything in them will be contained in a marvelous state of repose which is the same as that which they unconsciously admired in drama. The rush is temporary. The great and only possible dignity of man lies in his power deliberately to choose certain moral values by which to live as steadfastly as if he, too, like a character in a play, were immured against the corrupting rush of time. Snatching the eternal out of the desperately fleeting is the great magic trick of human existence. As far as we know, as far as there exists any kind of empiric evidence, there is no way to beat the game of *being* against *non-being*, in which non-being is the predestined victor on realistic levels.

Yet plays in the tragic tradition offer us a view of certain moral values in violent juxtaposition. Because we do not participate, except as spectators, we can view them clearly, within the limits of our emotional equipment. These people on the stage do not return our looks. We do not have to answer their questions nor make any sign of being in company with them, nor do we have to compete with their virtues nor resist their offenses. All at once, for this reason, we are able to *see* them! Our hearts are wrung by recognition and pity, so that the dusky shell of the auditorium where we are gathered anonymously together is flooded with an almost liquid warmth of unchecked human sympathies, relieved of self-consciousness, allowed to function. . . .

Men pity and love each other more deeply than they permit themselves to know. The moment after the phone has been hung up, the hand reaches for a scratch pad and scrawls a notation: "Funeral Tuesday at five, Church of the Holy Redeemer, don't forget flowers." And the same hand is only a little shakier than usual as it reaches, some minutes later, for a highball glass that will pour a stupefaction over the kindled nerves. Fear and evasion are the two little beasts that chase each other's tails in the revolving wire-cage of our nervous world. They distract us from feeling too much about things. Time rushes toward us with its hospital tray of infinitely varied narcotics, even while it is preparing us for its inevitably fatal operation. . . .

So successfully have we disguised from ourselves the intensity of our own feelings, the sensibility of our own hearts, that plays in the tragic tradition have begun to seem untrue. For a couple of hours we may surrender ourselves to a world of fiercely illuminated values in conflict, but when the stage is covered and the auditorium lighted, almost immediately there is a recoil of disbelief. "Well, well!" we say as we shuffle back up the aisle, while the play dwindles behind us with the sudden perspective of an early Chirico painting. By the time we have arrived at Sardi's, if not as soon as we pass beneath the marquee, we have convinced ourselves once more that life has as little resemblance to the curiously stirring and meaningful occurrences on the stage as a jingle has to an elegy of Rilke.

This modern condition of his theater audience is something that an author must know in advance. The diminishing influence of life's destroyer, time, must be somehow worked into the context of his play. Perhaps it is a certain foolery, a certain distortion toward the grotesque, which will solve the problem for him. Perhaps it is only restraint, putting a mute on the strings that would like to break all bounds. But almost surely, unless he contrives in some way to relate the dimensions of his tragedy to the dimensions of a world in which time is *included*—he will be left among his magnificent debris on a dark stage, muttering to himself: "Those fools. . . ."

And if they could hear him above the clatter of tongues, glasses, chinaware and silver, they would give him this answer: "But you have shown us a world not ravaged by time. We admire your innocence. But we have seen our photographs, past and present. Yesterday evening we passed our first wife on the street. We smiled as we spoke but we didn't really see her! It's too bad, but we know what is true and not true, and at 3 A.M. your disgrace will be in print!"

SUSANNE LANGER

The Dramatic Illusion

Most theoretical treatments of literature draw their material and evidence as much from drama as from lyric and narrative works. A serious analysis of literary art with only an occasional, passing mention of Shakespeare may have seemed to many readers a curious innovation. The reason for it, however, is simple enough, ... Shakespeare is essentially a dramatist, and drama is not, in the strict sense, "literature."

Yet it is a poetic art, because it creates the primary illusion of all poetry—virtual history. Its substance is an image of human life—ends, means, gains and losses, fulfillment and decline and death. It is a fabric of illusory experience, and it is the essential product of poesis. But drama is not merely a distinct literary form; it is a special poetic mode, as different from genuine literature as sculpture from pictorial art, or either of these from architecture. That is to say, it makes its own basic abstraction, which gives it a way of its own in making the semblance of history.

Literature projects the image of life in the mode of virtual memory; language is its essential material; the sound and meaning of words, their familiar or unusual use and order, even their presentation on the printed page, create the illusion of life as a realm of events—completed, lived, as words formulate them—events that compose a Past. But drama presents the poetic illusion in a different light: not finished realities, or "events," but immediate, visible responses of human beings, make its semblance of life. Its basic abstraction is the act, which springs from the past, but is directed toward the future, and is always great with things to come.

In using common words, such as "event" or "act," as analytic terms,

From *Feeling and Form* by Susanne K. Langer, pages 306–25. Copyright 1953 Charles Scribner's Sons. Reprinted by permission of Charles Scribner's Sons and Routledge & Kegan Paul, Ltd.

one runs the danger of suggesting far less general concepts, and indeed a variety of them, all equally inadequate to the purpose in hand. "Event," . . . is used in the sense given it by Whitehead, to cover all space-time occurrence, even the persistence of objects, the repetitious rhythms of life, the occasion of a thought as well as of an earthquake. Similarly, by "act" I mean any sort of human response, physical or mental. The word is commonly used, of course, in more specialized senses. It may mean one of the major divisions of a play—Act I, Act II, etc.; or it may refer to overt behavior, rushing about, laying hands on someone, taking or surrendering an object, and so forth, or it may mean a piece of dissembling, as when one says of a person that he feels one way and acts another. In the general sense here employed however, all *reactions* are acts, visible or invisible; so in drama, any illusion of physical or mental activity is here called an "act," and the total structure of acts is *a virtual history in the mode of dramatic action*.

An act, whether instinctive or deliberate, is normally oriented toward the future. Drama, though it implies past actions (the "situation"), moves not toward the present, as narrative does, but toward something beyond; it deals essentially with commitments and consequences. Persons, too, in drama are purely agents—whether consciously or blindly, makers of the future. This future, which is made before our eyes, gives importance to the very beginnings of dramatic acts, i.e. to the motives from which the acts arise, and the situations in which they develop; the making of it is the principle that unifies and organizes the continuum of stage action. It has been said repeatedly that the theater creates a perpetual present moment [1], but it is only a present filled with its own future that is really dramatic. A sheer immediacy, an imperishable direct experience without the ominous forward movement of consequential action, would not be so. As literature creates a virtual past, drama creates a virtual future. The literary mode is the mode of Memory; the dramatic is the mode of Destiny.

The future, like the past, is a conceptual structure, and expectation, even more obviously than memory, is a product of imagination.[2] The "now" created by poetic composition is always under the aegis of some historical vision which transcends it; and its poignancy derives not from any comparison with actuality, but from the fact that the two great realms of envisagement—past and future—intersect in the present, which consequently has not the pure imaginative form of either memory or prophecy, but a peculiar appearance of its own which we designate as "immediacy" or "now."

In actual life the impending future is very vaguely felt. Each separate act is forward-looking—we put on a kettle expecting it to boil, hand someone a bill and expect to be given change, board a bus with casual confidence that we shall leave it again at an intended point, or board an airplane with somewhat more conscious interest in our prospective exit from its inside. But we do not usually have any idea of the future as a total experience which is coming because of our past and present acts; such a sense of destiny arises only in unusual moments under peculiar emotional stress.

In drama, however, this sense of destiny is paramount. It is what makes the present action seem like an integral part of the future, howbeit that future has not unfolded yet. The reason is that on the stage, every thought expressed in conversation, every feeling betrayed by voice or look, is determined by the total action of which it is a part—perhaps an embryonic part, the first hint of the motive that will soon gather force. Even before one has any idea of what the conflict is to be (i.e. before the "exposition" has been given), one feels the tension developing. This tension between past and future, the theatrical "present moment," is what gives to acts, situations, and even such constituent elements as gestures and attitudes and tones, the peculiar intensity known as "dramatic quality."

In a little-known volume, bearing the modest, impersonal title: *Essays by Divers Hands* (a volume of "Transactions" of the Royal Society of Literature in England),[3] there is a very thoughtful philosophical essay by Charles Morgan, called "The Nature of Dramatic Illusion," in which he seems to me to have both stated and answered the question of what is created in the full-fledged work of dramatic art—the enacted play.

"With every development of dramatic technique," he wrote there, "and every departure from classical structure, the need increases for a new discussion which . . . shall establish for the stage not indeed a formal rule but an aesthetic discipline, elastic, reasoned, and acceptable to it in modern circumstances.

"It is my purpose, then, to discover the principle from which such a discipline might arise. This principle I call the principle of illusion." [4]

"Illusion, as I conceive it, is form in suspense. . . . In a play form is not valuable *in itself*, only the suspense of form has value. In a play, form is not and cannot be valuable in itself, because until the play is over form does not exist. . . .

"A play's performance occupies two or three hours. Until the end its form is latent in it. . . .

"This suspense of form, by which is meant the incompleteness of a known completion, is to be clearly distinguished from common suspense—suspense of plot—the ignorance of what will happen, . . . for suspense of plot is a structural accident, and suspense of form is, as I understand it, essential to the dramatic form itself. . . .

"What form is chosen . . . matters less than that while the drama moves *a* form is being fulfilled." [5]

"Fulfilled" is here the key word to the idea of dramatic form. Everything, of course, has a form of some sort: the famous million monkeys playing a million typewriters for a million years, turning out chance combinations of letters, would be rendering countless phonetic forms (though some of these might not encourage pronunciation); similarly, the most aimless conglomerate of events, acts, utterances, or what not, would *produce* a form when taken together; but before such collections were complete (which would be simply when, for any reason, one stopped collecting), no one could imagine their form. There has to be a sense of the whole, some anticipation of what may or even must come, if the production of new elements is to give the impression that "a form is being fulfilled."

Dramatic action is a semblance of action so constructed that a whole indivisible piece of virtual history is implicit in it, as a yet unrealized form, long before the presentation is completed. This constant illusion of an imminent future, this vivid appearance of a growing situation before anything startling has occurred, is "form in suspense." It is a human destiny that unfolds before us, its unity is apparent from the opening words, or even silent action, because on the stage we see acts in their entirety, as we do not see them in the real world except in retrospect, that is, by constructive reflection. In the theater, they occur in simplified and completed form, with visible motives, directions, and ends. Since stage action is not, like genuine action, embedded in a welter of irrelevant doings and divided interests, and characters on the stage have no unknown complexities (however complex they may be), it is possible there to see a person's feelings grow into passions, and those passions issue in words and deeds.

We know, in fact, so little about the personalities before us at the opening of a play that their every move and word, even their dress and walk, are distinct items for our perception. Because we are not involved with them as with real people, we can view each smallest act in its context, as a symptom of character and condition. We do not have to find what is significant; the selection has been made—whatever is there is significant, and it is not too much to be surveyed *in toto*. A character stands before us as a coherent whole. It is with characters as with their situations: both become visible on the stage, transparent and complete as their analogues in the world are not.[6]

But what really assures the artistic unity Morgan called "form in suspense," is the illusion of Destiny itself that is given in drama, and that arises chiefly from the way the dramatist handles circumstance. Before a play has progressed by many lines, one is aware not only of vague conditions of life in general, but of a special situation. Like the distribution of figures on a chessboard, the combination of characters makes a strategic pattern. In actual life we usually recognize a distinct situation only when it is reached, or nearly reached, a crisis; but in the theater we see the whole setup of human relationships and conflicting interests long before any abnormal event has occurred that would, in actual life, have brought it into focus. Where in the real world we would witness some extraordinary act and gradually understand the circumstances that lie behind it, in the theater we perceive an ominous situation and see that some far-reaching action must grow out of it. This creates the peculiar tension between the given present and its yet unrealized consequent, "form in suspense," the essential dramatic illusion. This illusion of a visible future is created in every play—not only in very good plays, but in everything we recognize as a play, and not as dance, pageantry, or other non-dramatic "theater art." [7] It is the primary illusion of poetry, or virtual history, in the mode peculiar to drama. The future appears as already an entity, embryonic in the present. That is Destiny.

Destiny is, of course, always a virtual phenomenon—there is no such thing in cold fact. It is a pure semblance. But what it "resembles" (or, in the Aristotelian language which has been lately revived, what it "imitates") is nonetheless an aspect of real experience, and, indeed, a fundamental one, which distinguishes human life from animal existence: the sense of past and future as parts of one continuum, and therefore of life as a single reality.

This wide awareness, which we owe to our peculiarly human talent of symbolic expression, is rooted, however, in the elementary rhythms which we share with all other organisms, and the Destiny which dramatic art creates bears the stamp of organic process—of predeterminate function, tendency, growth, and completion. . . . In every art [the abstraction of those vital forms] is differently achieved; but in each one, I think, it is equally subtle—not a simple reference to natural instances of that form, but a genuinely abstractive handling of its reflection in non-living or even non-physical structures. Literally "organic process" is a biological concept; "life," "growth," "development," "decline," "death"—all these are strictly biological terms. They are applicable only to organisms. In art they are lifted out of their literal context, and forthwith, in place of organic processes, we have dynamic forms: instead of metabolism, rhythmic progression, instead of stimulus and response, completeness, instead of maturation, fulfillment, instead of procreation, the repetition of the whole in the parts—what Henry James calls "reflection" in the parts,[8] and Heinrich Schenker "diminution," [9] and Francis Fergusson "analogy." [10] And in lieu of a law of development, such as biology sets up, in art we have destiny, the implicit future.

The purpose of abstracting vital forms from their natural exemplifications is, of course, to make them available for unhampered artistic use. The illusion of growth, for instance, may be made in any medium, and in numberless ways: lengthening or flowing lines, that represent no live creatures at all; rhythmically rising steps even though they divide or diminish; increasing complexity of musical chords, or insistent repetitions; a centrifugal dance; poetic lines of gradually deepening seriousness; there is no need of "imitating" anything literally alive in order to convey the appearance of life. Vital forms may be reflected in any elements of a work, with or without representation of living things.

In drama the *situation* has its own "organic" character, that is to say, it develops, or grows, as the play proceeds. That is because all happenings, to be dramatic, must be conceived in terms of acts, and acts belong only to life; they have motives rather than causes, and in turn motivate further and further acts, which compose integrated *actions*. A situation is a complex of impending acts. It changes from moment to moment, or rather, from move to move, as the directly imminent acts are realized and the future beyond them becomes distinct and fraught with excitement. In this way, the *situation* in which characters act differs from their "environment"—a term with which it is sometimes confused, through the influence of the social sciences that invaded the theater a generation ago and bred a teeming, if short-lived progeny of sociological plays, with a few real dramas among them. The environment wherein characters have developed, and whereby they are stunted or hardened, refined or falsely veneered, is almost always implicit (*almost* always, i.e. except where it becomes a conscious factor of interest to someone in the play). The situation, on the other hand, is always explicit. Even in a vague romantic world like that of Pelléas and Mélisande, removed from all actual history, and so ungeographical that the environment is really just castle walls and a forest, without population (the chorus of women in the death-scene simply springs up *ex nihilo*—there were no inhabitants in the background before, as there are in Shakespeare's castles), the situation that elicits the action is clear.

The situation is, indeed, part of the action; it is conceived entirely by the dramatist, and is given by him to the actors to understand and enact, just as he gives them the words to be spoken. The situation is a created element in the play; it grows to its climax, often branching out into elaborate detail in the course of its development, and in the end it is resolved by the closing of the action.

Where "environment" enters into drama at all, it enters as an idea entertained by persons in the play, such as the slum visitors and reformers of the "radical" problem play. They themselves, however, do not appear in an environment, because that sociological abstraction has no meaning for the theater. They appear in a setting. "Environment" is an invisible constant, but "setting" is something immediate, something sensuously or poetically present. The playwright may utilize a setting as Strindberg did in his earlier plays, to establish the feeling of everyday life, or he may put it to the opposite purpose of removing the scene from all familiar associations, as Wagner sought to do by his extravagant stage demands. The setting is a highly variable factor, which the poets of former ages used to entrust to those who put their plays on the boards; a practice which harbors dangers, but also speaks of a healthy faith in the power of the script to guide the theatrical imagination that is to project it. There is a grand freedom given with the simple indication: "Thebes."

Drama is more variable, more tolerant of choices made by performing artists, than any other art and mode. For this reason, the "commanding form," which is established by the playwright, must be clear and powerful. It has to govern the crisscross of many imaginative minds, and hold them all—the director, the actors, the designers of sets and lights and costumes—to one essential conception, an unmistakable "poetic core." But the poet must give his interpreters scope, too; for drama is essentially an enacted poem, and if the acting can only duplicate what the lines already effect, there will be unintended redundancy, and an apparent clutter of superfluous elements that makes the total form impure and opaque (such failures of clear conception, not the use of materials "belonging" to other arts, not bold secondary illusions, are the source of impurity in a work; if the commanding form is organic and its realization economical, the most abnormal materials will be assimilated, the most intense effects of abstracted space, time, or power will become part of the pure dramatic work).

If drama is not made of words as a piece of literature is, how can the poet, who composes only the "lines," be said to create the commanding form? "Lines" in a play are only the stuff of speeches; and speeches are only some of the acts that make drama.

They are, however, acts of a special sort. Speech is a highly specialized activity in human life, and its image in all modes of poetry, therefore, has peculiar and powerful uses. Verbal utterance is the overt issue of a greater emotional, mental, and bodily response, and its preparation in feeling and awareness or in the mounting intensity of thought is implicit in the words spoken. Speech is like a quintessence of action. Edith Wharton described its relation to the rest of our activities very aptly, when she indicated its use in her own poetic medium, prose fiction: "The use of dialogue in fiction . . . should be reserved for the culminating movements, and regarding as the spray into which the great wave of narrative breaks in curving toward the watcher on the shore." [11]

Mrs. Wharton's metaphor of the wave is more apt than her literal statement, because one naturally thinks of "culminating moments" as rare moments, high points of the story, whereas the culmination of thought and feeling in speech is a frequent occurrence, like the culmination and breaking of each wave in a constant surf.

If, moreover, one contemplates the metaphor a little more deeply, it conveys a further relation of speech to the poetic elements that surround it, namely: that it is always of the same nature as they, subject to the basic abstraction of the mode in which it is used. In narrative it is an event, like all the events that compose the virtual Past—the private events that culminate in "direct discourse," the public events that intersect in the speaker's experience, and those which the speech, as a new event, engenders. In drama speech is an act, an utterance, motivated by visible and invisible other acts, and like them shaping the oncoming Future.

A playwright who writes only the lines uttered in a play marks a long series of culminating moments in the flow of the action. Of course he indicates the major non-verbal acts, but that may be done with the

fewest possible words: *enter So-and-so, exit So-and-so,* or such laconic
directions as: *dies, they fight, excursions and alarums.* Modern playwrights sometimes write pages of instructions to the actors, even describing the heroine's figure and face, or the style of some character's
motions and postures (Strindberg tells the leading actor in *Miss Julie*
to look like a half-educated man!). Such "stage directions" are really
literary treatments of the story—what Clayton Hamilton called, "the
sort of stage directions which, though interesting to the reader, are of
no avail whatever to the actor," [12] because they do not partake of the
dramatic form. Ibsen prefaced his opening scenes with minute descriptions of persons and set; but his greatest interpreters have always made
free with them. The lines of the play are the only guide a good director
or actor needs. What makes the play the author's work is that the lines
are really the highlights of a perpetual, progressive action, and determine what can be done with the piece on stage.

Since every utterance is the end of a process which began inside the
speaker's body, an enacted utterance is part of a virtual act, apparently
springing at the moment from thought and feeling; so the actor has to
create the illusion of an inward activity issuing in spontaneous speech,
if his words are to make a dramatic and not a rhetorical effect. As a
very interesting German writer, Ferdinand Gregori, expressed it, "Gesture is older than words, and in the actor's dramatic creation, too, it
must be their herald. Whether it is visible to the audience or not, it
must always be the pacemaker. Anyone who starts with the words and
then hunts for the appropriate gesture to accompany them, lies to the
face of art and nature both." [13]

The need of preparing every utterance by some elements of expression and bearing that foreshadow it, has led many theorists and almost
all naive spectators to the belief that an actor must actually undergo
the emotive experiences he renders—that he must "live" his part, and
produce speech and gesture from a genuine passion. Of course the
stage-occurrence is not his own life, but (according to this view) he
must pretend to be the individual he represents, until he actually feels
the emotions he is to register. Oddly enough, people who hold this
belief do not ask whether the actor must also actually have the motives
and desires of his alter ego—that is, whether he must really intend or at
least wish to kill his antagonist, or to divulge a secret.

The imputation of bona fide feelings and emotions to the actor on
stage would be only a negligible popular error, were it not part and
parcel of a broader fallacy—the confusion of theatrical representation

with "make-believe," or pretense, which has always led both play-wrights and directors to misconceive the relation of the audience to the play, and saddled them with the gratuitous and silly problem of the spectator's credulity. The classic expression of concern is, of course, Castelvetro's warning in his *Poetics*, published in 1570: "The time of the representation and that of the action presented must be exactly coincident. There is no possibility of making the spectators believe that many days and nights have passed, when they themselves obviously know that only a few hours have actually elapsed; they refuse to be so deceived." [14] Corneille, a generation later, still accepted the principle, though he complained that to limit a dramatic action quite strictly to one room and the time span of a theater visit "is so awkward, not to say impossible, that some enlargement of place must of necessity be found, as also of time." [15]

An art principle that cannot be fully and wholeheartedly applied, but requires compromises and evasions, should be immediately sus-pect; yet the principle of making the spectators believe that they are witnessing actual happenings has been accepted down to our own day,[16] and though most theorists have seen its error, it still crops up in contemporary criticism, and—worse yet—in theater practice. We have fairly well recovered from the epidemic of naturalism, the stagecraft that sought to dispense with all artifice, and consequently borrowed living material from the actual world—"drugstore clerks drafted to impersonate themselves in real drugstores transferred bodily to the stage," as Robert Edmond Jones described this sort of dramaturgy. Now it is true that real art *can* be made with such devices; no device in itself is taboo, not even putting stage-beggars in clothes begged from real beggars (Edward Wothern, in his autobiography, recalls his acquisition of one such alluring treasure). But the theory that a play is a game of "make-believe" designed by the poet, carried on by actors, and supported by an audience willing to pretend that the stage history is actual, which still persists, and with it its practical counterpart—the principle of deluding the audience, aiding the public "make-believe" by making the play seem as real as possible—is another story.

The whole conception of theater as delusion is closely linked with the belief that the audience should be made to share the emotions of the protagonists. The readiest way to effect this is to extend the stage action beyond the stage in the tensest moments, to make the spectators feel themselves actually present as witnesses of the scene. But the result is artistically disastrous, since each person becomes aware not only of his own presence, but of other people's too, and of the house, the stage, the entertainment in progress. Rosamond Gilder reported such an experience in her comment on Orson Welles' staging of *Native Son;* describing the scene wherein Bigger Thomas is cornered by his pursuers, she said: "Here flashing lights, gun-play, shouting and shooting converge on the stage from balcony and boxes. The theatrical illusion, far from being increased, is shattered, and the scene becomes nothing more than a nineteen-forty-one version of Eliza crossing the ice." [17]

I, too, remember vividly to this day the terrible shock of such a recall to actuality: as a young child I saw Maude Adams in *Peter Pan.* It was my first visit to the theater, and the illusion was absolute and overwhelming, like something supernatural. At the highest point of the action (Tinkerbell had drunk Peter's poisoned medicine to save him from doing so, and was dying) Peter turned to the spectators and asked them to attest their belief in fairies. Instantly the illusion was gone; there were hundreds of children, sitting in rows, clapping and even calling, while Miss Adams, dressed up as Peter Pan, spoke to us like a teacher coaching us in a play in which she herself was taking the title role. I did not understand, of course, what had happened; but an acute misery obliterated the rest of the scene, and was not entirely dispelled until the curtain rose on a new set.

The central fallacy in such play production, and in the concept of drama that it assumes, is the total disregard of what Edward Bullough, in an essay that has become deservedly famous,[18] called "psychical Distance." All appreciation of art—painting, architecture, music, dance, whatever the piece may be—requires a certain detachment, which has been variously called the "attitude of contemplation," the "aesthetic attitude," or the "objectivity" of the beholder. As I pointed out in an early chapter of this book,[19] it is part of the artist's business to make his work elicit this attitude instead of requiring the percipient to bring an ideal frame of mind with him. What the artist establishes by deliberate stylistic devices is not really the beholder's attitude—that is a by-product—but a relation between the work and its public (including himself). Bullough terms this relationship "Distance," and points out quite rightly that "objectivity," "detachment," and "attitudes" are complete or incomplete, i.e. perfect or imperfect, but do not admit of degrees. "Distance, on the contrary, admits naturally of degrees, and differs not only according to the nature of the *object*, which may impose a greater or smaller degree of Distance, but varies also according to the *individual's capacity* for maintaining a greater or lesser degree.[20]

He describes (rather than defines) his concept, not without resort to metaphor, yet clearly enough to make it a philosophical asset:

"Distance . . . is obtained by separating the object and its appeal from one's own self, by putting it out of gear with practical needs and ends. . . . But it does not mean that the relation between the self and the object is broken to the extent of becoming 'impersonal'. . . . On the contrary, it describes a *personal* relation, often highly emotionally colored, but *of a peculiar character*. Its peculiarity lies in that the personal character of the relation has been, so to speak, filtered. It has been cleared of the practical, concrete nature of its appeal. . . . One of the best-known examples is to be found in our attitude towards the events and characters of the drama. . . ." [21]

This relation "of a peculiar character" is, I believe, our natural relation to a symbol that embodies an idea and presents it for our contemplation, not for practical action, but "cleared of the practical, concrete nature of its appeal." It is for the sake of this remove that art deals entirely in illusions, which, because of their lack of "practical, concrete, nature," are readily distanced as symbolic forms. But delusion—even the quasi-delusion of "make-believe"—aims at the opposite effect, the greatest possible nearness. To seek delusion, belief, and "audience participation" in the theater is to deny that drama is art.

There are those who do deny it. There are very serious critics who see its essential value to society not in the sort of revelation that is proper to art, but in its function as a form of ritual. Francis Fergusson and T. S. Eliot have treated drama in this vein,[22] and several German critics have found in the custom of hand clapping a last vestige of the audience participation that is really the public's lost birthright.[23] There are others who regard the theater not as a temple, but primarily as an amusement hall, and demand of drama that it shall please, delude us for a while, and incidentally teach morals and "knowledge of man." Brander Matthews extended the demand for amusement—any or every sort of amusement—to all the arts; but as his renown rests entirely on his dramatic criticism and teaching, his view of "art" is really a view of the theater casually extended to all other realms. "The primary purpose of all the arts is to entertain," said Matthews, "even if every art has also to achieve its own secondary aim. Some of these entertainments make their appeal to the intellect, some to the emotions, and some only to the nerves, to our relish for sheer excitement and for brute sensation; but each of them in its own way seeks, first of all, to entertain. They are, every one of them, to be included in the show business." [24]

Here we have certainly two extremes of dramatic theory; and the theory I hold—that drama is art, a poetic art in a special mode, with its own version of the poetic illusion to govern every detail of the performed piece—this theory does not lie anywhere between these extremes. Drama is neither ritual nor show business, though it may occur in the frame of either one; it is poetry, which is neither a kind of circus nor a kind of church.

Perhaps the greatest snare in the course of our thinking about theater is its free trafficking with the standard materials of all the other arts. People are so used to defining each art by its characteristic medium that when paint is used in the theater they class the result as "the painter's art," and because the set requires building, they regard the designer of it as an architect. Drama, consequently, has so often been described as a synthesis of several or even all arts that its autonomy, its status as a special mode of a great single art, is always in jeopardy. It has been treated as essentially dance, by confusion with pantomimic dances that have a dramatic plot; it has been conceived as tableau and pageantry heightened by speech and action (Gordon Craig held that the designer of its visual aspects was its real creator), and as poetic recitation accompanied by gestures, sometimes by dance-gestures. This last view is traditional in India, where it is supported by the obvious epic sources of Hindu plays (as usual, finding the source of a phenomenon is supposed to reveal its "real" nature). Hindu aestheticians, therefore, regard drama as literature, and judge it by literary standards.[25] Nietzsche found its origin in "the spirit of music" and consequently regarded its true nature as musical. Thornton Wilder describes it as an exalted form of narrative: "The theater," he writes, "carries the art of narration to a higher power than the novel or the epic poem. . . . The dramatist must be by instinct a story-teller." [26]

But story-telling, narration, is something quite different from story-enactment in a theater. Many first-rate story-tellers cannot make a play, and the highest developments of narration, such as the modern novel and short story, show devices of their own that have no meaning for the stage. They project a history in retrospect, whereas drama is history coming. Even as performed arts, narration and dramatization are distinct. The ancient rhapsodist, for all his gesticulations and inflections, was not an actor, and today, too, people who are known as good readers of poetry or prose need not therefore have any aptitude for the theater.

The concept of drama as literature embellished with concurrent appeals to the sense of sight is belied most convincingly in the very society where it enjoys its traditional vogue; the fact that in India the classic drama survived as a popular art for centuries after both the Sanskrit and the various Prakrits in which it was composed had become dead languages, understood only by scholars, proves that the stage action was no mere accompaniment, but was instinctively developed by the actors to the point of self-sufficiency, making the precise word meanings of the speeches dispensable; that this drama is, in fact, what Cocteau called "a poetry of the theater," as well as "poetry in the theater."

As for dance, though it probably preceded drama on the boards, and though it uses dramatic plots after its own fashion, it does not give rise to drama, not even to true pantomime. Any direct dramatic action tends to suspend the balletic illusion. The fact that Greek drama arose amidst ritual dancing has led several art historians to consider it as a dance episode; but the dance was, in fact, only a perfect framework for the development of an entirely new art; the minute the two antagonists stepped out of the choric ensemble and addressed not the deity, nor the congregation, but each other, they created a poetic illusion, and drama was born in midst of the religious rite. The choric dance itself was assimilated to the world of the virtual history they presented.

Once we recognize that drama is neither dance nor literature, nor a democracy of various arts functioning together, but is poetry in the mode of action, the relations of all its elements to each other and to the whole work become clear: the primacy of the script, which furnishes the commanding form; the use of the stage, with or without representational scenery, to delimit the "world" in which the virtual action exists; the need of making the scene a "place," so that often the designer produces a plastic illusion that is secondary here, but primary in the art of architecture; [27] the use of music and sometimes of dance to keep the fictitious history apart from actuality and insure its artistic abstraction; [28] the nature of dramatic time, which is "musical" instead of practical time, and sometimes becomes strikingly evident—another secondary illusion in poetry, but the primary one of music. The guiding principle in the use of so many transient borrowed illusions is the making of an *appearance*, not under normal circumstances, like a pretense or social convention, but under the circumstances of the play. Its total emotional tone is like the "palette" of a picture, and controls the intensity of color and light, the sober or fantastic character of the sets, the requirements such as overture, interludes, and what not.

Above all, that emotional tone guides the style of the actors. The actors are the chief interpreters—normally, the only indispensable ones —of the poet's incomplete but commanding creations. An actor does not undergo and vent emotions; he conceives them, to the smallest detail, and enacts them.

Some of the Hindu critics, although they subordinate and even deprecate dramatic art in favor of the literary elements it involves, understand much better than their Western colleagues the various aspects of emotion in the theater, which our writers so freely and banefully confuse: the feelings experienced by the actor, those experienced by the spectators, those presented as undergone by characters in the play, and finally the feeling that shines through the play itself—the vital feeling of the piece. This last they call *rasa;* it is a state of emotional knowledge, which comes only to those who have long studied and contemplated poetry. It is supposed to be of supernatural origin, because it is not like mundane feeling and emotion, but is detached, more of the spirit than of the viscera, pure and uplifting.[29]

Rasa is, indeed, that comprehension of the directly experienced or "inward" life that all art conveys. The supernatural status attributed to its perception shows the mystification that beset the ancient theorists when they were confronted with the power of a symbol which they did not recognize as such. Audiences who can dispense with the helps that the box stage, representational setting and costumes, and sundry stage properties lend to our poetic imagination have probably a better understanding of drama as art than we who require a potpourri of means. In Indian, Chinese, and Japanese drama—but most consistently in the Far Eastern—not only events and emotions, but even *things* are enacted. Stage properties exist, but their use is symbolic rather than naturalistic. Even the simulation of feeling may be sacrificed to enhance the formal value, the emotional effect of the play as a whole. Objects involved in the action are simply implied by gesture.[30] In India, some stage properties do occur—carts, dragons, even elephants—and are elaborately made of paper, bamboo, lacquer, etc.; others are left to the imagination. The deciding factor seems to be whether the action turns on the non-human element, or not. A king who quite incidentally mounts a chariot merely indicates its existence by an act, but in *The Little Clay Cart* the cart is really put upon the stage. European spectators at Chinese plays always find it surprising and offensive that attendants in ordinary dress come and go on the stage; but to the initiated audience the stagehand's untheatrical dress seems to be enough to make his presence as irrelevant as to us the intrusion of an usher who leads people to a seat in our line of vision.

On the Japanese stage, an actor may step out of his part by giving a signal and address the audience, then by another formal sign resume his role.

A public that enjoys such pure acting gives itself up to the dramatic illusion without any need for sensuous delusion. But sensuous satisfaction it does want: gorgeous robes and curtains, a rich display of colors, and always music (of a sort that Westerners often find no asset). These elements make the play dramatically convincing precisely by holding it aloof from actuality; they assure the spectator's "psychical Distance" instead of inviting him to consider the action as a piece of natural behavior. For in the theater, where a virtual future unfolds before us, the import of every little act is heightened, because even the smallest act is oriented toward the future. What we see, therefore, is not behavior, but the self-realization of people in action and passion; and as every act has exaggerated importance, so the emotional responses of persons in a play are intensified. Even indifference is a concentrated and significant attitude.

As every act and utterance set down in the poet's script serves to create a perceptible destiny, so all plastic, choreographic, or musical elements that are added to his play in the theater must support and enhance that creation. The dramatic illusion is poetic, and where it is primary—that is to say, where the work is a drama—it transmutes all borrowings from other art into poetic elements. As Mr. Jones says in *The Dramatic Imagination,* "In the last analysis the designing of stage scenery is not the problem of an architect or a painter or a sculptor or even a musician, but of a poet." [31] It is the painter (or architect, or sculptor) turned poet who understands the commanding form which the author has composed by writing the lines of the play, and who carries this form to the further state of visibility, and it is the actor-poet who takes the whole work—words, setting, happenings, all—through the final phase of its creation, where words become utterances and the visible scene is fused into the occurrence of the virtual life.

Histrionic imagination is the same fundamental talent in the playwright, the leading actors, the performers of even the smallest parts in so far as they are genuine actors, the scene and light designer, the costumer, the light controller, the composer or selector of incidental music, the ballet master, and the director who surveys the whole to his satisfaction or despair. The work on which they are engaged is one thing —an apparition of Destiny.

"From the Greeks to Ibsen the actor has represented, by elocution as well as by movement, human character and human destiny. . . . When drama takes on the abstract character of music or pure dance it ceases to be drama. . . .

"The dramatist . . . is a writer, a poet, before he is a musician or a choreographer. Wagner of course showed that many dramatic elements can be embodied in orchestral music; silent movies showed how much can be done with the visual element alone; but if you add Wagner to Eisenstein and multiply by ten you still do not have a Shakespeare or an Ibsen. This does not say that drama is better than music, dancing, or the visual arts. It is different.

"The defenders of the arts of the theater must be infected by the commodities of the theater if they can forget that all 'theater arts' are means to one end: the correct presentation of a poem." [32]

NOTES

1. For example, R. E. Jones in *The Dramatic Imagination*, p. 40, says: "This is drama; this is theatre—*to be aware of the Now.*" And Thornton Wilder, in "Some Thoughts on Playwriting," lists as one of the "four fundamental conditions of the drama" that "its action takes place in a perpetual present time." —"On the stage it is always now." (*The Intent of the Artist*, p. 83.)

2. Compare the observations of George Mehlis, . . . Mehlis mistook the nature of the "distancing" effect of memory and expectation, which he thought rested on people's tendency to leave out the unpleasant, and a consequent "aesthetic improvement" of the facts; but despite this error he noted truly the transformational power of both projections.

3. N. S. Vol. 12, ed. by R. W. Macan, 1933. The article in question covers pp. 61–77.

4. Ibid., p. 61.

5. Ibid., pp. 70–72.

6. A German critic, Peter Richard Rohden, saw this difference in our understanding of illusory and actual persons, respectively, as something of a paradox. "What," he wrote, "distinguishes a character on stage from a 'real' person? Obviously the fact that the former stands before us as a fully articulated whole. Our fellowmen we always perceive only in fragmentary fashion, and our power of self-observation is usually reduced, by vanity and cupidity, to zero. What we call 'dramatic illusion' is, therefore, the paradoxical phenomenon that we know more about the mental processes of a Hamlet than about our own inner life. For the poet-actor Shakespeare shows not only the deed,

but also its motives, and indeed more perfectly than we ever see them together in actual life." (See "Das Schauspielerische Erlebnis," in Ewald
Geissler's collection of essays, *Der Schauspieler*, p. 36.)

7. On this point Mr. Morgan might not agree with me. Having stated that
"form in suspense" is the dramatic illusion itself, and the suspense of form
something "without which drama is not," he speaks elsewhere of the dramatic illusion as a rare experience, "the highest reward of playgoing." I do
not know whether he uses two concepts or only one, somewhat different
from mine.

8. *The Art of Fiction*, p. 170.

9. Cf. Chap. 8, p. 129.

10. *The Idea of a Theater*, p. 104.

11. *The Writing of Fiction*, p. 73.

12. *The Theory of the Theatre*, p. 307. A few paragraphs later he remarked
on Granville-Barker's plays: "Barker's printed stage directions are little novels
in themselves."

12. "Die Vorbildung des Schauspielers," in Ewald Geissler's collection *Der
Schauspieler*. See p. 46.

14. Reprinted in *The Great Critics, An Anthology of Literary Criticism*,
edited by J. H. Smith and E. W. Parks. See p. 523.

15. Ibid., p. 531. From *A Discourse on the Three Unities*.

16. Strindberg, for instance, was convinced that the spectators in the theater
let themselves be deluded, tricked into believing or making-believe that what
they saw was actual life going on in their presence, and he was seriously afraid
of what popular education, and the general enlightenment it was expected to
bring, would do to people's credulity. In the famous preface to *Miss Julie* he
observes that "the theater has always served as a grammar school to young
people, women, and those who have acquired a little knowledge, all of whom
retain the capacity for deceiving themselves and being deceived," but that
"in our time, when the rudimentary, incomplete thought-processes operating
through our fancy seem to be developing into reflection, research, and
analysis, the theater might stand on the verge of being abandoned as a
decaying form, for the enjoyment of which we lack the requisite conditions."

17. "Glamor and Purpose," in *Theatre Arts*, May 1941, pp. 327–335.

18. "'Psychical Distance' as a Factor in Art and an Aesthetic Principle,"
British Journal of Psychology, June, 1912.

19. See Chap. 4.

20. *Op. cit.*, p. 94.

21. *Op. cit.*, p. 91. The attitude referred to is, of course, the famous "aesthetic attitude," here treated as an index to the proper degree of distance.

22. Cf. Francis Fergusson, *The Idea of a Theater*. A book so full of ideas,
scholarship and discernment that even in taking issue with it I would recom-
mend it to every reader.

   T. S. Eliot, in "A Dialogue on Dramatic Poetry" (in *Selected Essays, 1917–
1932*), p. 35, lets "E" say, "The only dramatic satisfaction that I find now is
in a High Mass well performed."

23. E.g., Theodor Wiesengrund-Adorno, "Applaus," *Die Musik*, 23 (1930–
31), p. 476; also A. E. Gunther, "Der Schauspieler und wir," in Geissler's *Der
Schauspieler*, p. 144.

24. *A Book About the Theater*, p. 6.

25. Cf. Sylvain Levi, *Le théâtre indien*, p. 257: "They [Indian theorists] are wont to consider drama as the juxtaposition of two arts, which simultaneously pursue their respective ends, namely poetry and mimetic dance. . . . Dance and mummery, stagecraft and scenery combine to heighten the illusion and pleasure by appealing to several senses. Representation, therefore, surpasses reading by a quantitative difference of emotion; there is no qualitative difference between them." See also A. B. Smith, *The Sanskrit Drama*, pp. 294–295.

26. "Some Thoughts on Playwriting," p. 86.

27. Cf. Jones, *op. cit.*, p. 75: "The energy of a particular play, its emotional content, its aura, so to speak, has its own definite physical dimensions. It extends just so far in space and no farther. The walls of the setting must be placed at precisely this point."

George Beiswanger, in a little article entitled "Opera for the Eye" (*Theatre Arts*, January, 1943, p. 59), makes a similar remark: "Each opera has its own ideal dimensions, and their illusion must be created whether the actual stage be large or small."

28. Schiller, in his famous preface to *Die Braut von Messina*, called the Greek Chorus, which he revived in this play, "a living wall" to preserve the Distance of the work.

29. Sylvain Levi, *op. cit.*, p. 295.

30. See Jack Chen, *The Chinese Theater;* A. E. Zucker, *The Chinese Theater;* Noel Peri, *Cinq no: Drames lyriques japonais.* The last-named gives the most detailed account of this technique.

31. p. 77.

32. From E. R. Bentley, "The Drama at Ebb," *Kenyon Review*, VII, 2 (Spring, 1945), 169–184.

BERTOLT BRECHT

from *On the Experimental Theatre*

Sympathetic understanding is a main support of the prevailing aesthetic. In the imposing *Poetics* of Aristotle we have a description of how Catharsis, that is, the spiritual purification of the spectator, was brought about through *mimesis*. The actor imitates the hero (Oedipus or Prometheus), and he does so with such suggestion and power of conversion that the spectator imitates him in the role and thus possesses himself of the hero's experience. Hegel, who, to my knowledge, drew up the last of the important systems of aesthetics, refers to the ability of man to experience the same emotions when faced with simulated reality as he does when faced with reality itself. What I want to acquaint you with now is that a series of experiments to establish a practicable view of life by means of the theatre's resources has led to the staggering question whether to achieve this end it is necessary, more or less, to surrender sympathetic understanding. Unless one perceives humanity, with all its conditions, proceedings, manners of behavior and institutions, as something stable and unchangeable, and unless one accepts the attitudes of humanity, as one has accepted them of nature with such success for several centuries, those critical attitudes, concerning change and the mastery of nature, then one is unable to utilize the technique of sympathetic understanding. Sympathetic understanding in changeable human beings, in avoidable acts, and in superfluous pain, et cetera, is not possible. As long as the stars of his fate hang over King Lear, as long as we consider him as being unchangeable, his deeds subject to nature without restriction, even presented as being fated, so long can we be sympathetically understanding towards him. To discuss his behavior is as impossible as a discussion of the splitting of the atom would have been in the tenth century.

If the intercourse between stage and public were to occur on the basis of sympathetic understanding, then at any given moment the spectator could have seen only as much as the hero saw with whom he was joined in sympathetic understanding. And towards particular situations on the stage opposite him he could only have such emotional responses as the "mood" on stage permitted. The observations, emotions, and perceptions of the spectators were the same as those which brought the characters on stage into line. The stage could scarcely generate emotions, permit observations and facilitate understanding, which are not suggestively represented on it. Lear's wrath over his daughters infects the spectator, that is, the spectator, watching him, could only experience wrath, not perhaps amazement or uneasiness, and the same holds for other possible emotions. The wrath of Lear, therefore, could not be tested against its justification nor could it be provided with a prophecy of its possible consequences. It was not to be discussed, only to be shared in. In this way social phenomena appeared eternal, natural, unchangeable, unhistorical, and did not hold for discussion. My use of the term "discussion" here does not imply a dispassionate treatment of a theme, a purely intellectual process. We are not concerned with simply making the spectator immune to the wrath of Lear. It is only the direct transplantation of this wrath that must be stopped. An example: The wrath of Lear is shared in by his faithful servant Kent. Kent soundly thrashes a servant of the thankless daughters, who is instructed to disobey one of Lear's wishes. Shall the spectator of our time share Lear's wrath and approve of it, while in essence sympathizing with the thrashing of the servant, carried out on Lear's orders? The question is this: How can this scene be played so that the spectator, on the contrary, flies into a passion because of Lear's wrath? Only an emotion of this kind which can deny the spectator sympathetic understanding, which generally only he can experience, and which generally could occur only to him, and then only if he breaks through the theatre's power of suggestion, can be socially justified. Tolstoy had excellent things to say on this very matter.

Sympathetic understanding is the important artificial means of an age in which man is the variable and his surroundings the constant. One can be sympathetically understanding only towards a person who, unlike ourselves, bears the stars of his destiny within him.

Human beings go to the theatre in order to be swept away, captivated, impressed, uplifted, horrified, moved, kept in suspense, released, diverted, set free, set going, transplanted from their own time, and supplied with illusions. All of this goes so much without saying that the art of the theatre is candidly defined as having the power to release, sweep away, uplift, et cetera. It is not an art at all unless it does so.

The question, then, is this: Is the artistic treat at all possible without sympathetic understanding, or, in any case, is it possible on a basis other than sympathetic understanding?

What could a new basis such as this offer us?

What can be substituted for *pity* and *terror*, the twin-yoked classical cause of Aristotle's Catharsis? When one renounces hypnosis to what can one appeal? What attitude should a spectator partake of in this new theatre, when he is denied the illusionary, passive, resigned-to-fate attitude? He should no longer be abducted from his own world into the world of art, no longer be kidnapped; on the contrary, he should be ushered into his own real world, with attentive faculties. Would it be possible, perhaps, to substitute for pity, helpful collaboration? Is it possible therewith to create a new contact between the stage and the spectator, might this offer a new basis for the artistic treat? I cannot describe here the new technology of playwriting, of theatre construction and of acting techniques, through which our experiments were carried out. The principle consists in introducing in place of sympathetic understanding what we will call *Alienation*.

What is Alienation?

To alienate an event or a character is simply to take what to the event or character is obvious, known, evident and produce surprise and curiosity out of it. Let us consider again the wrath of Lear over the thanklessness of his daughters. Through the techniques of sympathetic understanding the actor is able to present this wrath in such a way that the spectator sees it as the most natural thing in the world, so that he cannot imagine how Lear could not become wrathful, so that he is in complete agreement with Lear, sympathizing with him completely, having himself fallen into the same wrath. Through the technique of alienation, on the other hand, the actor presents the wrath of Lear in such a way that the spectator can be surprised at it, so that he can conceive of still other reactions from Lear as well as that of wrath. The attitude of Lear is alienated, that is, it is presented as belonging specifically to Lear, as something shocking, remarkable, as a social phenomenon which is not self-evident. This emotion of wrath is human, but it is not universally applicable; there are human beings who do not experience it. The experiences of Lear need not produce in all people of all times the emotion of wrath. Wrath may be an eternally possible reaction of the human being, but this kind of wrath, the kind of wrath which manifests itself in this way and which has such origins as those of Lear, is an ephemeral thing. The process of alienation, then, is the process of historifying, of presenting events and persons as historical, and therefore as ephemeral. The same, of course, may happen with contemporaries; their attitudes may also be presented as ephemeral, historical, and evanescent.

What do we achieve by this? We achieve the fact that the spectator need no longer see the human beings presented on the stage as being unchangeable, unadaptable, and handed over helpless to fate. What he sees is that this human being is thus and so because conditions are thus and so. And conditions are thus and so because human beings are thus and so. This human being, however, is capable of being presented not only in this way, as he is, but in other ways also, as he might be; conditions, too, are capable of being presented in other ways than as they are. As a result of this the spectator has a new attitude in the theatre. He has the same attitude towards the images of the human world opposite him on the stage which he, as a human being, has had towards nature during this century. He is also welcomed into the theatre as the great reformer, one who is capable of coming to grips with the natural and social processes, one who no longer merely accepts the world passively but who masters it. The theatre no longer seeks to intoxicate him, supply him with illusions, make him forget the world, to reconcile him to his fate. The theatre now spreads the world in front of him to take hold of and use for his own good.

The technique of alienation was developed in Germany through a new series of experiments. At the Theater am Schiffbauerdamm [1] in Berlin we attempted to develop a new style of production. The most gifted of the younger generation of actors worked with us. There were Helene Weigel, Peter Lorre, Oskar Homolka, Neher, and Busch. Our experiments could not be carried through so methodically as those of the foreign schools of Stanislavski, Meyerhold, and Vachtangov because we had no state support, but our experiments were, therefore, pursued more widely and not merely in the professional theatre. Artists participated in experiments of schools, workers' choruses, amateur groups, et cetera. From the beginning amateur groups were developed along with the professional. The experiments led to a vast simplification of apparatus, style of production and subject matter.

It was a question throughout of continuing the earlier experiments, and those of Piscator's theatre in particular. Even in Piscator's last ex-

periments the consequent development of the technical apparatus led
to the realization that the machinery which then dominated everything
might also permit a beautiful simplicity of production. The so-called
epic style of production, which we developed at the Theater am Schiffbauerdamm, revealed its artistic qualities relatively quickly and the
non-Aristotelian technique of drama set about working importantly with
important social subjects. Possibilities appeared for transforming the
dancelike elements and the elements of group composition of Meyerhold's school from something artificial into something artistic, and the
naturalistic elements of Stanislavski's into realistic elements. The art of
speech was joined with the art of movement, while workaday speech and
the recitation of verse were thoroughly fashioned from the so-called
movement principle. Theatre construction was completely revolution-
ized. Piscator's principles, freely employed, permitted not only an
instructive theatre but a beautiful one as well. Symbolism and Illu-
sionism might be liquidated in like manner, and the *Neher principle* for
the development of scenic design permitted the scenic designer, according to the needs determined in rehearsal, to gain profit from the acting of
the performers and to influence the acting in his own way. The playwright was able to propose his play to the actors and the scenic designer
in uninterrupted collaboration, to influence as well as be influenced.
Painters and musicians at once regained their independence and were
able through their own artificial means to make their presence felt on
the subject matter: the collective art project appeared before the spectator as a series of dissociated elements.

From the start the *classical repertoire* organized itself on the basis of
many such experiments. The artificial means of alienation opened a
broad path of approach to the vital importance of the dramatic works
of other ages. Through alienation it became possible to produce enter-
tainingly and instructively the worthwhile old plays without disturbing
elements of over-actualization and museumlike treatment.

Liberation from the compulsion to practice hypnosis is noted to be
particularly advantageous to the contemporary amateur theatre
(worker, student, and child actors). It is becoming conceivable to draw
boundaries between the performances of amateur and professional
actors without the need to relinquish one of the basic functions of the
theatre.

On the basis of the new foundation, for example, such divergent
acting techniques as perhaps those of the Vachtangov or the Ochlop-
kov troops and the Workers' troop could be joined. The heterogeneous

experiments of half a century appear to have found a basis for their utilization.

Nevertheless, these experiments are not so easily described, and I have simply to assert here that what we intend is to make the real artistic treat possible on the basis of alienation. This is not too terribly surprising since, seen from a purely technical point of view, even the theatres of past ages produced results through the use of alienation effects, the Chinese theatre, for example, the classical Spanish theatre, the popular theatre of Bruéghel's [2] time and the Elizabethan theatre.

Is this new style of production *the* new style, is it a technique which is complete and which can be surveyed as such, the definitive result of all the experiments? The answer is: No. It is *one* way, the way which *we* have gone. Experiments must continue. The same problem exists for all art, and it is a gigantic one. The solution which we are striving towards is only *one* of the perhaps possible solutions to the problem which is this: How can the theatre be both entertaining and instructive at the same time? How can it be drawn away from this intellectual narcotics-traffic and be changed from a place of illusion to a place of practical experience? How can the shackled, ignorant, freedom- and knowledge-seeking human being of our century, the tormented and heroic, abused and ingenious, the changeable and the world-changing human being of this frightful and important century achieve his own theatre which will help him to master not only himself but also the world?

NOTES

1. Brecht's theatre in Berlin.
2. Pieter Bruéghel (1520–1569), Flemish painter, known for his grotesque style.

Plot

The soul of drama, Aristotle says, is in its plot (*mythos*), and the dramatist must be first and foremost a maker of plots, only secondarily a poet, philosophic thinker, or creator of characters. Aristotle's demands on plot are exacting. Each phase must issue by causal necessity from that preceding it if the entire structure is to exhibit the unity of action he deems essential, and especially if it is to produce the cathartic effect which he regards as the proper object of tragic plots. A shrewd student of the kinds and techniques of plot employed in classical Greek tragedy, Aristotle makes it abundantly clear that plot is a major means by which dramatic material is given form and coherence.

But we need to remind ourselves that Aristotle spoke only of tragedy. Whether in obedience to Aristotle or not, tragic plots do tend to unfold the probabilities of a given situation, showing us a world harnessed to the relentlessness of cause and effect. Comedy, however, operates in a freer world. The tragic law of action and inevitable reaction gives way to comic lawlessness, to plots based on the principle that no action is irreversible and anything is possible. Neither conception of plot is of course better than the other, merely different; every literary genre, indeed every literary work, sets its own ground rules in the process of transforming reality in its special fashion.

277

And so, in a sense, do different ages. Despite Aristotle's great influence on dramatic theory during the Renaissance, playwrights of the period frequently abandoned the Greek practice of presenting a single story (as in *Oedipus Tyrannos,* for instance) in favor of developing multiple lines of action (as in *King Lear*). Shifting from the single to the multiple plot may result in a loss of concentration and sometimes of a sense of tragic inevitability, but on the other hand, a gain in variety and comprehensiveness. In the twentieth century, a good many dramatists have been less interested in multiplying plots than in eliminating the concept of plot itself. One reason for this is that they associate plot with a traditional, regulated, artificially "shaped" kind of drama that they want to move beyond—the kind of drama whose plots are too readily diagrammed in terms of "exposition," "complication," and "resolution," or some such structural scheme. In place of a rigorously controlled plot preordained by a godlike dramatist, they would substitute a sense of spontaneity and openness. Thus Harold Pinter, the modern British dramatist, says that he begins his plays simply by putting a couple of people in a room and then seeing what happens. What happens is a play with a minimum of action and an almost total absence of Aristotle's concept of causality.

If the notion of plot is to have any descriptive value for modern plays like those of Pinter, Ionesco, and others, it must be reconstituted somehow. Thus Elder Olson enlarges considerably on Aristotle's exclusively "uni-linear" conception of plot, taking account of various "multi-linear" plots found in post-Aristotelean plays and attempting to formulate a theory that will do justice to plays that eschew causal sequence in favor of the expanding situation or nonprogressive pattern. For this reason, Olson's remarks on plot lead naturally into the section above called "Form" and are especially pertinent to Marvin Rosenberg's essay on linear and contextual forms.

ARISTOTLE

Poetics

VII

These principles being established, let us now discuss the proper structure of the plot, since this is the first and most important part of tragedy.

Now, according to our definition, tragedy is an imitation of an action that is complete, and whole, and of a certain magnitude, for there may be a whole that is wanting in magnitude. A whole is that which has a beginning, a middle, and an end. A beginning is that which does not itself follow anything by causal necessity, but after which something naturally is or comes to be. An end, on the contrary, is that which itself naturally follows some other thing, either by necessity, or as a rule, but has nothing following it. A middle is that which follows something as some other thing follows it. A well constructed plot, therefore, must neither begin nor end at haphazard, but conform to these principles.

Again, a beautiful object, whether it be a picture of a living organism or any whole composed of parts, must not only have an orderly arrangement of parts but must also be of a certain magnitude, for beauty depends on magnitude and order. Hence an exceedingly small picture cannot be beautiful, for the view of it is confused, the object being seen in an almost imperceptible moment of time. Nor, again, can one of vast size be beautiful, for as the eye cannot take it all in at once, the unity and sense of the whole is lost for the spectator, as for instance if there were a picture a thousand miles long. As, therefore, in the case of animate bodies and pictures a certain magnitude is necessary, and a magnitude which may be easily embraced in one view, so in the plot a certain length is necessary, and a length which can be easily em-

From *Aristotle's Theory of Poetry and Fine Art* translated by S. N. Butcher, London 1895; 4th edition, New York, 1955.

braced by the memory. The limit of length in relation to dramatic competition and sensuous presentment is no part of artistic theory. For had it been the rule for a hundred tragedies to compete together, the performance would have been regulated by the water clock—as indeed we are told was formerly done. But the limit as fixed by the nature of the drama itself is this: the greater the length, the more beautiful will the piece be by reason of its size, provided that the whole be perspicuous. And to define the matter roughly, we may say that the proper magnitude is comprised within such limits that the sequence of events, according to the law of probability or necessity, will admit of a change from bad fortune to good or from good fortune to bad.

VIII

Unity of plot does not, as some persons think, consist in the unity of the hero. For infinitely various are the incidents in one man's life which cannot be reduced to unity, and so, too, there are many actions of one man out of which we cannot make one action. Hence the error, as it appears, of all poets who have composed a *Heracleid*, a *Theseid*, or other poems of the kind. They imagine that as Heracles was one man, the story of Heracles must also be a unity. But Homer, as in all else he is of surpassing merit, here too—whether from art or natural genius—seems to have happily discerned the truth. In composing the *Odyssey* he did not include all the adventures of Odysseus—such as his wound on Parnassus or his feigned madness at the mustering of the host—incidents between which there was no necessary or probable connection, but he made the *Odyssey,* and likewise the *Iliad,* to center round an action that in our sense of the word is one. As, therefore, in the other imitative arts, the imitation is one when the object imitated is one, so the plot, being an imitation of an action, must imitate one action and that a whole, the structural union of the parts being such that, if any one of them is displaced or removed, the whole will be disjointed and disturbed. For a thing whose presence or absence makes no visible difference is not an organic part of the whole.

IX

It is, moreover, evident from what has been said that it is not the function of the poet to relate what has happened, but what may happen—what is possible according to the law of probability or necessity. The poet and the historian differ not by writing in verse or in prose. The work of Herodotus might be put into verse, and it would still be a species of history, with meter no less than without it. The true difference is that one relates what has happened, the other what may happen. Poetry, therefore, is a more philosophical and a higher thing than history, for poetry tends to express the universal, history the particular. By the universal I mean how a person of a certain type will on occasion speak or act, according to the law of probability or necessity, and it is this universality at which poetry aims in the names she attaches to the personages. The particular is, for example, what Alcibiades did or suffered. In comedy this is already apparent, for here the poet first constructs the plot on the lines of probability and then inserts characteristic names, unlike the lampooners who write about particular individuals. But tragedians still keep to real names, the reason being that what is possible is credible. What has not happened we do not at once feel sure to be possible, but what has happened is manifestly possible; otherwise it would not have happened. Still there are some tragedies in which there are only one or two well known names, the rest being fictitious. In others, none are well known—as in Agathon's *Antheus*, where incidents and names alike are fictitious—and yet they give none the less pleasure. We must not, therefore, at all costs keep to the received legends which are the usual subjects of tragedy. Indeed, it would be absurd to attempt it, for even subjects that are known are known only to a few, and yet give pleasure to all. It clearly follows that the poet or "maker" should be the maker of plots rather than of verses, since he is a poet because he imitates, and what he imitates are actions. And even if he chances to take a historical subject, he is none the less a poet, for there is no reason why some events that have actually happened should not conform to the law of the probable and possible, and in virtue of that quality in them he is their poet or maker.

Of all plots and actions the episodic are the worst. I call a plot "episodic" in which the episodes or acts succeed one another without probable or necessary sequence. Bad poets compose such pieces by their own fault, good poets, to please the players, for, as they write show pieces for competition, they stretch the plot beyond its capacity and are often forced to break the natural continuity.

But again, tragedy is an imitation not only of a complete action, but of events terrible and pitiful. Such an effect is best produced when the events come on us by surprise, and the effect is heightened when, at the same time, they follow as cause and effect. The tragic wonder will then be greater than if they happened of themselves or by accident, for even coincidences are most striking when they have an air of design. We may instance the statue of Mitys at Argos, which fell upon his murderer while he was a spectator at a festival and killed him. Such events seem not to be due to mere chance. Plots, therefore, constructed on these principles are necessarily the best.

X

Plots are either simple or complex, for the actions in real life, of which the plots are an imitation, obviously show a similar distinction. An action, which is one and continuous in the sense above defined I call simple when the change of fortune takes place without reversal of intention and without recognition.

A complex action is one in which the change is accompanied by such reversal or by recognition, or by both. These last should arise from the internal structure of the plot, so that what follows should be the necessary or probable result of the preceding action. It makes all the difference whether any given event is a case of *propter hoc* or *post hoc*.

XI

Reversal of intention is a change by which the action veers round to its opposite, subject always to our rule of probability or necessity. Thus in the *Oedipus* the messenger comes to cheer Oedipus and free him from his alarms about his mother, but by revealing who he is he produces the opposite effect. Again, in the *Lynceus*, Lynceus is being led away to his death, and Danaus goes with him, meaning to slay him, but the outcome of the action is that Danaus is killed and Lynceus saved.

Recognition, as the name indicates, is a change from ignorance to knowledge, producing love or hate between the persons destined by the poet for good or bad fortune. The best form of recognition is coincident with a reversal of intention, as in the *Oedipus*. There are indeed other forms. Even inanimate things of the most trivial kind may sometimes be objects of recognition. Again, we may recognize or discover whether a person has done a thing or not. But the recognition which is most intimately connected with the plot and action is, as we have said, the recognition of persons. This recognition, combined

with reversal, will produce either pity or fear, and actions producing
these effects are those which, by our definition, tragedy represents.
Moreover, it is upon such situations that the issues of good or bad
fortune will depend. Recognition, then, being between persons, it may
happen that one person only is recognized by the other—when the
latter is already known—or it may be necessary that the recognition
should be on both sides. Thus Iphigenia is revealed to Orestes by the
sending of the letter, but another act of recognition is required to
make Orestes known to Iphigenia.

Two parts then of the plot—reversal of intention and recognition—
turn upon surprises. A third part is the tragic incident. The tragic
incident is a destructive or painful action, such as death on the stage,
bodily agony, wounds, and the like.

ELDER OLSON

The Elements of Drama: Plot

We generally speak of the action of drama as *plot:* unfortunately, however, we tend to use that term in a variety of senses, some of them less accurate, or at any rate less useful, than others. Perhaps it would be wise to look into these before we do anything further.

The most general meaning of *plot* is that of the argument, synopsis, or summary of a narrative or drama. In this sense you tell someone the "plot" of a movie. The fact that you are frequently surprised and disappointed by your listener's reaction shows that your synopsis is not really the "plot" devised by the dramatist. Had your listener seen the movie himself, his reaction would have been similar to yours, in all probability. A synopsis or summary never precludes the possibility of opposite emotional effects; a plot is always aimed at some definite effect. A synopsis of the Pyramus and Thisbe play in *A Midsummer Night's Dream* is closely similar to a synopsis of *Romeo* and *Juliet.* In both plays we have "two star-crossed lovers," parents averse to their union, clandestine meetings, the lover killing himself on the mistaken supposition that his beloved is dead, but it would be absurd to say that these plays have the same *plot;* one is comic, the other tragic.

For the same reason, plot is not a system of bare events or incidents in complete abstraction from character. Birth, marriage, parenthood, poverty, riches, death—any event, as *mere* event—can produce any number of different effects upon us, and thus no determinate effect. The death of a tyrant can bring joy, the marriage of an innocent girl to a villain can bring sorrow, though we commonly think of death as a sorrowful and marriage as a joyful event.

We also apply the term *plot* to a myth, legend, or series of historical happenings. This, too, seems inaccurate usage. Sophocles, Seneca, Corneille, Dryden, Voltaire, Hofmannsthal, Gide, and Cocteau all composed plays about Oedipus; can we say with any accuracy that all of these plays have the same *plot?*

Again, plot hardly appears to be mere intrigue or "conflict," although post-Elizabethan theorists often made it synonymous with the former, and nineteenth-century theorists often equated it with the latter. There are many plots—that of Sophocles' *Oedipus Tyrannus,* for example—which involve no intrigue whatsoever; similarly, there are plots in which no conflict is involved. What basic conflict can we find in *Our Town?*

Finally—and this is a subtler matter—plot is not the dramatic representation, or what we have just called the *scenario.* Parts of the plot, indeed crucial and central ones, may be omitted from the representation, that is, may occur off-stage; the murder of Duncan, the death of Lady Macbeth and of Macbeth himself are obviously important parts of the plot, but they are not shown on the stage. Conversely, events may be shown on the stage which form no part of the plot. For example, Act I Scene i of *Julius Caesar* is not a part of the plot. It has no effect whatsoever upon the train of consequences which make up the action; it is merely an expository scene, intended to exhibit the fickleness of the Roman rabble, and so establish the probability of important events which happen later.

Other considerations go to show the difference between plot and representation. The plot may begin before the representation, or after it, or simultaneously with it; similarly, the plot may end before or after or simultaneously with the ending of the representation. It would be wearisome, perhaps pedantic, to illustrate all of this: I may simply remark that the representation in *Hamlet* begins long before the plot, which has its initiating incident in the information which the Ghost gives to Hamlet; that of *King Lear* begins almost immediately before the initiating incident of the plot, which is Lear's questioning of his daughters; while the representation of *Oedipus Tyrannus* begins after the beginning of the plot.

Further, the incidents of the plot are *time-bound,* that is, must occur in a given chronological order, and are consequently not convertible. The incidents of the representation are not time-bound, and conversions of chronological order are common. The commonest instance is the flash-back; only a little less common is the successive representation of simultaneous events—the well-known "In the meantime" of the silent movies. There is even what we might call the "flash-ahead," such as the Prolog to *Marco Millions*, which depicts events twenty-three years *after* the events of Act I Scene i.

If the matter is still not clear, one further reflection should set it beyond all doubt: when the dramatist has completed his plot, he must still determine what he will show upon the stage, in what order, on what scale. The scenario or representation cannot possibly be devised until the corresponding parts of the plot have been invented, for the representation is *what represents*, whereas the plot is *what is represented*. They are thus, obviously, distinct.

Both representation and plot are actions, and dramatic actions. But the representation is a "dramatic action" primarily, in the sense precisely which we discovered in Chapter I, whereas a plot is "dramatic" secondarily, in the sense that it admits of being set before us by the representation. In other words, *any* plot is a dramatic one—regardless of the "actability" or "stageability" of the incidents which comprise it —so long as a dramatic scenario can be contrived to imply it. It is, thus, secondarily dramatic, as contingent upon the possibility of devising a dramatic scenario or representation. Henry James failed as a dramatist, not because he could not contrive dramatic plots, but because he could not contrive dramatic scenarios. The great success of some of his plays, as reworked by competent dramatists, establishes this beyond question.

If plot is evidently neither the representation nor any of the other things we have been considering, what is it? For simplicity's sake I shall define it first and argue the definition afterward. *Plot is a system of actions of a determinate moral quality*. I use the word "actions" in a very general sense, to include the inner workings of the soul as well as external actions. In this sense, any actualization of a capacity for thought, emotion, or action is to be considered as "action."

I say "system of actions" because it seems unlikely that anyone would ever consider a single action or incident as a plot. A single, absolutely simple and indivisible activity, such as we find in the simplest forms of imagistic poetry, has never been called "plot" by anyone, so far as I know. Indeed, I suppose a good many people will balk at the notion of a plot as containing two, perhaps even three or four, incidents only. I shall come back to that later; for the moment, I say "system" as implying an activity (1) divisible into at least two activities, and (2) made into a system by some unifying principle. In saying "*some* unifying principle," I mean of course to imply that there are different possible ones.

The matter of "actions of a determinate moral quality" threatens to give us a little trouble. I shall simply give you the reasoning which leads me to insist upon this. I assume, as I said before, that plot is always aimed at some specific effect; that it is absurd to say that a tragic and a comic version of one and the same story have identical plots. If we then respond differently—as in fact we do—to events which in general synopsis are identical, that difference of response must be due to the different particular presentations of the events. Now, if we feel different emotions at the sight of the fortunes or misfortunes of characters in a play, we are of course feeling pleasures or pains, for the emotions are forms of mental pleasures or pains. Why do we feel these pleasures or pains? Because what we are seeing is in accordance with or in opposition to our wishes for the characters. What leads us to wish good or bad fortune for characters whom we have never known, and whose forturnes or misfortunes could never conceivably affect our own? Because we favor some, and hold others in disfavor. Why should we hold in favor or disfavor absolutely fictitious persons who exist in absolute detachment from our own self-interest? I can find only one answer to this last question: We feel toward them, this way or that, upon precisely the same grounds on which we feel one way or another toward persons who have existed in remote periods of history, or who are otherwise absolutely detached from our advantage or disadvantage; that is, upon *grounds of moral approval or disapproval.* But an action which incurs moral approval or disapproval must itself be possessed of a certain moral quality; thus the foundation of emotional effectiveness in plot must clearly be moral, and plot itself is morally determinate action.

Certain objections offer themselves at once to this view. As I see them, they appear only for immediate dismissal. First: Why should not we simply say that all our emotional reactions in drama are based upon general human sympathy? This can mean one of two things: that we feel, emotion for emotion, precisely what the character is feeling, or that our reactions are based upon the general love of man for man. The latter is patently false, for drama is filled with characters toward whom we feel the extremest antipathy. The former is false, too. Time and again we feel emotions which are the very opposites of those felt by the character. For example, we do not share the wicked glee of the villain at the apparent success of his plan, nor do we share the calm confidence of the heroine as she moves among unsuspected dangers.

Well, then, cannot we simply say that we identify ourselves with the characters? This is another very widely held view, and it can also mean one of two things. It can mean that we absolutely "put ourselves into the shoes" of the characters, that is, imagine ourselves as them, or that we identify our own interests with theirs. Both again are false and contrary to fact. These may possibly be principles of certain schools of *acting;* they are positively not principles underlying the reactions of the *audience.* Do we, in fact, in watching a play, fancy ourselves now as Claudius, now as Gertrude, now as Hamlet, now Horatio, and now Polonius? Or identify our own interests with theirs? In that case we should view the outcome with very mixed emotions indeed. If we identify ourselves with some but not with others, on what grounds do we do so? For identification cannot itself then be the *principle* underlying our reactions: it requires something further to explain it. Do we, in fact, identify ourselves with *anybody?* Is it not rather manifestly the case that as we watch, absorbed in what we see, nothing is further from our thoughts than ourselves and our self-interest?

The fundamental fault in both of these views is that each assumes that we cannot be moved emotionally without reflection upon our self-interest, and that our attitudes towards others must consequently be based upon self-interest. Man does not happen to be so insensitive nor so self-concerned. I will leave the matter there; David Hume has beautifully argued the rest of the case for me; I will merely say that our feelings at a play are such feelings as we have, not for ourselves, but for others.

There is one other objection, which a very able British critic, Mr. John Holloway, has brought against my definition of plot as morally determinate action. This would apply, Mr. Holloway observes, to the crude plots of Saturday matinee movie-melodramas, and the naive "good-guy and bad-guy" reactions of the children who go to see them; if so, how can it also be the basis of the subtlest reactions to the greatest drama?

I must answer that, in the first place, the question is not one of good plots and bad plots, but of what is and is not plot. In the second place, a definition of plot must offer universal attributes of plot, ones common to the highest and to the lowest kinds. Mr. Holloway's objection, far from being a real one, seems to me rather to make for my case; I should be disturbed indeed if my definition did *not* cover the movie-melodramas. Besides, the possibility of a crude moral attitude in no way precludes the possibility of a more subtle and refined one. On the contrary, the subtle is possible only if the crude—or basic—attitude has been established.

Very well, then, we have our definition of plot, and we must ask another question: In how many ways may plots differ from each other?

First of all, they can differ in magnitude, in the extension of the action. The magnitude of the action is a function of the number of situations and of the number of characters which it contains. We can thus distinguish four kinds of magnitudes:

(1) the activity of a single character in a single closed situation

(2) the activity of two or more characters in a single closed situation

(3) the activity of two or more characters in a series of situations centering about a single principal event

(4) the activity of two or more characters in a series of situations involving more than one principal event.

The action involving a single character in a single closed situation is not common in drama as the whole action of a play. It can form a scene in a play, certainly; but as a whole action it is commonly found in lyrics, of which it is perhaps the commonest form of all. By a "closed situation" I mean one in which there is no external intervention of any kind; the character is as it were hermetically sealed off from the rest of the world, so that his action, thought, or emotion runs its uninterrupted course from beginning to end. This is the kind of action you will find in Keats's "Ode to a Nightingale," Milton's "Lycidas," Yeats's "Sailing to Byzantium," and similar lyrics.

The action involving two or more persons in a single closed situation is one that permits of many more possible developments, and so it is frequently found in short plays, and sometimes even in rather extended ones, such as Sartre's *No Exit* (*Huis Clos*). Even here, however, complication of the action can arise only out of the characters themselves, and not from external interruption or intervention. As a consequence, it is difficult to develop an extended action of this sort.

When external causes or agencies are combined with internal, however, the case is very different. If you have two characters in a given situation and can bring in a third who can change that situation, you can proceed indefinitely. The third may appear in person or may be represented only as the writer of a letter or someone invisible on the other end of the telephone; it does not matter. Whether or not he figures in the *Dramatis Personae*, he is still an agent in the drama; and it is obvious that as we multiply agents or agencies we multiply the possibilities of development and hence of extension.

The last two kinds of action, thus, as permitting external intervention, offer far greater possibilities of developing an action of some length. Suppose we call the action of situations centering about a principal event by the name of *episode*, and the one which centers about more than one principal event by the name of *grand plot*. They are clearly distinct: the action of the *Agamemnon* is an episode, with everything centering about the murder of Agamemnon; whereas the action of *Macbeth* is a grand plot, for it is impossible to designate in it any one event about which everything else centers.

So far as magnitude or mere extension of plot is concerned, I can think of nothing which goes beyond grand plot. But there is a matter of thickness or thinness, so to speak, as well as length. This is the matter of the number of lines or threads of action involved in a plot. A line of action is a chain of cause and effect, separable at least in part from other such lines. Plots are either linear or polylinear. The plot of the *Agamemnon* is linear, as consisting of a single line of action. The plot of *Oedipus Tyrannus*, on the other hand, is polylinear, and you can easily distinguish such different threads as Oedipus' investigations, the events happening at Corinth, and so on. When lines of action are such as to have an independent interest and constitute a story in their own right, they are called sub-plots, by-plots, or under-plots. The actions of Fortinbras and of Laertes in *Hamlet* I should consider lines of action simply; similarly, the successive actions of Albany in *King Lear* are merely a line of action, although a very important one. On the other hand, the Gloucester story is an under- or sub-plot.

Lines of action, whether or not they are sub-plots, either converge or diverge or run parallel. If you diagram a plot and find two or more lines of action stemming from a single cause or incident, this is divergence. If you find chains of causation concurring in a single effect or situation, this is convergence. If they are wholly independent of each other, they are parallel. Divergence is commonest at the beginning of an action, as permitting complication; convergence is commonest at the end, to achieve resolution. Threatened convergence is one way of obtaining suspense, when the convergence is such as to affect the outcome materially; sudden convergence is one way of obtaining surprise. In *King Lear,* for instance, Albany almost understands the true state of affairs at certain points, and since he has the power to put an end to the villainy, may help Lear's situation: his line threatens to converge with Lear's. The unexpected return of Lovewit in *The Alchemist* is an instance of sudden convergence.

When lines of action are not merely causally related, as producing complication or resolution, they serve to enhance the effect of the main line of action, either through resemblance to it or contrast with it. Thus a comic sub-plot in a serious play contrasts with the main plot, and conversely. There are other more subtle possibilities: the Fortinbras and Laertes lines in *Hamlet* both reflect the main lines as similars and contrast with it, for Fortinbras is like Hamlet a dispossessed prince, and Laertes is like Hamlet the son of a murdered father, and yet both act in sharp contrast to Hamlet. In the same manner the Gloucester line in *King Lear* is both similar and dissimilar to the main line.

You can see at once that this offers all sorts of possibilities. Plots can begin with a single incident which produces a divergence of lines which never meet again. In John Buchan's *A Gap in the Curtain,* five men, after participating in an experiment in prevision, work out their separate destinies. Plots can end in the convergence, in a single incident, of lines previously more or less independent, as in *The Bridge of San Luis Rey.* They can involve lines which converge and diverge repeatedly, like the lines of Henry and the Master in *The Master of Ballantrae.* They can have lines that start independently and converge halfway through, to diverge and become independent again, as in Barrie's *Dear Brutus;* they can diverge from a single incident, run parallel for awhile, and then converge in the denouement; and they can do many another thing besides, which you may work out on your own by drawing lines on paper in the form of hourglasses, diamonds, strings of diamonds, zigzags, and whatnots. You will only need to bear in mind that divergence is the stemming of separate lines from a single cause, while convergence is the coming together of lines in a single effect.

I want to move on to another aspect of plot: its unifying principle, the thing which makes it a system and a single system. This is one of the aspects of plot construction about which critics have been most dogmatic, and it is one of the things about which it is most dangerous to be dogmatic. To prevent dogmatism as much as we can, let us consider four plays and ask ourselves what makes the plot of each *one* plot. I choose *Macbeth, Our Town,* Schnitzler's *Reigen* (*La Ronde*), and *Ghosts.*

The plot of *Macbeth* has the unity of a train of consequences. The train has a beginning, an initiating incident (the meeting with the Witches), and it has a terminating incident (the killing of Macbeth and the passage of the crown to Malcolm). Everything in between is in some way an effect of the beginning and a cause of the end; the whole has the unity of a causal sequence. The plot of *Our Town* is quite different. There is a certain amount of causal relation, to be sure, but it is not terribly important, and it is not the unifying principle of the plot. The plot is intended to catch an image of life in a small American town, and it is complete when it has caught that image completely, at least in its more nostalgic aspects. In this respect it resembles the plot of Dylan Thomas's *Under Milk Wood;* only it attempts to capture the image of town life through the three phases of youth, marriage, and death, whereas Thomas's plot attempts to reflect its image in the activities of a townful of people on a single day. This difference of organization is unimportant, however; the significant thing about this sort of plot is that it is complete in the sense in which a description is complete when it has adequately described its object. The incidents are present in it, not because they have any necessary causal relation, but because they show different aspects of the object in view. The plots of documentaries, chronicle plays, and many historical, biographical, and pageant pieces are of this order.

Schnitzler's *Reigen* has a different sort of plot again. The events are in no way causes or effects of each other, and they do not deal with any one object. They all deal with the theme of sexual love, but they are not intended to offer any very adequate description even of that. There are ten scenes: The Whore has sexual relations with the Soldier, the Soldier with the Parlormaid, the Parlormaid with the Young Gentleman, the Young Gentleman with the Young Wife, the Young Wife with the Husband, the Husband with the Little Miss, the Little Miss with the Poet, the Poet with the Actress, the Actress with the Count, and finally, the Count with the Whore. There you are: A and B, B and C, and so on, till we come full circle back to A. What sort of unity has this? Why, none, I say—unless you are willing to admit that a circle has unity or, more generally, that a pattern has unity. We can call this the *pattern plot*. Of course there are many possible patterns.

The plot of *Ghosts* is of still another kind. There is a causal sequence, but Ibsen is apparently so little concerned with it that he allows things to happen by convenient coincidence—for example, the outbreak of fire at a particular time—rather than go to the trouble of making them probable occurrences. It is hard to say what the initiating incident is. Is it the marriage of the Alvings? Or Mrs. Alving's flight from her husband? Or her return? Or his catching syphilis? Or the birth of Oswald? Or what? And what is the end? Does she poison Oswald or not? There are elements of the descriptive, too; but the unity of the plot is hardly that of a description. There is even a pattern of sorts; but that isn't primary either. The play is a *pièce à thèse;* the action and the characters are designed to prove, by example, that in a society in which duty is invariably opposed to pleasure, the good must suffer or become corrupt, while the wicked flourish in hypocrisy.

We have, thus, at least four different kinds of unifying principle in plots: the consequential, the descriptive, the pattern, and the didactic. I say, at *least* four; there may be many more.

We are likely to think that a plot cannot be complete unless it deals with a complete, and therefore finite, action. But in fact this applies only to the consequential plot. It is perfectly possible for a finite plot to convey the idea of an indefinitely continuing, perhaps eternal, process. There are a good many examples of this: *The Long Christmas Dinner, The Skin of Our Teeth,* and *Huis Clos* come to mind immediately. Some plots are complete when they afford an adequate basis for a certain emotion, some when they have made possible a certain inference. Some plots are stories; others, considered as stories, have no story at all, or are chronicles of very small beer indeed. What they do have in common is some end or other in view, and it is important to consider what that end may possibly be, for it is in terms of that and nothing else that the plot is complete.

To return to the question of other differences among plots: they can differ in terms of their laws of probability. This is a very difficult and complex question, and I can only deal lightly with it here. What I have in mind is that events which are probable or even inevitable in fantasy may very well be impossible in realistic drama, and that events which are probable or inevitable in farce may be impossible in ordinary comedy. The various forms of drama are in a sense different universes regulated by different laws, and the beings and objects within them operate according to those laws. We can distinguish several different systems of such laws or probabilities. We think an event probable if it happens daily or usually or frequently, to most people, or to most people at some time or other, or at any rate to people of a certain kind; and we think an action probable if everyone or most people or people of a certain kind have the power and the inclination to do it. This is common natural probability, and it is the kind of probability on which realistic and naturalistic plots are based.

We also think that rare and unusual occurrences are probable too, in certain circumstances, providing we believe that adequate causes exist, or that there are adequate indications that the occurrences happened. This is conditional natural probability, the probability of the unusual. Tragedy depends on it, and so does melodrama of the better sort.

We also accept as probable certain things of a highly exaggerated nature, because we recognize that the exaggeration, patently preposterous as it is, is only figurative and contains an element of truth. This is hyperbolical probability, and it underlies farce.

We even accept as probable the actions of beings we know do not exist, or actions which existent beings could not possibly perform, provided these follow upon a certain hypothesis. *If* witches, ghosts, and fairies existed, they *would* do such and such; *if* a dog could talk, he *would* talk like that. This is hypothetical probability, and it underlies all fantasy and stories of the supernatural.

We will accept anything as probable which corresponds to something already accepted. Thus a plot which follows a familiar legend or a familiar version of historical events will be accepted as probable, even though these latter contain improbabilities or impossibilities. No one will question the feats of Paul Bunyan, or George Washington's cherry tree. This holds, too, of certain forms; for instance, we expect certain things to happen in a Western, improbable as they may be. This is the probability of custom, or conventional probability.

There is emotional probability, too. This may be completely irrational and in no way connected with logical probability. A given emotion predisposes us to believe certain things, even though they may be impossible. A man in a gloomy frame of mind finds it doubtful that anything good can happen; an audience in a certain emotional state will similarly accept things that in another it would question.

When I spoke earlier of "different universes regulated by different laws of probability," I did not mean to imply that these universes could not coincide, or at least impinge upon each other to some degree. They can, and often do. A plot of natural probability can turn to hypothetical probability (fantasy) and subsequently return to the natural: instances are A *Midsummer Night's Dream*, Dunsany's *If*, Barrie's *Dear Brutus*, and Shaw's *Man and Superman*. The natural probability can turn to the hyperbolical, as in Androcles' waltz with the lion in *Androcles and the Lion*. There are many other possibilities, one of the most fruitful of which seems to be the reversal of conventional probabilities; that is, the establishment of a different system of probabilities—within the framework of a legend or literary form—from those associated with that form or legend. This is one of Shaw's characteristic devices; he uses it in *Arms and the Man, Caesar and Cleopatra, Man and Superman, St. Joan,* and other plays. It has been used repeatedly also by Gide, Cocteau, Giraudoux, Sartre, and Anouilh to provide startlingly different versions of classical legend.

These shiftings of probabilities, or mixtures of them, seem to depend for their success upon a single principle; they must be required by the form, and themselves made probable within it. In *A Midsummer Night's Dream* separate lines are established at the outset, the human and the faery, each with its own probabilities. When the lines of action converge in the Wood, the natural and the hypothetical probabilities operate together; subsequently they draw apart again. The whole is probable because the convergence and the divergence have been made probable. In *St. Joan* an action which has been principally one of natural probability shifts, in the Epilog, into hypothetical. There has been much objection to the Epilog as "unnecessary," "improbable," and "destructive of the tragic effect"; I think these charges are very ill-founded. *St. Joan* is not tragedy, but a certain kind of comedy. As Shaw says, "The angels may weep at the murder, but the gods laugh at the murderers"; and he arranges matters so that Joan herself may have the last laugh—albeit a melancholy one. Her last laugh came with her canonization in the twentieth century, and so, if she is to enjoy the joke on her murderers, fantasy is required. The Epilog is essential to the play, for it contains the comic reversal; to delete it would be to alter the very form and significance of the play. This is a matter of the probability of form, and it underlies many of the great tragic denouements of Shakespeare.

If we consider probability in a different light, everything that is probable is so either intrinsically or through its connection with other things. In *St. Joan*, since we have been speaking of that, Shaw subverts the idea of the "miracles" as miraculous by supplanting them with events of intrinsic natural probability. The natural probability is always more probable intrinsically than any other. Normally we are more willing to believe that something is coincidence, or has been foolishly interpreted or knavishly misreported, than that it is actually miraculous. It would seem that this is the position of the Roman Catholic Church itself, since it submits all supposed miracles, I understand, to extremely rigorous tests.

On the other hand, extrinsic probability can very powerfully overcall intrinsic probability in some instances. Witch and fairy must do what witch and fairy would do, although both are impossible. Again, the spell of a particular emotion may be so powerful that under it we may doubt what we should normally believe, and believe what we should normally doubt.

There is probability even within the realm of accident and coincidence. That is, although we think of these as improbabilities, not all accidents are equally improbable. It is more probable that a car will collide with another than that it will be struck by a meteorite; that such-and-such will happen in the jungle than that it will happen in a city, and so on.

Plots of consecutive action are either simple or complex. A simple plot is one that moves in a single direction, as when the fortunes of the protagonist steadily decline or improve. A complex plot is one that involves a change of direction, as when the protagonist moves toward greater and greater good fortune, and then suffers reverses. A straight line and a bent line will give you the idea; the former is simple, the latter, complex. The complex is always divisible into distinct parts, while the simple is not: you can see that the bent line is made up of two discrete parts, but the straight line is continuous, and any point of division is arbitrary. The point at which the fortunes alter is the peripety or reversal. Discovery of some sort is usually associated with reversal, either as producing it or resulting from it. Someone learns that he has committed a dreadful mistake, or finds out in time to prevent it, and so on.

All complex plots involve at least two factors which we may call *force* and *counter-force*. The force is what carries the action initially in one direction; the counter-force is what produces the change of direction. Both must be probable, of course, as causes; but if the reversal is to be unexpected, the counter-force must be concealed, or made to seem improbable, while the force must be obvious and apparently irresistible. On the other hand, if the reversal is to be probable, the counter-force must be, in retrospect, far more probable than the force. The superiority of the complex plot lies in that it permits of the unexpected and hence of greater emotional power, since emotions that come upon us unexpectedly are always more violent and powerful.

Complex plots always involve complication, as their name suggests. There are two kinds of complication, the continuous and the incidental. The continuous operates from the first and throughout; the incidental operates only in a given part, is resolved and done with in that part, and another incidental complication must be introduced if further development is to result. The great Shakespearian tragedies involve continuous complication; Shaw chiefly uses the incidental. Thus in *Pygmalion* Doolittle appears, threatens to break up Lisa's arrangement with Higgins, and withdraws. All momentary obstacles are of this order. Continuous complication depends primarily upon extrinsic probability, and incidental complication depends primarily upon intrinsic.

Character

By "character" we mean the illusion of human personality and identity imparted by a dramatic role. "Illusion" because literary characters are of course fictive: it is no use puzzling ourselves about how Hamlet's childhood experiences contributed to his admiration for his father, since he had no childhood; he is born with his first speech in the play. When he leaves the stage for a scene or two he ceases to exist, even fictively, but we as audience are quick to fill in the gaps of his identity much as the mind fills in the gaps between the frames of a motion picture sequence. "He," then, is an imaginative construct, a more or less coherent set of inferences that we invest with "life" and wholeness. The bases for our inferences are speech and actions: what Hamlet says and what is said about him, what he does and what is done because of him. By their words ye shall know them: each speech of Hamlet's is not merely a communication of meaning but a verbal act selected from a great many other acts that might have been possible, a "choice" therefore that reveals the nature of the chooser, an act performed with a certain style that discloses the nature of the performer. Hamlet's second line in the play comes when Claudius, having assured Hamlet that he thinks of him as a "son," wonders why he still remains melancholy: "How is it that the clouds still hang on you?" Hamlet replies, "Not so, my lord; I am too much i' th' sun." As verbal statement, that says what it says; as verbal act performed in a certain style, it is a form of circumspect attack-by-rejection enabling us to infer that Hamlet is defensive, sardonic, witty, terse, self-protective (operating behind a mask of irony), conscious of public decorum (else he might have said bluntly "I don't like your sun-like *noblesse oblige* that condescends even as it claims closeness and equality"), etc., all of which suggests very quickly that the character "Hamlet" is elusively complex for us as well as for Claudius.

From this standpoint, "Hamlet" is a tissue of inferences that we draw from verbal actions written into the script by Shakespeare (without such inferences "Hamlet" becomes merely so many sentences with a common speech tag). But the medium of drama is also the stage, and from this standpoint "Hamlet" appears before us, standing, sitting in a certain posture, wearing certain clothes, gesturing in certain ways, his features thus and so, gazing at Gertrude perhaps, the floor, Claudius, a locket in which his father's portrait appears, etc. etc. But this is of course not "Hamlet" but an actor, who therefore need not be arrested after the play for the murder of Polonius. He provides us with a visual and an aural basis for drawing further inferences about "Hamlet" as a character. This "Hamlet," however, is only a "version" of Hamlet, the actor imitating a "Hamlet" that he has himself inferred from reading Shakespeare's text, and as a version it may be moodier, brasher, more diffident, more volatile than other versions we have seen acted. Where the "real" Hamlet is behind or within all the shifting interpretations and enactments of him on mental and actual stages is an epistemological issue of some fine complexity, which, fortunately, need not be resolved here. Perhaps in seeking the "real" Hamlet we do well to recall his own comment about the inviolability of the inner life:

> 'Tis not alone my inky cloak, good mother,
> Nor customary suits of solemn black,
> Nor windy suspiration of forc'd breath,
> No, nor the fruitful river in the eye,

> Nor the dejected haviour of the visage,
> Together with all forms, moods, shapes of grief,
> That can denote me truly. These indeed seem,
> For they are actions that a man might play;
> But I have that within which passeth show . . .

Thus far we have been concerned with "who" Hamlet is, with his psychological, emotional, moral, intellectual make-up as disclosed to us through Shakespeare's script and performances of it in the theater. An essay like J. L. Styan's on "Manipulating the Characters" reminds us that unlike real people literary characters do not gradually develop in response to the interactions of heredity and environment; their "heredity" derives from the dramatist's imagination, and their environment is the artificial world of the play. They "are" what the dramatist wants them to be and do what he wants them to do; however complex and lifelike they may seem, there is this very real sense in which they remain puppetlike, subservient both to the dramatist's abilities and to the technical requirements of the play. The dual nature of literary characters is brilliantly discussed by Harold Rosenberg, who suggests that they may be thought of in terms of "personality" and "identity." "Who" Hamlet is—the amalgam of human characteristics that constitute the distinctive Hamlet style—is his "personality," which we infer pretty much as we do the personalities of real people. "What" Hamlet is, however, relates to his dramatic functions within the play and constitutes his "identity." Personality and identity normally are consistent with each other, if only because the dramatist creates characters with certain personalities so that they can plausibly perform certain functions within the play. In personality, let us say, Hamlet is melancholy, introspective, meditative through much of the play, and these qualities, combined with his wit and eloquence, make him interesting in himself. From the perspective of identity, however, these qualities are important not in themselves but as they bear on his role in the development of the play as a whole, and in this connection they help make plausible his function of delaying the action, which is a central feature of Senecan revenge tragedy. Shakespeare might have invested him with a different personality that would have served equally well the identity of "delayer"; he might have made Hamlet a coward, a piously non-violent man, an ineffectually stupid man, etc. When he becomes reconciled to his task of revenge in Act V, it is less because his personality requires it, as Rosenberg points out, than because the play requires it; Hamlet must graduate from "delayer" to "revenger" if the play is to achieve its tragic end. Transformations of identity may or may not be wholly consistent with personality. In comedy "villainous" characters (who are so because they are needed to frustrate the union of lovers usually) very often become converted to congeniality not because such conversions are psychologically inevitable but because the happy ending makes them necessary. Personality is thus sacrificed to identity. In realistic drama, for the most part, personality and identity go hand in hand, but as drama becomes more symbolic or otherwise indifferent to psychological realism, identity and personality part company, the character's function as part of a formal or thematic structure dominating his function as a plausible representation of a real person.

J. L. STYAN

Manipulating the Characters

In drama "character" is not an author's raw material: it is his product. It emerges from the play; it is not put into it. It has an infinity of subtle uses, but they all serve in the orchestration of the play as a whole; and so character finds this place in the scheme. But we face probably the most difficult and confused problem, a real stumbling-block, in dramatic appreciation, and the most I can do is to offer some pointers to what seem to be the real issues for the playgoer.

Some of the dangers of falsely assessing character are obvious, but none the less awkward to avoid. We set up our own barriers to full appreciation if we take a misplaced interest in a fictional character for its own sake and out of context. Because of the peculiar sympathies a writer calls upon through character, we have a natural urge to talk about, say, Cordelia as a daughter or Edgar as a son. Because the figures do have human aspects in the play, we are encouraged to that extent to talk even of Strindberg's ghosts, Pirandello's fantasies or Yeats' masked symbols in terms of individual thoughts and feelings. We talk about what we are more sure of: human qualities and attributes.

It may be that in the frustrating task of defining a play for ourselves after seeing a performance, we take the easy way and search for a character as an absolute: we define the play *Hedda Gabler* by the qualities in Hedda the woman, *Macbeth* by qualities in the man. Perhaps we go so far as to assume it a mark of indifferent playwriting if we cannot do this. Perhaps up to a point Ibsen and Shakespeare ask us to do so: a dramatist who works with human nature as his material is surely interested in character? Yet every time we look for character as something which can be neat and complete and satisfyingly objective,

From *The Elements of Drama*, 1960, pp. 163–78. Reprinted by permission of Cambridge University Press.

we are liable to blind ourselves, and judge the play by character alone, perhaps by a self-created thing. Since Aristotle, the student of drama has been led into considering character as a separate entity, without full regard for its being cause or effect.

Natural as this is, at its best it represents a slacker criticism, something of a failure to envisage the broad complexity of a character's function in a play. At its worst, for an audience to grow to love a character as if it were an old friend is to reduce interest in the actor as a person. We have to beware lest any one element like character, whether because it is a particularly striking element, or because an actor's performance has been out of proportion to his part, becomes the false centre of attention, prompting us to garner illegitimate impressions. It might lead us away from the play; it might become the play itself.

In recent years the warnings against this habit have perhaps been rather too loud. Professor Wilson Knight offered a seminal concept about Shakespeare's characters, stating that "the persons, ultimately, are not human at all, but purely symbols of a poetic vision." But in some sense we *must* feel Lear, Macbeth, Hamlet are human. We pity or admire because we are throughout the performance in contact with humanity in human situations: the figures in the pattern are, after all, human figures in a human pattern. Lear, Macbeth, Hamlet speak for human beings; they speak for us—or what value is there in the play.

Professor L. C. Knights pursued this topic, and suggested that character was "merely an abstraction from the total response in the mind of the reader or spectator." He was rightly concerned that our proper interest in a play should not be deflected, lest we should "impoverish the total response"; his words were more guarded. But it was noticeable that in his analysis of a play that followed this statement, he made no reference to a physical stage or to a live actor embodying a character. He demolished actor with character and substituted another abstraction in its place. When he suggested that *Macbeth* had a greater affinity with *The Waste Land* than with *A Doll's House*, it was almost a case of throwing the baby out with the bath water.

Common sense cannot accept that a character is no more than a mouth for an arrangement of words. We are bound to examine the fuller contribution we know to exist. It would be irresponsible to ignore its strangely binding quality in commanding an audience's response. And that quality is tied up with the presence of the actor on the stage.

To solve these problems we appeal to experience. The unique contribution of the living actor is his ability to fill in the author's outline, retaining whatever symbolic and universal suggestion that outline carries while representing it to an audience as alive and urgent. The key-word here is *alive*. All values in art depend upon the power of communicating them, making them a wholly felt, breathing force to the recipient. This is the limitation on the symbol: the character must be sufficiently human for the actor congruously to present it in his own person and for the spectator to recognize it. It is the test of a good morality play that it should make human where its lesson is most abstract. Tragedy depends for its intrinsic effect on keeping its hero mortal. If the gods are called in, whether in Aeschylus's *The Eumenides*, or in Giraudoux's *Amphitryon 38*, they must think like people, as must ghosts and apparitions. And the test of the modern symbolic melodrama, say Betti's *The Queen and the Rebels*, like the test of classical tragedy, is whether the character can remain living while carrying an exceptional load of wide meanings. In this play, can Argia the self-seeking prostitute support a queenly martyrdom? The author's choice of such extremities is partly to offer unexpected hope for an abiding Christian dignity in life. To this we may wish to give consent, but not unless the character in the person of the actress can convince us of the truth in this particular human transformation. Living symbols will be judged by life.

But here is new danger. "Judged by life": does this mean the characters must be lifelike? Is it implied that our circumspect modern audiences will not find a character adequate if they cannot find a parallel within their own experience? In the words of Mr. Raymond Williams, "we must be careful that our judgement depends not on whether the characters are lifelike, but on whether they serve to embody experience which the actor has shown to be true." It is a safer approach that does not bring preconceived, external and invalid standards from real life to the judgement of an artificial arrangement like a play. But we do.

As before, it is easy to see why we do. We find differences between speakers labelled in the way they speak: idioms, inflexions, sometimes tricks of speech distinguish them. But whether this is for the purpose of identifying the speaker in the mind of the actor as he acts, or at the other extreme, of the reader as he reads, is irrelevant: representation of life is not an end in itself. The relevant question is to ask *why* Shakespeare makes recognizable in this or that form Beatrice or Mercutio or Juliet's Nurse or Shylock, naming some most commonly discussed as "living" individuals. Once such a question is asked, character slips into its proper place.

Another side of the same fallacy is the belief that the author who can convince the playgoer that a character has a life of its own has fulfilled a proper end of drama. The playgoer's *conviction* is held to be the mark of a good play. Such a theory must be to the detriment of all the plays not written in the realistic convention—the bulk of the world's output—if the nature of the conviction is not more closely specified. Different kinds of play anticipate different kinds of conviction. We are not asked to believe, for example, that Shaw's Joan or Anouilh's Antigone or Giraudoux's Hector in *Tiger at the Gates* would have been so up-to-the-minute in their thinking. Anachronisms have always been part of the stock-in-trade of a dramatist trying to impress timeless values on a contemporary audience. Such characters convince because they are *consistent* within the little world built for them, which may be fantastic or distorted, very wide or very narrow. Theirs is a truth probable to their own world. Conviction may be important to the success of a play, but it will be determined by the organization of all the elements within it and may not be directly related to character at all.

This is not to deny that realistic characterization may be important in itself if it suggests, like the iceberg, a depth not visible on the surface. Human psychology can itself constitute a theme. Provided this depth of characterization is relevant, that is provided the theme is dependent on this sort of conviction, common-sense would not deny it. In such a case the psychological overtones of the play may be the one source for the theatre experience, and must be valued as such. Thus Strindberg in his Preface to *Miss Julie* can justifiably write,

> An event in real life—and this discovery is quite recent—springs generally from a whole series of more or less deep-lying motives . . .
>
> In explanation of Miss Julie's sad fate I have suggested many factors: her mother's fundamental instincts; her father's mistaken upbringing of the girl; her own nature; the suggestive influence of her fiancé on a weak and degenerate brain; furthermore, and more directly: the festive mood of the Midsummer Eve; the absence of her father; her physical condition; her preoccupation with animals; the excitation of the dance; the dusk of the night; the strongly aphrodisiacal influence of the flowers; and lastly the chance of the two of them together

in a secluded room, to which must be added the aggressiveness of the excited man.

Thus I have neither been one-sidedly physiological nor one-sidedly psychological in my procedure.

In this play Strindberg wishes to stage a tragic struggle between heredity and environment. To do it he uses as a common point of reference modern understanding of psychology. In this struggle, Julie, carefully circumscribed by her background, is the author's realistic symbol for his purpose. Nevertheless, each of the factors Strindberg enumerates in explanation of Julie's behaviour plays a double part, for in addition to making this character in this situation credibly "real," each also represents a factor in the struggle. Thus each also represents a facet of the theme. It is unwise, even in realistic drama of the best sort, to separate the character from the play, the psychology from the theme.

We must avoid begging essential questions about the source of the experience. There is a distinction to be made between the *dramatis persona* of the scene and the personality which emerges as part of the impression we derive. Character in the usual sense of "personality" is not an agency for the writer as speech is. Even in a leading part it may indeed not exist, as many expressionistic dramas have shown; in the minor parts of even realistic drama we may not expect it. An impression of personality is more truly a by-product, a facet of the image, sometimes only an accident that happens because of the occasionally narrative turn of a play. In the weak play, we may be kept happy by the presence of personality when what that stands for cannot engross us. The author who is a cheat will tap associations from our own or typical acquaintance, till we give body to the pale shadow the author has made of his character. On the other hand, tapping our preconceived notions of character can be legitimate procedure, as in a play planned to upset those notions (we think of conventional Parson Manders in Ibsen's *Ghosts*), or in the modern play using old legend (the heroes in *Tiger at the Gates*). In the latter case, Giraudoux expects us to make his Helen and his Hector familiar figures, the better to remind us of their eternal existence. Yet even here the characters remain primarily *dramatis personae*.

A rule for one type of play may not apply to another. The real test is whether a character can do what the play requires of it. The type of play that designedly breaks realistic rules thus presents a set of special problems. How do we judge a character in a farce or an extravagant comedy? Standards from life can only distract. We agree to allow half-people like Sergius and Raina from *Arms and the Man* to be the head and tail of a pantomime donkey if together they serve their purpose. The mouthpieces of a Shavian discussion-drama may be rare folk among our drawing-room acquaintance, but may be valid on Shaw's stage. What place are we to allow for the masked characters of Greek or Roman drama or of the *commedia dell'arte?* Do we think less of majestic, unearthly Electra or of fragile insubstantial Millamant or of one-track, head-on-legs Jack Tanner because they do not display the same three-dimensional qualities of realism as Falstaff and Madame Ranevsky? We measure the adequacy of a character by the unity and completeness of the dramatic impression to which it contributes: if we can add nothing, nor wish to take anything away, the character has served.

The concept of character derives from the mask. The mask imposes a tight control upon one aspect of reality to present it simply. Basically, it dispenses with the need to "act"; for two antithetic masks juxtaposed upon one stage provide the substance of a situation and the plan for a play. The development of drama, as Archer might have maintained, seems to have been the gradual freeing of the actor from the restrictions of the mask, but as long as the author was still writing for an actor on a stage, neither has been totally free. Always the basic premise of theatre has remained, that a play must concentrate and confine life within fixed limits. An author happily acknowledges these limits—even today. One can understand the usefulness to authors of what, in the jargon, are called "types," especially in radio drama where distinctions of voice are essential to recognition by ear alone. An author frequently welcomes the readiness of a preconditioned audience to supply for him the villainy behind a pair of cruelly curling moustaches, or the innocence behind a bonnet and shawl. Moustaches may have been replaced by cleaner upper lips, bonnets and shawls by more fashionable frills, but in the eyes the seediness or the sweetness, as the case may be, is the same. The author relies upon a character to serve as a known quantity: if the audience will not furnish it, the author must establish it. From another point of view, there probably remains a preference among the acting profession for "character" parts, because, in one way, less effort is needed to satisfy the requirements of a character with definite, that is, more limited, life.

A sequence from *Arms and the Man* may help us rethink the nature of characterization, in particular in artificial comedy. This kind of play falsifies and overstresses some aspect of human nature so that its absurdities are thrown up and tested. So in Shakespearian comedy we are encouraged to laugh at and judge the romantic excesses of Hermia and Helena, or in Restoration comedy the affectations of Lord Foppington and the mock decorums of Lady Wishfort. Sergius and Raina in this passage are of a rather more complex order:

> RAINA, *very solemnly.* Sergius: I think we two have found the higher love. When I think of you, I feel that I could never do a base deed, or think an ignoble thought.
>
> SERGIUS. My lady and my saint! *He clasps her reverently.*
>
> RAINA, *returning his embrace.* My lord and my—
>
> SERGIUS. Sh—sh! Let me be the worshipper, dear. You little know how unworthy the best man is of a girl's pure passion!
>
> RAINA. I trust you, I love you. You will never disappoint me, Sergius. LOUKA *is heard singing within the house. They quickly release each other.* I cant pretend to talk indifferently before her: my heart is too full. LOUKA *comes from the house.* . . . I will get my hat; and then we can go out until lunch time. Wouldnt you like that?
>
> SERGIUS. Be quick. If you are away five minutes, it will seem five hours. RAINA *runs to the top of the steps, and turns there to exchange looks with him and wave him a kiss with both hands. He looks after her with emotion for a moment; then turns slowly away, his face radiant with the loftiest exaltation. The movement shifts his field of vision, into the corner of which there now comes the tail of* LOUKA's *double apron. His attention is arrested at once. He takes a stealthy look at her, and begins to twirl his moustache mischievously, with his left hand akimbo on his hip. Finally, striking the ground with his heels in something of a cavalry swagger, he strolls over to the other side of the table, opposite her, and says* Louka, do you know what the higher love is?
>
> LOUKA, *astonished.* No, sir.
>
> SERGIUS. Very fatiguing thing to keep up for any length of time, Louka. One feels the need of some relief after it.

In the words and actions of Shaw's puppets, every detail exemplifies his efficiency and economy in caricaturing human behaviour.

An audience seeing these words enacted does not trouble itself to entertain doubts about verisimilitude: in the theatre such a question does not arise. What then are we concerned about? Perhaps the manner in which their speech and gesture burlesque our own? This is a sophisticated reaction, which if it occurs at all, probably does not do so during the performance. The immediate wish of the audience is to follow the "logic" of the action, to guess by its own knowlege of human behaviour what prompts Raina or Sergius to say or do what Shaw makes them, to follow the play's general line of intention. Sergius and Raina have been so excessively applauding each other with a plethora of clichés,

> You have been out in the world, on the field of battle, able to
> prove yourself there worthy of any woman in the world . . . ,
> Dearest: all my deeds have been yours . . . ,

that it is almost impossible for the actors to do anything less than "ham" their lines. Their activity of gesture and movement—they greet each other impetuously, Raina suddenly sits demurely, Sergius kneels impulsively—suggests self-consciousness, because true emotions do not fluctuate so rapidly. Even if this means the audience is not aware of the false romanticism that marks these characters, the downright lie from Raina, "And you have never been absent from my thoughts for a moment," will convince it that one at least is posing. Such easy ironies are at work quite without conscious effort of thought on our part. We come prepared to enjoy the insincerities of characters presented as distortions of human beings, misrepresentations of life.

They proceed to the limits of the line they have begun to pursue, while we know instinctively that they have forced themselves into an impossible position from which the only return must be anticlimax. We are delighted when Raina, dropping her voice and her eyes, brings to the surface the thought that she has long been privately caressing: "I think we two have found the higher love." It is part of the Shavian method to have a character say, not what is likely to be said in life, but what is preposterously representative of its type of mind. "Higher love" implies a divinity which *this* representation cannot in any world exemplify. It is immediately belied by the next half-truth she utters: "When I think of you, I feel that I could never do a base deed, or think an ignoble thought." We are not to forget Raina's "poor darling" of the final moment in Act I as she protects Bluntschli from Catherine, nor her tell-tale dissimulation in front of Sergius and her father a moment before in Act II.

With the mention of "the higher love," a key has been struck, and Sergius takes the note from her in an effort to render feelings reverently in keeping with the style she has set: "My lady and my saint!" So they vie with each other to adopt the appropriate spirit for a heavenly occasion, the romantic debauch for which their sort of love stands. Unfortunately they have trouble in deciding who is saint and who is pilgrim. Their exchange grows to a stagey crescendo too embarrassing to sustain, and Shaw relieves them by the timely-untimely entrance of Louka. Divinity disperses in a flash: even the higher love must sometimes be aware of what the servants think. Raina, however, does not neglect to recover her poise with a satisfying excuse and a mollifying cliché: "I cant pretend to talk indifferently before her: my heart is too full." They part with gestures derived from their childhood story-books, to all appearances convinced that this is the correct behaviour.

The audience does not care whether Raina and Sergius are deceiving themselves or each other. But we are concerned to deduce, if there is to be any continuity of interest in the scene, that their little world is a false and fickle one. As such it must be clear, for our critical pleasure, that it will rapidly become too prickly to live in. That Sergius, released from the obligation of Raina's presence, reassumes what we take to be his normal manner of treating the opposite sex when he returns to Louka, is pleasing because it satisfies half-held expectations. In addition, it comments on his behaviour with Raina, revealing him as a *poseur* and in part explaining the exaggeration of his speech and gesture. With but a little pin he is deflated. And yet our hearts are oddly warmed towards him at the same time, both because Raina deserves the treatment she gets, and because Sergius suddenly becomes understandable within his own rules of conduct. One might almost have said he becomes human. His move to flirt with Louka effectively brings down the flimsy pack of cards he and Raina have been assiduously piling up. It does not worry us that he descends so hastily from the refinement of the higher love to the crudity of his addresses to a servant: we are content to feel, in the play's own bold terms, that this gesture might fairly represent a certain attitude of mind, itself not unfamiliar.

To some extent this excerpt exemplies the function of character in any play. Sergius and Raina are consistent within themselves. We give

Shaw the licence, and he makes use of it to manipulate his characters for particular ends. When he has established the quality for which each stands, we look to it for confirmation of our earlier impression; but what, ironically, we see, is that quality being exposed. The continuity of the character is all-important to the author if he is to communicate with us. The gross statement of Shaw's crashing anticlimax depends for its effectiveness upon our seeing the same Sergius who talked before with Raina talking now to Louka.

It is no great step from saying that characters have only that limited existence the play requires of them to saying that character is dependent upon the action it exists to enact. The only satisfactory way to understand character is thus to see it as a way of defining a dramatic impression. Our ultimate interest should not be in the character itself, though this may be a way of starting interest, of separating particular impressions, often of providing a continuity of an idea through the person of one actor. But the fastidious playgoer returns to the play. D. H. Lawrence's celebrated statement belongs to drama too:

> Again I say, don't look for the development of the novel to follow the lines of certain characters: the characters fall into the form of some other rhythmic form, as when one draws a fiddle-bow across a fine tray delicately sanded, the sand takes lines unknown.

As in the novel, so in the play. The form of the impressions determines and deploys the detail of characterization, shows us the perspective of the character. So before we look for consistency in a character, we look for consistency in the relationship between one and another. Just as two contiguous speeches project an image, so two characters contribute to its formation. Hamlet is not Hamlet without Claudius, without Gertrude or without Ophelia. He discharges his meaning in the context of a scene.

It is true that character *discloses* itself by physical appearance, by self-exposition (if we take it at face value) and by what others think. So in Chekhov's straightforward one-act farce *The Bear*, first we see Grigory Stepanovitch Smirnov as an overbearing, middle-aged landowner. Second, he talks about himself:

> Brr! How mad I feel today, how furious! I'm positively shaking with rage. I can hardly breath. . . . Ugh! my God! I'm almost fainting!

Third, Elena Ivanovna Popova says of him: "You're a coarse, ill-mannered fellow! Respectable people don't talk like this to a lady." But these technical aids offer no positive meaning apart from the particular presence of the other character—the widow with the dimples on her cheeks, Madame Popova, who resists his intrusion and makes him forget his pomposity his misogyny and his anger, who challenges him with her husband's pistols and her charm. The play creates the simplest of impressions, constructed on the "before-and-after" pattern. It reaches a ludicrous climax:

> A duel! Yes, that's equality of rights, that's emancipation! There's equality of sexes for you! I'll pop her off just as a matter of principle!

All the processes of the play have gone to force this crisis, and reality has been left far behind. But in a moment a touch of reality is introduced, and we recognize an affectation familiar to us. The pace halts, Smirnov pauses, and the anticlimax arrives: "But what a woman! . . . I'm almost sorry to have to kill her!" He capitulates. Her capitulation will follow, and, to our joy, her initial pose,

> I will never go out. . . . Why should I? My life is over. He lies in his grave—I have buried myself in these four walls. . . . We are both dead,

is equally shattered. We do not think chiefly of Smirnov, nor of Popova, but of the sparks flying between them. Character discharges its meaning in friction and reaction.

The reader may argue that character *develops*, which is not, he may say, something a mere "mask" allows. But the development of character is in fact nothing but a finer definition of the features of the mask. It is properly the development of the image that deludes us into seeing a development in the character. In some plays, like *King Lear* or *A Doll's House*, the idea of change in the character can itself be a central impression, but we must not receive an effect and take it to be a cause. We oblige the author by consistently linking together this aspect and that of the mask as it appears to us. This is facilitated by the continuous presence of the actor, and we are likely to go astray only if the author has not sufficiently provided for our natural desire to complete half-formed images, or if he has left the actor with words so empty that he must fill them out from his own resources, perhaps from his own personality: the abuse of a playwright's work may be due to a fault in the play itself.

Four consecutive speeches from the beginning of Strindberg's exceptionally closely knit play *Miss Julie* suggest in little how character is created and how it develops:

> JULIE. Thank you. Don't you want some yourself?
>
> JEAN. I don't care very much for beer, but if it is a command, of course—
>
> JULIE. Command?—I should think a polite gentleman might keep his lady company.
>
> JEAN. Yes, that's the way it should be.

Miss Julie is virtually alone with Jean her footman for the first time, since Christine the cook has fallen asleep. Thus anything said between them now takes on a meaning arising from a dramatic counterpoint: what these particular people say in private works against what a lady and her servant should say in public. Character emerges less from the seductive coyness of Julie's remarks and from Jean's reticence and embarrassment (secondary symptoms) than from the fact that this remark is made to this person in this circumstance.

Julie had asked for beer: "My taste is so simple that I prefer it to wine." She first slyly invites Jean to join her in drinking it. The seeming quibble about the social standing of beer or wine and the appropriateness of the drink to the drinker hints at the change in their relationship to come and partly prepare us to accept their perverse states of mind. Jean's reply is double-edged. He is unwilling to abandon his position of the man in the relationship, although he is still aware of his social inferiority. In the audience we await his reaction: had he replied "Yes," we should have assumed he was asserting his masculinity; had he replied "No," he would have been accepting his menial position. His actual reply, enhanced for us by the actor's momentary hesitation, establishes his indecision at this stage of his "development." But will she reduce him again to servant, or raise him to an open equality as between man and woman? Her words tell us she takes the second course: "I should think a polite gentleman might keep his lady company." By her voice, softer and more insinuating, she raises him to her level. They are now "lady" and "gentleman." Will Jean accept this advancement? Yes, but with a degree of reluctance in the implied conditional: "that's the way it should be." This last remark of his is potent with a sudden new regard he has for himself. It precipitates a vision of him as the dominant partner in a sexual relationship, but one with latent abnormalities.

Character implies relationship, and development of character suggests growth towards a more precise, evolving relationship, our guided deduction. It should not confuse the argument to call this relationship the situation. Both Jean and Julie seem to develop, more especially Jean in these lines, but it is properly the situation that has meaningfully progressed. Situation is manipulated by the author; character, involved by it, appears to grow. As character grows, in turn it reveals relationship.

"Relationship" is not being used here in the limited sense of a personal connection between people, but in the dramatic sense of a relative connection between characters, which can of course include a personal connection. We are asking not how characters affect one another, but how they affect the action. Once this is done, relationship between characters can be seen to exist even where they do not meet, as Falstaff, for example, does not meet King Henry but must by his behaviour put a construction upon what the King stands for. Neither does Macbeth "meet" his Porter; nor the Dauphin Baudricourt's Steward. But all have their place in the pattern.

A useful concept of recent coinage is that discussed by Dr. E. M. W. Tillyard as differing "planes of reality." One character can bear relationship to another even when it is presented at a lower or higher "level" within the play, not necessarily a social level, but an imaginative one. We respond to a similarity or to a contrast by making the association in the sequence of impressions: so Sir Toby is imaginatively linked with Orsino, Touchstone with Jaques. Looking for so-called "sub-plots" misleads us into falsely anatomizing a play's unity of feeling. Degrees of fiction in the shape of actors are set on the same stage and related dramatically, especially in the fantasies of artificial comedy. *A Midsummer Night's Dream* uses this freedom extravagantly.

Within the magic of the moonlit wood near Athens, Shakespeare is at liberty to play dramatic variations upon his motifs of love-sickness. In the first scene the varieties of moon imagery paint the thematic setting for this wedding play: it is the moon that "lingers desires," "the cold fruitless moon of chastity," which is opposed to the romantic moon that,

> Like to a silver bow
> New-bent in heaven, shall behold the night
> Of our solemnities.

This moon in turn weaves the spell that "hath witched the bosom" of Hermia. The world of *fancy* shall merge into the world of *fantasy*. Within this web of charmed love and fairy moon-madness, within this loose dialectic of verbal imagery, Shakespeare symbolizes his lovers and his fairies in the forms we know. Bottom and the mechanicals with their burlesque of Pyramus and Thisbe supply mongrel and preposterous elements that are caught up in the pattern and used to balance, criticize and complicate the luxury of sentiment the others display.

The theme is the irrationality of love, explored in the comic licence of the moonlit wood. There are five worlds of potential and actual lovers, and the formal illusion of the play is to make us wonder in which world we stand ourselves. Not in the literary world of Pyramus and Thisbe, nor in the regions of the supernatural of Titania and Oberon, nor in the grotesque circle of Bottom and his friends, nor among the tinsel passions of Lysander, Demetrius, Helena and Hermia. We can identify ourselves only with the rational onlookers Theseus and Hippolyta, who prompt us to look with the eyes of the newly-married couple for whom the play was possibly written. With their anticipation we shall speculate about romantic beliefs. Through the agency of Puck, all lovers' sincerities are forsworn, and all their protestations of faithfulness are disputed and denied; the delicate purity of ideal fairy love is repudiated by Titania's sophisticated relationship with Oberon, and coarsely soiled by Bottom the worldly lover; and Ovid's noble story of the perfect love of Pyramus and Thisbe performed by the ignoble cannot be other than burlesqued. No sentimenal sweet assumption we have had is allowed to rest. With what quizzical judgement Theseus concludes,

> Lovers and madmen have such seething brains,
> Such shaping fantasies, that apprehend
> More than cool reason ever comprehends!

Shakespeare is ironically asking whether we are prepared to acknowledge with "cool reason" the validity of all the fancies with which unreason comforts itself.

This is the disquieting virtue of the play, to allow us no moment of easy sympathy with any kind or degree of love. We can only detach ourselves with Theseus and Hippolyta. By travesty and burlesque, all pleasing preconceptions and misconceptions are fretted and disparaged. We are quietly told of our inadequacies—"But, howsoever, strange and admirable." This line from Theseus's lady suggests the lightness in the tone of Shakespeare's reprimand and the gentleness in the touch of his punishment.

This complexity could not have been secured had not the author felt himself free to caricature the lovers, the fairies and the clowns, free to colour each set of characters to clash with another. Laughter follows the shocks of the feather-weight irony. As each group, acting on its own plane of reality, taking its own standards of conduct so seriously, is juggled by the conjuror, romance is made an object of fun. When we examine the mechanism by which two of these caricatures, Bottom and Titania, are, at the master-stroke of Act III, scence i, thrown together, animal disporting with angel, fairy in love with ass, character has become a critical term of strictly limited usefulness, or else one so wide in its application that it must embrace the whole structure of the scene. In Shakespeare's romantic comedies, like *A Midsummer Night's Dream, As You Like It* and *Twelfth Night,* character is more structural than individual, more general and formal than personal.

Pirandello manipulates character in a highly original way, daringly asserting the freedom of the stage. *Six Characters in Search of an Author* provides a brilliant example. "What is true?" is Pirandello's basic question, and his play is a complex task for the analyst, especially since breaking down the play's objects into neat compartments, for example (i) how an artist creates, (ii) what reality there is in art, (iii) what reality there is in life, does not help, since these three and other problems are being dramatized simultaneously. In reading the play, one may find it jerky, without an organic centre and therefore unconvincing. This, I believe, is because one tends to tease out the separate strands of the theme from without. In performance, the play is smooth and interlocking, and the ideas move centripetally by the powerful magnetism of the play's emotion. Characters that in the text seem to divide the play, in performance bind it by being precisely placed in the structural relationships enacted.

See this play as one composed of dramatized, implicit discussions between characters, some of whom have the ability to speak with more than one voice. Two of the Six Characters in particular, both by being the centre of interest and by moving freely between all the worlds of imagination the play defines, encourage us to feel the meaning of the play as a unity. The Stepdaughter and the Father speak as characters in the absent author's play, while at the same time they imply what the absent author would have said in his own defence; so the relationship author-character is demonstrated and the processes of creative art are argued. When the Stepdaughter and the Father are seen as characters with more life than the actors who are to play, actor criticizes character and character criticizes actor, and the relationship character-actor is argued. Pirandello reserves his final cumulative shock when we are persuaded that the actors are but characters, that, in the final chaos of the play when the Stepdaughter goes laughing hysterically through the auditorium, the characters are but actors, and that we are but an audience, susceptible to anything we take for granted in the theatre or in life. This hits us with the horror of a blow in one's sleep. The game is one of trying to find the "right" viewpoint, the "comfortable" attitude towards any given idea. Are we in the play or in reality? Are we looking with the eyes of the author or the character or the actor or the audience? The play does not leave us with any consolatory answer. Our final queries are about life, not about art, and Pirandello's skill is positive by being negative, serving to enlighten us by confounding us.

A particular piece of analysis will indicate the variety of forces working upon the imagination at the same time. In the following scene, Madame Pace, the repulsive milliner brothel-keeper, remaining completely the character of the absent author's fiction, speaks a broken English, which amuses the watching group of actors and actresses and pleases the Director:

> DIRECTOR. . . . Yes, speak like that, Madame! It'll bring the house down! We couldn't ask for anything better. It'll bring a little comic relief into the crudity of the situation. Yes, you talk like that! It's absolutely wonderful!
>
> STEPDAUGHTER. Wonderful! And why not? When you hear a certain sort of suggestion made to you in a lingo like that. . . . There's not much doubt about what your answer's going to be . . . Because it almost seems like a joke. You feel inclined to laugh when you hear there's an "old señor" who wants to "amuse himself with me." An "old señor," eh, Madame?

MADAME PACE. Not so very old . . . Not quite so young, yes? And if he does not please you . . . Well, he has . . . *prudencia.*

MOTHER. *Absorbed as they are in the scene the Actors have been paying no attention to her. Now, to their amazement and consternation, she leaps up and attacks* MADAME PACE. *At her cry they jump, then hasten smilingly to restrain her, for she, meanwhile has snatched off* MADAME PACE's *wig and thrown it to the ground.* You old devil! You old witch! You murderess! Oh, my daughter!

STEPDAUGHTER, *rushing over to restrain her mother.* No, Mummy, no! Please!

What is the audience thinking as it listens to this? To make each remark carry meaning, it must first have decided where the character speaking stands in relation to the character commented upon. The spectator will also be trying to assess where the character stands in relation to himself. When the Director says, "Yes, speak like that, Madame! It'll bring the house down! We couldn't ask for anything better," we know he is speaking from a position *outside* the play-within-the-play in which we take Madame Pace to be, and in part speaking for us in the audience, since, like the choric group of actors and actresses on the stage, we are also watching the rehearsal he is conducting. But when he adds, "Yes, you talk like that! It's absolutely wonderful!" there is a shift of understanding and we take up a position outside *him,* because now he has started talking to a "character" as if she were an "actress," and we recognize that he is being deluded by the degree of reality Madame Pace possesses. From our superior position we criticize the inadequacy of his vision, and reflect momentarily upon our former limitation when we joined him in his approval of the cheap theatrical titillation of the broken English. The art of the theatre is under the microscope whenever the Director speaks. Nor is the Director's shortsightedness allowed to appear a human shortcoming, an understandable weakness. Because the situation of Madame Pace and the Stepdaughter is melodramatically emotional, it colours all attitudes not in keeping with melodramatic feeling, and we involuntarily condemn the Director and his company as culpable monsters whenever they speak for the theatrical profession.

We are thus prepared for the Stepdaughter's criticism of the Director, "Wonderful! And why not?" with which we now agree. We assume she is with us *outside* the rehearsal, as if in the audience looking on. We quite forget that the passion with which she turns on the Director, comes not wholly of a desire to criticize the ways of the theatre, but more of her own passionate concern with the part she must perform in the play-within-the-play, whose reality she never questions. The venom of her sarcasms should have passed the warning that she is only half outside the rehearsal. In giving her our sympathy we find ourselves making the mistake we have made already many times, as the author intends: the mistake of taking the Six Characters as real and the Director and his company as unreal. The emotions of the play-within-the-play are again made deliberately harrowing by the ugly euphemisms in the Stepdaughter's mimicry of Madame Pace. As soon as the Stepdaughter recreates the scene in her mind, her position shifts as if by the impulsion of her bitter thoughts. She addresses Madame Pace directly: "An 'old señor,' eh Madame?" Immediately we recognize that she is *inside* the play again, suffering in a second capacity.

When Madame Pace replies, her callous "Not so very old . . . Not quite so young, yes?" can only be spoken completely "in character." It is spoken directly to the Stepdaughter, showing she is quite oblivious of the critics around her in the persons of the actors and the characters and of us, the true audience. By her very obliviousness Madame Pace's reality comes in question. Yet because of the sincerity of the scene she is enacting, against which the Director and his actors seem petty, we tend unconsciously to question the substantiality of the others too. The play modulates through a discussion of the shams of the theatre to one of the relationship between character and reality.

The Mother, who has been looking at the scene as if it were the past resurrected, suddenly by the force of her emotion takes the past to be the present and the play to be reality. In a flash we are startled, as we were when Madame Pace made her supernatural entrance, into the illusion that the exchange between the Mother and Madame Pace is the only truth. This effect is enhanced by the credibility of Madame Pace's horror when her wig is thrown off. The Stepdaughter, deceiving us by her double role inside and outside the play-within-the-play, for a space suggests that her attempts to calm her mother are the attempts of a child to appease a parent, until we reflect this might also be the behaviour of a daughter conscious of her mother's making a *faux pas* in public, the public being the Producer and his company. This impression, that the Stepdaughter is farther outside the play than the Mother, is stressed when the Father's advice to the Mother follows:

"Calm yourself, my dear!" This reaffirms that she is moved by the presence of Madame Pace to the exclusion of all else. In performance, the half-existence of the Mother by contrast makes the Stepdaughter more "alive" than the play's structure would suggest.

The modulations of the action are easy. The audience turns its feeling and its critical intelligence elastically on this, then on that, aspect of the subject, because it is led through the play uncertain of the level at which it must feel and of what it is free to criticize. Through the vacillation of response to this or that character Pirandello is able to dramatize his abstract discussions.

The complexity of the play's suggestions increases rapidly. The ambiguities become bewildering in the scene of Madame Pace's shop which the Stepdaughter and the Father enact for the Director:

> FATHER, *coming forward, a new note in his voice.* Good afternoon, Miss.
>
> STEPDAUGHTER, *her head bowed, speaking with restrained disgust.* Good afternoon!

How are we to see these characters now? Are they merely representing the spectator's point of view, criticizing the professionals and showing them how it should be done? If this make-believe is a further comment on theatrecraft, then they are acting acting. But Pirandello means us to accept their performance as truth, for his direction to the Father is that he must at first look troubled and very pale,

> *But as he approaches from the back of the stage he smiles, already absorbed in the reality of his created life. He smiles as if the drama which is about to break upon him is as yet unknown to him.*

As the sequence develops, we are to be moved by a more realistic style of acting: actors of Pirandello must be "plastic" according to the distance of their speech and movement from the author's conception of the "true" reality. In 1925, the author wrote:

> The six characters must not appear as phantoms, but as "created realities," immutable creatures of fantasy. They are more real and consistent than the voluble actors.

And the play itself has provided for a subtle changeover by which the Stepdaughter and the Father are more convincing than the actors. We are to take the brothel scene as reality, so that when the Ingénue interrupts with "Oh, I say! Those are *our* hats!" we are shocked into recognizing that we are being deluded, and the discussion of our awareness of degree of reality is successfully dramatized. This aspect of the play is later emphasized when the Stepdaughter criticizes the Father's *performance*: and then again when the Leading Man and the Leading Lady attempt to re-enact the performance they have seen. They act now with a lesser realism, though Pirandello makes it clear that their acting must be near enough to accepted standards to make us consider it seriously as a possible interpretation:

> *The playing of this scene by the Actors will appear from the very first words as something completely different from what was played before, without its having, even in the slightest degree, the air of a parody.*

The Father's immediate reaction is to cry, "No!," and the Stepdaughter cannot restrain a burst of laughter. By this process of refining our standards of reality in dramatic statement and counter-statement, we are forced to argue about probability and credibility. Our thoughts are set wrangling with our feelings.

It would be unlike Pirandello to leave us complacent. Before we are allowed to go, he arranges it that the climax of the play-within-the-play coincides with the climax of our experience, and that the fictional reality of the characters becomes inextricably confused with the comparative reality of the Producer and the Actors. The end of the play introduces a revolver shot which is perhaps the most effective shot in drama. It effects a conjunction of the real and the unreal, hits off the climax of our emotions and sums up the play's puzzle. By this shot, shadow is made solid, and the spectator dizzy with a terror of the unknown.

> *Then first from one side, then from the other, the Actors re-enter.*
>
> LEADING LADY, *re-entering right, very much moved.* He's dead. Poor boy! He's dead! Oh what a terrible thing to happen!
> LEADING MAN, *re-entering left, laughing.* What do you mean,

> dead? It's all make-believe! It's all just a pretence! Don't get taken in by it!
>
> OTHER ACTORS, *entering from the right*. Make-believe? Pretence? Reality! Reality! He's dead!
>
> OTHERS, *from the left*. No! Make-believe! It's all a pretence!

These contradictory extremes compel our silence, not our laughter: they mark the subtlety with which the characters have been manipulated, and our absorption in the play.

To stifle *Six Characters in Search of an Author* with preconceived notions of what character may do in a play, or what degree of conviction it must carry, is to treat character as something external, hopelessly making nonsense of the experience. The playgoer can finally admit character only as a mask in its meaning and a puppet in its action, and judge it only by standards of reality and conviction which the orchestration and total purpose of the play demand.

HAROLD ROSENBERG

Character Change and the Drama

> "We have already seen Bernard change; passions may come that will modify him still more." ANDRÉ GIDE, *The Counterfeiters*

I

An egg with an ancestry, developing, changing its form, maturing; later, degenerating, dying, decaying, again changing its form; always in a slow gradual way except for the shocks of birth and death—such is the broadest metaphor of the human personality developed by the organic point of view and expressed in such studies of mutation as biology, biography, history, psychology. Whatever unity an organism maintains at the base of its tranformations is something mysterious: the single being may be compared with other organisms which it resembles, it may be classified, accounted for statistically, subsumed under a type; but its individuality can only be "felt." To the human person himself his own coherence is, as Herbert Read once put it, "an organic coherence intuitively based on the real world of sensation."

On the other hand, the concepts of morality or social law, applying exclusively to human beings and ignoring possible analogies with other living creatures, tend to define the individual not as an entity enduring in time but by what he has done in particular instances. A given sequence of acts provokes a judgment, and this judgment is an inseparable part of the recognition of the individual. Here too there is no final comprehension of the single person; but whereas the organic approach points towards the existence of individuals, each of whom can be grasped only by a nonrational operation, social legality operates as if it were unaware of them altogether, except as they are totally defined by their "overt acts." If the law is not always satisfied with itself, it is not because it feels the need at any time to discover more about the nature of individuals, but for the reason that it realizes all at once that acts are being performed for which it has no means of holding them responsible.

The law is not a recognizer of persons; its judgments are applied at the end of a series of acts. With regard to individuals the law thus creates a fiction, that of a person who is identified by the coherence of his acts with a fact in which they have terminated (the crime or the contract) and by nothing else. The judgment is the resolution of these acts.[1] The law visualizes the individual as a kind of actor with a role whom the court has located in the situational system of the legal code.

In contrast with the person recognized by the continuity of his being, we may designate the character defined by the coherence of his acts as an "identity." Representing the human individual as an actor, the term stands against the biological or historical organism-concept, which visualizes action as a mere attribute of, and clue to, a being who can be known only through an intuition.

The modern novel has more in common with the biological or historical view of character than with the legal. *Remembrance of Things Past* and *The Magic Mountain* are models of a literature of character metamorphosis, *Finnegans Wake* a high point in the rendering of organic texture.

As for the legal definition, its way of shaping personae with a hatchet causes it to seem at first glance far removed from the needs of imaginative writing. Without considering the symbolic, collective or residual ingredients of feeling or motive, the law comprehends its "characters" in terms of the most commonly ascertainable elements of their acts. Only information relevant and material to the legal "cause of action" may be introduced as bearing on the parties and their transactions. The law is forever fixed to that edge of individuality where particulars are caught in the machinery of the abstract and pulled into an alien orbit. Yet in the old tragedy, the individual was similarly torn away from himself by the force of an impersonal system.

There too, however, distinctions must be made: social law is not dramatic law. That the persons who stand before the bar of justice are identities, that they appear to be personifications of, and completely explainable by, the logic of their crimes, is the effect of a visible artifice of judicial thinking. In fact, of course, a man who has committed a murder may not have acted in a manner recognizable as murderous until that last instant when he pulled the trigger. That he meant to kill at that moment satisfies the law's demand for premeditation and homicidal malice; but since all the acts of the criminal were not of a criminal quality, there is forced upon our consciousness a lifetime of extenuating circumstances. All those common details of existence, gestures in every way resembling our own, even including those preceding the murder—entering an automobile, stepping on the gas, obeying the traffic lights—to say nothing of receiving certain influences, being molded by certain values, which go more to form part of the criminal in the innocence or "alegality" of his animal duration than of the relevant *res gestae* of his crime, the law takes into account only to fill in the scenic accompaniments of the last act and the rationale of its intent. So that dealing with identities rather than with personalities, the law is enabled to do so only by willfully converting persons with histories into emblems of unified actions of a given order. In other words, the law, like its victims, suffers from the discrepancy between being and action, the failure of the individual to conform in every respect to his role. Were this not so, law and justice could be synonymous.

If, however, the old drama, as contrasted with biographies of actual or of fictitious persons, succeeded, as has been asserted by ethical critics, in supplying a picture of action in which a kind of justice and a kind of law conform to each other, it must be because the dramatist started with identities. Like the judge he left aside personalities, their growth, their structural peculiarities; like the judge he established the particularity of a character only on the basis of the coherence of his acts with a chosen fact; like the judge he was interested in psychological phenomena not for themselves but only as bearing on the plausibility of the judgment with which he terminated the action. But unlike that of the judge, the dramatist's definition of the character was not an arbitrary superimposition that exchanged the emotional, intellectual and mechanical characteristics of a biological and social organism for some one deed that concerned the court; it constituted instead the entire reality of the character, avoiding the ruinous abstractness of the law by determining in advance that his emotions, his thoughts and his gestures should correspond with and earn in every respect the fate prepared for him . . . In short, because the dramatist had created his characters he could maintain the relation between their emotions, their thoughts and their destinies; while those who confront the judge on his dais were, unfortunately, born.

Its distinction between personality and identity, quietly implied by its mode of defining the individual as an identity, is what dramatic thought has in common with the legal. The characters of biography and the novel are persons with histories, but in the drama the characters are identities with roles. The distinction relates to a difference in purpose of biography and tragedy. Biography aims to picture a life as fully and precisely as possible with the type of exactness which is proper to history, that is to events visualized as successive in time. But drama, as a "poetical picture of life," is composed of events which, though seemingly related sequentially and causally, are chosen with reference to the application of specific laws leading to a judgment: the conventional coherence of these events, the suggestion to the spectator that they have actually happened or are at least within the range of probability, is superficial, and far from determining the outcome of the action serves only to connect in the mind of the audience the natural world of causal determination with the dramatic world of judgment. Those psychological explanations of the motivations of dramatic figures which form so large a part of criticism apply to this layer of causality which is the outer form of dramatic movement; they do not touch on the dramatist's act of judging,[2] derived from his conception of how the world is ordered, by which his characters are moved. Psychology can establish the plausibility of Macbeth's or Lear's behavior, but for the sufficiency of his motivation we must refer not to a possible Macbeth or Lear in "real life" but to the laws of the Shakespearean universe.

It is with respect to these laws that drama reaches objectivity, that the dramatist's image mirrors the lives of actual people. In "nature" individuals may evade any system of ends; but a dramatic identity is a creature in whom a judgment is involved at birth, a judgment which delivers him to pathos and gives meaning to it. In thus substituting identities, whose motor organs are judgments,[3] for personalities who live erratically within the freedom and hazard of moral laws not yet discovered, drama brings into being figures who are at once particular and general and its account of events appears as "more philosophical than history."

II

Religious thought also interprets the individual as an identity; it looks to the judgment that will establish his eternal role. To it the psychology of personality-development is irrelevant; for upon the fixed situation of an identity, mutations of the personality have no bearing. As in the bloody book of the law, there are in religion stirring examples of this division between identity and personality. For instance, in demoniacal possession identities usurped personalities: the demon, in all respects a new being controlled by the conditions of a supernatural world, subjected the individual to its own will.[4] The personality of the possessed remained intact. The demon was a character with a name of his own. His voice was heard from the mouth of a man—but he was not that man, any more than Hamlet was Barrymore. And he could be influenced only by means fundamentally identical in all contemporaneous cases of possession—there was one law for demons belonging to the same system. Exorcism was a contest between powers of a purely religious cosmos. The exorcist addressed the demon directly; no attempt was made to affect the psychological structure of the possessed. As we have said, it was irrelevant.

An identity is constant. In the worlds which give rise to identities, growth is excluded and change of character occurs above the rigid substratum of the identifying fact: whatever happens to the murderer, the murder still stands as his sign. Dramatic reversal of situation derives its overwhelming effect from this persistence of identity. Everything has turned inside out, yet the actor goes on doing the same thing. Were psychological adjustment to the new position possible, it would destroy the tragic irony and disperse the pathos.

Identity may be revealed more fully as a drama progresses. In such so-called character development, behavior rises or declines on the moral plane without, however, altering the fact by which the character is identified; we simply see a second side of the same character: e.g., the idling Prince Hal's "Well, thus we play the fools with the time" belongs to the same royal identity as Henry V's conscientious "Our bad neighbor makes us early stirrers, / Which is both healthful and good husbandry." Unchanging identity may also be present in the sudden reversals of moral direction that occur in *crise de conscience* episodes of novels and plays, moral reversal being merely a species of character development carried on at quick-time.

Yet identity itself may change in a drama, not through moral or psychological development, but through a process that causes the central fact which identifies the character to give place to one belonging to a different constellation of values. When such a shift of centers occurs, the fact to which the character's action was previously attached loses its power to move him. His moral nature may remain substantially the same, but his acts crystallize differently; he is a different dramatic individual; all his likelihoods have been recast.

It is especially in the substitution of one identity for another, or for a personality, that the type of coherence which marks the identity is clarified, since change of identity takes place, as we shall see, all at once, in a leap, and not as in personality through a continual transformation of elements.

To begin with the legal instance: the fact of the crime organized (by determining their relevance) the acts of the criminal and interpreted them. For the law he lived by that fact alone. Were it suddenly discovered that no crime had been committed, the coherence of his action would collapse and the prisoner, having been converted in an instant into the hypothetical and undefined figure of an innocent man, would no longer exist under the eye of the court. If thereafter he were charged with a different crime, his legal identity would depend upon this new fact and would be entirely unrelated to the one he had lost; he would emerge out of the void as a "new man."

In religion identity and change of identity have been, one may say, the dominant interest of the most significant and important ceremonies. Professor Guignbert writes in *Christianity:*

> In the Phrygian cult of Cybele and Attis, but not in that alone, for we find it in various other Asiatic cults and in that of Mithra, a singular ceremony, called the *taurobolium,* took place. It formed part of the mysterious initiatory rites exclusively reserved for believers.

Having given an account of the rites, Guignbert explains their transforming function:

> The pit signifies the kingdom of the dead, and the mystic, in descending into it, is thought to die; the bull is Attis, and the blood that is shed is the divine life principle that issues from him; the initiate receives it and, as it were, absorbs it; when he leaves the pit he is said to be "born again" and milk, as in the case of a newborn infant, is given him to drink. But he is not born the mere man again he was before; he has absorbed the very essence of the god and, if we understand the mystery aright, he is in his turn become an Attis and is saluted as one.

Guignbert then draws attention to the resemblance between these rites and the Christian baptism and eucharist.

The change consists then in both the legal and religious instances in (1) the dissolution or death of the previous identity through cancellation of its central fact [5]—this may involve the physical death of the individual (as with Ivan Ilych, whom Tolstoy abandoned on the threshold of change) or his symbolic death; and (2) a reidentification, wherein the individual is placed in a new status, is "reborn," so to say, and given a new character and perhaps a new name.

Drama is no more religion than it is law. But the fact that the phenomenon of religious conversion is the only one which actually [6] effects a change of identity in the living person, in which through the touch of death a course of living is annulled and another substituted without rupturing the organic continuity of the individual, relates religion and drama in a peculiar way. To present identity-replacement in a credible manner the dramatist must imitate the experience of religion and subject his character to the ordeal of death. But he may do so in terms of action alone and without adopting any metaphysical supposition as to the cause of the change. In a word, dramatic death and regeneration need not be involved in faith: [7] there is the death-laden incident; then occurs a transfer of identities within the single figure, a change of faces behind the mask.

The process appears with characteristic modifications in different literatures. A very early account of identity-change is the life story of the Biblical Jacob, whose character is built out of connotations of the word from which his name was derived, as when Esau complains in the Hebrew pun that he was "Jacobed" twice. A self-reliant trickster, he wins his way through ruses and negotiations until the threat of death descends upon him in the approach of the avenging Esau. Then "greatly afraid and distressed" he calls on God to save him and schemes to be the last of his company to die. Alone behind the encampment, however, he is met by the angel and wrestles with him until dawn. During this contest he receives the sign of the dislocated thigh and his name is changed to Wrestler-With-God. In the morning he advances to meet his brother, whose fury has been unaccountably—psychologically, that is, though enforcing the point of Jacob's new identity—transformed to love.

From that time the lone adventurer, gainer of property and wives, has disappeared; in his place sits the patriarch, and interest shifts to his children. In the next episode, the seduction of Dinah, it is his sons who plot and carry out the treacherous revenge. The transformed Jacob, Isra-el, his character "deducible" from his wrestle with God, is busy with the erection of altars.

This is an extremely simple picture of the process of identity-change. There is a minimum of action-detail, only the death threat and alteration by contact with the divine over-plot and by renaming.

In the next example, a personality is transformed into a dramatic identity. In it, the action of a person, which is the expression of a psychological condition, is contrasted with that of an identity, which always takes place in response to his role—which he performs as required of him by the plot, by the whole in which he is located. That this hero is a person at the outset means that the work begins as a species of biography; that he changes into an identity means that from that point on the biography-drama becomes a true drama.

In *Hamlet* there is a fusion of two forms of interpretation, the naturalistic and the dramatic. The argumentative, self-analytical Hamlet of "nonaction," describing himself in every speech, and using speech as a substitute for deed, is very much the figure of a personality, of a being insufficient for, *because irrelevant to,* the dramatic role offered to him.[8] Hamlet has all the qualities required for action; what he lacks is the identity structure which would fit him to be a character in a drama, a one-ness with his role originating in and responding to the laws of his dramatic world. Thus he is contrasted or "paralleled" [9] with Laertes whose situation is similar to his, "For by the image of my cause, I see / The portraiture of his," but who is characterized as an identity by his readiness to act; and the point is repeated in setting off his psychological diffusion against the acting-craft of the visiting players. It is not a weakness of personality that impedes his action but the fact that he is a personality. The revolving sword of judgment cuts him off at that point where he would force an entry into the dramatic cosmos. He has been exiled to a middle ground between the natural world and the dramatic; governed by contradictory laws, it is a playground of somewhat insane fantasies. Hamlet is inadequate to carry out the Orestean judgment because he has been permitted to retain a portion of himself. As a new kind of hero, the person who matches his self against his part, he thinks too much not because he is an intellectual but because it is impossible for him to do anything else. The mystery which surrounds him consists in that he is neither an identity nor a personality wholly but a combination of both, an hypothetical actor who has wandered by accident upon a stage.[10]

Clearly, then, this character must be changed if the play is to become a tragedy, if the action is to resolve itself and not to break down into a series of episodes exposing psychological layers. To arrive at a pathos, Hamlet must be given an identity which will alter his relation to the action and fit him into the drama. But there is only one way to represent such a change dramatically.

Until we meet Hamlet on his return from the voyage to England, where he had been sent to his death and narrowly escaped in the grapple with the pirates, we have to do with the standard figure of Hamlet-criticism. But after this immersion in symbolic death,[11] we encounter a new character, a regenerated man. In his next appearance on the stage, Hamlet takes death as his subject and discourses on it as an insider. More to the point, he has acquired a certainty with respect to his feelings and a capacity for action. "This is I," he announces, as he leaps into the grave of Ophelia, "Hamlet the Dane!" Having *named himself* he is at once attacked by Laertes but with unexpected firmness proclaims his dramatic equality.

> I prithee, take thy fingers from my throat;
> For, though I am not splenetive and rash,
> Yet have I something in me dangerous,
> Which let thy wisdom fear. Hold off thy hand!

With this "dangerous" new ability to act, he is no longer troubled by ambiguity of feeling: "Why, I will fight with him upon this theme. . . . / I loved Ophelia . . ." To his mother Hamlet's self-assured identity is unrecognizable; she sees him as he was before the change:

> This is mere madness,
> And thus a while the fit will work in him.
> Anon, as patient as the female dove
> When that her golden couplets are disclosed,
> His silence will sit drooping.

But Gertrude is mistaken. For Hamlet has commenced to act his role of self-purifying vengeance, had assumed immutably his dramatic being, at that moment when aboard the ship bound for England he had read his death-warrant. Then for the first time his mind had responded with the immediacy of the actor:

> Being thus be-netted round with villainies—
> Ere I could make a prologue to my brains,
> They had begun the play—

And now this hero who had looked with such passionate envy upon passion is "constant in his purpose" towards the King. The magical event barely indicated ("Had I but time, O, I could tell you") has released his forces. His action hustles the play to its tragic close and the apparently accidental character of his revenge serves to emphasize that he is controlled at the end not by the conflicting intentions of a self but by the impulsions of the plot. Transformed from the image of a personality into that of a dramatic identity, he has found at last his place in the play.

Our third example is from Dostoevsky's *The Brothers Karamazov*. This author's handling of change of identity follows more literally experience of typically religious conversion than does either that of the Old Testament or of Shakespeare; it is related directly to Christian beliefs and emotions.

The "Biographical Notes" of Father Zossima set out two parallel cases of identity-change. First there is Markel, Zossima's brother, whose conversion is briefly sketched to furnish a ground for Zossima's own conversion which comes later and is developed in greater detail. After his brother's death Zossima was sent to Petersburg to enter the Imperial Guard. From the house of his childhood, he records, he had brought none but precious memories of a religious import, but these grew dimmer in the cadet school and he became a "cruel, absurd, almost savage creature.". . . A disappointing love affair, an insult, and a challenge to a duel . . . "and then something happened that in very truth was the turning point of my life." The evening preceding the duel, he flew into a rage and struck his orderly so violently that his face was covered with blood. When Zossima awoke the following morning he went to the window and looked out upon the garden. The sun was rising. "It was warm and beautiful, the birds were singing." At that point the conversion began.

> What's the meaning of it, I thought, I feel in my heart as it were something vile and shameful? Is it because I am going to shed blood? No, I thought, I feel it's not that. Can it be that I am afraid of death, afraid of being killed? No, that's not it at

all . . . And all at once, I knew what it was; it was because I had beaten Afanasy the evening before!

Then Zossima recalls his converted brother, the deceased Markel. On the field of honor, risking his companion's contempt, he halts the duel after his adversary has fired. A short time later he becomes a monk.

This incident, turning on danger of death though fear of death is denied, stages the typical antecedent conditions listed by psychologists for cases of religious conversion; it may be assumed that, apart from his own experience after being threatened by the Czar's firing squad, Dostoevsky was familiar with the subject through books on the psychology of conversion. Yet Zossima's transformation arouses no suspicion that it is an ideological fable of the descent of Grace rather than a genuine dramatic happening. The change takes place through events which, for all their realism, are the equivalent of the legendary and picaresque circumstances of the Bible and *Hamlet*. In all three examples, the process underlying the character's change is the same, although the nature of the action accompanying it is different in each instance and explanations vary from angelic intervention to terror and remorse. In all three an identical anxiety is present. In the terse account of Jacob's transformation he is described as "greatly afraid and distressed," Hamlet recalls that ". . . in my heart there was a kind of fighting, / That would not let me sleep," while Zossima feels "something vile and shameful."

> The so-called psychic states preceding conversion seem all to have this in common, that they dissolve the economy of the individual, and excite the soul, but cannot satisfy it or allay its disturbance. They are psychic states which propound questions, but do not answer them; they initiate, but do not complete. They provoke a suspension of the soul in which they are being experienced.—*Religious Conversion*, Sante de Sanctos.

III

Individuals are conceived as identities in systems whose subject matter is action and the judgment of actions. In this realm the multiple incidents in the life of an individual may be synthesized, by the choice of the individual himself or by the decision of others, into a scheme that pivots on a single fact central to the individual's existence and which, controlling his behavior and deciding his fate, becomes his visible definition. Here unity of the "plot" becomes one with unity of being and through the fixity of identity change becomes synonymous with revolution.

Of this dramatic integration religious conversion, of all human conditions, supplies the most complete example, although only an example. Through conversion the individual gains an identity which revolves upon a fact that is subjective in its unifying effect upon him yet extra-personal in its relation to his world. In all converts, regardless of what they are converted to, there comes into being that surface coherence which is the sign of the dramatic character. To other individuals unity of action may be *attributed;* [12] the convert claims his oneness to be himself and compels his life to conform to his interpretation.

It is recognition of the individual as an identity that establishes the fundamental connection between religious and dramatic thought. In both, the actor does not obey his own will but the rules of the situation in which he finds himself. In both, change (and escape from the plot) can be accomplished through one means alone, the dissolution of identity and the reappearance of the individual in a "reborn" state. In thus reflecting the limits imposed by action, the "unnatural" processes of religion and drama correspond to those of actual life.

NOTES

1. Raskolnikov, for example, in *Crime and Punishment* sought judgment so that his act would be completed and he could take on a new existence.
2. Instead of the "dramatist's act of judging" we might refer to the "dramatist's act of seeing judgment as involved in and carried out by action." From the naturalistic point of view, there is no judgment impressed upon action, and the presence of judgment in the drama must therefore be attributed to an act of the dramatist; but from the "dramatic viewpoint" there is no action that is not an effect of judgment, whether of the gods, the fates or history, and the judgment is therefore seen as present in the real formula of the action, is said to be discovered by the dramatist, and not to be the result of his act.
3. The moral judgments of drama may, of course, not seem moral at all in the conventional sense; the dramatist may choose to execute a character because he is powerful rather than because he is wicked.
4. ... The cases reported in the Middle Ages, including the epidemic outbreaks of possession, are perhaps the most striking.
5. That the purpose of the law in executing a criminal is to avenge itself upon him or to deter others has long been denied by philosophers of the law. The logic of the execution becomes clear when we understand it as an attempt

to eliminate the criminal identity and thus to cancel the crime itself which that identity personifies. The death of the criminal is incidental to this aim of cleansing the past. Any other means equally certain of accomplishing the dissolution of the criminal identity would be, theoretically, as satisfactory.
6. The legal change is of course a purely formal one.
7. Death in the drama means only cessation of the character's action and the impossibility of his taking it up again. This stoppage may mirror natural death—the character has died or been killed; or, as in the impostor type of comedy, the death may apply to a fictitious identity—the individual continues to be present but through having been exposed as a fraud cannot go on with his old act.
8. Psychological criticism lays Hamlet's failure to act to the preponderance of one trait, usually the reflective one. Interpreting his character in terms of dramatic identity, we relate his incapacity to a structural insufficiency, that is, to his failure to be part of an action-system, a defect for which there is no psychological remedy.

> I do not know
> Why yet I live to say "this thing's to do,"
> Sith I have cause and will and strength and means
> To do 't.

9. "Save yourself, my lord." etc. The scene belongs in all respects to the rôle of Hamlet.
10. "For he was likely, had he been put on, / To have proved most royally."
11. "High and mighty," he writes to Claudius without apparent reason, "You shall know I am set naked in your kingdom."
12. This is rarely done by biographers, who stress the "human" aspects of a character. But contrast Prince Mirsky's biography of Lenin as a man who had almost no personal life.

Language

According to Aristotle, the soul of drama is its plot and the dramatist ought primarily to be a maker of plots. In his essay on "Dramatic Dialogue," however, Allardyce Nicoll argues that "a playwright essentially is, or should be, an artist in words." From this standpoint, the "ancients" necessarily triumph over the "moderns," especially if the principal witness for the cause of the ancients is Shakespeare. From Ibsen, Strindberg, and Chekhov to the present, few dramatic successes have been owing to the kind of verbal eloquence that Kenneth Burke finds essential to great drama (see his "Psychology and Form" above). There have been exceptions, of course—Yeats, Synge, O'Casey, Eliot, others—but the prevailing realistic mode has inevitably moved dramatic speech toward the lower edge of art, beyond which is the abyss of "real" speech in all its disordered and inarticulate barrenness. Even some nonrealistic modes like "absurdist drama" (see Martin Esslin's essay in the section on "genres") specialize in linguistic skepticism, dealing not in heightened language but in anti-language. Samuel Beckett, Harold Pinter, Eugene Ionesco, and Edward Albee repeatedly set up occasions that call for eloquence and then deliberately refuse to answer the call (as in the mute gesticulations of the "Orator" at the end of Ionesco's The Chairs) or produce mock-heroic parodies of eloquence (as in Lucky's pseudo-oration in Beckett's *Waiting for Godot*). Some critics, concerned about the fate of tragedy in the modern world, have wondered whether the depth, complexity, and grandeur of the tragic experience are any longer possible when characters are obliged to negotiate with the devalued linguistic currency of the Cabots in *Desire under the Elms* or Willie Loman in *Death of a Salesman*.

Dramatic language, however, is not merely a matter of eloquence. Eloquence in isolation from the developing dramatic context is only rhetoric, part of what Kenneth Burke calls the "psychology of information" rather than of "form." Language alone is not implicitly kinetic, nor is character; thus Moody Prior reminds us that action, which is kinetic, which necessarily implies consequences, is the governing principle determining what is said and who says it. That should also remind us of the point made in the headnote to "Character" about dramatic speeches functioning as "actions" from which certain inferences may be made. From this perspective, we can see why some of the most impressive dramatic occasions result not from the richness and expressive power of language but from the self-disclosing capacity of words-as-acts. Lear's "Pray you, undo this button" or Ferdinand's "Cover her face; mine eyes dazzle; she died young" (in Webster's *The Duchess of Malfi*) are not verbally impressive in the way Hamlet's soliloquies or Othello's major speeches are, yet with the accumulated dramatic weight of their plays bearing upon them they become profoundly revelatory of characters in crisis. This point, however, should be qualified by the observation that plays that have risen to verbal heights and have demonstrated a capacity to sustain eloquence throughout can capitalize on non-eloquence at key moments for effects that are unavailable to plays that have never risen above non-eloquence.

ALLARDYCE NICOLL

Dramatic Dialogue

Action is to drama what his body is to man; in its language resides the drama's soul. A playwright essentially is, or should be, an artist in words.

Despite this self-evident truth, comparatively little critical attention has been paid to dramatic dialogue, chiefly no doubt because the analysis of verbal forms presents far greater difficulties than the discussion of structural matters. Certainly the majority of theoretical writings on the nature of drama have tended to concentrate upon plot and character, catharsis and hamartia, concept and "meaning," leaving largely neglected examination of the dialogue by means of which these are expressed.

In approaching a consideration of this subject it is essential to bear in mind, first, that traditionally in the past the playwrights never dreamed of using anything save verse measures for their tragic characters, second, that, even when comedy turned from verse to prose, the form of prose it employed was definitely patterned and conventional, and, third, that thus both the tragic verse and the comic prose were entirely distinct from that simulation of common, everyday speech which later became the ideal of the realistic endeavour. The practice of the past, then, was completely distinct from the usual practice of the present.

This statement, in itself obvious, requires, however, some qualification. By the beginning of the twentieth century, it looked as though the earlier tradition had been completely and irrevocably overthrown; only a few lonely heretics, excommunicated by the theatres, dared to ask whether the drama, in abandoning the old, might not have impoverished itself. Then, during the thirties of our era something fresh

From *The Theatre and Dramatic Theory* by Allardyce Nicoll. Reprinted by permission of George G. Harrap & Co. Ltd., and Barnes and Noble.

began to stir; the tentative questions turned into asseverations; instead of almost apologetic whispers, we started to hear boldly voiced pronouncements. The past few decades have thus been marked by the appearance of numerous pleas for the reestablishment of "poetry" on the stage—and peculiarly impressive is the fact that these pleas have come not only, or even chiefly, from the poets, who might be thought to have a vested interest in the matter, or from the academic critics, whose opinions might be deemed influenced by their affection for bygone tradition, but also from within the professional theatre itself. We might have been prepared, perhaps, to pay but little attention to the pleas had they come only from a Lascelles Abercrombie, a Gordon Bottomley, even a W. B. Yeats or a T. S. Eliot, but we are bound to stop and ponder when we hear a Somerset Maugham saying

> I cannot but state my belief that the prose drama to which I have given so much of my life will soon be dead.[1]

Still longer are we compelled to stop and ponder when we hear the same sentiment voiced by actors [2] and scene-designers. "The theatre we knew, the theatre we grew up in," declares one of the most distinguished scenic artists of our time,[3]

> is dwindling and shrinking away, and presently it will be forgotten. It is essentially a prose theatre and of late has become increasingly a theatre of journalism.

ORDINARY SPEECH

Although these pleas are nearly always expressed in terms of "prose" and "poetry," basically the contrast in the minds of those who utter them is that between dramatic dialogue which reproduces more or less faithfully the speech of ordinary life, and dramatic dialogue which makes use of a definitely conventional form of language. For this reason, instead of talking rather indefinitely of "poetry" and "prose," it will be well here to think and talk of "patterned language" and "ordinary speech." Only by so doing is it likely that we shall be able to explore this theme adequately or to reach any valid conclusions. Use of the word "poetry" in connexion with drama is apt to bring to mind either Shakespeare or Stephen Phillips; use of the word "prose" is apt to obscure the fact that much of comic dialogue in the past (and some, indeed, in the present) is almost as far removed as "poetry" is from current speech forms.

There is, of course, no doubt that a play set in familiar, contemporary surroundings and presenting characters who are made to behave in lifelike manner must properly make these characters speak in equally lifelike manner. The one thing which is anathema for plays of this sort is anything which savours of the "literary" or "artificial." Where this simulation of ordinary speech is concerned with situations which are commonplace and unemotional, it provides a perfectly satisfactory, if often unexciting, medium. The world of the drama, however, is, or should be, the world of emotions, and every one knows that our common speech has no power to express our passions intimately. In ordinary life passion tends to make us tongue-tied or incoherent; the trite phrases, "stunned with grief," "spluttering with anger," and the like, testify to a universal recognition of this fact.

Because of this, when the realistic playwright, as inevitably at times he must, introduces scenes of emotional content, he finds himself confronted by a serious problem. He is, in fact, forced to adopt one among a limited number of inadequate procedures.

He may, if he is determined to remain absolutely faithful to the naturalistic principle, make his characters maintain precisely the tongue-tied silence they would display were they living persons. "Some of the post-Chekhovian style used in plays of to-day," remarks Ivor Brown,[4]

> is so scrupulously faithful to the suppressions and mutterings of ordinary conversation that it strains the ears of the audience and misses its heart.

The actors are "made mum."

This method, however, is obviously unsatisfactory for performers and spectators alike, and consequently other dramatists have deliberately sought to concentrate upon the depiction of persons whose unsettled mental conditions might warrant a greater loquacity. Without doubt this explains why we have lately had such a run of plays concentrating on hysterical and mentally disturbed characters, and why so often other modern dramatists present their main persons, at climactic moments, in a state of intoxication. A woman who suffers from some delusion or obsession is likely in real life to express herself more volubly than one who is sane; and a man who is a drug-addict or mentally biased may similarly gabble more than one who is better balanced. Such characters certainly offer to actors and auditors more than those who remain mum; but the stage cannot always be peopled by hysterics and mental cases and drunks.

Faced by this problem, numerous modern playwrights take a third path. They have their emotional scenes and they endeavour by a slight heightening to make them expressive. In attempting such a task, however, they find that they can do little else save rely on broken sentences and ejaculatory phrases, and the resultant sense of inadequacy becomes amply apparent when we note how the texts of these scenes are commonly bespattered with as many exclamation marks and underlinings as might disfigure a schoolgirl's letter.

To demonstrate this we need only glance at the climax scenes in almost any modern realistic play. When, for example, Lavinia confronts Orin in O'Neill's *Mourning Becomes Electra*, hardly a single sentence lacks its concluding mark of exclamation; hardly one is truly expressive. We move from

> LAVINIA (*furiously*): Stop talking about her! You'd think, to hear you, I had no life of my own!
> ORIN: You wanted Wilkins just as you'd wanted Brant!
> LAVINIA: That's a lie!
> ORIN: You're doing the lying! . . .

down to

> LAVINIA (*chokingly*): Stop it! I—I warn you—I won't bear it much longer! . . .

and

> LAVINIA: No!
> ORIN: Don't lie!

It is all rather pathetic. The whole of this scene struggles vainly on in a plethora of meaningless words; "garrulousness," as Lee Simonson has noted, rules in this realistic realm, whenever it tries to express more than statements intellectually conceived.[5] Exactly similar in essence is a climax scene in Tennessee Williams' *A Streetcar Named Desire*:

> That's how I'll clear the table! [*He seizes her arm*] Don't ever

talk that way to me! "Pig—Polack—disgusting—vulgar—greasy!"
—them kind of words have been on your tongue and your sis-
ter's too much around here! What do you two think you are?
A pair of queens? Remember what Huey Long said—"Every
Man is a King!" And I am the king around here, so don't forget it! [*He hurls a cup and saucer to the floor*] My place is
cleared!

Exactly similar, too, another scene from Arthur Miller's *Death of a
Salesman*:

I got so mad I could've torn the walls down! How the hell did
I ever get the idea I was a salesman there? I even believed
myself that I'd been a salesman for him! And then he gave me
one look, and—I realized what a ridiculous lie my whole life
has been!

Where the speeches dramatically should be expressive, should soar
high or plumb the depths, they shamble awkwardly along. And the
reproduction of ordinary speech, for serious purposes apart from the
communication of factual concepts, must in general inevitably shamble.

One is compelled to say "in general" because two authors, Ibsen
and Chekhov, did succeed in overcoming the obstacles. This they
managed to do by the adoption of a couple of special devices. The
first of these was the association of emotions with some selected objects charged with almost symbolic significance—Ibsen's wild duck
and church-steeple, Chekhov's seagull and cherry-orchard. By this
means emotions for which the realistic dialogue could give but slight
expression were evoked in the spectator's imagination. The cherry-
orchard is omnipresent; it becomes the spirit which is central to the
play, and its image in our minds enriches and deepens the words actually spoken. The second device is that employed by Chekhov, wherein
two characters conversing together pursue their own lines of thought
or feeling; through this a kind of counterpoint effect results, and once
again the auditors' imagination is stimulated into experiencing more
than the actual words directly convey.

While observing the force of these two devices, however, we must
admit that they strain the realistic method so far that it is carried almost into another sphere. "The paradox of Ibsen's naturalistic tragedy,"
it has been said, "is that it depends so much on the non-naturalistic

elements for its success"; [6] Chekhov's style has often been called "poetic"—and rightly so, because of its conventional utilization of material selected from life. Still further, neither Ibsen nor Chekhov can profitably be imitated. Both have carried their characteristic styles so far that they cannot serve as effective models; imitation is bound to mean only uninspired copying.

PATTERNED LANGUAGE

If the dramatist should be an artist in words, if the drama itself should deal mainly with emotional material, and if its limitations demand that playwrights should have the most perfect of instruments available for their use, then certainly the employment of our common familiar speech, even when carefully selected and manipulated, is not sufficient for dramatic dialogue. It is, of course, the realization of this that has led to the recent pleas for "poetry."

But vague pleas for "poetry," and especially pleas for what more than one writer has called the "ornament of verse," will not take us far. To assume that "poetry" is merely something pretty which can be added or left out misconceives entirely the foundation upon which the older dramatic tradition was firmly based. That tradition, so long as it remained vital, depended upon a central approach to drama which made patterned language the only possible medium for its expression. The design of the plays as a whole and the design of the dialogue were in harmony, and both were calculated to permit the presentation of an inner and emotional reality instead of a merely surface reality. Where the present-day realism continually keeps the characters associated with and bound to things—the tables and chairs, the teacups and saucers, the bottles and glasses of familiar surroundings, the Greek and Elizabethan characters inhabit a world in which material things are reduced to a minimum. The convention—and the drama must always depend upon conventions—was focused upon a human reality independent of time and place.

In so far as the dialogue was concerned, these dramas of the older tradition adopted and moulded to their needs a second kind of language the potency of which from time immemorial man had recognized—the language employed in primitive times for magical and incantatory purposes and later exercised for the communication of emotional experiences. Its peculiar quality resided in its dependence upon carefully determined form. In familiar everyday speech all that matters is the intellectual content; a particular thought may be phrased in any one of half a dozen ways; so long as the idea has been made reasonably clear no more is asked for. In the other kind of language, the pattern of the words, apart from their meaning, possessses a force of its own. Therefore the magical formula and the verses penned by a poet are fashioned in exact shapes which cannot be altered without destroying the whole. The pattern, in other words, becomes necessarily an integral and significant part of the formula.[7]

Needless to say, not any kind of formula will do, and that is one reason why vague demands for "poetry" may be dangerous. In particular, four things are demanded of the patterned language to be used for dramatic scenes—suitability for the actor's speech and the auditor's comprehension, consonance with the familiar current style of familiar speech, variety, and dynamic quality. A non-dramatic poet may pen stanzas difficult to recite and to understand; for a playwright such a formula would be fatal. Shakespeare's blank verse, in perfect accord with the everyday language of his time, lost its force when that every day language changed. A non-dramatic poet may win success in measures which, although modulated, have no bold variations within them, but measures of this kind would be tedious for an audience; and similarly he may felicitously produce a purely static effect, whereas the theatre constantly demands movement. This final requirement involves much more than the obvious necessity in dramatic dialogue for an adjustment and correspondence between the actor's words and gestures; it means that the language itself must contain within it a sense of dynamic action. In *Macbeth*, for example, the hero stands motionless on the stage after he has heard the news of his wife's death, yet the words given to him conjure up in the mind a motion unseen. The to-morrows "creep" in their "petty pace"; the fools follow a link-boy on their "way to dusty death"; life's shadow is "walking"; the poor player "struts and frets his hour upon the stage."

In these, and indeed in other, ways the formula, if it is to possess vitality, must be modified to suit the drama's needs. Yet basically it depends upon a triad of conventional devices common to all patterned speech, from the primitive magical incantation down to the poetry of to-day—definite rhythmical movement, concord of sounds, and associative imagery. As a general rule, those who plead for patterned language in drama stress two values in the use of these devices. They point out, rightly, that by using such means language can communicate emotional experience to the listeners; and they point out, too, that the sheer beauty thus created has a decided appeal in the theatre. Somerset Maugham, for example, speaks of the "specific dramatic value" of this style—a value which, he adds, "anyone can see by observing in himself the thrilling effect of a tirade in one of Racine's plays or of any one of Shakespeare's great set pieces"—a value "independent of the sense . . . due to the emotional power of rhythmical speech." 8

Without doubt, these values are centrally important, but other values, since they are commonly neglected, deserve to be stressed. Let us take the concord of sounds. In its simplest form, this device, one of the three bases of patterned speech, offers the dramatist a means of securing, without effort, effective emphasis, of fixing and riveting the auditors' attention:

> *F*air is *f*oul, and *f*oul is *f*air . . .
> *B*ring with thee airs from *h*eaven, or *b*last from *h*ell . . .
> These are but *w*ild and *wh*irling *w*ords, my lord—

the phrases, through the very boldness of their sound, startle the mind and fix themselves in the memory.

The importance of not discussing this question in terms of "poetry" and "prose" becomes evident when we note that in comedy's almost equally conventional speech the same effects are frequent:

> God hel*p* the noble *C*laudio! if he have *c*aught the Benedi*ck*, it will *c*ost him a thousand *p*ound ere a' be *c*ured.

And lest it be said that this is simply Shakespeare at work, we may listen to Congreve's Millamant:

> Vanity! No—I'll *f*ly and be *f*ollowed to the last *m*oment. Though I am upon the *v*ery *v*erge of *m*atrimony, I expect you *sh*ould *s*olicit me as *m*uch as if I were wa*v*ering at the grate of a *m*onastery, with one *f*oot o*v*er the thre*sh*old. I'll be *s*olicited to the *v*ery la*s*t—nay, and a*f*terwards.

Simple emphasis upon sound, however, indicates merely one value of this device. Even more significant is the way in which at times the dramatist has deliberately made sounds do the work of contrasting characters. In *Coriolanus,* for example, Shakespeare is confronted by a problem in the persons of Brutus and Sicinius. They are associated together in their functions; they both have to say fundamentally the same thing; there is no call to give them individual personalities—indeed, had that been done it might have broken the fabric of the drama. At the same time, if they are not distinguished from each other, they must certainly prove a dead drag on the scenes in which they appear. What Shakespeare does is to distinguish them by sound. In his first speech of seventeen lines Brutus splutters out words emphasizing both explosive *b* and *p* and harsh *k* and *ch:* "*b*leared . . . *p*rattling . . . ra*p*ture . . . *b*aby . . . *p*ins . . . '*b*out . . . *b*ulks . . . *p*ress . . . *p*opular . . . *p*uff . . . s*p*oil . . . *b*urning . . . *p*other . . . *p*osture . . . s*p*eak . . . s*p*e*c*ta*c*led . . . *c*ry . . . *ch*ats . . . *k*it*ch*en . . . mal*k*in . . . ri*ch*est . . . lo*ck*ram . . . ree*ch*y . . . ne*ck* . . . clam*b*'ring . . . *b*ulks . . . *c*ommit . . . dama*sk* . . . gawded *ch*ee*k*s . . . *k*isses . . . *c*re*p*t." That this is not merely coincidental becomes evident when, twenty-two lines later, the same concatenation of sounds once more is made to dominate: "*p*eople . . . *p*ower . . . *p*leaders . . . dis*p*ro*p*ertied . . . a*c*tion . . . *c*a*p*a*c*ity . . . *c*amels . . . *p*rovand . . . *b*earing *b*urdens . . . *b*lows." In contrast, Sicinius' words are given a constant hissing note; his first speech conveys a sound value quite distinct from that of Brutus':

> Thi*s*, a*s* you *s*ay, *s*ugge*s*ted
> At *s*ome time when hi*s s*oaring in*s*olen*c*e
> Shall touch the people—which time *s*hall not want,
> If he be put upon't; and that'*s* a*s* ea*s*y
> A*s* to *s*et dog*s* on *s*heep—will be hi*s* fire
> To kindle their dry *s*tubble.

Not by what they say, but by how they say it have they been granted their individual personalities.

Exactly the same effect has been secured by Goldsmith in the opening scene of *She Stoops to Conquer*. Mr and Mrs Hardcastle are revealed to us when the curtain rises. Naturally, we know nothing about them, but, since they are to be the principal opposed characters against which the love story and its adventures are set, the author has to use every means in his power to make us aware of the differences between them. Their sentiments, of course, are in contrast, but the contrast has been underlined and enriched by the very sound of their words. Mrs Hardcastle's speech is marked by hard stops and dentals, from her initial query,

> Is there a *creature* in the whole *c*ountry *b*ut ourselves that
> does *n*ot *t*ake a *t*rip *to* *to*wn now and then *to* *r*ub off the *r*ust
> a li*ttl*e,

down to her

> And all our en*t*er*t*ainmen*t*, your old *st*ories of Prince Eugene
> and the Du*k*e of Ma*rl*borough. I ha*t*e such old-fashioned *t*rum-
> pery.

Hardcastle's utterance, on the contrary, abounds in soft labials, from his
first sentence,

> Ay, and bring back *v*anity and a*ff*ectation to *l*ast them the
> who*l*e year,

down to his final speech,

> And I *l*ove it. I *l*ove e*v*erything that's o*l*d: o*l*d *f*riends, o*l*d
> times, o*l*d manners, o*l*d books, o*l*d wine; and I be*l*ie*v*e,
> Dorothy, you'*ll* own I ha*v*e been pretty *f*ond of an o*l*d wi*f*e.

A variant of this appears in the first scene of *The School for Scandal*,
although here Sheridan has been faced by a slightly different problem.
First, he has to establish the sibilant hissing of scandal in general, and,
secondly, he has to differentiate the two scandal-mongers. Like Goldsmith, he achieves much of his initial effect by an adroit use of sound;
the stress on *s* and *k* are made common to both Mrs Sneerwell and
Snake, but in the speech of the one the hiss is the predominant note, in
that of the other the hard stops are characteristic, while, in addition, the
latter is given an undertone of *f* largely absent in the former. Her opening sentence,

> The paragraph*s*, you *s*ay, Mr *S*nake, were all in*s*erted?

thus contrasts with his

> They were, madam; and as I *c*opied them myself in a *f*eigned
> hand, there *c*an be no suspicion whence they *c*ame.

Snake concentrates upon "the *c*ommon *c*ourse of things," "the *c*ause of six matches being bro*k*en o*ff*," and "*c*lose *c*on*f*inements," Lady Sneerwell upon "She *c*ertainly ha*s* talent*s*, but her manner *is* gro*ss*."

In all conventionally planned dialogue effects of this kind may be harmoniously introduced. Although Synge was inspired by actual peasant speech, the dialogue in his plays is almost as highly patterned as that in any poetic drama, and so it is entirely proper that, in *Riders to the Sea*, we should listen to the music of

> There's a great roaring in the *w*est, and it's *w*orse it'll be getting *w*hen the tide's turned to the *w*ind,

or

> Let you *g*o down now to the spring *w*ell and give him this and he passing. You'll see him then and the dar*k* *w*ord *w*ill be bro*k*en, and you *c*an say "God speed you," the *w*ay he'll be easy in his mind.

So, too, in the final part of *Back to Methuselah*, wherein Shaw deserts the argumentation and the familiar environment of the middle sections, Lilith's great peroration may appropriately take shape in a series of distinct movements—movements which Shaw himself said were composed under the inspiration of music and which make their advance with ever-modulated resonance:

> They have a*c*cepted the *b*urden of eternal life. They have ta*k*en the agony from *b*irth; and their life does not fail them even in the hour of their destruction. Their *b*reasts are without mil*k*; their *b*owels are *g*one; the very shapes of them are only ornaments for their children to admire and *c*aress without understanding.
>
> .   .   .
>
> I*s* thi*s* enough: or *s*ha*ll* I *l*abour again? Sha*ll* I bring *f*orth something that wi*ll* *s*weep them away and make an end of them a*s* they have *s*wept away the bea*st*s of the garden, and made an end of the crawling thing*s* and the *f*lying thing*s* and o*f* a*ll* them that re*f*use to *l*ive for e*v*er?
>
> .   .   .

> I had patience with them for many ages: they tried me very sorely. They did terrible things: they embraced death, and said that eternal life was a fable. I stood amazed at the malice and destructiveness of the things I had made.
>
> .   .   .
>
> Mars blushed as he looked down on the shame of his sister planet.

We follow the interweaving of changing sound in these and in successive paragraphs—the sudden stress in "The pangs of another birth were already upon me when one man repented," the movement to "I gave the woman the greatest of gifts," to "Lilith will be only a legend and a lay that has lost its meaning," and to the final sentence,

> and though of its million starry mansions many are empty and many still unbuilt, and though its vast domain is as yet unbearably desert, my seed shall one day fill it and master its matter to its uttermost confines.

Needless to say, passages of this kind can effectively be introduced only when they are in unison with their context. Ordinary speech rarely employs alliterative patterns except perhaps as a joke, and accordingly these patterns are in general avoided in realistic plays. Occasionally, however, the writer of such a play, desperately trying to secure an emotional effect, feels that he must intensify his lines—and the result is nearly always fatal. Thus, for example, in Clifford Odets' *Golden Boy* we find:

> What will my father say when he hears I murdered a man? Lorna, I see what I did. I murdered myself, too! I've been running around in circles. Now I'm smashed! That's the truth. Yes, I was a real sparrow, and I wanted to be a fake eagle! But now I'm hung up by my fingertips—I'm no good—my feet are off the earth!

Here, instead of listening to music we seem to be confronted only by a blatancy akin to that of an alliterative newspaper headline.

These examples will, perhaps, be sufficient to demonstrate that what we may call conventional dialogue—which includes both poetry for serious drama and patterned prose for comedy—offers opportunities to a dramatist which he absolutely needs, but of which he is deprived if he chooses to fetter himself by the mistaken notion of verisimilitude. And the diverse ways in which sound can be made to play its potent rôle form only one of the opportunities. The freedom offered by patterned language for the introduction of imagery inappropriate to the simulation of ordinary speech is equally significant.

Numerous studies published during the past twenty or thirty years have demonstrated to the full what powerful force the images exert in Shakespeare's dramas. No doubt the exact significance of these images becomes intellectually apparent only when the plays are examined meticulously in the study, but without a doubt they impinge upon the auditors' emotions and assist in creating the total effect of tragedy and comedy. And they do so in two ways. The over-all imaginative pattern comes first—the concentration upon light and darkness in *Romeo and Juliet,* upon disease in *Hamlet,* upon reverberating echoes in *Macbeth.* In addition to this, however, Shakespeare in his maturer plays was able to make use of imagery, much as he had made use of verbal melodies, for the purpose of intensifying and contrasting his characters. In *Othello,* for example, Iago's speech is characterized by his use of simile, that of Othello by his use of metaphor; Iago's images tend to be concrete and commonplace, Othello's vast and spacious; both refer repeatedly to the sea, but Othello's allusions suggest infinity and mystery, while Iago's descend to caracks and tackle.[9] It is perfectly true to say that

> as Shakespeare grows in poetic power, he employs his images, not only for ornament, but for far higher purposes; his metaphors, transmuted in his imagination, interpret and in a sense create the life he depicts.[10]

Comedy's conventional language admits of a kindred employment of imagic material, although with a very marked difference. In the serious drama metaphor rules: the object spoken of and the object with which it is compared become so fused in the mind that the distinction between them vanishes. In comedy, on the other hand, the simile proves more characteristic and apt: in spite of the comparison the two objects are held distinct in the mind and the differences between them, as well as the likenesses, are stressed directly or by implication. Two examples, one from Shakespeare and one from Congreve, may be used to illustrate the distinction. First, there is the famous description of Cleopatra:

> The barge she sat in, like a burnished throne,
> Burn'd on the water: the poop was beaten gold;
> Purple the sails, and so perfumed that
> The winds were love-sick with them; the oars were silver,
> Which to the tune of flutes kept stroke and made
> The water which they beat to follow faster,
> As amorous of their strokes.

The rich, subtle, palpitating rhythm obviously aims at identifying Cleopatra with the barge; the two become one in our imagination. From this we turn to Congreve:

> Here she comes, i'faith, full sail, with her fan spread and streamers out, and a shoal of fools for tenders.

The whole comic effect here rests in holding Millamant distinct from the ship to which she is compared and in mentally contrasting, not identifying, the one with the other. The first is emotionally imaginative, the effect secured by an association only indirectly implied; the second is intellectual, the effect secured by direct reference and emphasis. "The ship rides the waves" might be a phrase, if somewhat trite, incorporated in a poetic framework; but "He bumped up and down on his horse as if he were a freighter on a heavy sea" could be appropriate only to a comic atmosphere. When we hear Hamlet speaking of

> Exposing what is mortal and unsure
> To all that fortune, death and danger dare,
> Even for an egg-shell,

no picture of an actual egg is in our minds; but a line in *As You Like It*—

> Truly, thou are damned, like an ill-roasted egg all on one side—

has been so phrased as to cause us to hold two things at once distinct in our consciousness. So in comedy we have, from *The Way of the World*:

> He has brought me a letter from the fool my brother, as heavy

as a panegyric in a funeral sermon, or a copy of commenda-
tory verses from one poet to another—

or from *The Full Moon:*

I am feeling as if the five fingers of my hand to be lessening
from me, the same as five farthing dips the heat of the sun
would be sweating the tallow from—

or from *Patience:*

Do you know what it is to be heart-hungry? Do you know
what it is to yearn for the Indefinable, and yet to be brought
face to face, daily, with the Multiplication Table? Do you
know what it is to seek oceans and find puddles?—to long for
whirlwinds and yet have to do the best you can with the
bellows?

In modern plays wherein the comic spirit has dominated over the
realistic endeavour, similes of a kindred sort certainly appear, even
although often they may clash with other elements conditioned by the
desire to achieve a measure of a verisimilitude; but in serious dramas
written in the modern manner imagery becomes in general impossible.
Once more we find the playwrights inhibited and thwarted, denied
the opportunity of utilizing all the tools which ought to be at their
command.

VARIATIONS ON FORM

One further matter of intrinsic significance requires attention, and it
may best be dealt with by reference to Shakespeare's work. There is,
of course, no question of suggesting here that the Elizabethan forms
are suitable for or can be utilized in the present age; but possibly a
consideration in broad outline of the medium through which Shakespeare found dramatic expression may provide us with a few principles
to serve as standards, and at the very least we may derive from the
inquiry a mental picture of a great dramatist working under ideal conditions.[11]

When Shakespeare came to maturity as a playwright he found that
he had four chief instruments available for his dialogue, all inherited

in basic form from his immediate predecessors and all enriched by his own earlier efforts.

1. Blank verse, with its staple norm, the line of five "rising" feet, was basic, capable of variation in a thousand different ways, of which the chief were modifications in the foot measures, expansion or contraction of the usual ten syllables and the multiform diversity possible in the linking of line to line.

2. Secondly, Shakespeare had the possibility of using prose of different kinds, such as the comic prose of the clowns and the familiar speech of gallants in easy conversational moments—both subtly modified so as to harmonize with the general pattern.

3. Thirdly, he had available several sorts of rimed ten-syllable lines. Of these, the commonest were the simple couplets; next to them came the quatrains; next to them longer stanza units, of which the sonnet was chief.

4. And finally Shakespeare could on occasion employ shorter rimed lines, generally eight- or six-syllabled, and generally, too, in couplets or quatrains.

Between most of these, particularly in longer passages, the contrast, even when we hear the words spoken rapidly in the modern theatre, is patent. We thus will readily recognize the difference in measure between:

1. Now, fair Hippolyta, our nuptial hour
Draws on apace: four happy days bring in
Another moon; but O, methinks how slow
This old moon wanes! She lingers my desires,
Like to a step-dame or a dowager,
Long withering out a young man's revenue. . . .

2. Is all our company here? You were best to call them generally, man by man, according to the scrip. Here is the scroll of every man's name which is thought fit, through all Athens, to play in our interlude before the Duke and the Duchess on his wedding-day at night. . . .

3. Helen, to you our minds we will unfold;
To-morrow night, when Phoebe doth behold
Her silver visage in the wat'ry glass,

Decking with liquid pearl the bladed grass,
A time that lovers' flights doth still conceal,
Through Athens' gates have we devis'd to steal. . . .

and

4. Over hill, over dale,
     Thorough bush, thorough briar,
Over park, over pale,
     Thorough flood, thorough fire,
I do wander everywhere,
     Swifter than the moon's sphere;
And I serve the Fairy Queen
     To dew her orbs upon the green.

Even although Shakespeare's measures, born of the Elizabethan age, are far removed from us, we all recognize the differences here; but it cannot be too heavily stressed that the ears of Shakespeare's contemporaries were far more keenly attuned than modern ears to detect variations much subtler than these. These measures, for them, were the measures of their own age; the auditors were trained in an atmosphere of formalism and convention; the printed page, particularly in the shape of the daily newspaper, had not dulled their power of alert listening—all these combined to make their aural senses acute. We must even believe that Elizabethan audiences were able in a moment's flash to detect the pattern of blank verse: a single line was sufficient for them. In *As You Like It* Orlando enters and addresses the disguised Rosalind:

Good day, and happiness, dear Rosalind.

We certainly could not hope, in that passing moment, to identify these words as a line of verse, but Jacques' comment shows at once that the Elizabethans did:

Nay then, God buy you, an you talk in blank verse.

The point of the joke rests in Shakespeare's assumption that his audience will be as quick as Jacques to catch the measure.

The two facts, (1) that his blank verse provided a standard, and

(2) that it was immediately recognized for what it was, meant that Shakespeare could play with effects which, even if they still contribute much to our appreciation of the tragedies and comedies, have now less power than they had in his own time. At the first performance of *Macbeth*, for instance, the spectators saw three strangely clad, enigmatic figures appear before them, and heard those creatures uttering their lines:

> When shall we three meet again,
> In thunder, lightning or in rain?

Immediately the octosyllabic lines, in place of the normally-to-be-expected blank verse, must have suggested the supernatural, while the prevailingly trochaic or falling movement—

> Fair is foul, and foul is fair—

must have given the impression of inversion and, imaginatively, of the presence of evil. By the very rhythm, therefore, Shakespeare was enabled to make on his audience the initial impact he desired.

A similar effect is secured in the opening lines of *Hamlet*. In the first seven short utterances of that play there are three regular blank-verse lines:

> Nay, answer me: stand and unfold yourself. . . .
> You come most carefully upon your hour. . . .
> 'Tis now struck twelve; get thee to bed, Francisco.

This is the established norm; but the first speech-line is the brief, emphatic "Who's there?", and that is accompanied by three other broken lines, "Long live the King!", "Bernado?", and "He." To listeners keen and able to detect and evaluate variations in the medium, therefore, the impression created in rhythmic sound would have been precisely what the dramatist aimed at—a blank-verse world broken and disturbed by tension and nervous anxiety.

The passages from *Macbeth* and *Hamlet* illustrate the association of the verse forms with the content of a scene. In addition, the forms often are employed to secure contrast. In *Romeo and Juliet*, for example, we have the balcony scene, with its rich lyrical blank-verse ecstasy:

'Tis almost morning. I would have thee gone;
And yet no further than a wanton's bird,
That lets it hop a little from her hand,
Like a poor prisoner in his twisted gyves,
And with a silk thread plucks it back again,
So loving-jealous of his liberty.

The following scene introduces Friar Lawrence, and with him clearly the author requires to set a different mood. Comic prose might have been employed to provide a sharp distinction, but here nothing of the kind can be allowed: the atmosphere must be poetic, serious, and dignified. The effect he desires Shakespeare gains by boldly resorting to rimed couplets and by substituting for the light rhythms of the balcony-scene a heavy spondaic measure:

The gray-ey'd morn smiles on the frowning night,
Check'ring the eastern clouds with streaks of light,
And fleckel'd darkness like a drunkard reels
From forth day's path and Titan's fiery wheels.

Laboriously the phrases bear down upon us—"gray-ey'd morn . . . from forth day's path . . . night's dark dew . . . I must up-fill . . . in herbs, plants, stones, . . . naught so vile . . . aught so good . . . with that part cheers each part." Once more, by rhythm's sound alone Shakespeare conveys his emotional atmosphere to the audience.

Elsewhere the contrast may be in terms of character. A good example of this appears in the person of Caliban in *The Tempest*. More than one critic has suggested that the monster's speech beginning "Be not afear'd" shows Shakespeare extra-dramatically indulging in a little bit of lyric poetry put clumsily into an inappropriate mouth. The fact is, however, that, except when he is drunk, Caliban is consistently a blank-verse speaker and thus kept distinct from Trinculo and Stephano. His very first lines set the tone:

This island's mine, by Sycorax my mother,
Which thou tak'st from me. When thou cam'st first,
Thou strok'st and made much of me, wouldst give me
Water with berries in't, and teach me how
To name the bigger light, and how the less,

That burn by day and night; and then I lov'd thee
And show'd thee all the qualities o' th' isle.

The verbal music here may properly contrast with Prospero's polished
utterance; but the lines are verse, and through his use of that verse
Caliban is sharply differentiated from the clowns. He breathes an air
richer than theirs; and consequently it is entirely in keeping with his
whole presentation that the lyrical passage should finally tumble from
his monster lips:

> Be not afear'd. The isle is full of noises,
> Sounds, and sweet airs, that give delight and hurt not.
> Sometimes a thousand twangling instruments
> Will hum about mine ears; and sometimes voices,
> That, if I then had wak'd after long sleep,
> Will make me sleep again; and then, in dreaming,
> The clouds methought would open and show riches
> Ready to drop upon me, that, when I wak'd,
> I cried to dream again.

Even further can this method of contrast go; instead of applying
to the speaker it may apply to the object of his speech. In *Troilus and
Cressida,* the heroine enters with a servant who describes the various
warriors going to battle. His remarks on Hector are cast in blank verse:

> Hector, whose patience
> Is as a virtue fix'd, to-day was mov'd.
> He chid Andromache, and struck his armourer;
> And, like as there were husbandry in war,
> Before the sun rose he was harness'd light,
> And to the field goes he; where every flower
> Did as a prophet weep what it foresaw
> In Hector's wrath.

But when the servant comes to Ajax, his medium changes:

> This man, lady, hath robb'd many beasts of their particular
> additions; he is as valiant as the lion, churlish as the bear, slow
> as the elephant—a man into whom nature hath so crowded

humours that his valour is crush'd into folly, his folly sauc'd
with discretion.

One other aspect of this subject must be referred to. In many
Shakespearian passages we encounter broken lines in the midst of the
blank-verse utterance. To our audiences of to-day these broken lines
do not stand out; they pass us by unperceived; but we may well believe, first, that to the keener ears of the Elizabethans they marked
breaks in the music, second, that consequently they possessed a value
of their own, and, third, that they were deliberately introduced by
Shakespeare with a dramatic end in view.

This can be seen even in the planning of some single speeches.
When, for instance, we look at Hamlet's soliloquy "O what a rogue
and peasant slave am I!", we observe that five broken lines break the
speech into six sections—*For Hecuba!, Yet I, Ha!, O vengeance!,* and
A scullion! Even although not all of these are printed in the Folio
and Quarto texts as broken lines, obviously they are all extra-metrical,
and obviously, too, they are designed to play a significant part in the
flow of Hamlet's speech. If we look upon the soliloquy, not as something to be read in the study, but as something to be spoken by an
actor and heard by an audience, we must acknowledge that these
broken lines and the sections which they mark off from each other
exactly correspond with the changing emotions of the speaker. They
form signals and pointers both for the actor and for the listeners.

The first eight lines, with their sibilant emphasis, from the self-
contemptuous opening down to "And all for nothing!", express Hamlet's
wonder at the passion displayed by the actor:

> O what a rogue and peasant slave am I!
> Is it not monstrous that this player here,
> But in a fiction, in a dream of passion,
> Could force his soul so to his own conceit,
> That from her working all his visage wann'd;
> Tears in his eyes, distraction in's aspect,
> A broken voice, and his whole function suiting
> With forms to his conceit? And all for nothing!

The sudden final melodic drop in "And all for nothing!" prepares the
way for the break "For Hecuba!" As though this were the signal for a

change of thought, and of sound, another eight lines follow, with an insistent hammering stress on "weep . . . tears . . . cleave . . . . . . speech . . . free . . . indeed . . . ears," in which Hamlet imagines what this actor would have done had he had a real and not merely a fictional motive:

> For Hecuba!
> What's Hecuba to him, or he to Hecuba,
> That he should weep for her? What would he do,
> Had he the motive and the cue for passion
> That I have? He would drown the stage with tears
> And cleave the general air with horrid speech,
> Make mad the guilty and appal the free,
> Confound the ignorant and amaze indeed
> The very faculties of eyes and ears.

Once more a signal comes with "Yet I," and nine lines, with a new insistence on the sounds of *b*, *d*, and *p*, are devoted to the searching query as to whether Hamlet is not, in fact, a coward:

> Yet I,
> A dull and muddy-mettled rascal, peak,
> Like John-a-dreams, unpregnant of my cause,
> And can say nothing—no, not for a king,
> Upon whose property and most dear life
> A damn'd defeat was made? Am I a coward?
> Who calls me villain? breaks my pate across?
> Plucks off my beard and blows it in my face?
> Tweaks me by the nose? gives me the lie i' the throat
> As deep as to the lungs? Who does me this?
> Ha!

The exclamation "Ha!" clearly forms for the actor the rising broken close to this section of the speech: to print it as

> Ha, 'swounds, I should take it

destroys completely the effect that is being aimed at. The "Ha!", in its position here, becomes almost a note of defiance, contrasted with the sudden descent to the despairing " 'Swounds," which opens six lines of self-laceration and spluttering anger, ending with the broken "O vengeance!":

> *Ha!*
> 'Swounds, I should take it: for it cannot be
> But I am pigeon-liver'd and lack gall
> To make oppression bitter, or ere this
> I should have fatted all the region kites
> With this slave's offal: bloody, bawdy villain!
> Remorseless, treacherous, lecherous, kindless villain!
> *O vengeance!*

These two words in turn introduce a new movement wherein Hamlet casts scorn on himself for losing in words what should have been done in action:

> *O vengeance!*
> Why, what an ass am I! This is most brave,
> That I, the son of a dear father murder'd,
> Prompted to my revenge by heaven and hell,
> Must, like a whore, unpack my heart with words,
> And fall a-cursing, like a very drab,
> *A scullion!*

And "A scullion!" serves as a cue for the final words of the speech in which Hamlet plans the "Mousetrap" play.[12]

It appears that the broken lines have their proper artistic place in the composition of the soliloquy and that their inclusion was inspired by Shakespeare's awareness of his audience's keen appreciation of the poetic forms of which he was making use.

THE MODERN ENDEAVOUR

This cursory examination of some among the advantages which Shakespeare, and his companions, possessed has value not merely for further stressing the fact that a modern playwright who strives to pen serious dramas in terms of common speech does so with one of his hands tied firmly behind his back, but also, and more importantly, for pointing to the problems to be faced and the principles to be adopted by any dramatist of to-day who seeks to escape from such fetters.

The first problem clearly is to find a form of language which may have such a connexion with our debased common speech as the standard Elizabethan blank verse measure had with the richer, less stereotyped, and more expressive familiar utterance of that time. This problem, onerous in itself, is made the greater by its association with another. Shakespeare was in the advantageous position of being able to adapt for dramatic purposes much that already existed in the non-dramatic verse of his time. He could do so because the greater part of this non-dramatic verse was "public" rather than "private." No doubt there were poets in his time who, despising the vulgar, wrote obscurely for a small circle of like-minded friends, but, in the main, Elizabethan verse addressed itself to wider circles. Some of it was confessedly "easy"—the hundreds of ballads, for example, printed for common consumption and sung in the alehouses and market-squares; and much even of the poetry written by more ambitious authors for cultured readers, although it might be subtly invested with recondite allusions and associative values, had on the surface a direct and easily appreciated significance. We all know, however, that poetry has of late tended more and more towards the "difficult," often replete with private meanings unintelligible save to the initiate, and inclined towards introspection rather than towards "public" utterance. Hence, for the most part, modern non-dramatic verse offers little to the playwright that he can satisfactorily use.

Furthermore, this non-dramatic verse of our age has veered towards formlessness. "Free verse" instead of formal verse has become the characteristic style. Certainly there are poets to-day who put older measures to work, but the general stream of verse written during recent decades has had the effect of destroying the earlier sensitivity on the part of reader or listener to variations on established forms. It goes almost without saying, therefore, that many of the effects easily secured by Shakespeare are to-day impossible to reproduce, or at least reproducible only with the expenditure of severe effort.

Above all, the task which confronted Shakespeare and the task confronting any modern poetic dramatist are utterly at variance. Shakespeare and his early companions were faced with the problem of toning down. The rime royal and other stanzaic measures employed by the dramatists who had preceded them were too formal, too conventional for theatre use; and thus the blank verse, couplets, and occasional quatrains represented the reduction of an "elevated" style to more ordinary levels. In contradistinction, the modern dramatist who essays to write conventionally patterned dialogue starts with virtually nothing, and consequently he has before him the immeasurably harder task of building up. He is somewhat like a man set on a sandy waste, assigned the problem of erecting a firm structure without material or means apt to prepare a solid foundation for his walls.

A fundamental question concerning objectives arises here. In view of the difficulties and of the particular conditions operative in the modern theatre, should the dramatist take a bold course or should he work, as it were, by concealed infiltration? When, in 1935, T. S. Eliot produced his trumpet call, *Murder in the Cathedral,* he left his auditors in no doubt concerning the conventional nature of his dialogue. The opening chorus—

> Here let us stand, close by the cathedral. Here let us wait.
> Are we drawn by a danger? Is it the knowledge of safety, that draws our feet
> Towards the cathedral? What danger can be
> For us, the poor, the poor women of Canterbury? What tribulation
> With which we are not already familiar?

set the tone, and the later choral speech increased the poetic tension—

> There is no rest in the house. There is no rest in the street.
> I hear restless movement of feet. And the air is heavy and thick.
> Thick and heavy the sky. And the earth presses up against our feet.
> What is the sickly smell, the vapour? the dark green light from a cloud on a withered tree? The earth is heaving to parturition of issue of hell. What is the sticky dew that forms on the back of my hand?

Fifteen years later, however, Eliot had changed his views, and in his *Poetry and Drama* firmly he laid down another method for the cultivation of the poetic drama. In brief, he there argued that, instead of boldly exciting the audience to recognize and respond to verse dialogue, every endeavour ought to be made to conceal from the auditors that what they are listening to is verse. "The verse rhythm," he declares, "should have its effect upon the hearers without their being conscious of it," and the use of prose alongside of verse ought to be avoided precisely because its introduction would make the audience aware of the rhythmic quality of the other passages. Thus, he further explained, in *The Cocktail Party*

> I laid down for myself the ascetic rule to avoid poetry which could not stand the test of strict dramatic utility; with such success, indeed, that it is perhaps an open question whether there is any poetry in the play at all.[13]

If, however, there is any virtue in our cursory observations concerning the indebtedness of Shakespeare to his dramatic style and in the analysis of the conventional nature of dramatic art, it must be obvious that such an endeavour as Eliot's deliberately denies what the conventional pattern can most potently offer. When "poetic" drama is made to "enter into overt competition with prose drama," so that the hearers are, as it were, cheated into believing that no verse is present at all, the very foundations of that poetic drama are destroyed. Shakespeare's plays were given strength to endure not merely because Shakespeare was an outstanding poet, but also because the openly acknowledged verse forms which he employed were in close harmony with his dramatic objectives.

The only course likely to lead to a true revival is one concerning the orientation of which no one can be in any doubt. And there is a particular reason for this. The poetic play cannot make a profound impact in our time until the audience is given some basic form, equivalent to what blank verse was for the Elizabethans, which it can recognize and the music of which can be kept in its mind as a measure. In discussing Christopher Fry's work, J. L. Styan has asked:

> What are the advantages of Shakespeare's firmer metrical line?

and he answers:

> Mr Fry's rhythms are comparatively limp because he cannot fall back upon a standard of regularity from which any departure provides a rhythmic meaning to the ear.[14]

This question and answer, although specifically concerned with Fry's work, applies to all the modern attempts at the writing of plays of this kind, and they will continue to apply until some Marlowe of to-day succeeds, by his boldness and intensity, in startling his auditors into immediate acceptance of his measure.

The invention of the measure is unquestionably the most important thing, but with it, too, must come the subtly incisive metaphors and the inner sense of movement which gave strength alike to the Greeks and to the Elizabethans. In our present days, no single dramatic author has succeeded in fusing all the elements into a single integrated form of expression.

This becomes evident when we examine the work of those three men, Maxwell Anderson, T. S. Eliot, and Christopher Fry, who more than any others have won popular success in this sphere. First we listen to a passage from *Wingless Victory:*

> Why was this body gathered out of dust
> and bitten to my image? Let that day be evil
> when a lover took a lover to mould the face
> that stares up blind from my agony! Stares up
> and cries, and will not be still! Let all women born
> take a man's love with laughter, and leave it; take
> the coil of animals they give, and rise
> in mockery. And you dark peoples of the earth,
> cling to your dark, lie down and feed and sleep
> till you are earth again; but if you love,
> love only children of the dark—keep back
> from the bright hair and white hands, for they are light
> and cruel, like the gods', and the love that breeds
> between us is honeyed poison. Let no flesh
> of theirs touch flesh of yours; where they have touched
> the welt rots inward! They are unclean, unclean
> and leprous to us! To lie with them is sweet,
> but sweet with death! I bear that death in me
> in a burning tide that rises—choking—Oh, God—
> torture me no more!

One thing is vital here—the dynamic quality of the verbs. The lines drive forward with stress on "gathered . . . bitten . . . mould . . . leave . . . rise . . . cling . . . keep back . . . touch . . . rots . . . bear . . . rises." But that is all. The metaphors have no driving force; the language is repetitive and woolly. It has been said that "Mr Anderson's facility often betrays him into a willingness to accept emotional clichés as well as verbal ones," that in his work one has "the feeling that one has heard or seen it all before," that there is "the absence of any sense that one's thought or feeling is being anywhere enlarged." [15] And this is true: the speech quoted above has no patterning in sound; it is over-exclamatory; its imagery seems ornamental rather than organic.

The presence of a dynamic quality in Anderson's writing, however, aids in drawing attention to its lack in much of the dialogue penned by T. S. Eliot, an author far more distinguished as a stylist and gifted with a poetic imagination far beyond his. T. S. Eliot is indeed a great poet, but when we turn to, say, Thomas' climactic utterance in *Murder in the Cathedral* we must be forced to decide that his poetic style, because remaining static, has not been given true dramatic quality:

> Now is my way clear, now is the meaning plain:
> Temptation shall not come in this kind again.
> The last temptation is the greatest treason:
> To do the right deed for the wrong reason.
> The natural vigour in the venial sin
> Is the way in which our lives begin.
> Thirty years ago, I searched all the ways
> That lead to pleasure, advancement and praise
> Delight in sense, in learning and in thought,
> Music and philosophy, curiosity,
> The purple bullfinch in the lilac tree,
> The tiltyard skill, the strategy of chess,
> Love in the garden, singing to the instrument,
> Were all things equally desirable.
> Ambition comes when early force is spent
> And when we find no longer all things possible.
> Ambition comes behind and unobservable. . . .

Even those few words in this passage which suggest action have intellectual rather than physical connotations: "come in this kind" does not really imply movement; "the way in which our lives begin" is static, not active; "that lead to pleasure" has no sense of action; "Ambition comes," because of the commonplace quality of the verb, does not bring to the mind a physical, stalking figure. And this motionless quality becomes even more pronounced in the later plays. Sir Claude speaks in *The Confidential Clerk*:

I'm not so sure of that. I've tried to believe in facts;
And I've always acted as if I believed in them.
I thought it was facts that my father believed in;
I thought that what he cared for was power and wealth;
And I came to see that what I had interpreted
In this way, was something else to *him*—
An idea, an inspiration. . . . .

And Celia similarly expresses herself in *The Cocktail Party:*

I know I ought to be able to accept that
If I might still have it. Yet it leaves me cold.
Perhaps that's just a part of my illness,
But I feel it would be a kind of surrender—
No, not a surrender—more like a betrayal.
You see, I think I really had a vision of something
Though I don't know what it is. I don't want to forget it.
I want to live with it. . . .

Christopher Fry exhibits more theatrical vitality, and, particularly in his later verse, an inner movement is frequently suggested by his lines. Thus, for example, Henry's reflections in *Curtmantle* have a dramatic vigour that goes beyond the reflections of Eliot's Becket, Sir Claude, and Celia:

Dear Christ, the day that any man would dread
Is when life goes separate from the man,
When he speaks what he doesn't say, and does
What is not his doing, and an hour of the day
Which was unimportant as it went by
Comes back revealed as the satan of all hours,
Which will never let the man go. And then
He would see how the natural poisons in him
Creep from everything he sees and touches
As though saying, "Here is the world you created
In your own image." But this is not the world
He would have made. Sprung from a fraction of life,
A hair-fine crack in the dam, the unattended
Moment sweeps away the whole attempt,
The heart, thoughts, belief, longing

> And intention of the man. It is infamous,
> This life is infamous, if it uses us
> Against our knowledge or will. . . .

The day "goes separate"; the hour, having passed, "comes back"; the natural poisons "creep from everything he sees and touches"; the moment has "sprung from a fraction of life"; it is a crack in the dam; it "sweeps away the whole attempt." At the same time even Fry sometimes pens dialogue that suggests the passivity of ideas rather than the dynamics of forcible and energetic motion. Jennet in *The Lady's Not for Burning* thus is made to utter her thoughts:

> I am interested
> In my feelings, I seem to wish to have some importance
> In the play of time. If not,
> Then sad was my mother's pain, sad my breath,
> Sad the articulation of my bones,
> Sad, sad my alacritous web of nerves,
> Woefully, woefully sad my wondering brain,
> To be shaped and sharpened into such tendrils
> Of anticipation, only to feed the swamp of space. . . .

Fry has brought much to the drama of our time, and we may well feel that his particular form of patterned language comes closer than any other towards suggesting a measure appropriate for the modern theatre; yet this speech of Jennet demonstrates that even he has not been able to reach a complete solution of the problem.

It is true that the passage quoted above is concerned with the "wondering brain," but we have already noted with what ease Shakespeare gave dynamic movement to Macbeth's speculations, and perhaps, for purposes of contrast, even more impressive is another exhibition of the "wondering brain" in *Julius Caesar*. Brutus, like Macbeth, stands motionless on the stage:

> It must be by his death; and for my part,
> I know no personal cause to *spurn* at him,
> But for the general: he would be crown'd.
> How that might *change* his nature, there's the question.
> It is the bright day that *brings forth* the adder,
> And that craves *wary walking*. Crown him—that!
> And then, I grant, *we put a sting* in him

That at his will he may *do danger* with.
Th'abuse of greatness is, when it *disjoins*
Remorse from power; and to speak truth of Caesar,
I have not known when his affections *sway'd*
More than his reason. But 'tis a common proof
That lowliness is young ambition's *ladder,*
Whereto the *climber-upward turns his face;*
But when he once *attains the upmost round,*
He then *unto the ladder turns his back,*
Looks in the clouds, scorning *the base degrees*
By which he did ascend. . . .

The actor on the stage is still; but in imagination we see before us a figure spurning, changing shape—an adder crawling from its shell, stinging and doing danger—remorse disjoining itself from power—a youthful aspirant climbing a ladder to its topmost rung, turning from it, and raising his countenance to the sky.

The lack of such a dynamic quality as is exemplified in Brutus' soliloquy is perhaps the most important weakness in much of the poetic dialogue written by those modern poets who have turned to the stage; but there are others as well. Some of these are due to external conditions; there are some for which the playwrights themselves must be deemed responsible. That a certain feeling of strain is perceptible in many modern poetic plays is not the dramatists' fault; they are working in the midst of an atmosphere far different from that enveloping the Elizabethans, when all writers for the theatre were familiarly referred to as "poets" and when the audiences normally expected to listen to verse forms in the words given to the actors. The very fact that they are striving to offer to their auditors a kind of speech distinct from that of current theatrical fare means that, instead of the patterned dialogue taking shape naturally in their imagination—so that the shape itself becomes the only possible way of conceiving and expressing the themes and characters—the poets of to-day approach their writing with a sense of deliberate purpose, and thus, to a certain extent, the poetic form given to their dialogue at times may almost seem a mere ornament. For this we cannot blame the authors; they are attempting to do something which came easily and without effort to Shakespeare and his companions, but which to-day can be achieved only with extreme difficulty.

If, however, the dramatists are not responsible here, many of them are responsible for a failure to give to their works an immediately perceptible and firm outline. Among the plays which have recently been written in this style, a large proportion have proved difficult for audiences to grasp, partly because the plot-material was too subtle and intricate, partly because the dialogue itself did not possess the power of making a strong primal impact on the spectators' minds. No auditor, however unlettered he may be, can fail to understand the plot of *Hamlet, Lear, Twelfth Night,* or *Much Ado;* and modern revivals of such plays as *Œdipus Rex, Antigone,* and *Medea* have shown that even the Athenian dramas, dealing with legendary matter which was part of the cultural heritage of their original auditors, but which to-day is familiar to few save specialists, tell their stories in a manner readily understandable. In contrast with this, we find that the plots of many modern poetic plays are so complex, involved, and perplexing that even the most alert among the audiences find it impossible to grasp their implications.

In addition to this, numerous speeches assume forms which may not be too hard to unravel when read on the printed page, but which have not the power to convey a primal meaning when they are heard from an actor's lips. When Shakespeare makes Ulysses deliver his great orations to Agamemnon and Achilles, or when he causes Leontes to give explosive expression to his passionate jealousy, the exact significance of the words indeed becomes clear in our consciousness only after we have devoted to them a very great deal of minute scrutiny; but, even if we have never read them, when we hear an actor delivering the lines we know at once what he is talking about. Ulysses is telling Agamemnon how order ought to be maintained; he is warning Achilles how easily reputation may become tarnished; Leontes' jealousy is palpable. Even in the most distinguished of modern poetical plays we often listen to speeches, no doubt savouring their sound, but having not the slightest idea of what the actor, and the author, intend to convey to us.

The problems are many. Certainly the journalistic play of verisimilitude has little chance now of contributing vitality to the stage, both because it already has had its run and because it struggles against the true theatre's current; yet the task of establishing something to take its place remains full of hazards. Patterned language in drama means far more than just "poetry"; at the same time, it must draw its strength from the traditions of poetic utterance, moulding these to suit the conditions operative in the theatre of our time. And audiences will not be likely to acclaim the efforts until dramatists come along who can embody in modern forms the basic principles which impelled and inspired the Greek and Elizabethan playwrights, and who can speak directly and unequivocally to the modern ear. Manifestly, such a style, if it is to come, will not result from conscious ratiocination, but from intuitional awareness of the stage's requirements; nevertheless, an analysis of some of the basic principles (of which the foregoing discussion is merely a rough sketch) can assist us in reaching standards for the appreciation of what, we trust, the creative artists may have to offer.

NOTES

1. W. S. Maugham, *The Summing Up* (1938), pp. 144–146.
2. Sir Cedric Hardwicke (*Theatre Arts*, February 1939, p. 107).
3. Robert Edmond Jones, "Toward a New Stage" (*Theatre Arts*, March 1941, p. 191). See also Lee Simonson, *The Stage is Set* (1932), p. 436.
4. Ivor Brown, "After Checkhov" (*Drama*, Spring 1960).
5. Lee Simonson, *The Stage is Set* (1932), p. 431.
6. Eric Bentley, *The Playwright as Thinker* (1946), p. 121.
7. Among the Zuni Indians, for example, "the efficacy of the formula depends upon its absolutely correct repetition." (Ruth L. Bunzel, "Introduction to Zuni Ceremonialism" (*Report of the Bureau of American Ethnology*, xlvii, 1933, p. 492).
8. W. S. Maugham, *The Summing Up* (1938), p. 144.
9. W. Clemen, *Shakespeare's Bilder* (1936), pp. 166–182.
10. Logan Pearsall Smith, *On Reading Shakespeare* (1933), p. 79.
11. Some paragraphs in this section are reproduced from an article, "Shakespeare and Elizabethan Poetic Drama" (*Kwartalnik Neofilologiczny*, vi, 1959, pp. 1–15).
12. It should, of course, be observed that at various times attempts have been made to "regularize" the blank verse of this speech and to attribute to actors some of the extra-metrical phrases. Thus, for example, Harold Jenkins (in an essay on "Playhouse Interpolations in the Folio *Hamlet*" (*Studies in Bibliography*, xiii, 1960, pp. 31–81)) would reject "O vengeance!" on these grounds, seeking to argue that it is "condemned by its context." But it is by no means condemned by its context: the tenor of the speech demands this exclamatory conclusion to the frenzied verbal attack upon Claudius; in effect, it provides a moment of pause before the Prince turns upon himself with "Why, what an ass am I!"
13. T. S. Eliot, *Poetry and Drama* (1950).
14. J. L. Styan, *The Elements of Drama* (1960), p. 42.
15. J. W. Krutch, *The American Drama since 1918* (1939), pp. 291–293.

MOODY E. PRIOR

The Nature of the Problem

The general acceptance of prose as the appropriate medium for most drama, including tragedy, is relatively recent. Until the later years of the nineteenth century, it was taken for granted that plays of a serious nature would normally be written in verse and that prose would be the exception. With the revolutionary success, however, of Ibsen, Tchekov, and the playwrights of the realistic school in England and America, verse drama has everywhere become the exception and its composition is regarded with uncertainty and even suspicion. The term "poetic drama," which criticism in recent years has applied to older verse drama, is an indication of the special category to which the once standard form of serious drama has now been relegated, and implies in some cases that verse is a somewhat specialized and perhaps dispensable accessory.

These recent developments have not, however, had the effect of making verse drama a dead issue. On the contrary, they have given it a new importance, since for the first time it has become a matter of explicit critical concern whether for the serious dramatist verse is better than prose. For in spite of the remarkable vitality of modern drama, the tragedies about whose unquestioned greatness there is general agreement are in verse, and it has therefore been suggested that with the general abandonment of verse, modern drama may have lost something—whatever it might be—that enabled the Greek tragedians and Shakespeare to do greatly what later writers seem able only to do well. Partisan enthusiasts of the modern drama have been inclined to question whether verse was an essential element in the success of the older drama—whether, in fact, it was not a handicap. Though at times their discussions show traces of the rough and ready improvisations of controversy, they have served to bring the issue into prominence and to encourage more philosophic and dispassionate excursions into the problem. Some of these have sustained the apologists of the modern prose play to the extent of maintaining that the use of verse in drama is now an anachronism and that the dramatist of today must find his way to greatness without it. On the other hand, there have been a number of attempts to explore the nature of poetic drama, to discover the special function of verse and the advantages, if any, which accompany its use, and to consider the possibilities of its continued use in the modern play. And there have not been wanting attempts to make a trial of these possibilities. Verse drama continues to be written. For the most part, the dramatists in verse in recent years have written tentatively and experimentally and not with the requirements of the popular stage primarily in mind. Yet even in the commercial theatre, the efforts of Maxwell Anderson to find a verse form suitable for the drama of our times illustrate that at least one kind of poetic drama can still enjoy considerable popular success. Both in theory and practice, the question of verse drama is still an open one.

A good approach to the problem would appear to be the thorough understanding of the great classics of tragedy. On the particular questions involved in this study, however, most of the critical writings about these plays do not prove very helpful. There are many illuminating studies of origins and development, and analyses of action, character, themes, and other related matters. There are also admirable appreciations of their "poetry," style, and particular felicities of expression. But scarcely any rigorous efforts have been made to bring these characteristics of expression into distinct and close relationship with other aspects of these plays. We learn, for example, a great deal about Shakespeare the dramatist, and we are shown much to admire about Shakespeare the poet, but the precise relationship which exists between these two aspects of that comprehensive genius has not often been seriously and painstakingly studied.

Yet one of the distinctive qualities of great tragedy is its wholeness—the impression it leaves of being undivided and fused, of being the product of genius under the directing impulse of one impressive dramatic idea. If we are to understand the special virtues and peculiar possibilities of the use of verse as the conditioning factor in the style, we must start with the assumption that there is an essential relationship between the particular way in which words are used in these plays and the order in which they are used, and the totality of the final product.

Complete artistic wholeness could not have been achieved if the poetry had been added to a dramatic design as a kind of final adornment. Since the form is dramatic, then all the means used had to be ordered to dramatic ends. Under no other circumstances could artistic success have been possible.

The results of any inquiry into this matter are hardly likely to be very rewarding, however, if what is involved in the idea of the dramatic is reduced, as it often is in loose and popular usage, to exciting intrigue, movement and bustle on the stage, or those moments of maximum force and excitement which any good play will afford. It is with the idea of the dramatic in its most comprehensive formal sense that the problem must be approached.

This will involve repetition of familiar and elementary concepts, but it is best to start building from simple, even if commonplace, assumptions. As a first premise, drama—and more particularly tragedy—as an art form may be defined as the representation of a complete action of some sort.[1] There are many to whom this will appear a limited and old-fashioned notion. There are those who agree wholeheartedly that, as one writer puts it, "Everything in the drama of these days indicates the passing of the importance of plot"; [2] there are those who have criticized Aristotle for making the action the soul of tragedy since character is by far the most interesting and memorable feature of any good play; and there are those who believe that stressing the importance of plot and action confuses the serious dramatist since it interferes with his primary purpose of giving expression to his ideas about man and society. Nearly all such objections arise from at least partial misapprehension of what is involved in the definition. To say that action is the primary formal principle in a serious play is not the same as saying that the plot is the supremely interesting thing about it, or the feature which fascinated the dramatist most and provided the main inspiration to his efforts, or the aspect which provides the chief grounds for gratification and reflection: what is meant is that in a serious play, action is the principle of order and selection. It determines what is to be included, since the relevance of any given speech or episode may be judged by what it contributes to the progression of events as part of a beginning, middle, and end continuum; it determines the order of the speeches and episodes, since they must be introduced in such a way as not to confuse the progression. In this sense, action is the "soul" of the play.

The significance of this principle for the art of the drama can be further appreciated if, for the moment, character or thought is considered in the same way as the end of drama. Character as a principle of organization is looser and less exacting than action. If what may be included in a play is determined only by its appropriateness in illustrating or defining character, the possibilities in the way of what may be relevantly introduced become very great. In addition, if character is regarded as the end of the play, no clear scheme of order is implicit in the formal principle: as Johnson said of the descriptions in *Windsor Forest*, "Of many appearances subsisting all at once, no rule can be given why one should be mentioned before another." In consequence, the effect of finality or inevitability characteristic of good drama is less likely to result. Where thought becomes the primary end, character tends to become a point of view or an attitude toward the issues being discussed, further development being in the way of additional touches or flourishes to add interest and variety to the persons of the play and thus to arouse sympathy or antipathy to particular views. Action in such a case assumes the role of providing theatrical stimulation to keep one interested and awake to the ideas. In the first instance (character), the action would serve merely as a loose narrative scheme to provide a practical check on the extensive possibilities for inclusion. In the second (thought), action would function merely as a rhetorical device.

The idea of action as the end of drama is not, however, by itself, sufficiently comprehensive unless account is further taken of the principle that a dramatic action must be probable and necessary. Character, for instance, is an important factor in any scheme of probability and necessity in a play; what we know about a character gives us grounds for comprehending his actions and also restricts the way in which he will meet the contingencies of the situation. Moreover, though the character becomes more fully understood as the number of episodes in which he functions is multiplied, that very enlargement of our knowledge actually limits the probable ways in which the character can behave. For instance, the behavior of Othello when he dismisses Cassio for unbecoming conduct while on duty anticipates his judgment and murder of Desdemona, and so, once we take into account the intervening differences in circumstance between the two events, his horrible act of perverted justice and honor becomes a matter of necessity. Moreover, in any given dramatic situation there are only a finite number of possibilities within which the play may properly move, any one of which may be probably determinant in the outcome. As the progress of the action eliminates one or more of the possibilities, the others become increasingly probable. The importance of these considerations may be emphasized by raising the question of what distinguishes a thin and shallow play from one that is rich and profound, or what distinguishes two different plays based on precisely the same plot. It is in large part a matter of differences in the kinds of probabilities which are determinant in the action—differences of character, differences in the bearing which some particular factor has on the outcome, and the like. If broadly enough considered, the principle of necessary and probable action will be found to define the formal basis of most good plays.

It is unwise, however, to be dogmatic about this. Not everything which is capable of being put on the stage, not every work which uses the conventions of act and scene division and characters in dialogue is ordered by action, and failure to conform to this formal principle is not necessarily a mark of artistic error. Many excellent one-act plays, for instance, are not thus ordered, nor are certain modern expressionistic plays. Every work of art is in one sense *sui generis,* and must be approached in terms of the principles appropriate to it. Dogmatic insistence on a narrow definition or undeviating application of a single, restricted critical technique is not, however, the only danger: at the other extreme is the incorporation into the idea of drama of anything from the Catholic Mass to dancing. Two characters dressed as shepherds reciting in turn the stanzas from an eighteenth-century pastoral do not constitute a play. Neither does a dialogue of Plato, since, in spite of the characterization, setting, and movement of persons, the work is primarily a dialectical exploration. Aristotle's principle of action as the formal basis of tragedy is useful in establishing a category of works which are, in a formal sense, dramatic, and thus in affording a convenient instrument of analysis for works which come properly within its province.

Before seeking to establish the connection between language poetically used and a dramatic action as just defined, it is further necessary to consider what is involved in the use of verse as the normal conditioning feature of dialogue. A good deal of attention has been paid to the metrical nature of such dialogue. Rhythm of itself must certainly play an important part in the large currents of a poetic play. In *Othello,* for instance, the measured and orderly cadences of Othello's defense before the senate are a mark of his honesty and complete self-assurance; the broken and unbalanced rhythms of his speeches during the undermining assaults of Iago indicate not only the destruction of his peace of mind but also the temporary disorganization of his noblest faculties; the forced calmness of his speech before killing Desdemona reflects the reluctant resolution of his mind; and the fine cadences of his last speech mark a return to the Othello of the opening scenes.

But the use of verse has also the most important consequences on diction. The regularity of metrical language, even though the rhythms are freely manipulated, imposes a discipline on the order of words such as is not encountered in ordinary discourse, and represents a break, therefore, with the characteristics of informal speech. Verse establishes a condition which eliminates the standard of strict verisimilitude as the criterion of appropriateness for any given speech, and hence opens the way to exploitation of all the resources of language for whatever artistic needs may arise. This is a matter of fundamental importance: it has immediate consequences which affect everything about the play in an essential way. It is misleading to contend, therefore, that "The use of verse instead of prose because of its emotional effect is . . . resorting to an extraneous aid for doing what the plot itself should accomplish; but it is not as dispensable a device as the spectacle because the medium of the drama is language." [3] Since words are, in a sense, the material with which a play is created, what happens to language is of primary importance and in no way comparable to the spectacle, which in most conventional plays is theoretically dispensable. And in the last analysis, it is not the verse that is important but the consequences in the diction which are important. The use of verse may be regarded as a sign that the criterion of appropriateness in diction is not reportorial exactness, or even a freely interpreted concern with faithfulness to the actual circumstances governing dialogue in life, but the needs of an art; it represents an intention of using all possible means to gain appropriate artistic ends without being hampered by the demands of verisimilitude.

There are several difficulties in the way of becoming reconciled at once to this attitude toward the language of a verse play. One of these is inherent in the nature of drama itself. A play represents characters speaking and acting, and the performance gives us these characters as actual persons. To the extent that the stage illusion is successful, the audience will tend to construe itself as an interested spectator of other people's lives. Hence the opportunity is constantly present to relate the dramatist's account of these persons' experiences with one's own, and in the process to eliminate, and perhaps even to resent as extraneous and confusing, whatever features of the play interfere with the ready formation of judgments on this basis. This attitude is particularly common at the present time as a result of the prevalence of several decades of realistic methods in playwriting. Not only have these accustomed spectators to look for minute resemblances in the life being portrayed, but they have made the standard of "truth to life" a major criterion of excellence. It is, of course, quite natural to look in a play for anything which the author's experiences might contribute to one's own knowledge, to find illumination about life in it, and to despise an author who is evasive or guilty of falsehood and misrepresentation. Truth to life in a play might raise one's respect for the matter, and indirectly might be responsible for good artistry, since honesty and sincerity must be presupposed for any great creative effort as distinct from clever writing or competent craftsmanship. Yet of two plays each equally praiseworthy in the respect of truth to life—however the phrase is understood in any given context—the one which is a better play will be preferred. This is another way of saying that truth is not—of itself—an artistic merit. It is a condition of intelligibility and acceptability. The dramatist needs the experiences of life to write at all. To the extent that he knows what he is talking about and that he presents his material in a way which makes us recognize his competence as an observer, he has established a rapport between himself and his audience. The question of whether the play is good or bad, however, still remains to be decided. That is an artistic question.

It is necessary to labor this point because poetic drama has been brought into question as a result of the confusion about it. William Archer argued against the appropriateness of verse in drama at all, and regarded verse dialogue as, at best, an accomplishment inferior in kind to excellent management of normal discourse. His views illustrate how far critics had gone toward assuming that drama acquires excellence as it approaches observed behavior in detail. Even professed admirers of the older dramatists—to whom, incidentally, the term "poetic tragedy" would have seemed a redundancy—occasionally reveal in their literary judgments a tacit acceptance of principles made current by the dramatic traditions of the last half century. Levin Schücking, for example, finds fault with a figure of speech used by Laertes to Ophelia because "This comparison of the tender feelings of a girlish heart with the artillery fire of an army in battle seems to us almost absurdly artificial." [4] Not all the figures of speech in the older tragedies are unexceptionable by any means, but judgment of their merits cannot be made in isolation from the larger context of the whole play or in terms of the realistic ideal of verisimilitude, simply because in the best sense they are "artificial."

Even when it is recognized that the condition of diction in a poetic play requires a different kind of appreciation from that appropriate to a style purporting to reproduce informal speech, the various methods of analysis which can be used are not all equally successful in revealing the dramatic function of language poetically ordered. Artifices of expression may be regarded, for instance, as serving the needs either of decoration or of rhetoric. It is not possible in practice to preserve a sharp line of demarcation between these theoretical extremes, but distinction between them is not wholly arbitrary. If we can consider language being manipulated chiefly for its possibilities as ornament, the ultimate criterion of excellence would be conspicuous technical expertness in the formulation of devices of speech and pronounced pattern and design in phrasing. Euphuism, though not wholly the freak suggested by our hypothetical case, has the marks of a style for which such criteria of excellence are clearly in place. When criticism of poetical works is guided primarily by the search for patterns as patterns, the results are chiefly valuable only as they provide understanding of the mechanical organization of the means. Consideration of the rhetorical approach to language represents a more involved problem, since the term "rhetoric" has acquired many shades of meaning and is used with both complimentary and pejorative force. Rhetorical use does not imply any one particular style; under certain circumstances, for instance, the cultivation of ornament may indicate a special instance of rhetorical intention. In its classic sense, rhetoric is the art of persuasion, and rhetorical usage is seen as governed in any given instance by the difficulties of subject matter and circumstance which stand in the way of securing approval or conviction. From this point of view, the nature of the audience is an essential consideration in determining rhetorical appropriateness and excellence. It is easy to appreciate this fact in oratory and pamphleteering; it is less obvious, perhaps, that the same criteria may be applied to such forms as satire, whose end is to secure disapproval and ridicule for the objects satirized, to particular speeches of certain plays where the dramatist makes a partisan plea for sympathy, or even to special artistic devices designed to suggest the preservation of artistic properties. The cultivation of sententiousness in some Elizabethan tragedies illustrates one consequence of thinking of the problem of expression in rhetorical terms. Where the critic relies primarily on rhetorical principles, the result usually takes the form of demonstrating the special effectiveness of individual passages.

The most familiar method of dealing with the poetical aspects of verse drama takes the form of appreciative comment on individual lines or passages conspicuous for beauty and power and expressive of intense feeling or depth of reflection. The two modes of analysis just considered often play a part in such comment. The fine effects of emphasis which rhythmic phrasing produces, of richness of suggestion and strength of statement which result from figurative expression and heightened diction, are so pronounced in these specially brilliant lines that, though isolated from their context, they seem complete and almost final acts of composition in themselves. A great deal can be learned from viewing these great moments in detail, but the widespread use of the method has bred abberations of critical view; for instance, that the proper function of poetry in drama is simply the expression of passion, or that the great speeches are lyrical interludes or "extra-dramatic moments." It seems unlikely, however, that a sensitive dramatist could write a play wholly or largely in verse only so that he might be ready for a few special utterances of fine frenzy, particularly if these moments represent an indulgence in fine writing distinct in function from other speeches. There are many magnificent lines in the best verse tragedies which one wishes to recall by themselves, and there are mediocre and poorly managed verse plays which are saved only by a few speeches of great splendor. But these considerations should not get in the way of the main critical problem. Isolation of the notable passages, special consideration of devices of expression by themselves, leaves the main question of relationship to the whole still unanswered, if indeed it does not definitely stand in the way of its solution.

For this reason, it is necessary to regard the work as a whole in order to understand the artistic role which the constituent elements must play in it. Where the diction of a play is poetically conceived, a dramatic understanding of its function, in the most comprehensive sense, must be arrived at through a consideration of the relevance of any given speeches, words, images, or figures to the work considered as a developing form.

The circumstances of a lyric make it altogether simpler to illustrate this way of looking at the problem of diction and form. By way of analogy, consider, for instance, Keats's use of "requiem" in "Ode to a Nightingale":

Now more than ever seems it rich to die,
    To cease upon the midnight with no pain,
        While thou art pouring forth thy soul abroad
            In such an ecstasy!
        Still wouldst thou sing, and I have ears in vain—
            To thy high requiem become a sod.

The word "requiem" is appropriate here because it fits in with suggestions of death and at the same time of music. But to realize the artistry
in the use of "requiem" it is necessary to recall the poet's desire at the
outset to be free of the sorrow and mutability of life and to identify
himself somehow with the song of the nightingale, which is established
as the symbol of joy and permanence. The poet's desire to resolve the
discrepancy between these two planes is conveyed through the interplay of images which oppose and balance suggestions of sorrow, pain,
death, and mutability against those of joy, beauty, life, and permanence.
Even when the poet, on the "viewless wings of poesy," finally imagines
himself at one with the nightingale in the forest, the description of the
beauty of the setting is still haunted by suggestions of death, change,
and opiate oblivion—"embalmed darkness," "fast fading violets," "mur-
murous haunt of flies." These suggestions lead directly to the reflections
of the next stanza: death is the appropriate ending of this moment, a
permanent, though imperfect, avenue of escape. This momentary resolution in the development of the poem is preceded by the extreme contrast between "rich to die" and "ecstasy" and it is effected in the word
"requiem"—the one word which could at once sustain the symbolic significance of the nightingale's song and the poet's preoccupation with
death, and thus bring to a focus the tragic paradox of his most hopeful
solution. The word demands the whole preceding development, just as
the whole preceding development demands the word.

The extraordinary concentration of lyric poetry makes such demonstrations a comparatively easy matter. In tragedy, however, such
effects and associations may appear to be more difficult to uncover—one
may justifiably wonder if they are possible at all, since tragedies are so
often based on violent and even brutal plots and are generally intended
to endure the harsh test of performance before a miscellaneous audience. Yet a principal consequence of writing drama in verse is precisely
that it opens the same resources of language to the dramatist as to the
lyric poet. Because words are freed from the limitations of versimilitude,

all these resources become available for supporting, illuminating, and magnifying the action. Imagery of all kinds, ambivalences of meaning and suggestion, words made uniquely potent and momentous by the circumstances of the context, figures of speech, in particular metaphors —all these become available to the dramatist to be used as his artistic needs require. And if one of the distinctive qualities of great tragedy is its wholeness, then it is permissible to assume that when poetic tragedy approaches perfection in the proper adaptation of means to ends, the question of propriety in diction may be determined by asking whether a given word or image has been put to use in such a way as to contribute to the development of a dramatic form. In the light of our definition of tragedy as a necessary and probable action of a particular sort, diction in poetic tragedy may be regarded as essentially related to the factors of necessity and probability which determine the form as an action.

Though detailed illustration of the nature of such relations must be reserved for the discussion of individual plays to follow, some of the general conditions governing them may be briefly stated. If we can imagine, for a moment, establishing a hierarchy of the devices of speech and special ways of using words available to the poet, metaphor would be at the apex as the type-form which the diction of poetry might be said to approach as a limit. The language of poetry is generally directed away from the literal and toward the symbolic, and it functions so as to increase the relevant implications and suggestions at any given point and to establish associations and correspondences between analogous or unlike things. Metaphor performs such functions with the most concentration. Aristotle regarded the ability to create illuminating metaphors as the one thing the poet could not learn but must have from nature. The importance of metaphor and of the other devices of language which imitate or approximate its function lies in the fact that poetry begins where the possibility or likelihood of literal exactness ceases. "Metaphorical language," says Shelley, "marks the before unapprehended relations of things and perpetuates their apprehension." The poetic functioning of language is in itself a symptom of and a contribution to an extension of our experience: it is, in a sense, a form of discovery, a pushing of the bounds of apprehension beyond the limits of exact observation and into areas where literal certainty and systematic knowledge do not provide the appropriate answers. This may be Shakespeare's meaning in a well-known passage from *A Midsummer Night's Dream:*

> And as imagination bodies forth
> The forms of things unknown, the poet's pen
> Turns them to shapes . . .

There need not be anything mystical about this, though some writers have not hesitated to approach metaphor as the key which might unlock the mysteries and show us what God and man is. Insights into aspects of experience which because of their obscurity or complexity cannot be readily reduced to explicit propositions can be expressed analogically or symbolically in such a way as to reveal an imaginative grasp of their nature and their emotional weight and moment. Things hitherto unrelated can be brought into association and disparate things shown in relationship.

For the dramatist, the advantages of such an instrument of expression and exploration are evident. Motives, conflicts of will, and emotional responses to events are in their nature too involved, even too little understood, to be reduced to plain and self-evident clarity without destroying their essential nature or giving them a narrow and false simplicity. Had the tragedies of Shakespeare and of the ancients not been poetic tragedies, the impression of depth and vividness which their characters convey would have been impossible. Another quality to which critics have repeatedly called attention, particularly in the case of Shakespeare's tragedies, is their largeness and grandeur and the sense they convey of having somehow touched on great and obscure truths about life. In part this impression is the result of the extension of the implications of a limited and unique action through the operation of figurative diction. Figures of speech, ambivalent words, and the like involve a reference to at least two aspects of reality or experience seen in relation to one another. In a richly poetical play the dramatist draws from so wide a range of impressions for his figures and gives to individual words so many special and intensified accents that by the accumulation of association and implication the simple action of the play seems to reach out to the most remote boundaries of human experience. The effect is, on the one hand, to endow the limited story with great generality (universality is a common term for expressing this quality), and, on the other, to endow the action with great magnitude.

Undisciplined use of these devices of speech could well lead to inflation, bombast, and diffuseness. It is, therefore, only when they operate within the restricted scheme of probabilities which govern the action and thus exert a directive force on the determinant elements of the play that they assume their most effective role in a dramatic form. Since character is one of the most important of such determinant elements, figures and images which apply to character can be made to enlarge our understanding of it or give additional force and expectation to what we know. When Bosola, in *The Duchess of Malfi*, says of the Duke and the Cardinal,

> You have a pair of hearts are hollow graves
> Rotten and rotting others,

he has illuminated them and their role in the play and the life of the court of which they are the center, and done so with a concentration and economy unattainable by any attempt to disclose the same things explicitly. Where the language of a play is through and through poetic, it can stay within the restricted scheme of the play and yet develop great complexity of reference. Enobarbus' description of Cleopatra's barge which "burned on the water" is something more than a highly decorative piece of reporting. The paradoxical phrase not only calls attention to the splendor of the barge, but it glances also at the queen, and the whole vivid picture is part of the contrast between Rome and Egypt which occupies an important place in the play and is an aspect of the dilemma in which Antony is caught.

Such effects, moreover, occur not only in the notable passages: where poetic language is integral to the play, the whole fabric of the work becomes affected, and the most inconspicuous speech may perhaps contribute to the probabilities of character and situation. In a relatively unimportant speech in *Macbeth*, Ross says,

> . . . by the clock 'tis day,
> And yet dark night strangles the travelling lamp.

The use of the word "strangles" to suggest the diminution of the light in the dense and unnatural darkness is part of an elaborate scheme in the diction which continuously reinforces the impression of the unnaturally violent world of the play. And, finally, since a play is an action, a progressive movement of events, the diction can properly reveal something of this dynamic development. When Cassius dies in *Julius Caesar*, Titinius says:

> O setting sun,
> As in thy red rays thou dost sink tonight,
> So in his red blood Cassius' day is set;
> The sun of Rome is set. Our day is gone;
> Clouds, dews and dangers come; our deeds are done.

The action continues briefly from this point until Brutus, defeated and left with only a handful of friends, takes his own life. Just before he runs on his sword, Brutus says:

> So fare you well at once; for Brutus' tongue
> Hath almost ended his life's history.
> Night hangs upon my eyes; my bones would rest
> That have but labored to attain this hour.

The night image has relevance to the final completion of the action as the sunset image has to the partial completion of it in the death of Cassius. The two images derive additional significance, moreover, from other developments within the play. The reader of *Julius Caesar* will recall the passionate nature of Cassius, who in the storm, for instance, had bared his bosom to the lightning "in the aim and very flash of it," who had a heart "dearer than Pluto's mine, richer than gold." He will recall, too, that it is Brutus who broods disquietly over each issue and who, from the time that Cassius urged him against Caesar, could not sleep. The images thus have relevance both to character and to the status of the play at the moment they appear.

These few illustrations are merely suggestive of the way in which the resources of diction available to poetic tragedy can be made to cooperate with those determinant elements which direct the action in a necessary and probable way. It is almost inevitable that most of them should be drawn from Shakespearean tragedy. To assume, however, that all poetic tragedy must do things in precisely the same way would be dogmatic and incorrect. Any alteration in the conditioning elements which operate to shape a given drama, whether in the nature of the materials used, or even in the construction and mechanics of the theatre for which the play is intended, will demand some modification in the manipulation of the means and in the conventions employed, and will produce a reorganization of the whole structure which will affect every detail, diction included. And since the devices and methods employed by Shakespeare can not be expected to function without change in the tragedy of any other age, the precise critical technique useful in discovering relations of diction and form in Elizabethan tragedy must not be assumed to be applicable in every detail and without modification to all verse drama whatsoever. Nevertheless, critical study of the great poetic tragedy of the past, as well as theoretical consideration of the potentialities of the form, seems to point to the general conclusion that, whatever material differences may exist between individual plays or types of plays, artistic success in the use of verse in tragedy, or of any style which attempts to approximate verse or take advantage of the effects possible through it, is contingent on an essential formal relationship between a diction poetically conceived and ordered and the dramatic character of the work. A play is, of course, not a lyric; and the language of a play—a verse play as much as any other—must conform to all of the practical and artistic requirements of the form: it must be adapted to the exigencies of performance, since drama is determined in many respects by the limits and conventions of a given playing stage; and it must be properly adjusted to the emotional demands of crucial moments—it must satisfy many conditions and demands which may, in one sense or another, be thought of as dramatic.[5] But in the most comprehensive sense, the diction of poetic tragedy becomes dramatic only when, after satisfying all other necessary demands, it contributes to the form as a necessary and probable action.

NOTES

1. The premises about drama which underlie this study show an obvious dependence on Aristotle's *Poetics*. However, the theoretical discussions should not be looked upon as an interpretation of, or commentary on, Aristotle. Opinion continues to differ as to the meaning of the *Poetics*, and the question of whether the present study represents a legitimate way of understanding that treatise or a proper extension of its principles should not be made to stand in the way of considering the present analysis on its own terms.
2. T. H. Dickinson, *Playwrights of the New American Theater* (New York, 1925), p. 251.
3. Mortimer Adler, *Art and Prudence* (New York, 1937), p. 644, note 164.
4. Levin Schücking, *The Meaning of Hamlet* (London, 1937), p. 52.
5. Granville-Barker has an excellent analysis of those qualities of Shakespeare's verse which are dramatic in the sense that the verse is adapted to the exigencies of the actor's speaking of the lines, the accentuation of vital words and phrases, and the building up of emotional heightening. See *On Dramatic Method* (London, 1931), pp. 67-112.

Imagery

Imagery is normally associated with the verbal dimension of drama and defined as figurative language that makes its appeal primarily to the senses. It is essentially from this point of view that Miss Ellis-Fermor discusses the multiple functions of imagery in poetic drama, where it is of course most abundantly found. In all literature, but especially perhaps in drama, imagery must transcend ornamentality to become genuinely contributive to the structure of meaning. When it does so in drama, it may imaginatively expand the "scene" (which is limited by theatrical necessity to what the stage can show), help unify the play by creating a pervasive mood, reveal character, act as a shorthand device for conducting arguments or lines of thought otherwise cumbersome to develop, etc. But drama is visual as well as verbal; thus "image-ry," which embodies this dual aspect of drama, is a good transitional concept to examine between language (in the foregoing section) and enactment (in the subsequent section). Alan S. Downer underscores both aspects of imagery by treating it as an element of poetry and as part of what he calls the "languages" of props, setting, and action—"languages" that are too easily unheard when we are reading rather than attending a play.

UNA ELLIS-FERMOR

The Functions of Imagery in Drama

The three plays or groups that we have already considered have shown how seemingly incompatible subject-matter may be shaped into dramatic form, a supreme work of art winning a victory, where least expected, by transcending the normal limitations. But victory of this kind on the grand scale is rare, and there are less remarkable triumphs over limitation which are made possible by skilful and unobtrusive technique. These are almost all matters of detail rather than of basic structure and generally work by extending the scope through suggestion and implication without modifying the presentation of the matter. Imagery and prosody, together with certain bold conventions and even devices of setting, serve in various ways to overcome the disadvantages of that brevity which is essential to the concentration and immediacy of drama. A play in which any or all of these are richly used conveys an impression both of magnitude and of subtlety, while the dramatist who uses fewer of them must (like Ibsen in the social dramas) compensate the resulting austerity by some other means, such as the power and skill of the architecture. It is hardly necessary to point out that the average sound theatre play, whether of the present age or of any other, does neither; its potency is thus commensurate with its necessary dramatic brevity; it may be effective in the theatre, but it will not grow in the mind as will a great imaginative work of art.

Of these ways of deepening the imaginative significance of a play without increasing its length or bulk, imagery is perhaps at once the most simple and the most powerful.[1]

In approaching this question we take almost inevitably as our point of departure the finest poetic drama, such as that of Shakespeare's maturity, in which the imagery seems to be entirely functional. Such

From *The Frontiers of Drama* by Una Ellis-Fermor. Reprinted by permission of Methuen & Co. Ltd.

imagery, that is to say, is an integral part of the play, just as is the theme or the structure; it is there, just as they are, because it is essential to the play, because it has a function belonging to nothing else but imagery, because without that imagery the play would be the poorer from whatever aspect we regarded it. At the other extreme from this there are admittedly plays (which perhaps qualify but doubtfully for the title "poetic") in which such imagery as there is is wholly or partly decorative and not an integral part of the play. There are also many plays, probably the greater number, in which the relation between the whole work of art and the imagery occupies a position intermediate between these two, in which the imagery is at times an aspect of the whole and at other times only incompletely related. But unless we are concerned mainly with the historical side of the subject, with tracing the development of this relation, our interest will almost certainly turn first to those plays in which the functional value of imagery is most fully revealed.

When we speak of imagery in this way we generally find that we are using the term in that stricter and somewhat limited sense which recent writers have tended to adopt when considering Shakespeare,[2] taking it, that is, either as co-extensive with metaphor or at most with the figures closely allied to metaphor. This is, I believe, advisable, even though, in the special case of drama, there are sometimes reasons for extending it to include the frontiers of symbolism, description, or even, it may be, the setting itself, when, as in much modern drama, the playwright relies upon that to express a part of his intention.[3]

Can we, then, within these limits, describe what are or have been some of the functions by which imagery helps drama to overcome the limitations inherent in its brevity?

All imagery that has a functional relation with a play increases dramatic concentration. In common with all genuine metaphorical expression, it reveals a significant and suddenly perceived relation between an abstract theme and a subject closer to the experience of the senses in such a way as to transfer to the rightly apprehending mind the shock, the stimulus with which the union of these two stirred the mind of the poet himself. Strong emotional experience is stored in the brief space of an image, and its release illuminates powerfully the emotions, the reflections, the inferences which it is the purpose of the passage to evoke. There is thus an artistic economy in imagery hardly to be equalled by that of any other kind of verbal expression, with the possible exception of irony; in each the potency comes from the high charge of implicit thought or feeling. Moreover, dramatic imagery tends to be the most strongly charged of all kinds; the concentration natural to drama impressing itself upon the imagery, just as the imagery in its turn enables the drama to increase its native concentration.[4]

A play which contains little or no imagery is not necessarily shorter than a play which carries a high charge of it. The concentration of imagery in a poetic play operates rather by enabling the play, without overrunning its brief form, to extend its scope and strengthen its texture. Lacking the leisure and the digressive privileges of the narrative and reflective forms, drama is sometimes in danger of poverty of implication or detail. This is true even of the finest type of drama, which maintains severely its proportioning and the magnitude of its theme. Even here, without the support of functional imagery, there is danger of thinness of character, absence of suggestive comment and lack of passionate significance in spite of richness of event. More often than we should readily believe, we find the presence or absence of imagery to be the immediate technical explanation of those differences in content, in fullness and in amplitude in plays otherwise similar in dimension, theme and structure.[5]

Imagery, as we have said, has certain functions which can compensate drama for the heavy liabilities inherent in its form. Without losing the intensity and compactness which is its virtue, the poetic drama of Aeschylus, of Shakespeare or of one of the modern poetic dramatists, such as Synge, depends largely upon functional imagery for its breadth and scope, for our awareness of a wider setting than that in which the actual events occur. Again, while still preserving its rapidity of pace, drama may, by virtue of the charge carried by its imagery, achieve some of the fullness and elaboration of detail in the revelation of character or of thought which, in narrative or reflective verse and prose, can be revealed at leisure by the descriptive method.

These several functions may be seen at work in the Greek drama as in that of the Elizabethans, at intervals in the drama of the Continent down to the present day and in England again since the revival of the poetic drama in the twentieth century.

Imagery, in such drama, often reveals the presence of a surrounding or accompanying universe of thought or experience which cannot otherwise be included, however essential to its poetic purpose, without forfeiting the rapidity and compression in which the artistic strength of drama chiefly lies. This is often also effected by symbolism, setting or incidental description,[6] but imagery, in the strict sense of metaphorical speech, is a more powerful means; more passionate than symbolism, more flexible than setting, more concentrated than descriptive digression.

This function of imagery may be traced in many of Shakespeare's plays, where the vastness of the issues involved, of which the action — that is shown us is but a part, is kept constantly before us by the imagery. As early as *Romeo and Juliet* the vastness of love is illuminated for a moment by an image whose revelation remains with us throughout the sequent action:

> My bounty is as boundless as the sea,
> My love as deep.

Just so, the universal, all-enveloping horror of Macbeth's crime, its unutterable and inescapable consequence, is borne in upon us, not only by the pitiless relation of cause and effect revealed in the action, but by images that light up, by potent analogy, the nature of the deed:

> This my hand will rather
> The multitudinous seas incardine
> Making the green one red.

Macbeth's mind, in which "function is smothered in surmise," is a microcosm of the "state" whose ordered processes are, by the consequences of his deeds, as surely smothered. He thinks instinctively of "the seeds of time" and "Nature's germens," thus flashing before us in single images the surrounding universes of time and of causality through which the events move.

In Timon's mind the themes of disease, misgeneration, and robbery image themselves in the elements; the earth, the sea, and the great processes of nature. We are never long without this reminder of the universal nature of calamity and evil:

> The sun's a thief and with his great attraction
> Robs the vast sea; the moon's an arrant thing
> And her pale fire she snatches from the sun.

In *Troilus and Cressida* again there is constant reference out from the affairs of man, in which the action consists, to the surrounding universe of being to which they transfer and from which they derive their sickness. The polity of man mirrors the order or disorder of the cosmos, and universal disjunction and disintegration are there imaged with a rapidity and power that could not be compassed in long passages of descriptive analysis. Much of the tempest imagery in *Lear* has a like function.

In *Antony and Cleopatra* there is brought before us by the imagery first the world-wide power of Rome and of Antony, "the triple pillar of the world," and later the presence of the infinity of time and space which dwarf that world. For Cleopatra there is

> Nothing left remarkable
> Under the visiting moon.

while, in the memory of Antony,

> His voice was propertied
> As all the tuned spheres.

Her longings are "immortal," and Charmian has leave to play till doomsday.[7]

If we look for a modern parallel to these we may find something similar in Synge's peculiar use of nature imagery, especially in his later plays, in which it suggests the world surrounding the action but not directly presented in it. This is especially noticeable in *The Playboy of the Western World*, where it reveals the background of the characters and their actions. Synge does not attempt, like Aeschylus and Shakespeare, to reveal a vast, surrounding world of being. He contents himself with using it (most precisely) to reveal an accompanying, but separate part of the experience of his characters.[8] Its presence is an essential part of the natures of the people and of their conduct. That they are, unlike the people in *Riders to the Sea*, unaware of the moulding power of the world outside Flaherty's shebeen, adds subtlety and significance to the functional power with which Synge invests their unconscious references and images. The dialogue is full of brief pictures, either in description or in metaphor, of the empty, isolated, and yet beautiful countryside of Mayo. Inside the bar are the drunken peasant farmers with their dreary lives and their starved but inflammable imaginations. The desolation of the country has crushed their enterprise, its beauty has kept their imaginations living. Out of the conflict comes their aptitude for intoxication, whether by the liquor of Kate Cassidy's wake or by the saga of Christy Mahon's heroic exploit. Synge has presented in the setting of the play the inside of the shebeen, only one of the two worlds they live in. He has thrown upon the imagery and allusions the entire function of revealing a world outside, by which this has been conditioned.

But these are only various forms of one function of imagery, that which reveals the relations between the world of the play and a wider surrounding world or universe. Far more frequent in poetic drama are those functions by which imagery enriches the content and implications that lie within the play itself. And of these perhaps the most frequent is that which reveals or keeps in mind the underlying mood. This not only knits the play together but emphasizes by iteration—and by iteration whose appeal is always to the emotions—the idea or mood which had guided the poet's choice of theme and shaping of form. It may be urged that this second function of imagery must always be at work in any poetic drama which has become a complete work of art; the main preoccupation of the poet's mind must be revealed in greater or less degree by all the aspects of a play that is the issue of that preoccupation. And it is true that iterative imagery, the peculiar function of which is to keep the dominant mood of the whole before us throughout the succession of parts, may be found, in some degree, in any work in which the poet's expression has issued in full artistic expression. But this, in special cases, becomes so clear as to form a continuous and recognizable undertone throughout the play; the undertone of moonlight and woodland in *A Midsummer Night's Dream,* of light and darkness in *Romeo and Juliet,* of sound and movement in *Much Ado About Nothing.*[9]

The function here is clear. A play is fuller and richer in significance because we are continually in the presence of certain elements in nature, themselves the reflection of the mood in which the play is written. This kind of imagery is distinct from, though it may harmonize with, setting or its Elizabethan equivalent, incidental description. For though the subjects of the images may seem to reproduce the setting, as in *A Midsummer Night's Dream,* much of their potency derives from the fact that they *are* images, called forth not by the immediate need to represent a scene but primarily in response to the poet's perception of a fundamental identity between them and his theme. When Lorenzo exclaims, "How sweet the moonlight sleeps upon this bank!" we recog-

nize it as a direction to the Elizabethan audience to imagine the setting that could not be presented; it is perhaps hardly more significant
than the finest of modern moonlight effects. But when Othello says,

> It is the very error of the moon.
> She comes more near the earth than she was wont
> And makes men mad,[10]

the passage is suffused with a spellbound bewilderment, half of enchantment, half of nightmare, like that which sometimes follows the
awakening from deep unconsciousness into the strange radiance of
moonlight. Othello's mind is revealed to us in one brief piece of metaphorical illumination, the moon linking his vision of oncoming madness
with the familiar, cognate physical experience in which it is imaged. In
just such a way, the iterative imagery of moonlight in *A Midsummer
Night's Dream* has, because it *is* imagery, the power to release associations of far fuller content than could be achieved by a long expository
analysis. The picture of virginity, "Chanting faint hymns to the cold,
fruitless moon," illuminates with its implications and charged associations a play whose central action is a tangle of cross-purposes and
apparent frustrations in love.

Closely related with this service, that of qualifying and enriching
each part of a play by continually recalling the mood or preoccupation
from which all derive, are certain functions whereby imagery helps to
amplify, to make subtler and more detailed the nature or relation of
events, the bases of character, the content or processes of thought,
which might else suffer impoverishment from the rapidity and compression of the dramatic form.

In the opening scenes of a play in which events are to move swiftly
we often find a kind of anticipation, not only of the mood of the subsequent action, but of the very events themselves; some hint, in the
subject of an image, of the course of the action, which, though we may
not notice it consciously, sinks into the mind and prepares us to accept
more rapidly some series of events which is to follow. This is a genuine
dramatic function; imagery, that is to say, which is thus used in drama
is functional to a high degree.

One of the Jacobean poetic dramatists, John Webster, seems to have
developed almost consciously this function of imagery; we may notice
that the action of his plays is of precisely that copious and rapid kind
which most needs such aids as this if it is to maintain depth and sig-

nificance. In the first scene of his *Vittoria Corombona,* where the fate of Lodovico reveals in miniature the passions and forces at work on the main action of the play, the speeches are shot with imagery that is prophetic not only of those passions, but of the kinds of events which they may (and in fact do) draw down:

> Fortune's a right whore:
> If she gives ought she gives it in small parcels,
> That she may take away all at one swoop.

This is not unusual Elizabethan image and it is only one of many that might have satisfied Lodovico's hatred of fortune, but it is not insignificant that one of the first words that rings out distinctly in this scene is "whore," which is to be bandied to and fro around Vittoria through the rest of the play and sums up one interpretation of the main part of the action. And the swoop of destruction is the fit image of the sudden turns of fortune and of the final catastrophe. Fortune in the later part of this image has already become in part a bird or beast of prey. In the next lines Lodovico's "great enemies" become "your wolf," the fitting embodiment of the predatory and ruthless figure of Flamineo, who guides and twists the action to his ends, only himself to founder in swift-moving destruction. "An idle meteor," Gasparo calls Lodovico, to be "soon lost i' the air"; and we have another image of the later action, in the brilliant and blazing careers of Vittoria, Brachiano, Flamineo, which vanish into sudden extinction, "driven I know not whither." And the images from knives, swords, and daggers here, "I'll make Italian cut-works in their guts," "Great men sell sheep thus to be cut in pieces," point on with sinister precision to the details of the final havoc.[11]

Sometimes a still subtler form of this use may be found in Shakespeare's works. In the first and third scenes of *Cymbeline* there is a series of images connected with or spoken by Imogen, which unobtrusively conveys her isolation, her exposure to the pricks of malice and of evil eyes,[12] and does this more quickly and more fully than would much direct comment from other characters. By helping so to convey her position, it helps also to convey the balance of the situation, the hostility surrounding her, upon which much of the subsequent action depends.

Closely akin to this use, though probably more usual and possibly more powerful, is the aid given by imagery to the rapid and significant revelation of character. How much more impressive and vivid are the brief imagistic summaries of character given at the beginning of *The Duchess of Malfi* than, for instance, Ben Jonson's lucid and often exquisitely balanced character analyses in *Cynthia's Revels*. How much deeper, indeed, than the impression made by these intellectual expositions is that of the imaginative picture of Ben Jonson's own Volpone?

> A fox
> Stretched on the earth, with fine delusive sleights,
> Mocking a gaping crow.

This, or some part of the picture called up by it, stays in the memory for the rest of the play and guides us, quicker than pages of character study, to the right interpreting of Volpone's character in the action which immediately follows. Just such is the function of the image, in *The Duchess of Malfi*, which introduces the Cardinal and Ferdinand; they are "plum-trees that grow crooked over standing pools; they are rich and o'er-laden with fruit, but none but crows, pies, and caterpillars feed on them."

In all these the function of revealing character has fallen upon the associations of the subject in which it is imaged. But there is another and sometimes subtler use of image which occurs also in a large number of Jacobean dramatists. In this the characters reveal themselves by their instinctive choice of subjects in which to image their thought and often also by the form of the image, by the relation, that is, between subject and theme. The work of Webster, Tourneur, and Shakespeare is full of imagery which has this profoundly dramatic function.[13] Shakespeare's later characters, and in some degree those of his middle period, have their individual imagery. It is related inevitably to the underlying mood out of which the play is, like the characters, generated, but is yet subtly distinguished, within the limits of that character's relation to the whole. Hamlet, Claudius, and Gertrude; Macbeth, Lady Macbeth, Macduff, Ross, and even the murderers have their own trend of imagery in subject or in form or in both; so again have Timon, Lear, Edmund, Antony, Cleopatra, Prospero.[14]

The imagery of Claudius and Gertrude furthers, without our necessarily being aware of the means, our understanding both of their characters and of their relationship. Indeed, certain of the "problems" of the play might with advantage be referred to the findings of a detailed analysis of these two significant groups. A brief indication of their function may perhaps serve here to indicate the value of the direct and unobtrusive revelation of character which can be made by imagery. The imagery of Claudius's public speech differs from that of his speech in private, though there are some fundamental resemblances. On formal occasions it is brief, superficial, and commonplace, illustrating his statements in a clear, efficient way that is hardly ever imaginative. The subjects of the images are homely, drawn from everyday life, frequently from warfare or military life, and sometimes from the operations of justice. He seldom surprises us by revealing anything beneath this surface, though he can sometimes, as in endeavouring to conciliate Laertes, become inept.[15] In private life, when he is alone, with Gertrude whom he can deceive easily or with certain courtiers such as Polonius whom he deceives hardly less easily, it is more vigorous and reveals more and more of the obsessions against which he struggles. It is still simple and generally homely, the index of a mind that is astute and practical rather than speculative or imaginative. But it is no longer superficial or perfunctory. The disturbance and sickness of his mind betrays itself in ever-recurring images of pestilence, infection, poison, and disease, especially hidden disease that feeds on the "pith of life," to reveal itself suddenly. The habit of concealment and the dread of discovery find their release in images of painting and false colouring like that of the "harlot's cheek"; sin is "rank" and "smells to heaven."

In Gertrude's speech there are remarkably few images, and those generally colourless and drawn almost entirely from commonplace themes. They have little vigour and hardly ever call up a vivid picture: the images of a mind that has never received sharp or deep impressions, that is, in fact, incapable of any imaginative effort. Some light is perhaps thrown upon the boundaries of these two natures and of the place at which they meet by even a cursory glance at the mental habits revealed by the images.

Most, as I have suggested, of the characters of Shakespeare's maturity will be found to have in some degree their native imagery. The contrast between that of Macbeth and Lady Macbeth is too clear to justify a brief examination; a full study of each character could, like Miss Spurgeon's picture of Falstaff,[16] be built up from the images alone. Even in subsidiary characters or in those which closely resemble each other, some traces of individual imagery can be found, contributing, whether we recognize it or not, to our quicker apprehension of their distinctive qualities; in the speech of Regan there is a slight preponderance of images drawn from calculation, wealth contrasted with poverty; in that of Goneril a similar preponderance of images drawn from passion and the uncurbed experience of the senses. In the speech of Edmund, images from disease and maiming conflict (especially at the beginning of the play) and alternate with those drawn from the elemental energies of nature, and both are crossed again by others, from the exercise of skill, of adroit and successful manipulation. With him, as with Claudius, the native strain is stronger in solitude and subdued or disguised in public.

The same poetic revelation of character and mental preoccupation may be traced in dramatists of far more limited range than Shakespeare, who are also, within their limits, capable of nice distinctions in this field. One of the most consciously precise of his contemporaries is Cyril Tourneur, whose *Atheist's Tragedy* offers a group of characters all differentiated by this means. In spite of Tourneur's conscious psychological exposition, a great part of our understanding of the characters is actually due to our largely unconscious assimilation of what is revealed by their images. D'Amville's character, the most potent and virile in the play, is revealed in outline by his actions and his cogent and fiery commentary; but in the last analysis it is mainly to the subjects and the form of his images that we owe an impression of a character in which power of imagination has been deliberately balanced by the playwright against a scientist's approach to and treatment of fact. Brief but highly charged poetic images are followed by the lucid, often sustained illustrative or intellectual imagery in which Tourneur delighted.[17] In marked contrast with D'Amville's is the imagery of Sebastian in the same play; plain, pithy, and with excellent relating of theme to subject, but the imagery of a shrewd and energetic practical mind. In marked contrast again is that of Levidulcia, which, in addition to being voluble and commonplace, shows a loose linking of subject and theme, not in a single instance and to indicate a momentary uncertainty, as with Claudius, but so constantly that we realize it as the very habit of her mind. Her conduct throughout the play testifies to a slipshod mental process; the structure of her own images reflects it.[18]

This, which is one of the most important of the dramatic functions of imagery, is frequent in the Elizabethan drama. It can be traced in much other poetic drama, whether in verse or prose, but falls into abeyance, as does all living imagery of whatever function, in prosaic and naturalistic drama. It returns, as do those other kinds, with the revival of poetic drama in our own century, though the absence of live metaphor in the common speech of our time has an inevitable reaction upon the language of our drama and upon the playwright's choice of themes and characters. A conscious and deliberate use of imagery to fulfill this and other cognate functions is to be found in certain kinds of analytical drama, in expressionist drama, especially when this approaches surrealist technique, and in plays of specific psychological theme. But even in these it is less abundant, I think, than in the drama of the great poetic period; Strindberg, Kaiser, and O'Neill (to instance only a few) do not use it so amply as the Elizabethans.

There is yet another function of dramatic imagery which, though less usual than those we have already considered, is still of great service in giving fullness of content despite dramatic compression; that in which imagery does the work of argument or reflection. A discussion or process of deduction may appear full or complete without the tedious and undramatic dilation that we should at once observe if it were in fact complete. In Hamlet's soliloquies imagery, rather than abstract terminology, is generally the medium for the expression of reflection, and when he speaks of "the native hue of resolution" as "sicklied o'er with the pale cast of thought", we apprehend in two brief lines a condition of mind which would need many lines or indeed speeches were it to be expounded. And so, throughout the soliloquy, moods and states of mind are revealed by single images or groups and related to each other by the apposition of the images and the transitions from one to another. The effect of a long psychological diagnosis is thus given in one speech, without diluting the dramatic concentration.

In certain other passages in Shakespeare's plays [19] the way in which the images are placed in relation to each other implies a train of thought linking image with image which is, upon analysis, found to be itself an argument. The original train of thought is thus started afresh in the minds of an audience who can catch the successive implications of the images, so that at the end of the speech they have experienced the equivalent of a long argument in the compass of a relatively brief speech, simply by virtue of the power with which imagery is charged to stimulate and to illuminate the imagination. Almost the whole of the conversation between Achilles and Ulysses (*Troilus and Cressida*, III, iii) is of this kind; imagery is used by both speakers (but chiefly by Ulysses) not only to express single reflections but also to imply the relationship between a sequence of reflections. This is perhaps most clear in Ulysses' central speech (III, iii, 145–90), where the transition from image to image—from the oblivion caused by ungrateful Time to perseverance which "keeps honour bright," from past virtue, which is "to hang Quite out of fashion" to the fierce competition of the narrow way of honour—give by the shock of their juxtaposition, the stimulus which stirs the imagination not only to apprehend the image but to apply the inferences to which these deliberately contrasted images are designed to lead us. Though this function appears perhaps most frequently and most powerfully in *Troilus and Cressida,* that play is by no means alone in this respect. Parts of *Hamlet* and much of *Measure for Measure* on the one hand and of *Timon* on the other depend for their effect upon this function.

In reflective and in religious poetry we often find images used not only (as in Hamlet's speech) to express an idea, but also to reveal spiritual experiences which, it would appear, could not have been expressed (or not by that writer) in the language of abstract statement. When Wordsworth says,

> For I must tread on shadowy ground, must sink
> Deep—and, aloft ascending, breathe in worlds
> To which the heaven of heavens is but a veil,

we are in the presence of imagery of this kind. Sometimes, but not often, drama enters this territory, and when it does we often find that it is to imagery that the poet turns as the quickest and most potent —sometimes, it may be, the sole—means of expressing a thought impossible to convey in disquisition or in action unless these were intolerably and undramatically extended. When Chapman's Byron in the hour of death reflects that he is seated "betwixt both the heavens," he takes leave of the world in a series of pictures which attempt to image the approaching disintegration of the mind in death, an experience which neither Chapman nor his hero would have found easy to expound or to analyze in abstract terms:

> Wretched world,
> Consisting most of parts that fly each other,
> A firmness breeding all inconstancy,
> A bond of all disjunction; like a man
> Long buried, is a man that long hath lived;
> Touch him, he falls to ashes: for one fault,
> I forfeit all the fashion of a man.

> Why should I keep my soul in this dark light,
> Whose black beams lighted me to lose myself?

Shakespeare's Troilus, revealing to Ulysses his conception of his state, uses imagery in the same way; his need is in fact even more imperative than Byron's, for, though our imaginations receive his meaning readily enough through the medium of the image, it is hard to give either a clear account of the subject apart from the theme or a statement in abstract terms of his precise conception of the relations between the various aspects:

> Oh madness of discourse,
> That cause sets up with and against itself;
> Bifold authority! Where reason can revolt
> Without perdition, and loss assume all reason
> Without revolt.

In just such a way as this Mr. T. S. Eliot, in *The Family Reunion*, leaves to imagery the function of revealing much of the thought or of the spiritual experience which would else prove well-nigh inexpressible within the limits of dramatic form. But the function of the imagery here is even more vital than in either of the two other cases, for these thoughts and these experiences are the main stuff of the play, sometimes its sole action. Here, then, is a play in which this peculiar function of imagery is exercised so fully that it would be hard to find a parallel outside the narrative or reflective poetry of mystical experience; yet it is an integral part of the action and thus essentially dramatic in function:

> There are hours when there seems to be no past or future,
> Only a present moment of pointed light
> When you want to burn. When you stretch out your hand
> To the flames. They only come once,
> Thank God, that kind. Perhaps there is another kind,
> I believe, across a whole Thibet of broken stones
> That lie, fangs up, a lifetime's march. I have believed this.

This is not incidental description or commentary; it is the centre of the action because it is the central experience of the chief characters; it is the subject of the play.

The functions of imagery which we have here considered [20] are among the most rapid and potent means of deepening the imaginative significance of a play and thereby helping to transcend the natural limitations of the form. Metaphor, being almost inseparable from poetic expression, must find some place in poetic drama and thus, as the art matures, be drawn into closer and closer functional relation. The functions I have tried to indicate here will, I believe, be found to exist whenever poetic drama rises to a height in any way comparable with that of the Greek and of the Elizabethan. (Nor do I doubt that there are other functions that I have not yet discerned in the drama that I have studied and have been unable to experience in that which I have not.) Many, as I have suggested, are already reappearing to-day in the poetic drama of Europe and America, and their presence there appears to indicate the operation of a fundamental law of dramatic aesthetics.

Indeed, that this should be so is not improbable, since the history of dramatic form is in one sense a history of its conflict with its own inherent limitations. That imagery should be one means of circumventing these is, it would appear, as inevitable as that certain technical devices, to be examined in detail in the following chapter, should be evolved for a similar purpose. The conflict of dramatic form with its potential content calls into being the peculiar functions of imagery that have been indicated here. The conflict between content and medium leads to the various devices which must now be considered.

NOTES

1. We should, however, be on our guard against under-estimating the corresponding function of prosody in verse drama.
2. This, as I interpret them, is the view of H. G. Wells, Middleton Murry, S. J. Brown, Elizabeth Holmes, C. F. E. Spurgeon, G. W. Knight, and Wolfgang Clemen, among others.
3. A familiar instance is the work of H. Lenormand in the present century.
4. Moreover, as Mr. Robert Nichols has recently pointed out to me, a high proportion of the imagery in Shakespeare's plays is dynamic and is distinct in this from the static imagery of the sonnets. Here again is reciprocity: action, which is characteristic of Elizabethan drama, is reflected as movement in the functional imagery of that drama.
5. An example or two may help to make this clear. Ibsen largely (though by no means entirely) discards imagery (as distinguished from symbolism) in *The Pillars of Society* and the succeeding social plays. But he achieves

strength of texture by that close interlocking of event and character that cost him so many revisions. Mr. Eliot, in *The Family Reunion*, to take an opposite case, derives great extension of scope from a specialized use of imagery. Galsworthy's *Strife* appears to separate the two functions, obtaining a certain strength of texture by methods not unlike Ibsen's and a certain enriching of meaning by the images of a few of his characters. But in Shakespeare's work both scope and texture are served by imagery, and the plays would be knit together by it even if the structure were unsure.

6. We may remind ourselves here of the recurrent symbolism of Ibsen, Strindberg or Maeterlinck, the fragmentary allegory and personification in the early Elizabethans, and the dreams and visions in the work of some of the Jacobeans (notably of Webster and Tourneur); of the expressionism of Strindberg and the succeeding German school, represented in our own day by Toller and Kaiser; of the setting which itself becomes an image of a mental state in parts of *Macbeth, Lear,* or *Timon,* or in such contemporary plays as Mr. O'Neill's *Emperor Jones,* M. Lenormand's *Simoun, A L'Ombre du Mal* and, somewhat similarly, in *Le Temps est un Songe* and *L'Homme et ses Fantômes.* (A detail similarly used to excellent ironic effect in our own realistic drama is the firescreen at the beginning of Galsworthy's *Strife.*) We may finally notice how incidental description plays this part in many of the early Elizabethans, most gracefully perhaps in the work of Peele. All these fulfil the function of extending the experience of the reader beyond the actual events, passions, and thoughts presented in the play to include a wider experience equally necessary to a full understanding of what is contained within the play.

7. These images are not incidental or scattered, as may be suggested by so brief an indication, but constant and frequent, forming, in all these plays and in many others, continuous motives or undertones. (C. F. E. Spurgeon notices, to take a specific case, that in *Antony and Cleopatra* there are no fewer than forty-two recurrences of the word "world" in the imagery. See *Shakespeare's Imagery,* p. 352.)

8. See, on Synge's nature imagery and its functions, my *Irish Dramatic Movement,* Chapter VIII.

9. This has been revealed by the full and lucid analysis of Professor Caroline Spurgeon, to whom I am indebted for the summaries above. See "Shakespeare's Iterative Imagery" (*British Academy Proc.,* 1931) and *Shakespeare's Imagery* (Cambridge, 1935), especially Part II, "The Function of Imagery as Background and Undertone in Shakespeare's Art."

10. It may be questioned whether this is strict imagery. Whether it is or not must depend upon the extent to which we credit Othello with a literal belief in the influences of the heavenly bodies upon human destiny. If we assume in him the qualified belief common to many Elizabethans, the "influences" would already have become half allegorical and the words therefore metaphorical. It is so that I take them.

11. These are only a few of the images that are, I think, charged with this power of anticipating by pictures or associations the nature of the events that follow. The same functional use can be found in the opening scene of Webster's second play, *The Duchess of Malfi,* in both of Tourneur's (especially the *Revenger's Tragedy*) and, in an elementary form, as early as Mar-

ston's *Antonio and Mellida.* It was, I think, well understood (though not necessarily consciously understood) among many of the dramatists of the early Jacobean period.

12. "Evil-eyed," "tickle," "wounds," "hourly shot of angry eyes," "gall," "a pinch . . . more sharp," "a touch more rare," "a needle," "prick," "sharp as any needle," "gnat," etc.

13. C. F. E. Spurgeon has made a detailed analysis of the imagery of Falstaff, showing in what ways and to what extent it reveals his character (*Shakespeare's Imagery:* Appendix VII). It will be seen in this examination that the character could be reconstructed from the images alone, with their revelation of the content of the mind.

14. I have instanced here only a few out of many characters. Upon some of these, and upon others that I have not cited, see Wolfgang Clemen: *Shakespeare's Bilder,* especially pp. 149–51, 176–79, 207–11, 222–24.

15.

> The great love the general gender bear him;
> Who, dipping all his faults in their affection,
> Would, like the spring that turneth wood to stone,
> Convert his gyves to graces. (IV, vii.)

This is the result of an over-anxious effort to persuade and convince. And Shakespeare had doubtless observed that this effort sometimes causes even so astute an intelligence as Claudius's to lose itself in words. Claudius seldom uses extended metaphors, and I know of no other passage in which he has constructed one whose two sides are not aptly related. The changing of wood into stone by a petrifying spring is a highly unsuitable picture of the transforming of Hamlet's punishment into additional grace or charm by the affection of the people. If it says anything, it says the opposite of what Claudius would have it mean—the inflexible stone replacing the live and flexible wood is a process the reverse of that by which the encumbering fetters add to Hamlet's graces.

I have examined this one passage in some detail because, taken in conjunction with the rest of Claudius's imagery in public speech—plain and straightforward as it usually is—this is a delicate indication of the fumbling uncertainty of his mind in this scene.

16. See above, p. 87.

17. Special reference may be made to certain passages: *The Athiest's Tragedy,* II, iv, 104–8, 203–4, IV, iii, 244–58, and V, i, 94–100. For a fuller analysis of Tourneur's imagery in a somewhat different connection, see my article, "The Imagery of *The Revengers Tragedie,* and *The Athiest's Tragedie," The Modern Language Review,* July 1935, and for his use of imagery to reveal character, mood, and temperament see my *Jacobean Drama,* pp. 160–61.

18. This culminates and is best illustrated in the soliloquy before her suicide, where the confusion between the various rivers, fountains, and oceans and their relation to the passions and deeds that they are called upon to image defy elucidation. There is, of course, no question but that Tourneur's art here is conscious and deliberate.

19. Upon a cognate but slightly different use of imagery as a general medium for reflection in Shakespeare see Wolfgang Clemen: *Shakespeare's Bilder* (Bonn, 1936), Section ii, "Reflexion in Bildern." "Bilder," according to Clemen, "werden mehr und mehr zu einer Hilfe der Gedanken der Menschen, zu einer bedeutsamen Kristallisation ihres Nachdenkens" (p. 105). And see also Section III, especially pp. 131–32, 149–51.

20. Like all students of this subject, I have a considerable debt to the clear thought and the imaginative analyses of Dr. Clemen's study of Shakespeare's imagery. The functions I have considered are not always those to which he attaches most importance and my categories differ somewhat from his, while sometimes overlapping. For his interesting and exhaustive examination of Shakespeare's early imagery, the reader is referred to the first part of his book (*Shakespeare's Bilder*), especially to pp. 30–1, 46, 50, 52, 57, 62, 71, 73, 82, 85–6, 105; for the analysis of the imagery of the great tragedies, to the later parts, especially sections III and IV.

ALAN S. DOWNER

The Life of Our Design

> Why, there you touch'd the life of our design.
> (*Troilus and Cressida*, II, 2, 194.)

THE FUNCTION OF IMAGERY IN THE POETIC DRAMA

In discussing poetic drama one has to begin with a number of negative generalizations: there is no such thing; there once was such a thing; it is a lost art, though not necessarily a dead one. Perhaps it is dormant because it has been defined as if it were a joining of two elements, poetry and drama, when actually it is only one: poetic drama. That is, it will not be resurrected by a poet, like Byron or Stephen Phillips, writing a play, or by a playwright, like Sheridan Knowles or Maxwell Anderson, trying to write a poem. Poetic drama must be written by dramatic poets. If the truism is chiastic, truth yet lies in the figure.

But if the definition of poetic drama is schismatic, so too is its criticism and analysis. In Miss Bradby's fascinating and infuriating little anthology of *Shakespeare Criticism,* 1919–1935, the critical lines are drawn: on the one side is the Shakespeare-as-a-dramatist brigade commanded by Granville-Barker and J. Isaacs; on the other, Shakespeare-as-a-poet, better equipped and manned, and officered by Spurgeon and Murry and G. Wilson Knight. The strange thing about this general confrontation of critical armies is that although the roll is taken on each side, and all are present and as fully armed as possible, no attempt seems to be made to join battle. Mr. Barker will occasionally take issue in a footnote with Professor Bradley, and a minor officer like Eric Bentley speak a few ill-mannered words about the enemy, but nothing conclusive ever happens. Not a shot is fired, not an attempt is made to storm the barricades, or on the other hand to sign a treaty of friend-

From *The Hudson Review,* II, 2 (Summer 1949). Copyright 1949 by Alan S. Downer. Reprinted by permission of the author and *The Hudson Review.*

ship and mutual aid. It is as if each side felt that something too precious to risk might be involved in either engagement or compromise. As a consequence, both sides are impoverished, and the neutrals uneasily trade with both at once in a state of utter uncertainty. Yet Union is possible with Honor and without Compromise; and it could stem from a recognition of the true nature of poetic drama.

The drama is a unique form of expression in that it employs living actors to tell its story; its other aspects—setting, characters, dialogue, action and theme—it shares with other forms of communication. But the fact that the dramatist is not dealing with characters merely, but with three-dimensional persons is paralleled by the fact that he is not dealing with a setting verbally described but three-dimensionally realized, with action that actually occurs in time and space, with dialogue which is spoken by human voices for the human ear: so many tools, so many tribulations. One of the very real problems of the dramatist is just this, that he, unlike the poet, must deal with the thingness of things; to him a mossy stone must be a mossy stone and a ship tossed on an ocean a ship tossed on an ocean, not a synonym for *peace* or *turmoil.* But the point is, surely, that for the poetic dramatist the stone is more than a stone without ever losing its stoniness, and the tempest may be a highly symbolic one without losing its reality. So, although the drama in general makes considerable use of physical objects—"props"—to tell its story, the higher drama transmutes the physical prop into a symbol, gaining richer meaning without expansion. The poetic drama relates the dramatic symbol to the poetic image, intensifying the unity of the work, and gaining still greater richness without greater bulk, compression being the ever-present necessity of the form.

It is my present purpose to examine the function of imagery in poetic drama, the language of poetry, and its relation to the essentially dramatic devices which might be similarly named the language of props, the language of setting, and the language of action. In the interests of communication I have chosen most of my illustrations from Shakespeare.

The more perceptive of the poetic critics have recognized the existence of this dramatic language, if they have refused to see its true relation to the verbal. Coleridge, for example: "Shakespeare as a poet was providing in images a substitute for that visual language which in his dramatic works he got from his actors." The definition of action as visual language is so illuminating that one wonders why Coleridge did not see by its flash the limitation of the earlier portion of his statement.

In the same chapter of the *Biographia Literaria* he gives the cue to most of his successors: the poetic power, he declares, consists in part of "reducing multitude into unity of effect, and modifying a series of thoughts by some one predominant thought or feeling." In particular this inspired Caroline Spurgeon in her counting and analysis of Shakespeare's images to determine, where possible, the "iterative images" of the plays. Using *image* broadly to cover every kind of simile and metaphor, she produced a documented and be-graphed volume which is the happy hunting ground of the anti-theatrical critics. Miss Spurgeon, however, felt that the results of her study could be used as a more general tonic. In her estimation the iterative image is a revelation of the writer's personality, temperament and quality of mind, and it throws fresh light on individual plays by serving as Background and Undertone, raising and sustaining emotion, providing atmosphere, and emphasizing a theme. It reminds one of the old patent medicines which cured everything from sterility to toothache. From her analysis, for instance, Miss Spurgeon concludes that Shakespeare was more sensitive to the horror of bad odors than to the allure of fragrant ones, and to the loathsomeness of bad cooking than to appreciation of delicate and good, presumably because he had "more opportunity of experiencing the one than the other." There is no other evidence that Miss Spurgeon had a sense of humor.

On the other hand, her extended discussion of the martlet image in *Macbeth* very nearly penetrates to the heart of Shakespeare's dramatic technique. The martlet is a foolish bird and Banquo notices him on Macbeth's castle:

> no jutty, frieze,
> Buttress, nor coign of vantage, but this bird
> Hath made his bed and procreant cradle.

Martlet was a slang word for dupe, like the word gull; that is, a metaphor. But in the *Macbeth* scene the bird is imagined to be present as part of the "setting," and therefore becomes, not a poetic image, but a dramatic symbol, of the "guest who is to be 'fooled'." Into dramatic symbolism, even when it is so intimately linked with the poetic imagery of the play, Miss Spurgeon will not go. She is, for instance, rather annoyed at the gardener's scene in *Richard II* because "no human gardeners ever discoursed like these," though she recognizes its importance in, as she says, "gathering up, focussing and pictorially presenting," the leading theme of the play.

The other school of modern interpretation of Shakespeare is perhaps best represented by Granville-Barker's essay on *King Lear*, in which he restores the play to the stage and demonstrates that it is essentially theatrical. "The whole scheme and method of its writing is a contrivance for its effective acting. The contrast and reconciliation of grandeur and simplicity, this setting of vision in terms of actuality, this inarticulate passion which breaks now and again into memorable phrases—does not even the seeming failure of expression give us a sense of the helplessness of humanity pitted against higher powers? All the magnificent art of this is directed to one end; the play's acting in a theater." The reactions to this kind of statement are violent and equally dogmatic—mere theatricalism, declared one reviewer.

It is surely too late to go around saying that *King Lear* is not adapted to theatrical representation. Is it not also too late to declare that poetic drama cannot reveal its meaning and depth and implications on the stage as fully as any other work of art in its own medium?

In seeing Shakespeare on the modern stage, we take immediate pleasure in the story and a secondary pleasure in the characterization. But certain critical writers have suggested that there is a third and more important pleasure—the meaning as interpreted by the interplay of images. Since we are reasonably deaf to spoken poetry, it would seem that this is a pleasure reserved, as the critics suggest, for the study. Aside from the fact that this makes Shakespeare look a little foolish, like a composer who writes a quartet to be performed by a one-armed violinist, is it true? I believe that it is not; that Shakespeare, if he began as two characters, the Poet and the Playwright, managed to unite them somehow as the Poetic Dramatist; if he began by using the language of action *and* the language of poetry he soon learned to use the language of *imagery in action* which is the major characteristic of poetic drama.

Perhaps the theatricalist and the reader of poetry can find common ground in a consideration of dramatic symbolism. At any rate, in this subject there is less excuse for the automatic or reflex sneer at the other's expense, since symbolism is as basic to drama as imagery is to poetry.

Symbolism grows naturally out of the materials of the drama. The successful unravelling of the plot dilemma in a Greek tragedy or a

Roman comedy frequently depended upon the manipulation of some physical object, some prop, a piece of cloth, a footprint, a birthmark, a chest. In the more intricate popular drama of the last century, a cache of gold, a missent letter, a list of conspirators might be the mainspring of the action. In such plays, however, one tires very quickly of the mere ingenuity by which the eventual discovery of the gold, or arrival of the letter is held off.

It was a considerable step up the ladder of dramatic interest and intensity in the nineteenth century when Ibsen discovered that the game of "pistol-pistol-who's-got-the-pistol" could not only make a fascinating plot but could suggest the relation of the action to some aspect of the experience of the audience. When Hedda Gabler produces a case of pistols at the beginning of her play, it is basic dramatic economy that she should give one to Lövborg to commit suicide with, and use the other to put an end to her own wretched life. Further, it is nicely ironic. But when the point is carefully made that these pistols are her sole material heritage from General Gabler, a parallel avenue of suggestion is opened. She has inherited her personal characteristics from the old general, and the pistols are symbols, not only of the spiritual heritage but of the order which shaped it—the empty, decadent life of the military caste. At the end of the play it is clear that Hedda's environment and heredity shaped all her actions, drove her to urge Lövborg's suicide and finally caused her own death. The pistols are not merely the means of the action, but the meaning of the action.

Lest it be objected that such an interpretation of a dramatic symbol stems from the study rather than the stage, a current example may be added. One of the earliest and sturdiest of the successes of the 1947–1948 season on Broadway was William Wister Haines's *Command Decision*. There is no pretense about this play: it is a tightly constructed, efficient product, intended for the open market. Yet despite its employment of stereotypes, conventions, and elements of melodrama, the audience is caught up in the movement of the play: we who have usually been asked to worry only about the problems of the doughboy and GI Joe, are suddenly emotionally involved in the problems of majors and brigadier-generals, hitherto satirized or portrayed as villains.

The action takes place in a Nissen hut, headquarters of an airforce command in England. The setting is narrow: the back wall, only a few feet from the footlights, is papered with a huge geodetic survey map of

Western Europe. Throughout most of the performance, this map is covered, the curtains being withdrawn only when it is necessary to explain current operations. At such times the audience sees the major target cities to be destroyed and the pitifully short arc of fighter cover. The decision, which the title reflects, is whether the destruction of the targets warrants the certain loss of American soldiers.

These soldiers, whose lives are at stake, and who would be the main concern of the conventional war play or film, we never see. We see only the men whose responsibility it is to send them out and who are popularly supposed to die in bed. Yet humanity is never remote. The whole world of the action is brought into the Nissen hut; each revelation of the map creates increasing tension. At its first showing, it is merely expository: this is where we must operate. At its second, it begins to become symbolic: this is the awful dilemma which presses upon the leading character. Finally, it symbolizes the underlying meaning of the play; the desperate nature of any decision for any man under competing pressures. The map as symbol enables the audience to participate in the emotional tension of the play, serves as a unifying force, and reveals the deeper significance of what might all too easily have been a routine piece of theatrical journalism. It is, further, the best kind of dramatic symbol in that it is never obtrusive, being equally germane to the action and the theme.

It may very well be that Mr. Haines stumbled upon this dramatic symbol quite unconsciously. There is nothing in his work as a novelist to indicate that he is particularly concerned with form in that medium. His experience in Hollywood working with a medium which deals largely and conventionally in visual symbols may have led him unawares to the device. The point is that the device is there for the use of the most prosaic dramatist and it serves to enrich his work by requiring the mechanical aspects of the play to do double duty.

This "language of props" is equivalent to the simpler uses of imagery in poetry, but it can become highly complex in the poetic drama. For the sake of familiarity, if for no other reason, one turns to Shakespeare for illustration. Since it is, however, somewhat unfair to the authors of both works to juxtapose *Richard II* and *Command Decision,* a contemporary of Shakespeare's may be used as bridge and buffer. The simpler uses of dramatic symbolism in the poetic drama are clearly exhibited in the first part of Marlowe's *Tamburlaine.* The Scythian tyrant is obsessed with the idea of power as symbolized in the "sweet fruition of an earthly crown." It is not surprising that the crown—a common-place symbol, wholly apart from its use in the drama —figures largely in the action.

In the first scene, Cosroe is crowned emperor. In the second act, foolish Mycetes rushes on stage seeking to hide his crown in a simple hole. Tamburlaine overtakes him:

> TAM. Is this your crown? (*Taking it*)
>
> MYC. Ay, didst thou ever see a fairer? (*Relinquishing it*)
>
> TAM. (*Ironically*) You will not sell it, will you?
>
> MYC. Such another word and I will have thee executed. Come, give it me!
>
> TAM. No, I took it prisoner.
>
> MYC. You lie; I gave it you.
>
> TAM. Then, 'tis mine.
>
> MYC. No, I mean I let you keep it.
>
> TAM. Well, I mean you shall have it again.
> Here, take it for a while: I lend it thee,
> Till I may see thee hemmed with armed men;
> Then shalt thou see me pull it from thy head:
> Thou art no match for mighty Tamburlaine.

Later, as Cosroe dies, Tamburlaine puts on his crown; a banquet of crowns is introduced; and the play ends with the triumphant crowning of Zenocrate. Throughout all this action, the symbol remains as simple as possible—verbalized, the crown stands for "perfect bliss" and "sole felicity," its

> virtues carry with it life and death;
> To ask and have, commond and be obeyed.

The crown is the symbol of the king's rank, the ruler's god-like power.

The crown which is handled so dramatically in the deposition scene of *Richard II* is, to be sure, the symbol of the king's rank. But it is not simply the sole felicity in which Tamburlaine displayed such interest. It is the symbol of the condition of England, as in the words of Gaunt:

> A thousand flatterers sit within thy crown
> Whose compass is no bigger than thy head;
> And yet, incaged in so small a verge,
> The waste is no whit lesser than thy land.

And Northumberland proposes to "Redeem from broking pawn the blemish'd crown." Further, it is the symbol of Richard as actor:

> within the hollow crown
> That rounds the mortal temples of a king
> Keeps death his court; and there the antic sits,
> Scoffing his state and grinning at his pomp;
> Allowing him a breath, a little scene,
> To monarchize. . . .

It is a symbol of that "divinity doth hedge a king":

> For every man that Bolingbroke hath press'd
> To lift shrewd steel against our golden crown
> God for his Richard hath in heavenly pay
> A glorious angel. . . .

The divinity which the crown symbolizes is strengthened by a second image, the king as the sun:

> knowst thou not
> That when the searching eye of heaven is hid
> Behind the globe, that lights the lower world,
> Then thieves and robbers range abroad unseen. . . .
> But when from under this terrestrial ball
> He fires the proud tops of the Eastern pines. . . .
> Then murthers, treasons, and detested sins,
> The cloak of night being pluck'd from off their backs,
> Stand bare and naked, trembling at themselves?
> So when this thief, this traitor Bolingbroke,
> Who all this while hath revell'd in the night
> Whilst we were wand'ring in th'Antipodes,
> Shall see us rising in our throne, the East,
> His treasons will sit blushing in his face,
> Not able to endure the sight of day,
> But self-affrighted tremble at his sin.

The image is extended and explicit. Even the dullest in the audience must have been impressed by it. At any rate, Bolingbroke is not slow to seize upon it:

See, see, King Richard doth himself appear,
As doth the blushing discontented sun
From out the fiery portal of the east. . . .

At this moment (III, 3) Richard is standing upon the walls of Flint Castle, which is to say the upper stage, and Bolingbroke is on the ground. At the end of the scene in response to his opponent's demands, Richard descends to the main stage, with still another reference to the sun image:

Down, down I come like glist'ring Phaeton,
Wanting the manage of unruly jades. . . .

He sees himself no longer as king, but an unsuccessful pretender to the title.

The climax of the action of the play, in which the complexity of the image is finally revealed, is the deposition of Richard. In the drama, the whole Parliament is assembled, with the lords and bishops of England providing not only a larger audience for the display of Richard's theatrical talents, but a more impressive background for the action. When the great moment comes, Richard makes the most of it, in a scene which should be compared with Tamburlaine's taking and returning of Mycetes' crown.

Give me the crown. Here, cousin, seize the crown.
(*As Bolingbroke hesitates*) Here, cousin,
(*A pause; Bolingbroke steps to him, and Richard
holds the crown between them*)
   on this side my hand, and on that side yours.
Now is this golden crown like a deep well
That owes two empty buckets,

and so on. How carefully Shakespeare has pointed the action here; not simply a passing of the crown from one hand to the other, but a tableau, and an extended simile to illustrate it. So the visual symbolic exchange of the crown, to quote Miss Spurgeon's words on another matter, "gathers up, focusses and pictorially presents" the downfall of a man whose nature was ill-suited to kingship, and who has to some extent come to realize the fact.

There are striking uses of this "language of props," the realization of the verbal image in dramatic terms, in later Shakespearean tragedy. For example, in *Macbeth* Miss Spurgeon found repeated iteration in the dialogue of the idea of ill-fitting clothes. Mr. Cleanth Brooks has related the image somewhat more closely to the play by seeing it as an interpretation of Macbeth's position as usurper: he is uncomfortable in garments not his own. Actually, the image suggests disguise. Macbeth is an unhappy hypocrite who declares before the murder of Duncan, "False face must hide what the false heart doth know," and before the murder of Banquo, "We must . . . make our faces vizards to our hearts, disguising what they are."

But the image is more than a mere verbal one. It is *realized*, made visual in the action of the play.

The first four scenes are various moments during and after a battle. In them, Macbeth will naturally be wearing his warrior's costume, his armor, as much a symbol of his nature and achievements as is Duncan's crown. When he defeats Norway, for instance, he is "lapped in proof," but when Ross and Angus greet him as Thane of Cawdor, he protests, "Why do you dress me in borrowed robes?" The image continues, verbally, as Banquo observes, half-jesting,

> New honors come upon him
> Like our strange garments, cleave not to their mold
> But with the aid of use.

Under pressure from his wife, however, he resolves to seize the kingship, to cover his warrior's garments and the golden opinions that went with them with the clothing that was properly Duncan's. The murder is committed with constant reference in the dialogue to the clothing image (skilfully interpreted by Mr Brooks) and the scene as marked in the Folio ends with the flight of Macbeth and his Lady from the crime as she urges him to

> Get on thy nightgown, lest occasion call us
> And show us to be watchers.

When next Macbeth enters he is wearing his dressing gown, and if the actor is wise it will be such a gown as calls attention to itself, for at this point the change in costume, the disguising of the armor, dramatizes both the change in Macbeth's nature and the iterated poetic image. From now until nearly the end of the play, Macbeth is cowardly, melancholic, suspicious, and unhappy; the reverse of all the qualities that had made him the admired warrior of the early scenes. He cannot buckle his distempered cause within the belt of rule; and Macduff's fear is prophetic, "Adieu, lest our old robes sit easier than our new," prophetic not only for the unhappy Scots, but for Macbeth himself.

One of the achievements of this highly skilful play is the maintaining of interest in, if not sympathy for, the central figure; assassin, evil governor, usurper, and murderer. Shakespeare maintains this interest not merely by portraying Macbeth as a man in the control of wyrd, or too susceptible to uxorial suggestion, but, I think, by making us constantly aware of the armor—the honest warrior's nature—under the loosely hanging robes of a regicide. Until Act II, scene 3, Macbeth is quite possibly dressed as a warrior. From that point, until Act V, scene 3, he is dressed in his borrowed robes. But in the latter scene, with his wife eliminated as a motivating force, and with the English army moving against him, he begins to resume some of his former virtues: his courage returns, his forthrightness, his manliness. "Give me my armor," he cries, and in a lively passage with the Doctor, he makes grim jests about the power of medicine as Seyton helps him into his warrior's dress. He is all impatience to be back at the business he understands as he does not understand government:

> MACBETH. Give me my armour.
> SEYTON. 'Tis not needed yet.
> MACBETH. Give me my armour.
>   Send out moe horses, skirr the country round;
>   Hang those that talk of fear. Give me mine armour. . . .
>   Throw physic to the dogs, I'll none of it!—
>   Come put mine armour on. Give me my staff.—
>   Seyton, send out.—Doctor, the thanes fly from me.—
>   Come, sir, despatch.—If thou couldst, doctor, cast
>   The water of my land, find her disease,
>   And purge it to a sound and pristine health,
>   I would applaud thee to the very echo,
>   That should applaud again.—Pull't off, I say.—

The tragic fall of this good man is dramatically underlined in his attempts to resume his old way of life. His infirmity of purpose cannot be more strongly presented than in his donning and doffing of the armor, and his bragging exit, with the equally revealing order:

> Bring it after me!

This is not an isolated, but only a more complex use of costume as symbol in poetic drama. For subtlety it might be contrasted with the costume changes of Tamburlaine, who, appearing first in his shepherd's weeds, casts them off contemptuously at his first triumph:

> Lie here ye weeds that I disdain to wear!
> This complete armour and this curtle axe
> Are adjuncts more beseeming Tamburlaine;

and who later wears in sequence white, scarlet, and black armor to indicate the stiffening of his attitude towards his victims. This is a simple dramatic device. In *Macbeth* the costume change is related to the iterated image to make concrete Macbeth's state of mind, and related also to the larger problem, the power of evil to corrupt absolutely, with which the play is concerned.

Without insisting too strongly on this kind of relation of image and symbol to clothe the idea of the play in reality, a few familiar instances may make the process clearer. *Hamlet*, for example, establishes in its opening scene, with the ghost, and the references to decay and unwholesomeness, what Mr. Knight calls "the embassy of death." The hand of death is upon the play from the very start and references to it are constantly reiterated. However, it is death of a particular sort, not just Hamlet's musings upon the possibilities of suicide. Hamlet speaks of the sun breeding "maggots in a dead dog," the king compares his nephew to a foul disease, and describes his subjects as "muddied, Thick and unwholesome in their thoughts and whispers." The idea is repeated over and over in the play which has been made explicit at the very start, "Something is rotten in the state of Denmark."

But if we have missed it through insensitivity, Shakespeare presents his symbol of the state of Denmark dramatically, in terms of the theater, before our eyes: *Enter two clowns*, who discourse learnedly of death and suicide and toss skulls and bones about the stage remarking on the pocky corpses they now must deal with; "Faith, if 'a be not rotten before 'a die," catches up the very word Marcellus had used earlier to describe the condition of the state.

It is this same kind of symbolism that Miss Spurgeon noticed with some surprise in the Gardener's scene of *Richard II,* in which the "leading theme . . . (is) gathered up, focussed, and pictorially presented." As she points out, this could hardly be missed by any careful reader. The lines of the play are larded with images of nature gone awry, the ugly clouds flying in the fair and crystal sky, the flourishing branch cracked and hacked down, and the summer leaves faded; there is a fearful tempest, a flood tide;

> The bay trees in our country all are withered,
> And meteors fright the fixed stars of heaven;
> The pale-faced moon looks bloody on the earth. . . .;

an unseasonable stormy day causes rivers to flood. But where the other characters of the play refer to the disordered political conditions in England in terms of unkempt nature, the Gardener reverses them by comparing the task of ordering his garden to the task of the governor of a commonwealth.

> O what pity it is
> That he had not so trimm'd and dress'd his land
> As we this garden!

Miss Spurgeon declares the scene to have been "deliberately inserted at the cost of any likeness to nature, for no human gardeners ever discoursed like these." To demand verisimilitude in what is obviously a poetic device is to apply to Shakespeare the standards of David Belasco. Probably even the most theatrical of theatricalists would be willing to grant the rightness and the effectiveness of the device, for it does realize dramatically and visually in terms of character and action the theme of the play. On reconsideration it may seem over-deliberate, super-imposed, introducing as it does two totally new characters for the sole purpose of the device, but Shakespeare had not yet learned dramatic economy. In *Hamlet,* the gravediggers belong to the plot as well as to the imagery.

The repeated pictures of natural conditions in *Richard II* introduce a second important function of the image in Elizabethan poetic drama. We are all convinced, I suppose, that the dramatist was forced to work without the benefit or incumbrance of representational scenery, and that the formal nature of the background of the Globe is the excuse for so many of those

> Barkloughly Castle call they this at hand

speeches, and such more extended and always (on the modern stage) intrusive passages in which we are informed,

> The grey-eyed morn smiles on the frowning night,
> Check'ring the Eastern clouds with streaks of light,

together with other meteorological data. But perhaps the Elizabethan playwright was more fortunate than his cabined, cribbed and confined successor. Not only could he shift his scene at will, or indeed not bother with a "scene" at all, but he could in his images create a world for his action more complete than any producer could provide, and uniquely adapted to the needs of both his play and his theme.

In *Richard,* for example, the action transpires not before painted sea-coasts and cardboard castles, but in an envelope which is at once scenic and emotional. The cumulative effect of the nature images is not merely to suggest the political condition of England, but the kind of world in which such a conflict as that between Bolingbroke and Richard could take place. The device is not very skillfully used, perhaps, for *Richard* is close to being an apprentice play. In the later works, the setting as an emotional envelope is more artfully handled.

Lear is a case in point and a particularly striking contrast to *Richard.* Instead of giving magnitude to his action (as in the other tragedies) by relating the struggles of the protagonist to affairs of state, in England, Rome, or Denmark, Shakespeare creates a world of his own, a special world of King Lear, and he creates it by means of imagery.

It is the worst of all possible worlds. The animals which inhabit it are dragons, curs, rats, geese, kites, wolves, vultures, tigers. It is a world of disease, of plagues, carbuncles, boils. Whatever happens in this world happens in the most violent manner, wrenched, beaten, pierced, stung, scourged, flayed, gashed, scalded, tortured, broken on the rack. All this has been noted before by Miss Spurgeon and others. The world of Lear is a world of torment, a world unfriendly to man. In such a world the events of the play are entirely natural, possible, logical. The imagery, better than any possible stage setting, provides a background for the action, enriching the language of the play and serving to unify its execution.

For what, strangely enough, does not seem to have been commented on is the realization of this metaphorical world in the action of the play, in the tempest which runs through its center and in the torturing and blinding of Gloucester. Both scenes have come in for critical attack as incapable of presentation or too horrible for effective use. But it is clear that both are as essential to the play's action as to its theme, and that the blinding of Gloucester—detailed as it is—is made as horrible as possible for a purpose. If we experience an emotion of disgust, or terror, it is because both elements are present, not simply in the action, but in the world of the play. It is the dramatization of the image which makes the meaning of the play evident. If Richard's crown is the "language of props," Lear's tempest is the "language of setting."

The most difficult of the dramatist's devices to appreciate in the study is his primary device, the "language of action." Our modern playwrights are at some pains to render the action clear in extended stage directions, separated from the dialogue by italics and parentheses. Now Shakespeare resorts to a stage direction only rarely, most of the movement in his plays being implicit in the poetry. The significance of this lies less in the freedom of interpretation permitted the actor than in the indication of a further unity between the devices of poetry and the theater in the poetic drama.

For a simple and clear instance of this we may again turn to *Richard II*. The plot of this play, the conflict between Richard and Bolingbroke, might be diagrammed by tracing the letter X and letting the downward stroke stand for the king, the upward for the usurper, and the point of crossing the deposition scene. It is curious to note how the dominance of first the king and then the usurper is symbolized in their positions on the stage as well as in the imagery and the plot line. For three acts, Richard is in the ascendant. Whatever Bolingbroke's activities, Richard maintains his position as king. This is indeed symbolized by his appearance "on the walls" of Flint Castle, while Bolingbroke and his followers remain below. His descent to Bolingbroke's level is accompaied by a punning speech:

> Base court, where kings grow base,
> To come at traitors' calls and do them grace;

but his recognition of the true state of affairs is indicated as Bolingbroke kneels and Richard raises him up. In the deposition scene the shift in positions is completed, and verbalized by Richard in a final allusion to the sun image:

> O that I were a mockery king of snow,
> Standing before the sun of Bolingbroke
> To melt myself away in water drops.

It is a sign of the maturing artist that as his skill increases in each of the dramatic forms he elects to try, Shakespeare relies more and more upon the essentially dramatic materials available to him, the actors, their movements and physical relationships. In the most perfect of the histories, for instance, *1 Henry IV*, he has involved himself in a highly complex plot, the handling of which is a constant source of wonder and admiration. Ostensibly, Shakespeare is relating the events of a portion of the reign of Henry IV, a revolt engineered by the Percy family, and the waywardness of the Prince of Wales. But the two problems confronting the king are brought into significant relationship to one another, and the facts of history are made to serve the purposes of art. The subject of the play is not English history, but the general education of princes. Events have been so modified that the play actually confronts two ways of life—Hotspur's and Falstaff's—and presents the dilemma of Hal in choosing between them. Although a good deal of ink has been spilled over the character of Falstaff, and a number of romantic female tears over Percy, Shakespeare's intention is clear from his manipulation of the characters in a crucial scene. In Act V, Scene 4, Douglas enters, challenges Henry IV, they fight and, *"the King being in danger, enter Prince of Wales."* One must perhaps visualize the scene in the Elizabethan theater—a broad platform projecting into the audience with entrance doors on each side at the rear. Douglas and the Prince fight, and *"Douglas flieth"* through one of the doors. As the King goes to join his troops, enter, through the opposite door, Hotspur. The two youths exchange challenges; *"They fight."*

> *Enter Falstaff.*
> FALSTAFF. Well said, Hal! to it, Hal! Nay you shall find
>   no boy's play here, I can tell you.
>   *Enter Douglas. He fighteth with Falstaff, who falls down as*
>   *if he were dead. (Exit Douglas.) The Prince killeth Percy.*

Percy dies, still prating romantically of his honor and his proud titles which now accrue to Hal; Hal speaks his eulogy and turns from the body to go to the nearest door. But on his way, *"He spieth Falstaff on the ground."* As in *Richard II* the positions of the characters in the scene are symbolic. Hal has, seemingly, been presented with a choice between the way of life represented by Hotspur and the way of life represented by Falstaff. And here they are, two (apparent) corpses on the ground, one on either side of him. The choice is to make, and he chooses— neither. Having bid farewell to Percy, he now bids farewell to Jack, confirming the promise of his first soliloquy and anticipating the rejection of Falstaff at the end of Part II.

Significant illustrations of this "language of action" could be chosen from nearly any of the plays. Indeed, nearly all the most familiar, most memorable scenes involve some kind of symbolic action. Not merely in tragedy, with Lear buffeted by the tempest, or Hamlet leaping into the grave of Ophelia, but in comedy, with Titania fondly caressing the hairy snout of ass-headed Bottom, or Feste torturing Malvolio into a realization of his humanity. The very essence of the tragic idea of *Hamlet* and *Lear* and the comic idea of *A Midsummer Night's Dream* and *Twelfth Night* is contained in those moments of action. This is not to say that the poetry is superfluous. These are further instances of the complete welding of the elements of poetry and the elements of theater which constitute successful poetic drama.

Enactment

Of the six formative elements of tragedy discussed by Aristotle—plot, character, diction, thought, song, and staging—the first four are literary, the last two theatrical. The least artistic of the six, Aristotle claimed, is staging, since tragedy can exist independent of the theater—in narrative forms such as the novel, for instance. Whether tragedy is possible in nondramatic forms is open to question; but there is no doubt that drama itself can exist independent of the theater, that it can be "enacted" by a reader in the theater of the mind. Whether drama is best read or witnessed is an issue of recurring disagreement between the theater-minded and the literature-minded, each of whom is likely to feel that the work is somehow diminished when subjected to the other's mode of experiencing. Shakespeare is often the battleground: as poetic *dramas* his plays are great theater; as dramatic *poems* they are great literature. On the one hand, literary criticism has effectively demonstrated that there is vastly more to Shakespeare's plays than any audience, no matter how sophisticated, could apprehend in the theater. On the other hand, Shakespeare himself seems to have been utterly unconcerned about providing accurate texts that would preserve his work for a reading public, as though he regarded theatrical performance as their final end and only mode of existence. Rather than exercise ourselves over the problem of whether the study or the theater provides us with a more definitive experience of the play, it would probably be wiser to be thankful that great drama is available to us in different modes.

A section on "Enactment" might well have included essays on directing, designing, costuming, lighting, acting, etc. However, we are less concerned here with the ingredients of enactment than with enactment itself, with the theatrical situation, which is rather more than the sum of its parts. (For an excellent discussion of the way in which some of the elements of theater coalesce at various stages of dramatic development, the student should see the essay by Richard Southern in the section on "Origins.") Thus the excerpts from the diary of Max Frisch, a contemporary Swiss playwright, tend to stress the vitalizing effect of the theater as a visual medium in which the audience itself plays a creative role. Eric Bentley's essay reduces enactment to its most elemental forms in order to analyze the psychology of play as a universal phenomenon from which dramatic art issues.

ERIC BENTLEY

Enactment

TO IMPERSONATE, TO WATCH, AND TO BE WATCHED

The theatrical situation, reduced to a minimum, is that A impersonates B while C looks on. Such impersonation is universal among small children, and such playing of a part is not wholly distinct from the other playing that children do. All play creates a world within a world—a territory with laws of its own—and the theatre might be regarded as the most durable of the many magic palaces which infantile humanity has built. The distinction between art and life begins there.

Impersonation is only half of this little scheme. The other half is watching—or, from the viewpoint of A, being watched. Even when there is actually no spectator, an impersonator imagines that there is, often by dividing himself into two, the actor and his audience. That very histrionic object, the mirror, enables any actor to watch himself and thereby to become C, the audience. And the mirror on the wall is only one: the mirrors in the mind are many.

What is it to want to be watched? Impossible to ask such a question these days without eliciting the word: exhibitionism. To want to be watched is to be exhibitionistic. Is this merely to say: to want to be watched is to want to be watched? Not quite. "Exhibitionism" is a clinical phenomenon, and the word carries a connotation of the socially inappropriate as well as the mentally unhealthy. Which, I am afraid, only makes it the more applicable to the theatre. Wishing to be watched, sometimes and in a small way, is one thing, but wishing to become an actor is wishing to be watched all the time and in a big way. Such a wish would take a lot of justifying and even more explaining. It is bizarre, and brings to mind Thomas Mann's notion that there is a natural affinity between art and pathology.

Is the Folies-Bergère the quintessence of theatre? That depends, I think, on how one takes the Folies-Bergère. Sir Kenneth Clark has distinguished between the naked and the nude. A nude body is one that calls for no clothing; a naked body is a clothed body temporarily stripped of its clothing. Sir Kenneth's interest in the distinction lies in the fact that the arts he is professionally concerned with—painting and sculpture—deal, not with the naked, but with the nude; in fact (so far as Europe is concerned) they invented it. Not so the theatre, however. Even in places and at times which had nothing against the body, the method of the theatre has been concealment by mask and costume. True, one of the archetypal acts of the theatre is to remove this concealment. But one can only take off what is on. Or, in Sir Kenneth's terms, theatre can present the naked, but never the nude. When therefore the girls of the Folies-Bergère are made a highbrow tableau of in the likeness of classical nude paintings, in trying to be nude they succeed in being untheatrical. When, on the other hand, they take off their clothes for us, or parade around in *almost* no clothing, they become theatrical through the act or simulation of unmasking. In short, if these girls are nude, they are art; if they are naked, they are theatre. Parts of the French audience take them to be nude, or try to. The foreign tourists take them to be naked. That is because the tourists have "dirty minds." But the tourists are right. The nudity is spurious; the nakedness, genuine.

Hence, theatre has less in common with the tradition of the nude in painting than with the tradition of the striptease in "vulgar" entertainment. Theatre is shamelessly "low"; it cannot look down on the body, because it *is* the body. If you want the soul, why pay to see chorus girls? Why pay to *see* nonchorus girls? To begin to understand and accept theatrical art, we must be willing to say, yes, it's true, we *do* wish to see, and we do wish to be stimulated by seeing bodies—we decline to say "titillated" because the word "titillate" belongs to the puritan enemy of the theatre. We must be willing to aver, further, that the bodies we wish to see are not "spiritualized" as Sir Kenneth Clark says nudes are, they are "naked," their spiritual credit is nil, their appeal is "prurient." We are prying into filthy secrets: the police department and the post office can begin to shift uneasily in their shoes.

How indecent the theatre is! Yet, for our peace of mind, the indecency is in general placed at a remove: the nakedness is usually of the soul, not the body—and it is Phaedra's nakedness we see, not Gypsy Rose Lee's. For once that we see Salome remove her seven veils in Wilde's play or Strauss's opera, we see the veils removed a thousand times in other operas and plays from the individual spirit, from society, from the universe.

The problem with this is that to show the naked spirit is impossible. Only the spirit's envelope can be shown, and this is the body. And though a philosopher may represent the body as a mere shadow of a more substantial spiritual reality, and a playwright may follow him in this, our crude retort is inevitably that the shadow is itself pretty substantial. "Can spirit set to a leg? No. Or an arm? No." Platonic thoughts can be entertained in the mind, but not lived by from breakfast to lunch. And though the great nakednesses of the theatre are spiritual, the immediate reality of theatre is aggressively physical, corporeal.

The physical world is real for every artist, and is that through which even a St. John of the Cross must communicate his antiphysical philosophy. Still, literature maintains some restraint in addressing its physicalities to the mind's eye only. Even painting and sculpture maintain some restraint in that the skin tints of the one have no skin under them, and the solidities of the other have no flesh or bone. Only theatre thrusts at its audience the supreme object of sensual thoughts; the human body. And while in the theatre it will never be nude, and will seldom be naked, its clothing is the more erotic in its double function of concealing and revealing, canceling and enhancing, denying and affirming.

That clothes may be used to heighten the sexual appeal of bodies, rather than reduce it, is a familiar enough fact. The exhibitionism of the actor is not so crudely sexual. He may even make himself theatrically more interesting by being less sexual: what has more appeal than Hamlet's funereal black? At worst, an actor or actress will concentrate on secondary sexual characteristics: a sensual mouth, a soulful eye, a rich head of hair, a slim waist, a well-shaped leg. He or she exhibits the body, but not for its beauty. In this the actor is closer to the acrobat than to the artist's model, since he exhibits his body largely for what it can do. And what an actor's body can do is expressive rather than lovely, and may be expressive, indeed, in the least lovely mode, such as grotesque comedy.

Does an actor exhibit *himself?* There has been much discussion on this head. Educators usually tell students of theatre that the actor does not exhibit himself: that would be egotistic. He submerges himself in his roles: a noble example of self-discipline, if not self-sacrifice. Louis Jouvet was saying as much when he stated that to embody a role the actor disembodies himself. One knows what he meant. When Sir Laurence Olivier plays Justice Shallow, the noble Olivier face and erect body are gone. Yet the very fact that I put it this way proves that I am not looking at the performance as I would if it were played by an actor who did not have a handsome face and an erect carriage. Does this signify only that I am a gossip, unable to concentrate on the show itself? I think not. The knowledge that an acrobatic trick is difficult is not irrelevant to the experience of watching it. On the contrary. We know it is easy for many creatures to fly up and down at great speed: the interest is *only* in seeing men and women do it, because it is not easy for them to do it. To see Olivier as Shallow is to see comparable difficulties overcome, comparable laws of nature defied by human prowess. Hence we are not enjoying the role alone, but also the actor. And he, on his side, is not exhibiting the role alone, he is exhibiting his prowess, he is exhibiting himself. Nor is the self-exhibition confined to the skill with which he portrays someone we define as "so different from himself." To wear a heavy, senile make-up and hunch the shoulders would not be enough if there were not a Justice Shallow in Olivier, if Shallow were not something he might yet become, or might have become. In such roles the actor is exhibiting the many different possibilities of being that he finds in himself.

No need to say anything about actors who all too evidently exhibit nothing but themselves. I am saying that even the actor who seems to be at the opposite pole from this is still exhibiting himself. Exceptional in Sir Laurence is the talent. Unexceptional is the original, naïve impulse that said: Watch me!

What of the pleasure of watching? In some respects, there is no difference between the theatre spectator and the "consumer" of other arts—the listener to music, the reader of novels. It might be imagined that his position is identical with that of the observer of painting, sculpture, and architecture: all are onlookers. But the phenomenon is less straightforward. If theatre is a visual art like painting, it is also a temporal art like music. The watcher is also a listener—the voyeur is also an eavesdropper.

Such words as *exhibitionist* and *voyeur*—though some will discount them as jargon—add to the purely descriptive words an implication of guilt.

> I have heard
> That guilty creatures sitting at a play

Have by the very cunning of the scene
Been struck so to the soul that presently
They have proclaimed their malefactions.

Literal-minded persons will find Hamlet's ideas on crime detection
somewhat far-fetched, but poetic drama deals in essences, and here
Shakespeare, Hamlet, and all audiences of *Hamlet* take it that the
essence of theatre is to strike guilty creatures to the soul—or, as we
would say in prose cliché, to play on the guilt feelings of the audience.
Seen in this way, the logic is good.

The play's the thing
Wherein I'll catch the conscience of the king.

—because plays *are* things wherin consciences are caught.

This makes it sound as if watching were very unpleasurable indeed
—as, for King Claudius, it was. Hamlet plotted to defy the distinction
between art and life, to exploit the possibility of a leap from art to life.
When that happens we are no longer dealing with drama but with the
destruction of its main convention. If we are not King Claudius, and
have not literally killed our brother, we are also spared his reaction.
Instead of calling for lights and making our exit, we stay on to "enjoy
the show." Is our conscience *not* caught, then? Are our withers un-
wrung? It is. They are. But in art, not life. Such is the paradox of pain
in drama: we do and do not suffer. We are suffering; we are also enjoying ourselves. When we watch, though we do not watch in the way we
watch actual happenings, neither do we watch in the spirit of "scientific
detachment" but always with some degree of emotional involvement.
I am suggesting that this involvement is not an innocent one.

It would be impossible to draw the line between drama and gossip,
drama and scandal, drama and the front page of the worst newspapers
—which, understandably enough, claim to be dramatic. Even what is
called pornography is by no means in any separate realm from the
realm of the tragic and comic poets. All these things are enjoyed by
human beings, and to all some measure of guilt is attached. Perhaps if
one took the guilt away, the dirty picture, so called, would lose much
of its appeal, and perhaps if one took from theatre the element of
voyeurism, the occasion would lose much of its appeal.

Certainly that element has been on the increase in modern times.
The Greek, Elizabethan, and Spanish theatres were less voyeuristic

because the plays were put on in broad daylight. It is the modern age that worked out the idea of a pitch-dark auditorium. Scholars call the modern stage the peepshow stage. The corollary is that this is a theatre for Peeping Toms. It is; and the classical criticism of it is that, from the eighteenth century to Tennessee Williams, it has been so too crudely. It has been, all too often, a theatre of domestic triviality.

The pleasure of looking on is in itself an equivocal thing. It includes such delights as feeling one has committed the crime yet is able to escape the penalty because the final curtain descends and one finds "it was all a dream."

What is pornography? One element in it is that forbidden wishes are seen gratified—the punishment being escaped because the man on the "dirty picture" is not oneself. The literature that is called pornographic often has another feature: following forbidden pleasure, condign punishment. Does not Tennessee Williams' *Sweet Bird of Youth* afford us the pleasure of being a gigolo for three quarters of the evening and then in the last part giving him the punishment that exactly fits the crime? Affords *us* the pleasure but gives *him* the punishment: which is to say, affords us the pleasure, but finds us a whipping boy. This might well be called pornography. It also has a lot in common with high tragedy which from its beginnings has presented crime and its punishment, the punished protagonist being a scapegoat for the audience. Pornography is continuous with art; and the pleasure of watching is continuous with the pleasure of peeping.

SUBSTITUTIONS

Such is the infantile basis of theatre. When he impersonates B, A is an exhibitionist, and when C looks on, he is a voyeur. But of course A does not need B if exhibition is all he desires for he could exhibit himself, and necessarily that is one thing he does exhibit.

B, the person impersonated, who is he? Originally, he is the little actor's father, the mother, and the siblings. Any other persons are likely to be members of the household interchangeable with a parent or a sibling. The interesting thing is that this continues to be true in adult theatre. There the persons impersonated are the work of a playwright. But the classic preoccupation of the playwright has been with the family. Comedy has often shown the family in the making. Both comedy and tragedy have often shown the family in the unmaking, and from the

Agamemnon to *Ghosts,* from *The Mandrake* to *Candida,* have dealt with marriage and the threats to it.

It was the psychoanalysts who pointed out that the family was often still the subject even when it seemed not to be. Otto Rank, for example, maintained that Julius Caesar is about parricide and that Brutus, Cassius, and Marc Antony are, symbolically speaking, Caesar's sons. Such a thing cannot be directly demonstrated but it comes to seem likely if we follow a certain line of reasoning. It is a matter of those other persons in the household whom, when we are children, we take to be members of the family, the nurse who is a kind of mother, the uncle who is a kind of father, the cousin who is an older or younger brother. The fact is that we continue to enlarge our family in this way as long as we live or, putting it the other way round, we assign all our acquaintances membership in the family which we knew as children. The play of life, as each of us writes it, has a very small cast—though for each role there may be innumerable understudies. If we felt our own father to be tyrannical, the role known as Father may be played by anyone we feel to be tyrannical. If we had the coddling kind of mother, the role known as Mother may be played by anyone, even a male, who coddles us. And so on. In short we have made ourselves a list of very definite types and, far from being tenuous and nebulous as types are reputed to be, they suggest to us strong emotion and clear-cut attitude.

IDENTIFICATIONS

There is a peculiarity about these little systems. One does not include oneself in the cast of characters, and so it is impossible for one to identify a whole class of people with oneself. It is the other way round. Unable to see oneself at all, one gropes in the dark, one guesses, one decides one is like some other person. One does not identify others with oneself but oneself with others. Again, the family is likely to play a guiding role. A little boy is likely to identify himself with his father. In this there is another source of tragic art: oneself as the great god Daddy. Here is the root of the idea of the hero: identification with strength.

The world, I have been saying, consists of oneself and others. One makes a cast of characters out of the ensemble, and a play out of living. A tragedy can well be made out of oneself and one's identification with Father, a comedy out of one's sense of those few archetypes, "the others." Two psychological processes are involved: *substitution* of all and sundry persons for the few in one's own original background, and *identification* of oneself with someone else. To analyze any "interpersonal" situation, one might well ask: who has been substituted for whom? and: with whom am I identified?

It would be hard to overestimate the influence of the identifications we all make. Though certainly we do not become the people we model ourselves on, what we become depends upon the people we model ourselves on. This is an element in upbringing which the Victorian age understood better than ours. Identifications, at home, and later at school, are everything. Central in the dynamics of living and growing up, they are central in this so intimately human art: the drama. Even Broadway knows as much. Its reviewers know how to account for the failure of a play by its lack of anyone in the cast they can identify themselves with. Precisely in its crudity, Broadway dramaturgy is suited to illustrate an argument I am presenting in broad lines only: a Broadway cast of characters consists of the person one identifies oneself with plus the rest of one's family put there in the form most quickly recognizable, old Uncle Tom Cobley and all.

Broadway producers presuppose in their audience very little spiritual ambition. They don't expect people to identify themselves with anyone of any stature. The old melodramas were more enterprising, because there, for the space of two hours, one could make a Douglas Fairbanks of oneself. At the other pole, there is the kind of protagonist who probably *is* beyond one's reach—T. S. Eliot's Becket, for example. In *Murder in the Cathedral* Mr. Eliot put in a chorus of women for us to identify ourselves with. They are slightly better than half-witted. In this way the "highbrow" playwright reaches a conclusion not dissimilar to that of the "lowbrows"; and indeed this play achieved a certain popularity.

EMPATHY AND ALIENATION

In challenging the traditional principles of the drama, Bertolt Brecht has in our day questioned the value of identification. The word was *Einfühlung*, translated as *empathy*. As used early in this century, by Vernon Lee, for example, the word empathy had to do with the mental process by which we say that a mountain rises from the plain. Since then it has come to bear one of the meanings Vernon Lee said it should not bear: more or less the literal meaning of *sich einfühlen*, "to feel oneself into." It is sympathy without the moral implication or the sentimental overtone. It is identification.

Brecht also had a word for what he saw as the theatrical alternative to sympathy. This is *Verfremdung*—Alienation or Estrangement. Brecht asks that we not identify ourselves with his characters but that we stand back from them. Object is to be seen as object, with astonishment. Brecht claims to derive this latter clause from science. Most people take for granted that apples fall; Isaac Newton was astonished. In the Brechtian theatre, the playwright is to be an Isaac Newton, and make Isaac Newtons of his audience. There was really no need to go outside the drama for such an aim. Corneille would have understood it well; and something of the sort is implied in most comedy.

Brecht is perhaps overconfident in assuming that when we abandon empathy we can see "the object in itself as it really is." He reckons without the process of substitution as I have described it. And failing to notice the inescapability of identifications, he himself makes them only unconsciously. Indeed his unconscious identification with his supposed enemies becomes a source of unintended drama.

THE ADULT AND THE INFANTILE

This comment on Brecht brings to a head my presentation of theatre as an infantile system. Brecht's objection is precisely to infantility. His Epic Theatre would be a completely adult theatre *if such a thing were possible*. As he writes in his Prospectus of the Diderot Society:

> Only in recent decades did a theatre develop which placed greater value upon a correct presentation of the world, whereby, to fit this correctness, objective, non-individual criteria should be allowed. No more did the artist feel himself bound to create "his own world" and, taking the actual world as known and unalterable, feel bound to enrich the catalogue of images which are really images of the image-makers; rather did he feel himself bound to take the world as alterable and unknown and to deliver images which give information more about the world than about him. . . . The "inner eye" needs no microscope or telescope, the outer eye needs both. For the visionary the experiences of other people are dispensable. Experiment is not in the repertoire of the seer. No, the artist who takes up the new task must, when he seeks to communicate images, deny himself the methods of hypnosis and even at need the customary empathy. . . .

In which it is taken for granted that a man "of the age of science" can become independent of the primitive side of his own nature by taking thought.

Everything in Brecht's theory of theatre—from the white light to the "presentational" acting—is dedicated to the same end: replacing a magical theatre with a scientific one, a childish theatre with an adult one. There is obviously a good deal to be said for this. What you cannot say for it, however, is that it is possible. For "growing up," so far as mental growth is concerned, is only a manner of speaking. The most mature person bristles with immaturities; the least neurotic person is still neurotic. The human race cannot reasonably be divided into two groups, the childish and the adult, because the child is not only father of the man, he is the man's Siamese twin.

The only odd thing is that an artist should not know it, since the child lives on more unabashedly in the artist than in any other class, and many artists are rather too happy about the fact. If I went back to infantile psychology in order to introduce the subject of this chapter, I did so in the interests not of simplicity but of relevance. For the theatre of grownups is much closer to the little system that children work out than the casual observer would think, the reason being, as Richard Sterba has put it, that "the pleasure of acting and looking on at a theatrical performance is a very narcissistic one, through regression to the early childhood stage of magic world creation." Brecht, who welcomed the blow to the world's narcissism that was administered by Galileo, should not have been above admitting that there are regressive and narcissistic and magical elements in all effective theatre, including of course his own. They have their negative side (immaturity is immaturity) but "becoming again like a little child" has its positive side too, and is a requirement not only of higher ethics but of higher theatre. . . .

WHAT THE ACTOR GIVES THE PLAYWRIGHT

Should a novelist turn to playwrighting, he might well feel that he has made certain sacrifices, even if he does not go all the way with Henry James, who envisaged the novelist-turned-playwright as throwing out the cargo to save the ship. However, if his plays were very well acted, such a writer might conclude that his losses had been recouped.

What does acting add to a play? Many things. Let me mention, first, one of the simplest but not least interesting: that the actors' eyes meet.

This is probably not true of some of the older theatres, and some of the Oriental ones, but in our modern Western theatre it is a well-established, if not essential, feature. Though some today may think of it as a product of the Stanislavsky Method, or even of the movies, one can in fact trace it much further back. There is, for example, an eighteenth-century comment on the actress Mrs. Clive, which reads:

> Mr. Garrick complained that she disconcerted him, by not looking at him in the time of action, and neglecting to watch the motion of the eye; a practice he was sure to observe to others. I am afraid this accusation is partly true; for Mrs. Clive would suffer her eyes to wander. . . .

Watch the acting of any intimate scene between a man and a woman—say, the last scene of *Pygmalion*. One can imagine an ancient Greek or a more recent devotee of classical Chinese theatre or Kabuki finding in our acting of *Pygmalion* a lack of formality and pattern, no special significance in where the feet are going, no special beauty in the way the body moves or stands. "Why, they're not doing anything," any of these visitors might say, "but alternately looking at each other and looking away." And this is essentially true. Acting, in such an instance, has come to concentrate itself in the eyes. And the eyes are subject to this physiological paradox: that to go on looking cancels out a look. To keep a look going, one has to interrupt it, and then look again; hence, in the various interruptions, all the looking away. A look is more dynamic as it is beginning to happen than when it actually happens; and having happened, it slows down into stony stare or sentimental gaze. As between persons, a look has its consummation when it is returned. The meeting of eyes constitutes a kind of center of human communication. The contact established is more personal than touch. What is communciated may be in doubt, but what is not in doubt is the aliveness of the lines of communication. On stage this is an aliveness of the actors, which they add to the much less directly physical life of the script. Spectators who might have difficulty with the written script have none responding physically, by empathy, to actors looking at each other. The stage, which renders things physically, neurologically, sensuously, is a great instrument of legitimate popularization. Conversely, the overliterary spectator who has seized Bernard Shaw's ideas all too readily, may not have lived through the drama of a Shavian scene until he, too, receives it from the actors' lips, through the actors' bodies, and especially through the actors' eyes. Usually, when we speak of seeing something through another's eyes, we are speaking only of the mind's eye. In the theatre, the actors' eyes guide us through the labyrinthine ways of the scenes; and all that joins us to the actors' eyes is the magnetics of looking. In the theatre, we may not be led by the nose: we *are* led by the eyes.

If a play in the theatre should prove hallucinatory in its vividness, it is the actor who finally has brought it to that pitch, adding to the play, one might put it, the crowning touch. Again, if a role is skeletal—and this I shall go into later—it may be possible for the actor to put some flesh on the bones. Some actors spend a lifetime filling in for inadequate playwrights. If they are stars, one often hears them disparagingly spoken of as mere personalities. The disparagement is misplaced, as "mere personality," in the sense here suggested, is exactly what the circumstances require.

And as we have seen in the chapter on Character, a good play may also have what novel-readers consider thin characterizations. If they do not need filling in, it is because the play survives by its plot or by a combination of plot, style, and theme. What the actor can contribute to a good play is not to fill up gaps—there may not be any he could fill —but *to intensify its effects*. Stanislavsky is right: it is fundamentally a matter of being able to "live" on stage. And Stanislavsky correctly assumed that what most people do on stage is not alive. Projection is lacking, and on stage not to project is not to live.

Pirandello points up this contrast wittily in *Six Characters* when two of the Characters speak without projecting their voices because people in real life do not project their voices. The result is that these Characters are not alive in the theatre. Now projection of the voice is a comparatively mechanical matter, and it does not follow that, if the voice is projected, the whole performance has "projection." We must take it that Pirandello here offers the part for the whole. To "live" on stage means to do more than live offstage, it means to give off life, to make it audible and visible, to make of it a projectile which is thrown out into the auditorium and reaches the back row of the balcony. "The point," says Jean Cocteau, "is not to put life onto the stage but to make the stage live."

What the actor has intensified when we out front have an "hallucination" is the illusion. Such is the acting of the tragic tradition, which in this century found its spokesman in Stanislavsky. What comic actors intensify is not the illusion but the aggression. (The comic tradition has recently been renewed by that most aggressive of playwrights—Brecht.) The comic aggression may take the form of satire and be called realistic, or it may take the form of high spirits and celebration and earn the description of fantastic. In either case the actor's fundamental contribution is not mimicry but vitality.

What indeed is that limited kind of acting which is so effectively practiced by friends of ours at parties in the way of malicious mimicry? The degree of likeness to what they mimic is a minor matter compared to the degree of wickedness with which they do it. A very little observation will suffice, provided very much fantasy and malice are superadded. Fantasy and malice are in this case the vehicles of vitality.

What acting testifies to in dramatic art is not in the first place its imitative character but its exaggerative character. The dramatist is immoderate. He likes to push his effects to the limit. The actor aids and abets him, adding powder to the bomb. The great actor resembles the great plays in that, beneath the formal calm which must be his normal aspect, he makes an immense violence felt. The impression given is that of living at great speed. And perhaps that, as Hebbel said, is just what the actor does—he lives "at speed, at unimaginable speed." Hebbel's idea is helpful for the understanding of all dramatic art. Rather than describe drama as an abridged, abbreviated form, as if something were missing from it, we should speak of it as an art in which more ground is covered in less time.

WHAT THE PLAYWRIGHT GIVES THE ACTOR

If the actor helps the playwright by adding his presence and his vitality (not to mention his craft), the playwright helps the actor by writing, not just a character, but a role. This is perhaps the most overlooked of all the playwright's tasks, at least among students of literature. It is understood only to the extent that the differences between playwright and novelist are understood. The novelist uses artifice, but in a setting of nature—natural scenery and natural characters. The playwright uses artifice in a setting of artifice—stage roles amid stage scenery. Such are the rules of the game, the controlling conditions of this art. While the novelist has the illusion of seeing actual characters in actual settings, the playwright has to learn to visualize the actor of the character and visualize him in that most unnatural of all settings: a theatre.

A character is not a role until, to begin with, it can be put across in a few acted scenes. Any idea for a character which cannot be put across at that velocity and by that method is unsuited to dramatic art. Conversely, an idea for a character which suggests opportunities for several self-explaining and violent stage encounters can prove effective even though it be lacking in depth and complexity. This second proposition begins to explain the success of certain roles, such as that of Marguerite Gautier, which are by no means great characters. To create *dramatis personae* which are great both as roles and characters is to be, in this department at least, a great dramatist.

The matter is a subtle one and has not been sufficiently studied, partly because the full possibilities of a role are only revealed by first-rate acting, and partly because histrionic phenomena have not traditionally been found worthy of the detailed study that is lavished on many lesser subjects. Anyone can see, for example, that Goethe was a greater genius than Schiller, yet Schiller was able to write characters that were also great roles. Goethe only managed it occasionally—as with his Mephisto who saved *Faust* for the theatre.

There is a moment when we might all feel, with Etienne Souriau, that the dramatist's heroic deed is to give existence to characters. This is the moment when these characters go out on stage and demonstrate that existence—it is *the moment when the characters show themselves to be roles*. That is the eating which is the proof of the pudding. It is as if, in the theatre, the physical existence of the actor were necessary to complete the sense of the verb *to exist*. This moving, speaking incarnation of character which is an acted role is an instrument of such unique power that, for the time being at any rate, we cease to long for the vaunted advantages of other forms and arts.

Which comes first, the character or the role? We tend to think of a writer starting with a character and, if he is playwright enough, going on to make sure it is a role as well. That is because we live in a literary age. In a theatrical age, it was the other way around. The actor was there and needed lines. One handed him a role. Only when he was lucky did he get anything that deserved the name of a character. Inquiring further back in history, we find a repertoire of fixed roles which actor-writers would refurbish as effective characters. Such was the *commedia dell'arte*.

PLAY, PLAY-ACTING, ACTING

The greatest part of our energy is expended in repeating what we and others have done many times before. To all appearances the aim of life is to make sure that tomorrow shall duplicate today. The same round of little duties and meals, followed by the same spell in bed! Our early education had only this kind of thing in mind. Toilet training was at first to repeat what our elders did, and later to repeat what we ourselves had begun to do. To learn language was nothing if not to repeat what the others said. To learn gesture was to repeat what the others did with their arms. So much indeed would seem to be necessary to the life process. But as if this were not enough of repetition, we add more. Repetition is a leading feature of our pleasures too. To learn a little dance is to learn a small figure which is then repeated *ad libitum*. We learn a tune in order to sing it a thousand times, not to mention that in most songs the theme is repeated even within one verse. We attach prestige to repetition. "Solemn occasions" are occasions on which oft-repeated words and music are repeated again. Ritual would not be itself if not constantly repeated. And so, if life is action, it should not seem surprising that play-acting—going through our actions again—is a universal art.

Of this art it can confidently be said that, if it became extinct, it would be re-invented again by children of two and three. Children of that age, giving up as hopeless the notion of being grownups on the full scale, become little imitation grownups and, as such, play-actors in the human comedy. This can be regarded, and often has been, as part of the educational process. We learn to grow up by pretending to be grown-up. To which some psychologists add that play-acting in children is also experimental. This means not only that we acquire (for example) a grown-up vocabulary by repeating the grown-up vocabulary but that the world of play is a workshop or laboratory for experiment by trial and error. There is no doubt a defensive side to it as well. Not having mastered the "real" world, by play-acting we construct a refuge from it, a haven whose inviolability we jealously guard.

Play, play-acting, acting: it is hard, in observing three-year-old children, to say where play leaves off and play-acting begins. Pure play would seem to belong more especially to a later age where rules are understood and adhered to. Games are a kind of abstract art, all geometry and numbers. What the three-year-olds mostly do has an element of pretending in it, and so of play-acting: there is a role and there is a drama. But it is not acting because there is no audience: it is not there to be looked at, noted, appreciated, enjoyed. Children, notoriously, are audience-conscious, they wish to be noted, appreciated, enjoyed, but what they at first exhibit to their audience is precisely not

their make-believe dramas but their conquests of "reality." If the
grownup is to be included in the drama he must be included as a fellow
actor, not observing the fantasy, but entering into it. Only when the
impulse to play-act is combined with the impulse to be watched and
appreciated can a child be said to be not just play-acting but acting.

It would be a naïve psychology indeed that saw acting as a device
of childhood to be later discarded. "All the world's a stage, and all the
men and women merely players," or, in the words written up at the
Globe Theatre: *totus mundus facit histrionem*—"all the world plays the
actor." Even everyday talk concedes that grown people are often "just
acting," "putting on an act," "doing a song and dance," and the Ger-
mans even say: "*Machen Sie keine Oper!*"—"Don't make an opera!" The
limitation of this popular understanding of acting in everyday life is
that it is marked with disapproval, applies only to hypocritical activity,
and presupposes that most action is not acting. More sophisticated
opinion allows that acting tends to characterize human behavior in
general. Indeed to make this allowance in Anglo-Saxon countries is
itself to *be* sophisticated, since our tradition in these matters is puritanic and philistine. It is for an Irishman like Shaw to tell us that the
actor is the least hypocritical of men since he alone admits he is acting.
It is for Irishmen like Wilde and Yeats to explain to us that our choice
is not between mask and face, but between bad masks and good. And
it is for the Spaniard Santayana, as provoked by Boston and Harvard,
to represent, with hauteur, that the mask is the only alternative to the
fig leaf, the fig leaf being "only a more ignominious mask."

> In this world [Says Santayana in the *Soliloquies in England*],
> we must institute conventional forms of expression or else
> pretend that we have nothing to express.

And again:

> What . . . could be more splendidly sincere than the impulse
> to play in real life, to rise on the rising wave of every feeling
> and let it burst, if it will, into the foam of exaggeration? Life is
> not a means, the mind is not a slave nor a photograph: it has a
> right to enact a pose, to assume a panache, and to create what
> prodigious allegories it will for the mere sport and glory of
> it. . . . To embroider upon experience is not to bear false

witness against one's neighbor, but to bear true witness to oneself.

Such a philosophy, which might be traced all the way back to a passage in Plato's *Laws*, makes us see play, play-acting, and acting, not only as natural and childish, but also as a human achievement and an adult goal. If, as phenomena of childhood, they seem to clinicians merely the preparation of unplayful adulthood, the philosopher can question the value of unplayfulness—the Puritanic notion of maturity—and place at the goal of experience a renewed childhood, a second playfulness, a regained innocence. Such an idea has even as good a claim to orthodoxy as the contrary, Puritan notion (latterly adopted more, perhaps, by scientific than religious folk), for what is the traditional conception of heavenly bliss? Its image, in its familiar if vulgar form, is that of angels sitting, harp in hand, on clouds—angels playing, angels performing. Condemned, as we may see ourselves, to eat bread in the sweat of our brow, we do so only in the hope of a celestial songfest or heavenly hootenanny.

MAX FRISCH

On the Nature of the Theatre

EXCERPTS FROM THE DIARY OF MAX FRISCH

Among those concepts which I use with partiality, without knowing
precisely what they mean, which need mean nothing at all, but which
might have a meaning, there belongs the concept of the theatrical.

Wherein does it exist?

On the stage there stands a human being, I see his physical form,
his costume, his countenance, his gestures, as well as his wider surroundings, all of them things which, by chance, I do not have in a
reading, at least not as sensible perceptions. And then something else
is added: speech. I do not merely hear noises, in keeping with sensible
perceptions, but speech. I hear what this human being says, which is
to say that a second thing is added, another image, an image of another
sort. He says: The night is like a cathedral! Besides that manifest image
I also receive a verbal image, one which I gain not through perception,
but through a mental image, through fancy, through imagination,
evoked through the word. And I possess them both simultaneously:
sensible perception and imagination. Their playing together, their relation to one another, the sphere of tension which is produced between
them, this, it seems to me, is what one might designate as being the
theatrical.

.   .   .

Hamlet with the skull of Yorick:—

When this scene is narrated one must conceive of both things, must
imagine them both, the skull in the living hand of Hamlet and the jokes

"On the Nature of the Theatre" by Max Frisch, translated by Carl Richard
Mueller, reprinted by permission of the translator, *The Tulane Drama
Review*, and Suhrkamp Verlag, Berlin and Frankfurt am Main.

From *Tulane Drama Review*, VI (March 1961). Translated by Carl R.
Mueller. Reprinted by permission of *The Drama Review* and Carl R. Mueller.

of the dead Yorick, of which Hamlet reminds himself. The narration, in opposition to the theatre, rests wholly and completely in language, and everything which the narrator has to impart reaches me on a single plane: namely that of imagination. The theatre performs in an essentially different way: the skull, which is only an object, the grave, the spade, all these things I already possess through sensible perception, involuntarily, in front of me, inevitably at every moment, while my imagination, wholly reserved for the words of Hamlet, has only to call up the vanished life, which it is capable of doing all the more intelligibly, since I use it for no other purpose. The past and the present, the once and the now: divided between imagination and sensible perception. . . . The poet of the theatre therefore uses two antennas in playing with me, and it is evident that the one, a skull, and the other, the jokes of a jokester, are of little significance in and of themselves; the complete statement of this scene, everything about it which moves us, rests in the relationship between these two images, and only herein.

. . .

It can be said of many a playwright who fails on the stage, that he possesses a more individual, a stronger, a more intrinsic language than Gerhart Hauptmann; nevertheless he drowns on stage, while a Hauptmann, whose magic is scarcely to be sought in individualistic language, is buoyed-up by this very same stage, much to our amazement. It seems as though language for the playwright were, after all, only a part. The other part, the sensibly perceptible part, which belongs essentially to the theatre, has the ability to be present even when the playwright forgets it, to be powerful even when the playwright fails to use it—to be against him, and indeed so much so, that no language, none whatever, may save him.

The most eminent example that language alone cannot bring this off is of course the second part of *Faust*, that felicitous marriage of the German language, which is playable only here and there: not because the statements of this poem are too exalted—Shakespeare is also exalted—but because they are not theatrical.

. . .

Theatrical diagnosis: what I see and what I hear—have they any relationship to one another? If not, if perhaps the statement lies exclusively in the word, so that in reality I could close my eyes, then the stage is fallow, and what, in this case, I see on the stage, when of course I do not close my eyes, is not a theatrical situation, but a superfluous sight, an apparently meaningless meeting of speakers, epic, lyric or dramatic.

(The dramatic, that dialectical wrestling match, wherein one may here and there perceive the sole possible theatre or at least the quintessence of the theatre, is desired by the stage only insofar as the stage actually always possesses something of the wrestling ring, of the arena, of the circus ring, of the public courtroom.)

.   .   .

The multiplication table of the clown: that at the moment when he appears heroic and respectable he stumbles over his own feet—I read once that the essence of the comic resides in the disproportionate, the inconsistent, the incongruous. In the case of the clown: the incongruous resides not within his utterance, but between his utterance and our perception. Self-confidence is not comical, stumbling is not comical; they are comical only when seen together. The incongruous, the disproportionate, which constitute the essence of all things comic, is divided between word and image, and particularly the theatrically comic—from the clumsy to the refined, from the clown to Shakespeare: we hear how blissful and tender are the phantasies of Titania in love, we hear her magnificent words, which are anything but witty, and we smile with delight because at the same time we see how with these selfsame sweet words, which enrapture us as well, she wins nothing more than the head of an ass—we see it.

.   .   .

The overwhelming aspect in Shakespeare is the way in which the situation (who stands opposite whom) is generally already composed as such, it is already significant as situation, so that nothing remains for the word to do but what is the most delightful of all: to reap, to pluck, to reveal the significance which is already present.

Who stands opposite whom.

The style itself of the classical plays indicates how essential this question is, even in the printed texts every entrance is noted, whereas very little else. Scene Ten: The King, the two Murderers. This is what is perceptible when the curtain rises, and when the two Murderers have their instructions, so that they leave the King alone, that which is perceptible changes; every entrance is a caesura. The King alone! If he says something now which reveals the burden of his increasing solitude, then it has the whole stage to itself, the emptiness of the stage—congruity between the outer and the inner situation. Another theatrical realization is the contrapuntal: Macbeth experiences the burden of his guilty solitude during a festive social gathering, he alone sees the ghost of Banquo, his solitude becomes manifest to such an extent that all his words which he wants to be sociable are powerless, the gathering disappears, only Macbeth and his Lady remain, each guilty in his own degree; again the entire working of a scene is visibly outlined, the ghost of the murdered Banquo says nothing—which is to say: I do not look in vain at the stage.

.   .   .

In the second play of Friedrich Duerrenmatt [*Der Blinde*] . . . there exists the following scene: a blind man, who does not perceive the destruction of his duchy, believes that he is still living in his secure fortress. In his belief, in his imaginaton, he rules over an unscathed and spared land. Thus he sits in the midst of ruins, which he of course, being blind, cannot see, surrounded by all kinds of the dissolute rabble of war, mercenaries, prostitutes, robbers, pimps, who in wanting to make a fool of the blind duke now deride his belief while allowing themselves to be received as dukes and generals, the prostitute, however, as a persecuted abbess. The blind duke addresses them in such a way as he imagines they deserve. We, however, see the repulsive individual whose blessing as abbess he believingly begs for—on his knees. . . . Model example of a theatrical situation: the statement resides wholly in the opposition between perception and imagination. Here the theatre can play alone.

.   .   .

In the Basel Museum there hangs a painting by Arnold Böcklin: *Odysseus and Calypso,* the relations between man and woman. He is in blue, she in red. She is in a hidden grotto, he on a projecting rock, his back towards her, as he looks out across the breadth of the open sea. . . . On my journey here I saw this painting again, without looking for it, and was amazed that the sea, the subject of his longing, is almost non-existent. There is only a tiny blue wedge of it. In my recollection it was a picture of the full sea—precisely because the sea is not shown. No theatre, any more than a painting, is capable of showing the breadth of the sea. It must be left to the imagination. In Sartre there is a scene in which Zeus puts on airs concerning his starry firmament, in order to attract Orestes, the mortal, to a belief in the gods. Sartre does the only thing possible, he describes his starry firmament with words. Now if a director, as I have seen done, wants suddenly with these words to turn on a heaven of electric bulbs, thus wanting to make the stars sensible perceptions, then naturally the magic of the theatre is made a joke of; the starry firmament which Zeus has to describe is made so childish thereby that the scorn of the unbelieving Orestes is in itself made to seem foolish. The backbone of the scene is broken—despite good actors —broken by a brainstorm which fails to appreciate the limitations of the theatre.

The field of action is always the human soul! All things are subject to its decrees. One of these decrees: Compensation. If I perceive a dungeon, then the word which describes an open and cheerful landscape finds me particularly responsive; the sight of Calypso housed in a grotto, which wants to hold me there, makes me particularly responsive to each tiny word which speaks of the open sea and foreign coasts; my imagination, which desires this, answers my longing. Or if I perceive a happy and high-spirited festival, a voice which mentions death will have particular power; the imagination which desires it answers my fear. The theatrical relationship—the opposition between perception and imagination—will be particularly compelling, particularly productive, particularly positive, if it follows the wants of the human soul, if, by way of example, it is composed of compensation.

. . .

The enticement of the theatre for even the non-dramatic poet, perhaps the lyric poet: the stage will supply him, if he masters it, with a heightened background for the word.

. . .

No play will be constantly theatrical. It is scarcely important as regards its theatrical potency, whether it is often theatrical in its development. The realization of the theatrical, I believe, always concerns the infrequent, the rare, the eye on the surface of a face. What may be decisive is whether the essential or only the accessory statements become theatrical. In the latter case, where the theatrical remains incidental, accessory, eccentric, every production, even the consummate one, will, without fail, signify a distortion, a falsifying displacement of accent. The theatre, the playwright will then say, is in my opinion a terrible means whereby a word is made crude! Of course it is that, but it is not the fault of the theatre if such an occurrence, which never seems to destroy a Shakespeare, becomes more than what it is, that is, if it grows into distortion, disfigurement, misrepresentation, into a destruction of the poetic. It is not the fault of the theatre if the poet cannot make use of it. Whoever works for the stage and fails to use it will find the stage against him. By making use of the stage I mean: not writing *for* the stage, but *with* the stage.

.   .   .

I went to another rehearsal today, and since I arrived an hour too early I withdrew into a private box, which is dark as a confessional. Fortunately the stage was cleared and without wings, and I knew nothing of the play which was to be rehearsed. There is nothing so stimulating as nothing, at least now and then. Just by chance a worker crossed the stage, a young man in brown overalls; he shakes his head, remains standing and scolds another, whom I cannot see, and the speech which sounds from the stage is utterly conventional, anything but literary—shortly thereafter an actress appears eating an apple, while with her coat and hat on she crosses the empty stage; she says good morning to the worker, nothing further, and then again the silence, the empty stage, the occasional rumble of a streetcar passing outside. This tiny scene, repeated a thousandfold on the street outside, why is it so different here, so much more powerful? These two people, just as they crossed the stage, had a being, a presence, a destiny, which naturally I know nothing of, nevertheless it was here, even if only secretly, it had a presence which filled all this large space. I must note, too, that there was the customary work-light, a light pale as ashes, devoid of magic, devoid of that so-called atmosphere, and so the entire impression produced was that nothing else existed save this little scene; all that surrounded it was night; for a moment's time there existed only a stagehand, scolding, and a young actress, yawning and going into the checkroom; two human beings, who met in space, who can walk and stand upright, who have resounding voices; and then everything is past, inexplicably, as if a human being had died, inexplicable that he ever existed, that he ever stood in front of us for us to see, that he spoke, conventionally and without consequence, but nevertheless stimulatingly.

There is something in this small event which seems significant to me, it also reminds me of the experience of taking an empty frame and hanging it tentatively on a bare wall, in a room perhaps in which we may have lived for a number of years: now, however, for the first time, we notice how the wall is really plastered. It is an empty frame which compels us to look. Our reason, of course, tells us that the plaster which I have framed can be no different from that on the rest of the wall; as a matter of fact, it is not the least bit different; but it becomes evident, it is there, it speaks. Why then are pictures framed? Why do they have a different effect when we release them from their frames? It is simply that they no longer set themselves off from the contingencies of their surroundings; for once removed from their frames, they are suddenly no longer secure; they no longer depend wholly on themselves; one has the feeling that they are falling apart, and one feels somewhat disillusioned in the fact; they suddenly appear worse; worse, that is, than they are. The frame, when it is there, severs the painting from nature; it is a window into an utterly different sphere, a window into the spirit, where the painted flower is no longer a flower which can fade, but the essence of all flowers. The frame places it beyond time. To that extent there is an exciting difference between the surface lying within a frame, and the surface which, as it were, is endless. It is a bad artist indeed who depends on a frame to rescue his work; it is not meant that everything, merely because it takes place within a frame, will assume the significance of a symbol; yet it assumes, whether it wills it or not, the claim to such a significance. It says: Look at me; here you will see something worth looking at, which exists beyond chance and impermanence; here you will find a lasting significance, not the flower that fades, but the likeness of all flowers, or as has already been said: the symbol.

All this holds good for the frame of the stage as well, and naturally there would be other examples which would explain, at least here and there, the stimulating impression which even the empty stage makes; one need only think of those display-windows which exhibit whole supplies of wares, display-windows which could never attract our attention, and then of those other windows which circumscribe themselves to a modest peephole: we see there a single watch, single bracelet, a single necktie. And this unusual thing appears to us from the very first to have value. There are small windows such as these, which at times are like tiny stages, one enjoys standing in front of them, looking into another world, which at least gives the appearance of having value. And its relation to the real stage lies in this: that on the stage I do not see thousands of fools, but only one, whom I can still love, not thousands of lovers, whose loves with their interminable protestations become obnoxious, but two or three, whose vows we can take as seriously as our own. There is profit in looking at them. I see people; I do not see millions of workers. In doing so, I would, unfortunately, no longer see the individual person. Rather, I see this individual who represents the millions and who alone is real: I see a stagehand, who scolds, and a young actress, who eats an apple and says good morning. I see what I would not otherwise see: two human beings.

.   .   .

One must naturally, having spoken of the frame of the stage, also speak of the stage's apron, which is a part of every such frame, and, indeed, the critical part. A stage without an apron would be a gate. And it is precisely that which it does not want to be. It keeps us from entering. It is a window through which we are allowed only to look. As part of a window it is called a sill, and there is a whole series of arrangements which serves that single purpose. All kinds of pedestals are possible. The concern is always with the separation of image and nature. There is a group by Rodin, the famous *Citizens of Calais*, which was conceived of without a base; the intention obviously lay in this, that the image presented by those bravely sacrificing Citizens of Calais was meant to be taken up into everyday life, as an example, and therefore it was placed on the same level as the living, who were to follow them, on the pavement of a public plaza. This is a special case, but for all that, it testifies in its own way, in the desire to avoid the pedestal, to the effectiveness and importance of this arrangement. It is well known that the temples of antiquity, too, stood on a pedestal of three or five or seven steps; steps are made for the precise purpose of being tread upon, as an aid for one who might hesitate at the thought of reaching the top elevation; it is only when the attempt is made that one realizes the steps are far too high; one may clamber up them, but a dignified gait is not possible, a gait with which one approaches a temple, and such an approach is indeed the very opposite of that which the pedestal desires. It severs the temple from us; but not only from us, rather from the countryside as well, from the contingencies of the region; it does not trouble itself over the incline of a hill, as, for example, we do when we build a country house. There it is our aim to nestle our house into that particular countryside in such a way that would not be possible anywhere else, but only in this solitary spot. That is: we recognize our limitations, and we make the most of them. There is a single Greek temple from the Golden Age which is adapted to the countryside, which plays with the summit on which it is placed, the Erechtheum on the Acropolis. All others, however, have the pedestal, which disregards the countryside, which dissociates the temple from the contingencies of the solitary countryside, which raises it above all earthly restrictions, which places it in another sphere: in the sphere of the Absolute.

Is this not universally the situation?

Time and again there are playwrights who reject the limits of the stage's apron; there is no lack of examples of actors approaching the stage from the orchestra floor, or of an actor stepping onto the apron and speaking into the orchestra, as though there were no gulf there, of which the apron is only a weak symbol; I am thinking of Thornton Wilder, of the time when Sabina turns towards the spectator with the passionate plea that he give up his seat to the fire so that Mankind may be saved. Here, too, just as with Rodin's sculpture, an example is to be carried out into real life, since the art-work is placed on the same level on which the spectator himself stands and walks. The question is whether the example becomes more effective when it rejects its removal. At all events, it has, when we consider Sabina's appeal, the momentary gain of surprise; that it can only be momentary is a fact which Wilder, too, realized: he has the curtain fall immediately thereafter. It serves as an exception rather than as a rule. Every gesture which rejects the limits of the apron loses in magic. It opens the locks, which is stimulating; but it is scarcely done so that thereby the artistic form can stream out into the chaos which it wants to change, rather chaos rushes into the sphere which we call by another name, into the sphere of poetry, and the poet who demolishes the apron surrenders himself.

Does he do so because it is a vogue?

Does he do so out of desperation?

Perhaps it is no accident that it was precisely Sabina who occurred to us as an example. Sabina, who, with her appeal across the apron, wants to save Mankind: the self-surrender of poetry, which recognizes its own weakness, which shows it owns weakness, has about it something which suggests a final alarm, which is all it has left.

.   .   .

Yesterday again we went to a puppet-play, and after it was over we were permitted to go behind the small stage. It is a narrow room filled with stale air. We regarded with astonishment the hanging puppets, somehow incredulous whether they were really the same ones which had just enchanted us. Even the devil hangs on the batten now, shabbier than we had expected. During the play they have a completely different effect, always in keeping with the scene, always in keeping with the word, which they themselves neither speak nor hear. This is established through the changing incidence of light, through the various positions of the head, and so on. Somehow one remains undeceived while the father-puppet soaps his hands, washes them, dries them and tells of further plans. Or at least one is silently disconcerted with the way in which the puppets suddenly stare into a void, lifeless, senseless, as though they no longer recognize us. . . .

.   .   .

What astonishes us everytime:

How easy it is for marionettes to succeed in representing other-than-human beings, an earth-spirit, a goblin, monsters and fairies, dragons, spirits of air and that which the heart desires. It can even happen that such forms must appear on the large stage as well, long-tailed monkeys or an Ariel; in this, however, there is always the danger that it will become embarrassing, and at best the actors can only succeed in not becoming ludicrous; nevertheless, the hoped for effect, namely ultimate horror or supernatural delight, which is supposed to emanate from such other-than-human beings, can scarcely be attained by the stage as long as it is bound to the use of human actors. Marionettes could carry it off. There is much to be said for the fact that this puppet which represents a human being, and that other puppet which represents an earth-spirit, are made of the same stuff. This means that the marionette which represents the earth-spirit for us is equally as believable or as unbelievable as the other which we are to believe a human being. On the large stage, I think, we cannot believe in the earth-spirit, because he is no match for the human being: because the human being who plays opposite him is really a human being, who is by nature of flesh and blood. The other, the earth-spirit, in comparison with him, remains an image, a symbol. And therewith the scene, however admirably it may be acted, plays from the very start on two different planes, which are not believable in the same manner. In the puppet-play there is a single level of belief. It is the same as in the drama of antiquity with its use of masks: when Athena and Odysseus both wear masks, when they both remain equally improbable and symbolic, then we can believe in the goddess.

.   .   .

Another thing which enthuses one about marionettes is their relation to the word. Whether one wills it or not, the word in a puppet-play is always heightened, so that it can never be confused with our everyday speech. It is supernatural, just because it is separated from the puppet, because it is filled with activity over and above it; to that end, it is a larger language than ever the wooden chest of the puppet could make it. It is more than the accompanying noises which daily emanate from our mouths. It is the word, which was in the beginning, the autocratic, the all-creating word. It is speech. The puppet-play cannot for one moment confuse itself with nature. There is one possibility only, namely the world of poetry; that remains its only sphere of action.

.   .   .

The comparison with the theatre of antiquity, which also possessed these rigid masks, forces itself upon us in many respects. Both theatres, the large and the small, operate through the means of an altered dimension. In the theatre of antiquity it was the mask wherewith one magnified figures, and later also with the cothurnus; in the puppet-play one reduces the figures. And the impression produced is essentially the same: we can no longer stand, shoulder to shoulder, beside the acting figures, nor should we be able to; on the contrary, the altered scale prohibits every such familiarity: we are here, and they are there, and whatever happens on the stage, we see across an irreconcilable distance, no matter whether this is achieved through magnification or through diminution. We then observe with amazement that the marionettes, the longer their play succeeds, become alive for us in a compelling sort of way; after a while we completely forget that they are smaller than we, dwarfs, and, indeed, dwarfs made of wood, whom we might catch up in our hand and cast from the play; we discover, we observe the proportions of all outward dimensions, including our own, and as long as their play is not interrupted through some prank or other, through some accident of gesture, which falls beyond the frame of the stage, and which thereby betrays that frame, just that long will the spirit of the thing remain unbound to any scale of measure. These wooden dwarfs, while playing, take possession, as it were, of our being. They become more real than we ourselves, and there are moments of true magic; we are, quite literally, beside ourselves.

And when it is all over:

How shabbily they hang there on the batten, now that they no longer are in possession of our being, now that we are again in possession of ourselves.

.   .   .

Christ as a puppet?

I recall as a student seeing a puppet-play in which the Last Supper was represented. It was deeply affecting. It was holy to such a degree that it would be thoroughly impossible for any human actor, trying to simulate a Christ for us, even to approach it. A Christ of linden-wood, such as Marion * makes: if we consider a crucifix, then we will sense nothing blasphemous in the puppet; the puppet, in opposition to the human actor, meets us from the very first as form, as image, as a creation of spirit, which alone is able to represent that which is Holy. The human being, even when he plays as image, always remains a man of flesh and blood. The puppet is wood, an honorable and a fine piece of wood, which never lays claim to the deceitful pretension of presenting an actual Christ, nor should we take it to be such; it is merely a symbol, a formula, a text, which signifies, without wanting to be that which it signifies. It is play, not deception; it is spiritual in such a way as only play can be.

* A contemporary Swiss sculptor.